THE STRANGER
in the MIRROR

CONTENTS

PART THREE
INSIDE STORIES

PART FOUR
BEFRIENDING THE STRANGER

ACKNOWLEDGMENTS

I AM DEEPLY GRATEFUL to the many people who shared their lives and their heroic journeys of survival with me. Hundreds of people have generously given me permission to share their stories in the hope that others will not have to suffer as they did. In particular, I am grateful to three patients—"Nancy," "Linda," and "Jean"—whose detailed histories are included in this book.

I would also like to thank my longtime friends and colleagues, Pamela and Ollie Hall, who encouraged me to present my work to the public. Many other friends, family, and colleagues supported my work in the early days, helping me pursue my observations and to blaze new trails. They include Christine Amis, Elizabeth Bowman, Domenic Cicchetti, Phil Coons, Jildy Gross, Richard Kluft, Marie Matheson, Diane and Alan Sholomskas, Jan Simpson, Annie Steinberg, Robert Miller, Bruce Rounsaville, and Moshe Torem. Special thanks go to Steve Dickinson for his ongoing support and wisdom.

I also wish to thank Diane Reverand at HarperCollins Publishers, whose guidance was critical to this project, and Janet Dery for superb editorial assistance. Thanks also to my coauthor, Maxine Schnall, whose unique writing talents helped me to incorporate eighteen years of research and clinical work in this book, and to our agent, Mary Tahan. Finally, I wish to acknowledge the National Institute of Mental Health, whose support made possible this research, which I hope will continue to improve the prospects for trauma recovery.

INTRODUCTION

Tここ HERE ARE SOME things you learn in medical school that you spend the rest of your life *unlearning.* My adventure in this eye-opening process of discovery began in 1981, when I was a first-year intern in psychiatry at Jacobi Hospital, an affiliate of the Albert Einstein School of Medicine in New York City. At that time dissociation—by which I mean a state of fragmented consciousness involving amnesia, a sense of unreality, and feelings of being disconnected from oneself or one's environment—was a relatively new concept. As an emerging field, it was largely an unmapped territory, remote, fascinating, exotic, and considered to be off limits for all but the most intrepid explorers. We had yet to establish that dissociation, as part of our standard response to trauma, is a near-universal reaction to a life-threatening event and that mild or moderate experiences of dissociation are as common in otherwise normal people as anxiety and depression.

Furthermore, we thought that dissociative disorders were exceedingly rare, as many still mistakenly do today. The only cases that caught anyone's eye were the most extreme forms of the severest dissociative disorder, then called multiple personality disorder, now known as dissociative identity disorder, or DID. It was assumed that every multiple behaved like the sensationalized heroines of *Sybil* or *The Three Faces of Eve,* floridly switching among dozens of separate personalities inside them. We had no idea that this dramatic switching is *atypical* and that multiples typically behave with far more subtlety and control, using compensatory techniques that make them indistinguishable in public from the figurative neighbor next door.

Unfortunately, this myth of the multiple as a freak of nature persists even today. It certainly prevailed in the early eighties, when I was an intern at Jacobi Hospital, and our introduction to a DID case had all the high drama and voyeuristic thrill of a theatrical event. Jacobi was an urban referral center for a very large mental health catchment area in the Bronx, serving an inner-city population of working-class people who were too poor to afford insurance. The psychiatric ER was a drab warren of interview cubicles and a crowded, noisy waiting room. Police officers were constantly bringing in belligerent, disoriented, or intoxicated drug users or alcoholics who needed to be restrained and were often hand-cuffed to chairs.

As part of our training, my fellow interns and I made rounds with a psychologist who was a senior member of the faculty at Einstein and wanted us to observe an inpatient he suspected had multiple personality disorder. The first day we were simply to meet Gloria, and the next day we were to watch if alternate personalities emerged. We were told that this would be a unique experience since Gloria's condition was so rare that we would probably never encounter more than one or two such cases in a lifetime of practice.

When we first saw Gloria, a Hispanic woman in her early thirties with caffe latte–colored skin and a mass of curly dark hair framing her thin face, she seemed depressed and anxious but not remarkable in any dis-cernible way. She conversed intelligently as a mature woman, revealing that she was a single mother supporting three children with part-time work as an office clerk. Her erratic behavior involving speaking like a child and slashing her wrists after a fight with her boyfriend caused her to be hospitalized.

The following day, when we went back to see Gloria, she was hooked up to an IV through which sodium amobarbital (Amytal) was being infused. Amytal is a barbiturate that has a sedating effect and lowers inhi-bitions. The idea was to relax Gloria sufficiently so that her guard would lower and her alternate personalities—if they existed—would emerge, thereby confirming the suspected diagnosis.

We watched, wide-eyed, as the Amytal worked with startling effi-ciency. In a matter of minutes Gloria switched to a tearful adolescent alter she called Carmelita, sadly complaining in a high, girlish voice about the hopelessness and oppressiveness of her life. This weeping teenager, tossing her hair back from her face and wringing her hands, was a completely different person from the woman we had met the day before. Suddenly Gloria switched again. This time she regressed into a more childlike state, CeeCee, and began babbling in baby talk about "bad booboos that Mommy and Daddy did," and about her mother's yanking her ponytail and part of her ear out of her head and making her jump from one rooftop of a building to another to escape her drunken father, who was chasing them with a drawn fishing knife. All the while she was wailing and pounding her fists on the bed in fear and rage. Then, in the blink of an eye, we heard, "Can I talk to you? It's me, Laura," as another alter spoke up in a polite, reasonable tone. "I think it was unfortunate that we needed CeeCee to bear the brunt of all of that crazy stuff that everybody said was a lie, but somebody has to carry all of it inside; otherwise we're going to go crazy."

When we left Gloria's room, I came away shaken by what I had seen. I wanted to learn what the course of treatment for her would be. When I inquired about her later, I was told that she fled the hospital the next day after the Amytal had induced her alters to surface before a group of gawking residents. I could understand why. How frightened, embarrassed, and humiliated she must have been. Regret for the insensitivity she'd suffered under the rubric of "training" turned this unfortunate event into a defining moment for me.

It was obvious that presenting Gloria to us like a dancing bear who could produce alters on demand was of no therapeutic value to the patient. Surely she would have preferred being in control of her personality states herself. What need was there to induce them by using drugs without treating these personalities once they were out? I vowed that this would not be the diagnostic method of choice for me if I ever came across a multiple again. Given the opportunity, I would work with such a person gently, helping her to learn about the different parts of herself and to feel comfortable with them so that she could talk about them openly and eventually accept and unify them. That opportunity seemed only a remote possibility.

I left Jacobi at the end of my internship and went to Yale in 1982 to finish my residency. During my first year at Yale my clinical supervisor, Francine Howland, M.D., introduced me to the treatment of dissociative symptoms and disorders. She was one of a tiny minority of professionals who gave such work any credence. Having been previously told how rare multiples were, I was astonished to identify three people that year who exhibited all of the symptoms of multiple personality disorder, now called dissociative identity disorder or DID. I wondered why I, a junior resident, was encountering so many of these cases whereas more experienced clinicians rarely did. Others questioned my diagnoses, provoking electrifying controversy about them, but the symptoms were irrefutably present.

I uncovered another, even bigger surprise. The symptoms were present not only in the most extreme cases like Gloria's, but in many much more subtle but nonetheless significant dissociative experiences. Over and over again I heard about these symptoms from people in all walks of life—professionals, business people, college students, laborers, homemakers, artists and writers. They spoke of episodes of "zoning out" or having "blank spells"; of "acting like some other person"; of "feeling apart from myself and watching myself from afar"; of "not allowing myself to feel anything"; of "just going through the motions"; of feeling "foggy" or "not feeling like a real person"; of "hearing myself talking as if someone else is speaking"; of thinking "nothing around me looked real"; of feeling "confused about who I am." The prevalence of these experiences was stunning. Was it possible that dissociation was far more common than psychiatrists thought? If so, what was I doing to identify it that others were not?

When I heard that an organization called the International Society for the Study of Dissociative States/Multiple Personalities (now called the International Society for the Study of Dissociation) was holding its first conference in Chicago, I was very excited. I assumed I would be in a supportive environment though not many people would be attending. Curiously clinicians who had never seen cases of dissociative disorders thought that the descriptions were too bizarre to be believed. This defied logic: people usually form opinions about what they know; they do not develop strong beliefs about a subject before they have any knowledge of it.

I arrived in Chicago late at night on the eve of the conference and checked into the downtown hotel where the conference was being held. The lobby was empty, and so was the elevator that took me to my floor. It was late, but there seemed to be so few signs of life that I wondered whether the conference had been called off for lack of attendance.

In the morning I walked into the conference room with my Styrofoam cup of coffee in hand and was amazed to see at least four hundred people there, milling about excitedly or already seated, waiting expectantly for the conference to begin. These attendees from throughout the United States were all practicing mental health professionals—psychiatrists, psychologists, social workers—who had been working with patients who had dissociative disorders. This was the validation I needed. The presence of so many clinicians who had actual experience with this condition helped confirm my belief that dissociative disorders were not so rare after all.

Such pioneers in the field as Richard P. Kluft, M.D., Helen Watkins, M.A., John Watkins, Ph.D., and Cornelia Wilbur, M.D., presented findings based on years of clinical experience that gave me valuable insights. They documented the close association between dissociative disorders and childhood abuse—emotional, physical, and/or sexual—as Gloria's case had suggested, and offered important guidelines for treatment. After three days of listening to presentations, attending workshops, and networking with the other professionals there, I still felt that something was missing in the way of a scientific instrument for diagnosis.

It seemed to me that the reason I'd already seen a few multiples as a novice, although experienced people hadn't come across them, was related to the group of questions I was asking every patient I saw. The questions were specifically planned to detect this disorder. Therapists generally were not asking their patients about dissociative symptoms at all. They were asking about the symptoms of depression, panic disorder, manic-depressive illness, attention deficit hyperactivity disorder, obsessive-compulsive disorder, and every other disorder except dissociative disorders. No wonder these disorders were thought to be so rare: hardly anyone was screening for them.

Back at Yale I continued asking patients my questions about dissociative symptoms and discovered that they not only were widespread, but fell along a continuum from mild (normal) to moderate to severe. Many people experienced them fleetingly from time to time with no sign of any psychiatric problem; other normal people experienced them as a transient response to a life-threatening accident or a near-death event; still others had dissociative episodes that occurred in times of stress or temporary crises; and there were those whose episodes were of such frequency and severity that they clearly indicated a dissociative disorder.

The most common experiences included not recognizing oneself in the mirror (hence the title of this book); staring into space and losing track of time; being uncertain whether a memory was from a dream or reality; feeling outside oneself as both an observer and a participant; feeling that one was watching a movie of one's progression through life; experiencing a numbing of emotions; missing parts of conversations; and being unable to remember something one had just done. After hearing about these symptoms repeatedly, I realized that even when they weren't alarming, they were still important occurrences people needed to talk about to a therapist as part of a comprehensive assessment. Very often these symptoms signified deeper issues that were not being treated appropriately, because neither the patient nor the therapist had recognized their importance. This was especially true if the symptoms recurred from time to time or happened frequently, caused distress, or became disruptive to a person's life.

There were other, somewhat less common symptoms that were more likely to be associated with a dissociative disorder, depending upon how persistent and troubling they were. These included the feeling that other people and the world around a person were not real; finding oneself in a place with no idea of how one got there; and feeling as if one were looking at the world through a fog.

And then there were the more bizarre phenomena around which a whole mythology had arisen. Besides the assumption of different personalities, there were past lives and alien abduction experiences. Though these dramatic episodes seized upon the public's imagination, from an analytical standpoint, they were all episodes of dissociation.

As I kept hearing about these symptoms from patients, I realized what a hidden epidemic dissociation is. I saw that the psychiatric community and the public were laboring under the misperception that dissociation was an all-or-nothing matter—either you were a "Sybil" or you were free and clear. What was missing from the equation was the *continuum* of dissociation, the same mild to moderate to severe range that occurs in depression or anxiety.

A person who is mildly depressed, for example, might go through a day or two of having "the blues" and snap out of it naturally without needing professional help. Further along the continuum, a moderately depressed person in a deeper or longer funk might need therapy and/or medication to lift the mood, and someone who is severely depressed might need to be hospitalized. Similarly, a person who has a slight case of nerves before an anxiety-provoking event may not need psychotherapy, whereas someone with a moderate or severe level of anxiety might find it hard to function without treatment. The same continuum holds true for dissociation. Everyone dissociates at times, just as everyone feels depressed or anxious on occasion. There are some everyday normal dissociative symptoms that are benign, but there is a whole range of other symptomatic experiences that have to be looked at with a skilled eye. Even someone who is not severely dissociative may need help for these symptoms and greatly benefit from it.

Determining whether a person had a dissociative disorder or not, I found, was all a matter of asking questions about dissociative symptoms and evaluating the answers. How many of the symptoms did someone have? How often did they occur? Did they cause distress? Were they disruptive to the person's life? The answers gave a snapshot of the inner workings of a person's response to trauma or repeated abuse in much the same way that a chest X ray gave a picture of someone's lungs. To put it another way, just as the X ray detected shattered bones, my interview detected symptoms of a fragmented sense of self. Clearly the questions that I was asking were yielding crucial information necessary for an accurate diagnosis—data that could turn what was then an uncertain art into a science.

One day on a train ride from New Haven to New York, I jotted down the interview questions from memory. When I returned to Yale, I began thinking about a research project to look at the questions and validate them in the form of a standardized psychiatric interview. I wanted to seek funding in order to turn my set of questions into a diagnostic instrument that any trained clinician could administer independently and find the same patterns I did—one pattern for those people who might dissociate on occasion but have no disorder and another for those who do have a dissociative disorder.

In my fourth year of residency I went to see a well-respected expert in administrative psychiatry and inquired about fellowship and research options to carry out my plan. He heard me out with an inscrutable expression on his face. When I was done talking, he cocked an eyebrow at me quizzically, paused for a long moment, and said in the most tactful, well-meaning way, "Marlene, I would advise you that if you are interested in a career in research, find another subject."

His answer took me aback, but I knew he was only looking out for my interests. Given the skepticism in the air, I was facing an uphill battle. No one had ever been awarded a large grant to do research in dissociation, so the odds were not in my favor. Still, this was where I wanted to go. My colleague kindly referred me to the two people who could help me get there: Bruce Rounsaville, M.D., a renowned expert in substance abuse and diagnostic testing of substance abusers, and Domenic Cicchetti, Ph.D., a widely recognized expert in testing the reliability and validity of psychiatric diagnostic tools.

With the assistance of Bruce and Domenic I was able to conduct the field testing for a diagnostic tool that could be replicated throughout the world. The test became known as the SCID-D (*Steinberg Clinical Interview for DSM-IV Dissociative Disorders*). In 1989 I was immensely pleased to be awarded the first of two very substantial grants from the National Institute of Mental Health. These grants were the first ever given to a researcher in dissociation, and they allowed me to conduct field trials of the SCID-D during a period of seven years. Three hundred and fifty people were interviewed by five experienced clinicians, producing over one thousand hours of videotaped interviews. Again the symptoms covered a wide spectrum of experiences and behaviors, ranging from the benign to the more severe. In this book you'll find gripping stories of three people at the upper end of the scale and discover the heroic inventiveness and creativity of the human mind fighting to survive inhuman cruelty and exploitation.

The questionnaires at the end of each chapter on each of the five core symptoms, adapted from the SCID-D, will enable you to tell where you or a loved one rank on the scale from normal experience to evidence of a deeper problem for which appropriate treatment is advisable. You may be surprised to find that experiences you've written off as inconsequential are actually dissociative symptoms. Though they may not be severe, they could still indicate the need for a full assessment by a professional and a new kind of therapy described in this book. This therapy will help you get to the bottom of hidden parts of yourself that you may not have fully understood or been able to control up until now. With the proper treatment even DID, the most severe form of the dissociative disorders, has a good prognosis for recovery.

If you are concerned about your own psychological health or that of a loved one, you should not be without the information in this book. You need to know that just as we developed earlier instruments for screening conditions like depression, attention deficit hyperactivity disorder (ADHD) and obsessive-compulsive disorder (OCD), we now have a breakthrough diagnostic tool for dissociation that has been rigorously tested scientifically—the SCID-D. The mental health community has embraced it as the most comprehensive and widely used "gold standard" with which all other tests of this type must be compared, but our emergence from the Dark Ages of dissociation has only recently begun.

This book will give you a context for recognizing symptoms of a condition that, through a conspiracy of silence, misunderstanding, and ignorance, has become the secret epidemic of our time. The material in its pages will finally shine a light on what could very well be the underlying cause of the anxiety, depression, manic-depression, panic attacks, ADHD, OCD, or even schizophrenia that you or a loved one may have been diagnosed with mistakenly. Based on a recent study *over 30 million people, or 14 percent of the general public, experience "substantial" dissociative symptoms.* You may be one of the millions whose symptoms have been undetected and untreated, because you couldn't identify them to report them to a therapist or were not asked about them. This may be the reason why you feel stuck in life or are wandering lost in therapeutic circles, not making any significant headway or achieving long-lasting improvement.

One of the trickier aspects of dissociation is that the more chronic some symptoms are, the less stress they may cause because you've adapted to them and they've become as normal to you as breathing. The information and tests in this book adapted from the SCID-D will help you identify them. No matter where your symptoms fall on the continuum, you need to know why you dissociate and whether your experiences are a clue to a deeper problem.

Since dissociation touches the lives of all of us as a universal coping mechanism in response to high stress or trauma, as a society we cannot afford to keep it in the closet one more day, a dark secret cloaked in ignorance, bias, and myth. This book will dispel popular misconceptions about dissociation and tell you the truth about it—a truth more creative and deeply human than stereotypes would have you believe. It will give you a working knowledge of this fascinating defense: why we have it; what causes it to go out of control; how to distinguish normal experiences of dissociation from problematic ones. And it will inform you of the latest advances in diagnosis and treatment.

It is no exaggeration to say that just as hysteria was the dominant psychiatric illness in Freud's time, and depression reigned in the late twentieth century, dissociation is *the illness* of today. Indeed, most people who have a dissociative disorder enter into therapy complaining of depression. As many as one in three women and one in five men in the United States who were sexually abused or exploited as children—more than 70 million people—are highly vulnerable to some dissociative symptoms or disorder. More cases of DID, the most severe of the disorders, have been reported within the last ten years than in the preceding two centuries, and it is estimated that 1 percent of the general population or 2.5 million people are suffering from it. Were it not for the fact that so many people who actually have a dissociative disorder are misdiagnosed and mistreated for something else, the reported numbers would skyrocket to reflect their true epidemic proportions.

Wherever your symptoms rate on the continuum of dissociation, you can be helped to a better understanding of yourself, and a richer life, through this book. Dissociation is a universal language of buried feelings and memories. Only by getting in touch with the hidden parts of yourself that may be thwarting the full realization of your talents or fulfillment in your personal relationships can you prevent or end unnecessary pain. This book can open a portal—one closed for far too long—onto a transformative path toward enlightenment, healing, and joy.

PART ONE

DISSOCIATION

What It Is and Is Not

1

IN THEIR OWN WORDS

dis·so·ci·a·tion: an adaptive defense in response to high stress or trauma characterized by memory loss and a sense of disconnection from oneself or one's surroundings

WHAT DOES THIS mean to you? Here's how a cross section of people who've experienced dissociation describe it:

"When I become engrossed in a good book, I lose all track of time."

—ALICE M. 33, TRAVEL CONSULTANT

"I feel that somehow my body is not doing what my head wants it to be doing."

—ERNEST P., 51, ENGINEER

"My mind wanders, and I go in and out. I just go away to myself. Nowhere, really, just not there."

—SANDRA N., 19, COLLEGE STUDENT

"I have trouble remembering what I said in a presentation after I've made it."

—JOHN T., 41, SALES DIRECTOR FOR INTERNET FIRM

"I was at home with my mother, and the whole thing was unreal. I knew she was my mother, but I just had a feeling that she wasn't really my mother."

—CINDY M., 32, TELEVISION PRODUCER

"I'm like a filter—who I am on a particular day depends on what's coming into me and what's going out. I don't feel connected internally all the time."

—JEAN W., 41, BATTERED WOMEN'S COUNSELOR

"I'll explode at my husband, and afterward I can't remember what I said."

—GAYLE T., 32, AEROBICS INSTRUCTOR

"It's not feeling real or feeling that I'm just doing things automatically."

—JIM Z., 37, ALCOHOL COUNSELOR

"I feel like a girl most of the time; other times I feel more like a guy."

—CARLY B., 19, COLLEGE STUDENT

"It's like watching a movie in my head. You know, like when you're watching a movie and you get all absorbed in the movie. And you forget who you are, where you are, what time it is, what's going on in your life."

—DONNA E., 41, NURSE

"I can become so totally concerned about what people are thinking of me or expecting from me when I'm talking to them that I become lost—I lose me."

—GEORGE N., 53, FINANCIAL PLANNER

"I couldn't remember whether it really happened or I imagined it."

—SUZANNE O., 35, HOMEMAKER

"It's like being shell-shocked—you know that you're doing something, but you feel that somebody else is doing it. You're watching yourself from a distance. Doesn't everyone have that feeling sometimes?"

—ROBERT A., 51, SCHOOL ADMINISTRATOR

"I don't feel like myself; I feel like some other person inside me."

—VICKI B., 44, MEDICAL TECHNICIAN

"I didn't let myself feel anything about my divorce until after I was divorced. The emotional side of me just shuts down under stress."

—FRED D., 42, BOND RATINGS ANALYST

"I've been in a shell, and I feel empty inside."

—LINDA A., 33, TEACHER

"A very powerful wave of emotion comes over me, and I don't feel in control of myself. I feel that this person is going to do what she wants and I'm over in a corner, helpless, waiting to see what happens."

—PENELOPE J., 54, FREE-LANCE WRITER

"I act differently with different people."

—MARSHA G., 36, FASHION CONSULTANT

Are you surprised to find that you've experienced some of these symptoms of dissociation yourself? You shouldn't be. *The fact is that dissociation is a healthy adaptive defense used almost universally by people in response to overwhelming stress or life-threatening danger. What's more, many normal people experience mild dissociative symptoms on occasion when their lives are not in immediate danger.*

Dissociation is not always the worst case scenario you may mistakenly think it is. It runs along a continuum. Most of us experience mild symptoms of it in our everyday life, like Alice, the travel consultant, who loses all track of time when she becomes engrossed in a good book—a mild form of amnesia. Then there are many other people who experience a moderate degree of symptoms but do not necessarily have a dissociative illness unless their symptoms are associated with distress or dysfunction. Of course, "moderates" who've adapted to their symptoms and compensated for them—sometimes unhealthily—may not regard them as distressing or realize their damaging effects. Fred, the bond ratings analyst, is a cautionary example. A man who doesn't let himself feel anything, a manifestation of a dissociative symptom, may adapt by burying himself in his work and not experience distress in an intimate relationship until it has ended.

Severe symptoms are found mainly in people who have a dissociative disorder, but even at its most extreme this illness is not the catastrophic affliction that it's often made out to be. In the most basic terms dissociative identity disorder, or DID, formerly called multiple personality disorder, is what happens when your "inner child" or some other hidden part of yourself operates independently, seizes control, and makes you act inappropriately or impairs your ability to function. Vicki, the medical technician, who says, "I don't feel like myself; I feel like some other person inside me," is describing a severe dissociative symptom because in her case that internal "other person" is a separate personality state. If that's true for you, like Vicki, you can have DID and still complete your college education, hold down a responsible job, get married, be a good parent, and have a circle of close friends. And best of all, you can recover.

Dissociative symptoms and disorders are far more prevalent in the general population than previously recognized for a good reason: a great many people don't report their symptoms to therapists because they can't identify them! Research has shown that these symptoms are as common as those of depression and anxiety, but the person who is unfamiliar with them may not regard them as significant. If someone doesn't know that "not feeling like a real person" or feeling "apart from who I am" is a dissociative symptom that might indicate a problem, why would that person report it?

The public's unfamiliarity with dissociative symptoms and inability to identify them has caused dissociation to become the silent epidemic of our time. Besides all the people who have an *undetected* dissociative illness, there are countless others who've been diagnosed with the *wrong* illness.

People go to a therapist's office describing symptoms they can recognize as such: "I have wild mood swings," or "I feel sad," or "I have panic attacks," or "I'm easily distracted," or "I keep washing my hands over and over again." If the therapist doesn't ask any questions about dissociative symptoms, the presenting problem—manic-depression, depression, panic attacks, attention deficit hyperactivity disorder, obsessive-compulsive disorder—becomes the diagnosis. Without being tested for dissociative symptoms, the person whose problem has an undetected dissociative basis can be in therapy for a long time without making any real progress. If you're that person, until the root cause of your problem is detected and treated appropriately, full and long-lasting recovery simply won't happen.

Why take that chance?

2

A HEALTHY DEFENSE GONE WRONG

A THIRTY-TWO-YEAR-OLD man was driving on an icy road late at night when his car suddenly skidded out of control, spun around and around like a ride in an amusement park, and finally slammed into a tree, pinning him against the wheel.

"I saw it all happening," says the man, "as if I were a bystander watching from the side of the road. I saw myself turning around in the car and heading straight for the tree, and I was sure I was going to die. But for some strange reason, I felt no emotion. I wasn't scared because it didn't seem real. It was like watching a slow-motion car crash in a movie. A minute seemed like an hour, and I could see details clearly, even specks of dust on the windshield. But the tree looming up in front of me seemed small and far away. When the crash thrust me against the wheel and the horn started blaring, I snapped out of it and reached for my cell phone to call for help."

A fifty-seven-year-old woman was rushed to the hospital for emergency triple-bypass heart surgery. On the operating table she went into cardiac arrest. She recovered, but at the time she thought she was going to die. As people often do during near-death experiences, she had an out-of-body episode, a common manifestation of a dissociative symptom (the dissociative nature of near-death experiences is covered at length in Chapter 15). The woman describes the event this way:

"I floated out of my body and hovered in the air, looking down on the doctors and nurses working on me. I felt detached from what was going on. It was like watching a medical show on TV. One of the doctors was pounding on my chest with big paddles, and I thought, 'I'm not going to make it.' I should have been frightened, but instead this wonderful feeling of peace came over me. Time stood still. Scenes from my childhood of happy times that I'd forgotten all about passed before me in quick succession, and I felt that I was actually reliving them. Pleasant memories of my husband, my children, and my grandchildren flew by, too. I felt sad leaving them, but I had complete peace of mind. I saw myself already entering a new life filled with joy."

A twenty-eight-year-old secretary was working at her desk in the Alfred P. Murrah Federal Building in Oklahoma City on April 19, 1995, when a bomb exploded, killing 168 people and injuring hundreds more. Severely burned and bleeding from flying glass, she was able to make her way out of the building to safety.

"I felt that what was happening around me was like a scene from a war movie," she says. "I was observing it, but I wasn't participating in it. It all seemed so strange and unreal. I saw my burns and the blood pouring out from a deep gash on my arm, but I didn't feel any pain. I was numb, and everything around me was a blur—the noise, the screaming, the smoke. My thoughts started moving a mile a minute, thoughts like where was the nearest exit, how could I get there, how much time did I have before the whole building collapsed. I felt myself moving automatically, almost like a robot walking through a fog, and the next thing I knew, I was outside."

All of these accounts describe episodes of dissociation experienced by normal people in response to a life-threatening traumatic event. Believing that they were in extreme danger or were about to die, these people dissociated—that is, they activated altered states of consciousness that helped them marshal the inner resources to cope with a situation that otherwise would have been overwhelming. During these altered states they experienced a number of phenomena:

- a sense of detachment from oneself and one's body
- feelings of unreality
- a numbing of emotions
- a sharpening of one's senses
- changes in perceptions of the environment
- a slowing of time
- a quickening of one's thoughts
- automatic or robotic movements
- a revival of buried memories as if one were reliving them

Survivors of life-threatening trauma convey these phenomena in images that are familiar to anyone who has looked death in the eye. "I floated out of my body" and "It was like watching myself in a movie" are common ways of describing the feelings of disconnection and unreality that diminish the threat of death by allowing the person facing it to view the scene as a detached observer. "I felt numb" and "It didn't seem real" depict the characteristic lack of emotion. Saying that "everything around me was a blur" or that threatening objects seemed "small and far away" describes the dulling of certain perceptions of the environment that many survivors experience along with a heightened perception of others or the ability to "see details clearly." Such stock phrases as "Time stood still" and "Every minute seemed like an hour" speak to the familiar slowing of time, whereas speeded-up thoughts are "moving a mile a minute." These thoughts are usually directed at "the nearest exit," toward which the survivor moves automatically, like "a robot walking through a fog," then arriving at a safe place without any knowledge of how she got there. And, finally, there is the rapid retrieval of memories "I'd forgotten all about," so vivid that the person has the feeling of "actually reliving them." This commonplace near-death, my-whole-life-passed-before-my-eyes phenomenon, technically known as "panoramic memory," distracts the survivor's attention from the gravity of the situation and helps her maintain her serenity. Panoramic memory may also be a way of searching for data from past experiences that might be of help in the current situation.

People in life-threatening circumstances have reported experiencing these phenomena so repeatedly that we now understand them as part of the normal human trauma response—a healthy coping device in everyone's psychological repertoire. As a natural reaction to trauma, dissociation has the remarkable capacity to intensify alertness greatly while splitting off from awareness emotions that would paralyze or unhinge the person. The sense of unreality and distorted perceptions of the environment, blurring some features and accentuating others, distance the endangered person from the more terrifying aspects of the situation. Feeling that the clock has stopped in the outside world gives the person the latitude to focus on quickening thoughts of self-preservation. The numbing of emotions stills anxiety and wards off panic, allowing the person to perform automatically, as if some higher power had taken control. In all, these perceptual alterations combine to enable someone in grave danger to defy death or, failing that, to accept it gracefully.

By dissociating, the man in the auto accident was not done in by fear and had the presence of mind to reach for his cell phone and call for help when he returned to a normal state. The woman in cardiac arrest achieved a state of extraordinary calm and peacefulness by dissociating from the straits she was in and was able to accept what she thought was imminent death with equanimity. And the young woman in the Oklahoma City bombing incident used dissociation to block out the horror around her, allowing her to concentrate on escaping from the building before it collapsed.

From these examples we can see what an ingenious adaptive device dissociation is to a life-threatening trauma. To help us survive, certain perceptions, feelings, sensations, thoughts, and memories related to the trauma are split off from full awareness and encoded in some peripheral level of awareness. Miraculously, dissociation alters reality but allows the person to stay in contact with it in order to help himself. This duality is evident in the metaphors people use to describe their feelings of detachment from reality during dissociative episodes. They repeatedly use the phrases "as if" and "it was like"—"I saw it all happening as if I were a bystander," or "It was like watching a medical show on TV." Their language clearly shows that although people in a dissociative state feel that what is happening to them is not real, on another level of awareness they know that it is. When they return to a normal state, the dissociated material is less accessible, but it might be lying in wait to resurface.

NORMAL DISSOCIATION VERSUS ABNORMAL DISSOCIATION

My pilot study group for the SCID-D, the interview test I developed for diagnosing dissociative disorders, included normal subjects as well as people who had been diagnosed with various psychological disorders. The findings revealed a surprising fact: *dissociative episodes are very common among normal people even when they're not in any danger.*

Usually these episodes are a reaction to stress. "I was having a day when the pressure of my job really got to me," reports Annette, thirty-six, a trial lawyer and the mother of two young children. "I could hardly drag myself out of bed in the morning, thinking of all I had to do. When I was getting dressed, I looked in the mirror and thought, 'Who is that? Do I know you?' The person I saw looking back at me was totally unfamiliar. I knew it was me, and yet it wasn't me. It was scary, so I snapped myself out of it and finished getting dressed in a hurry. It never happened again."

Josh, a twenty-nine-year-old stockbroker, describes a similar dissociative response to nerve-fraying stress he once had. "I was sitting at my computer in the office, watching intraday trading on a day when the market was fluctuating wildly. The phone didn't stop ringing. My clients were going crazy. Orders were flying at me left and right: buy, sell, put, call. I looked around me and saw everybody else going through the same thing. Then a funny thing happened. I knew these people, saw them every day, but they didn't look real to me. The whole scene didn't look real. It was all very strange, like something out of a dream. That only lasted maybe thirty seconds or so, and then I was back to normal, taking another order on the phone."

Although these people were in no life-threatening danger, the stress overload made them feel as if they were dangling over the edge of an emotional precipice and triggered a momentary trauma response. They felt as if they had to escape, and they did it by detaching themselves from their body or the world around them in much the same way that a person in an auto accident or some other cataclysmic situation goes out-of-body or sees the environment as unreal.

The SCID-D gives a clear picture of the difference between normal people who are experiencing dissociation, whether in response to life-threatening trauma or to less calamitous stress, and those diagnosed with a dissociative disorder. "Normals," like Annette and Josh, experience episodes that are brief, are rare, and have a minimal effect on their ability to function socially or on the job. People with a dissociative disorder, on the other hand, have episodes that are persistent, recurrent, and disruptive to social relationships or job performance.

Normal people rate their dissociative episodes on the "mild" end of the spectrum in terms of duration, frequency, and the amount of distress and dysfunction they cause. By contrast, those who have a dissociative disorder rate their episodes as "moderate" or "severe." People with DID, the most extreme form of the dissociative disorders, have the highest ratings for all of the symptoms, including the one that defines their illness—identity alteration or the assumption of different personalities.

Another striking difference between normal and abnormal dissociation is related to memory. The life review or panoramic memory phenomenon experienced by normal people dissociating in a close brush with death does not occur in people with a dissociative disorder. Instead they have amnesia for traumas and persistent and recurrent episodes of unaccountable "lost time" or large memory gaps for a period in their lives that may stretch for years. Though the life review for normal people is composed mostly of pleasant, long-forgotten memories spilling out disconnectedly like cards from a shuffled deck, for people with a dissociative disorder the intrusive memory fragments are alarming, terror-filled, repeated "flashbacks" or replays of the trauma itself long after the event has passed.

"Mental clouding" is another cognitive difference that distinguishes normal dissociation from abnormal. Normal people experience a speeding up of mental processes in times of extreme danger, whereas people with a dissociative disorder often suffer mental confusion. Their amnesia may cause them to "blank out" at times and may interfere with their ability to recall important personal information. Knowledge or skills they've acquired may also intermittently be forgotten as if they suddenly vanished without a trace through a trapdoor. A person who was a skilled pianist for many years, for example, may be dumbfounded to sit down at the piano and suddenly not know how to play at all.

On an emotional level there is a distinct difference, too. For normal people facing a life-threatening trauma, the numbing or dulling of feelings they experience is gratifying because it keeps their fear and anxiety under control and enables them to stay calm. For people with a dissociative disorder this emotional numbness has the opposite effect of heightening their anxiety to the point of panic at times. Their feeling of inner deadness, of lifelessness and emptiness inside, can be terrifying at its worst—if not a continuing cause of depression. For them the inner deadness is associated with a disconnection from the dreadful traumas they experienced in childhood.

Essentially the difference between normal and abnormal dissociation is a matter of too much of a good thing. An *adaptive,* even life-saving, response to a traumatic event posing grave danger to a person somehow persists and recurs long after the danger has passed and becomes *maladaptive.* How and why does this happen?

In terms of processing incoming information, research on rats has shown that the brain is like a post office with two different tracks for local and out-of-town mail. All information from the outside world is first received by the thalamus, the brain's sensory-input center. From there messages can be sent along either one of two separate systems of nerves: one going to the frontal cortex of the brain, where conscious thinking and analysis take place, and the other going to a thimble-size bit of tissue at the base of the brain called the amygdala. Fear determines which set of sensory information goes where.

When danger is perceived, fear-inducing information is split off from the rest of the input in the thalamus and in twelve milliseconds is sent to the amygdala for emergency processing. Instantaneously, before we're aware of having given it a thought, the amygdala sets off the trauma response. This tiny nerve center sends messages along the neural pathways running out from it to increase heart rate, blood pressure, and respiration; lower body temperature; and otherwise press our bodies into full-scale counterattack mode. It does this blindly, without the capacity to judge the seriousness of the threat and decide on the most appropriate course of action from a number of options. Not only that, the amygdala stamps its own fear-driven images on the bundle of traumatic information and stores it in a different memory bin from the one where factual information processed by the thinking part of the brain is kept.

From this two-track memory system—one track for emotionally charged material and the other for factual information—we can see a physiological basis for dissociation. The way the brain separates out emotional memories from factual ones is a forerunner of the splitting off in dissociation, in which the fragmentation is more complex and extensive— not only are emotionally charged memories split off, but so are parts of one's very sense of self.

Normally, as we've seen, this detachment during a *transient* episode of dissociation in response to a life-threatening event, such as an auto accident or cardiac arrest, is immensely helpful. For some people exposed to intense trauma or severe and ongoing abuse in childhood, the dissociative response becomes fixed and automatic. The enormous stress related to the traumatic memories makes it exceedingly hard for the brain to defuse and integrate them when there is no longer any threat of danger. So triggers keep the danger signals raucously blaring and blaring like a burglar alarm tripped by someone who doesn't know how to turn it off.

One example of this jarring repetitiveness can be seen in how the "replay button" operates in normal people as opposed to those with post-traumatic stress disorder (PTSD), an illness that is primarily dissociative in nature. In the aftermath of a traumatic event, people commonly replay memories of it over and over again. Repetition helps them drain the power from the trauma until it loosens its grip, and they can put it aside. This is a healthy use of the mechanism for a limited time. The person with PTSD gets trapped in the machinery, and the replay continues indefinitely with no abatement of the original terror. Intrusive images and memories of the trauma recur obsessively in nightmares and flashbacks and are so terrifyingly real that the person experiences them not as memories, but as events in the present.

For people whose trauma response system is out of control, the past becomes indistinguishable from the present. Any reminder of the trauma can set off a Pavlovian reflex, as it does in the shell-shocked combat veteran who hears an automobile backfiring in the street and runs into a closet to hide. Over time any stressor, even one not remotely reminiscent of the trauma or abuse, can trigger a similar response.

Living in a continual state of battle alert or hypervigilance erodes emotional stability. Nameless fears and anxiety abound in people with a dissociative disorder, and they become caught up in a desperate struggle to control the spin cycle of their emotions, constantly revolving from high to low. Since they've lost the ability to regulate their emotions, they often overreact to stress, with either temper tantrums or panic attacks, and dissociate in an effort to numb their emotions and quell their anxiety. They may also try to numb their emotions with drugs or alcohol and channel their anxiety into food obsessions or self-mutilation rituals. This habitual dampening of their feelings may eventually bring about physiological changes in the brain, impairing its ability to process emotions and leading to a sense of sadness and hopelessness characteristic of depression.

When people who have DID seek therapy, the problem that looms large is usually the one that is treated—the panic attacks, the mood swings, the obsessive-compulsive behavior, the depression. Their out-of-control trauma response, the real villain, is often ignored because many clinicians are not trained to look for the dissociative symptoms that signal its dysfunction. Also, people with DID may find their dissociative symptoms difficult to describe or may have memories so fragmented by trauma or abuse that they no longer remember what actually happened to them.

Sexual abuse is so ravaging to a child's psyche that dissociation, meant to be a defense, holds the child hostage, and the survivor is made a prisoner of its symptoms. A child who is sexually assaulted by a parent the young person trusts implicitly and totally depends upon for protection is facing unimaginable terror. The jumble of fear, love, rage, pain, and shame at the forbidden sexual excitement can shatter the soul.

Overwhelmed by the assault, the ego passively allows itself to fall apart, saying, in effect, "This is too much pain for any one person to survive, so I'll split off a part of myself and create another person to help me bear it." This is different from repression, in which the ego expels inner threats from consciousness and preserves the person's sense of self intact. In dissociation the ego falls to pieces and causes the person to experience the self as more than one. Repressed material kept out of awareness is unlikely to reemerge as a separate personality, but the dissociated part of the mind can be experienced as a separate center of consciousness capable of organized thinking—in other words, a personality.

The young child who is being sexually and emotionally abused or physically beaten is afraid that she will either die or go insane. She can't run *and* she can't hide. She can't even confide in anyone about the abuse for fear of retaliation. Since physical escape is impossible, the child escapes mentally. She floats out of her body, imagining that somebody else is being raped or beaten, and turns off her emotions, saying, "This isn't happening to me."

As the abuse goes on, dissociation becomes routine. The child continues to detach and float outside her body and create an imaginary person inside her to carry the abuse memories. Though a normal child may have an "imaginary friend" at age four or five who goes away, for the abused child the imaginary friend becomes fixed and continues throughout life. With habitual dissociation other distinct parts of the person may come along, each with its own name, memories, thoughts, feelings, abilities, chronological age, handwriting, manner of dress, and so forth, and may take control from time to time, often without the person's awareness. What was once a healthy adaptive defense on rare occasion is now an automatic response to everyday stress or any trigger suggestive of the abuse memories—and it never goes away.

For most people, brief, mild episodes of dissociation are a part of everyday life. Take memory, for example. Automatically driving a car and not remembering the ride, because only a split-off part of the mind was on the road, probably happens to normal people every time they drive home from work. Another common experience is the frustrating "tip of the tongue" phenomenon. When pressed, we can't recall a familiar name, only to have it pop back into consciousness when we're *not* thinking of it.

Multiply these quirks a thousandfold, and you might get some idea of how the memory of a person with a dissociative disorder has been impaired. People with DID may look whole on the outside, but inside their sense of self and connection with the outside world has been splintered into bits and pieces. Every day is a quietly heroic struggle, not only to keep unthinkable memories hidden from consciousness, but also to conceal frightening symptoms from others. No matter what their level of education or socioeconomic background, all these people have an extravagantly rich and creative inner world. Not surprisingly, many high-functioning multiples are gifted writers and artists, who, as they heal, are able to find an aesthetic outlet for the sealed-off rage and pain they have not allowed themselves to feel.

WHO IS AT RISK?

Not every abused child becomes a multiple, but a history of childhood abuse has been found in more than 90 percent of all diagnosed multiples. Although more women than men are diagnosed with DID, it's believed that many adult males with DID are *undiagnosed*. Men often attempt to deal with problems on their own rather than seek treatment for them. They may relieve stress and inner symptoms by drinking, using drugs, or engaging in compulsive sex. Since drinking alcohol, using drugs, or being sexually overactive may be socially acceptable initially, it may take longer for a man to enter into treatment and have his psychological issues evaluated. Frequently it takes a sudden loss—the death of a child, the breakup of a marriage, getting fired—to impel a man to seek treatment. If men were as treatment-oriented as women, just as many men as women would probably be diagnosed with a dissociative disorder.

It's not hard to understand why dissociative symptoms are so widespread, considering that as many as one in three women and one in five men in the United States were sexually abused or exploited before age eighteen—more than 70 million people—are highly vulnerable.

Especially at risk are the 28 million children of alcoholics in America who grow up in homes where violence, abuse, or neglect is often the norm. Add to that the unusual kinds of traumatic incidents we have in modern life—terrorist bombings of buildings or airplanes, mass shootings in the subway or in schools—and you begin to get the picture.

The pressure on college students today makes them another group who tend to get high scores on dissociative screening tests. In a 1984 study 34 percent reported episodes of depersonalization or feelings of being unreal or separate from one's own body, apart from times when they were under the influence of drugs or alcohol and were more likely to have them. One study of five hundred university students taking an under-graduate psychology class produced the bombshell that 12 percent—about one in eight—had at least once dissociatively cut, burned, or similarly harmed themselves. So prevalent is self-mutilation among young women, in fact, that campus cutters have dubbed it "the new anorexia."

Dissociative symptoms and the disorders they might signify need to be taken seriously, but they can't be dealt with realistically until we dispel the myths about them. Since the field of dissociation has been so demonized and misrepresented to the public, what you "know" about the disorder probably isn't true.

3

⌁

DEBUNKING THE MYTHS

DURING MY NINETEEN years of scientific research devoted to dissociation, I have been amazed at the amount of *misinformation* that has been dispensed to both the public and the professional community. No other field of medicine in modern times has been buried under such a mudslide of misconception, skepticism, and plain ignorance.

Part of the problem lies in the nature of dissociation itself. Dissociative disorders are so fascinating because they express the universal language of pain in an intensely imaginative and metaphorical way, yet at the same time they seem so bizarre and theatrical as to arouse incredulity. Before the SCID-D, diagnosing dissociative disorders was more of an art than a science. With no valid and reliable tool for accurate assessment, wary clinicians tended to shy away from treating dissociative disorders or deny their existence.

Another basis for the skepticism many clinicians have toward dissociative disorders, especially DID, can be found in the philosophical underpinnings of their traditional training. The presence of a variety of personality states that take control of a person's thoughts and behavior at different times contradicts a long-held assumption. For years the thinking was that we should have one unitary personality, and skeptics are reluctant to question such a fundamental concept.

Yet another reason for clinicians' skepticism toward dissociation may be their difficulty in accepting a history of trauma in their own lives. A growing number of therapists have acknowledged that they were attracted to the helping professions because as children they learned how to survive abuse or to be caretakers in compromised families. The connection between childhood trauma and dissociative disorders challenges them to look at themselves and their own histories from a potentially painful perspective. Rather than explore such anxiety-provoking issues, they may take cover in a mantle of skeptical "objectivity."

We all know how nature abhors a vacuum. Unfortunately in the absence of scientific findings about dissociation disseminated to a public largely undiagnosed and untreated for the symptoms, mythology has rushed in to fill the breach. Following are the seven most common myths.

MYTH #1
DISSOCIATIVE SYMPTOMS SIGNIFY A SERIOUS DISORDER

On the contrary, every one of us has probably experienced a perfectly normal dissociative episode any number of times in our lives. These include losing oneself in a novel and completely forgetting where one is; daydreaming while driving a car and arriving somewhere with no idea of how one got there; blanking out and forgetting a familiar name or missing part of a conversation; staring into space and losing track of time; not knowing whether a memory is real or from a dream; not being able to remember what one has just done; feeling as if one were a participant in what is happening and an observer watching it happen; looking in the mirror and seeing oneself as unfamiliar; moving automatically, like a robot; feeling as if one were watching oneself in a movie; having a dream-like or unreal feeling about other people, objects, or the world around one; feeling that time is standing still.

Most often these symptoms occur as a natural reaction to trauma or stress or having a lot on one's mind, pass quickly, and do *not* indicate the presence of a psychiatric disorder. For example, a study of ninety men and women reacting to the 1989 earthquake in the San Francisco area found that two-thirds had some kind of dissociative symptom, such as a distorted sense of time or a perception of the world as dreamlike. One in ten reported having an out-of-body experience, and close to half found themselves staring at an object in space, for example, a tree, and not knowing why.

In all, close to 25 percent of the general population have been found to experience mild to severe episodes of dissociation. If these episodes are short-lived and and do not recur often enough to become a cause of distress or dysfunction, they don't signify the presence of a disorder. Dissociative symptoms are indicative of a serious disorder only when they have become maladaptive or recur persistently after they are no longer necessary for self-protection and adversely affect a person's well-being or ability to function in daily life.

MYTH #2
DISSOCIATIVE DISORDERS ARE RARE

Recent studies have shown that far from being rare, dissociative disorders are much more prevalent than previously realized. Multiples, the most seriously affected, number as much as 1 percent of the general population, or more than 2.5 million people. This is a conservative estimate in light of how widely underdiagnosed dissociative disorders are. The true figure for the dissociation disorders is probably closer to 10 percent—as high as the one-year prevalence of major depression or generalized anxiety disorder, for which the dissociative disorders are often mistaken.

Few people make dissociative symptoms their primary complaint, because they are elusive and hard to describe, involving as they do a strange absence of feeling or a curious sense of reality. The symptoms may also remain hidden or silent because people vary greatly in how they experience them—some becoming so acclimated to them that they no longer find them disquieting and assume everyone has them. Sometimes the symptoms have such a demoralizing effect on people's self-esteem that they develop an attitude of resignation toward them, throwing their hands up in the air and saying, "That's life." Actually, this feeling of helplessness is one reason why so many persons with dissociative disorders have been misdiagnosed as depressives.

Another factor that makes it hard to diagnose DID without administering a test like the SCID-D is that people suffering from a dissociative disorder often have a huge amount of denial. The garish stereotype of a multiple that has been implanted in their minds by *Sybil* and *The Three Faces of Eve* has had a chilling effect. Their worst fear is that if they talk about their symptoms to a therapist, they'll immediately be labeled a freak or a crazy person.

Very often people who have separate parts of themselves keep them hidden, because they don't think of them as well-defined personalities, but more as "aspects" of their own personalities or different internal "voices" or puzzling "sides" of themselves with which they're not in touch all the time. If they perceive these fragments as vague, amorphous, or shadowy—no matter how troubling—they may dismiss them as simply figments of an overheated imagination. The reason many multiples are misdiagnosed as manic-depressives is that the uncontrollable mood swings and "temper tantrums" they complain of are actually the outbursts of a personality fragment carrying all of the rage associated with childhood abuse.

Although people are rarely quick to complain about their dissociative symptoms to their therapists, the fact is that these episodes occur in many patients who have been diagnosed with other psychiatric problems. They may well indicate a more fundamental dissociative disorder that has to be dealt with before any lasting recovery can be achieved.

MYTH #3
MULTIPLES ARE EASY TO SPOT

The person suffering from a dissociative disorder is a far cry from the distorted image of the bizarre multiple grossly switching from one personality to another on sensationalistic TV talk shows. The fact is that multiples run the gamut from Ph.D.'s to prostitutes and are generally highly intelligent, creative, brave, articulate, and likable. Many are accomplished professionals, married, raising children, and holding down responsible jobs. Most of the time they don't engage in public displays of shocking, uncontrollable behavior. If they switch at all, it is usually in the privacy of their own home or in confidential sessions with a therapist whom they've learned to trust. Otherwise the changes in voice, speech patterns, comportment, and dress signaling that an alter personality has taken control are subtle.

Multiples are able to function at a high level and "pass" as healthy by dint of an elaborate inner world and exhausting always-on-guard compensatory strategies for avoiding detection by others. Tortured by an unspeakable past, they endure the daily agonizing struggles of a present lived in secret shame. The person you'd be least likely to expect—a neighbor, loved one, friend, coworker or boss—might very well be someone secretly struggling with the demons of a dissociative disorder.

MYTH #4
MOST MEMORIES OF ABUSE ARE CREATED IN THERAPY

The fact is that most abuse survivors seek treatment due to memories of abuse that existed *prior* to treatment. Though abuse of children is widespread, disbelief about its existence continues. In the United States, close to 1 million children were victims of confirmed child abuse and neglect for each year from 1900 to 1997. Add to that the 4 million women who are victims of severe assaults by boyfriends and husbands each year, as reported by the American Medical Association, and it should come as no surprise that when these people enter treatment, they will report having memories of being abused. Over half of survivors entering therapy report that they have had continuous memories of childhood sexual abuse. Intrusion of traumatic memories often leads people to seek psychotherapy. Because what survivors experienced in childhood was too painful for them to bear, survivors may have partial amnesia for some aspects of their abuse and may not necessarily remember details, such as dates, but will remember the overall gist of their trauma.

In recent years, the controversy over recovered abuse memories has created a groundswell of bias and misunderstanding about trauma and dissociation and is an unfortunate diversion from legitimate claims and treatment. Accusations of therapists' induction of false memories have magnified limitations in the field that no longer exist. Thanks to advances, clinicians now have the benefit of diagnostic and screening tools, cutting-edge research on the physiological effects of trauma, and specific treatment guidelines. By asking nonleading, open-ended questions that result in spontaneous responses from patients about their traumatic experiences, both in the SCID-D diagnostic process and throughout treatment, therapists can minimize the risk of false memories.

Even "retractors"—people who retrieve memories of abuse, only to claim later on that some memory they retrieved is false—may have some abuse or trauma in their histories. The accuracy of abuse memories has been confirmed in some cases with police or medical reports and by witnesses of the abuse. Today's more sophisticated and stringent guidelines for assessing and treating dissociative disorders, however, should result in earlier detection of dissociative symptoms and an increasing number of successful outcomes for abuse survivors. Currently, appropriate treatment would focus on helping the patient reduce the severity of dissociative symptoms, alleviate stress associated with whatever memories of abuse he or she has, and restore functioning rather than focusing on identifying specific memories.

Claims of false memories and retractions of abuse have to be seen in the context in which they are made. Even when there are confessions by perpetrators and substantial physical evidence of abuse, children can retract their disclosures as a way of dealing with their confusion and psychological pain. Adult victims who confront their families about the abuse are often met with denial and coercion to retract their allegations. Parents, siblings or grandparents who have abused a child in the family may be so ashamed of what they've done that they cannot admit it to themselves. Clinical experience shows that *perpetrators* are far more likely to suppress the truth about their abuse than their victims are to fabricate it.

MYTH #5
A PERSON WHO WAS REALLY ABUSED WOULD NEVER FORGET IT

Pressure to remain silent about traumatic events plays a significant role in provoking amnesia for them. When a father repeatedly forces his young daughter to have sex and warns her, "If you talk about this, I'll kill you," or the girl reports the abuse and is told, "You're lying," the girl is prompted to split the memory of the trauma off from consciousness. She forgets it, because she fears being driven crazy by acts of betrayal too painful to bear. Forced to live with a terrible secret and made mute by the fear of reprisal, she is unable to find comfort or enlist anyone to come to her rescue.

The failure to report abuse does not mean that people have forgotten it. The fact is that most victims do not report abuse at all. In a study conducted at the University of Colorado at Boulder in 1995, researchers found that only 8 percent of men and 22 percent of women who described experiencing sexually abusive events in childhood identified themselves as "abused." Of those who described experiencing physical abuse, including being beaten, punched, kicked, and threatened with a weapon by a parent, only 5 percent of men and 9 percent of women identified themselves as "abused." A 1994 study of 129 women with sexual abuse histories (documented by ER visits) found that when they were interviewed seventeen years later, 38 percent of these women did not recall their abuse. These were women whose abuse was so severe that it necessitated visits to hospital emergency rooms. We can only imagine how many others suffered in silence at home.

People with histories of childhood abuse are not eager to talk about it. Or they can't. For every person who has a supposedly false memory of abuse, there are millions of people who've been so debilitated by childhood abuse, whether they are mentally impaired, in chronic psychiatric institutions, or homeless on the street, that they will never speak a word of it to anyone.

Ironically, researchers' findings that people forget the details of a traumatic event but not that it happened best answers the question so often asked by skeptics: How can a person completely forget something as outrageous as sexual abuse and then suddenly remember it years later? The point is, the person doesn't forget it completely. Many adults with histories of childhood abuse have times during their lives when they've forgotten or nearly forgotten the abuse, but very few have consistently forgotten about it throughout their lives. What generally happens is that they experience a breakthrough of intrusive but fragmented impressions of the abuse with intermittent periods of forgetting. Most disclosures of sexual abuse are not based on "recovered" memories magically pulled from storage like rabbits out of hats, but on a process of remembering, forgetting, and remembering that is customary for recalling traumatic memories.

Memories like those of sexual abuse have a life of their own. As fear-imprinted memories, they are not recorded coherently on a mental "videotape," as factual memories are encoded by the thinking part of the brain. Incapable of thought, the tiny mass of gray matter called the amygdala shapes and stores traumatic memories in the limbic part of the brain, which processes emotions and sensations, but not language or speech. As a result, survivors of childhood abuse may carry implicit physiological memories of the terror, pain, and sadness generated by the abuse but may have few or no explicit factual memories to explain their flashbacks and the feelings and sensations they arouse. They live with the repercussions of the event without having a narrative—this is what happened at this time at such-and-such a place—to provide a back story. Memories of traumatic experiences are not retrieved so much as they intrude. They pop up in jagged impressionistic fragments overloaded with sensations and emotions that can distort the details. The memory that abuse occurred usually remains intact over time—and is real.

Another question often heard from people who doubt the veracity of abuse disclosures is, Why do some trauma survivors remember their experience without any blanks at all, and others have amnesia for it? In other words, why doesn't everyone dissociate the memories of trauma? Obviously those who are more driven to avoid the stressful thoughts and feelings related to the trauma are more likely to have memory blanks for the event or its most threatening aspects. There are three main factors that influence this propensity toward dissociative amnesia: the nature of the traumatic events, their frequency, and the age of the person experiencing them.

A child sexually abused by a parent who warns that disclosure means death has good reason to develop amnesia for the trauma. By comparison, a woman raped by a stranger who slips into her apartment and assaults her at knife point may suffer severe posttraumatic stress, but if her family and friends rally around her and offer sympathy and support as she recounts the dreadful experience, she has no need to dismiss it from memory.

Random disasters, like earthquakes or plane crashes, are impersonal in nature and less likely to be dissociated than trauma inflicted on someone willfully by another human being, such as sexual abuse or torture. A traumatic single event, such as a rape or witnessing of a violent death, or narrowly escaping the loss of one's own life in an accident, is less likely to be dissociated than repetitive traumas, such as ongoing physical or sexual abuse or lengthy military combat, which often result in amnesia. Adults who experience traumatic events are not as likely to dissociate memories of them as are children who experience trauma. Since a child's brain and central nervous system are too immature to process the overwhelming fear, pain, and excitement that repeated sexual trauma engenders, the younger a child is when the trauma occurs, the more likely it is that the event will be dissociated.

MYTH #6
DID IS NOT A REAL ILLNESS

All scientific investigations support the fact that DID is a real illness with a consistent pattern of symptoms, a characteristic course, and chronic impairment if untreated. The SCID-D field trials provided evidence that DID is a real illness with clinically measurable symptoms. Subjects gave elaborate descriptions to substantiate all dissociative symptoms they claimed to have. Independent researchers around the world, using the SCID-D and a variety of other measures, have documented virtually identical symptom profiles in people with DID. On the other hand, the myth that DID is not a real illness is based on anecdotal information or misinformation as well as unjustified conclusions by investigators who do laboratory research on college student volunteers rather than psychiatric patients. Although these experiments show that isolated symptoms, like using an alternate name, can be shaped by asking leading questions, they offer no proof that the full clinical syndrome of DID can be faked.

The idea that people can successfully fake or exaggerate multiple personalities was soundly disproved by Dr. George Fraser, M.D., and associates in a 1999 study. Using the SCID-D and other psychological tests, the research project detected individuals asked to fake multiple personalities in a group consisting of the pretenders, DID patients, schizophrenics, and normal people. On the SCID-D 100 percent of the true DID patients were diagnosed with DID, and none of the pretenders or the normals was.

People who are now professing that "Sybil" was not a real multiple, but a highly suggestible person who was faking her symptoms to please her therapist, are guilty of hearsay and pseudoscience posing as authentic research. Her psychiatrist, Dr. Cornelia B. Wilbur, M.D., former professor of psychiatry at the Medical School of the University of Kentucky, has since died and is unable to defend her diagnosis and treatment of her famous patient. Sybil's therapy took place in the days before we had modern tests that would have proven whether she was a real multiple or not. However, her symptoms described in the book based on her case are typical of patients who have been accurately diagnosed with DID.

Myth #7
DID can't be cured

DID patients have a good prognosis for recovery once they are accurately diagnosed and treated appropriately. The problem has been the failure of many clinicians to make an accurate diagnosis. Now, with the SCID-D, this problem can be eliminated. The questionnaires in this book will make it possible for you to identify symptoms in yourself or in a loved one that might have been unnamed or unnoticed before and were therefore untreatable.

The most effective treatment for DID is a combination of highly specialized psychotherapy and drug therapy. Antidepressants and antianxiety medication are frequently used to help alleviate the emotional numbness, depression, or turmoil associated with the disorder. The psychotherapy, contrary to a popular misconception, is not concentrated on recovering memories of abuse. It isn't necessary for a person to dredge up more memories than she is prepared to handle, nor to remember all the details. What *is* necessary is knowing how to comfort oneself when distressing memories or emotions emerge.

Recovery is a challenging process that takes time—an average of three to five years of weekly sessions. The results can be enormously gratifying and transformative, especially when you consider that many people with DID spend long years of their lives in treatment for panic attacks, OCD, depression, anxiety disorders, bipolar disorder, ADHD, and even schizophrenia without this kind of progress.

The in-depth case histories of three of my patients that appear later in the book are enlightening examples of how people with a dissociative disorder *can* recover. They're proof of the extraordinary power of the human mind both to defend itself against inhumanity and to recover from the wounds sustained in that life-or-death battle.

PART TWO

RECOGNIZING THE SIGNS AND RATING YOUR SYMPTOMS

4

THE FIVE CORE SYMPTOMS

A FTER YEARS OF working with abuse survivors and listening to
them talk about their symptoms, I discovered the key that unlocked the
elusive mystery of dissociation—the presence of five core symptoms.
These symptoms are universally experienced by people, to varying
degrees, after exposure to trauma.

The core dissociative symptoms are:

1. amnesia
2. depersonalization
3. derealization
4. identity confusion
5. identity alteration

Amnesia is the inability to account by memory for a specific and significant block of time that has passed. You may think of it as "gaps" in
memory or "lost time."

Depersonalization is a feeling of detachment from yourself or looking at
yourself as an outsider would. You may also feel separated from parts of your
body or feel detached from your emotions, like a robot or an automaton.

Derealization is a feeling of detachment from your environment or a sense that the environment is unreal or foreign, often involving people who were previously familiar to you.

Identity confusion is a feeling of uncertainty, puzzlement, or conflict about who you are. You may feel as if a continuing struggle is going on inside you to define yourself, including your sexual identity, in a particular way.

Identity alteration is a shift in role or identity, accompanied by such changes in your behavior that are observable to others as speaking in a different voice or using different names. You may experience the shift as a personality switch or loss of control over yourself to someone else inside you.

After identifying these major symptoms, I developed ways to evaluate their severity, by crafting a concise definition for each that characterized its essential features. In particular, I used the terms "identity confusion" and "identity alteration" to describe how trauma affects one's sense of self. Equipped with the SCID-D, clinicians could, for the first time, assess all five symptoms comprehensively to determine whether a person had a dissociative illness or not. Different constellations of these five core syndromes defined the particular dissociative disorder a person had.

1. **dissociative amnesia** (loss of memory for your identity or past, characterized by the inability to recall important personal information)
2. **dissociative fugue** (sudden, unexpected travel away from your home associated with identity confusion leading to distress and dysfunction)
3. **depersonalization disorder** (persistent and recurrent severe episodes of feeling detached from yourself, parts of your body, or your emotions, leading to distress and dysfunction)
4. **dissociative identity disorder or DID** (the existence of distinct, coherent identities within yourself that are able to assume control of your behavior and thought)
5. **dissociative disorder not otherwise specified** (DDNOS, an early stage or less serious form of the other disorders that often precedes a diagnosis of DID)

The SCID-D interview provides a well-defined snapshot of the health of a person's trauma response system. At one end of the spectrum are people whose dissociative defense is normal. Their symptoms are mild—rare, of short duration, and not distressing or disruptive to their lives. In the middle of the scale are those with moderate symptoms that occur more frequently and last longer, including some that cause dysfunction or distress, and indicate the need for a professional assessment. Many people in this range have been in therapy for something other than a dissociative symptom or disorder—depression or panic attacks, for example—and will not enjoy a full recovery unless their dissociation is recognized and treated. At the opposite end are those with severe symptoms that are more frequent and result in more dysfunction than moderate symptoms, and are present in people with a dissociative disorder.

The most important distinction for you to make is between mild dissociative experiences that are normal and experiences that range from moderate to severe. If your symptoms fall anywhere in the moderate to severe range, you should have the full SCID-D done by a qualified professional who can make an accurate diagnosis. With appropriate treatment, the chances of recovery from a dissociative disorder are very good.

Determining whether your dissociative response is healthy or not depends upon your ability to recognize certain experiences—memory blanks, feelings of unreality, emotional numbness, out-of-body episodes, automatic movements, and the like—as signs of one of five core dissociative symptoms. Once you fully understand how and why these symptoms manifest themselves, you can identify your experiences of them and determine whether they're normal or rise to a higher level of moderate to severe.

An accurate diagnosis of a disorder should be undertaken only by a specially trained clinician. The purpose of the material in the next chapters on the core symptoms is to tell you enough about them so that you'll be able to understand and recognize your own experiences of them. After you've read all the material about each symptom, you can answer the questionnaire adapted from the SCID-D at the end of the chapter on that symptom. When you've completed each questionnaire, you'll be able to assess whether your symptoms are serious enough to warrant seeing a therapist. If you're in therapy now, you should draw these symptoms to your therapist's attention, particularly if they're at all disturbing, and ask to have the entire SCID-D done. The interview usually takes less than three hours. This little bit of time can save a person twenty years of misdiagnosis and inappropriate treatment.

You'll find that some of the items in the questionnaires are signs of normal dissociative symptoms. For example, forgetting where you put personal belongings like your keys or glasses is a normal kind of amnesia, and finding it hard to juggle all the different roles in your life is a normal form of identity confusion. Experiences like these shouldn't be a cause for concern. If you've experienced any of the other items several times, particularly if the symptom is associated with dysfunction or distress, a more complete evaluation by a professional is recommended.

The following illustrations, reprinted from my *Interviewer's Guide to the SCID-D,* will give you a graphic picture of how the presence of dissociative symptoms determines a disorder. The first four graphs show how the five core symptoms combine to form a particular dissociative disorder. The last one shows the wide divergence in the severity of symptoms between normal people and those with a dissociative disorder. Symptoms in normal individuals are mild or absent, whereas symptoms in people with a dissociative disorder are mostly moderate or severe. In the middle between the two groups are the "moderates"—people who have any one of a number of psychiatric conditions but have a higher degree of dissociative symptoms than normal people do. These symptoms are often unreported or overlooked in therapy to a patient's detriment.

Your answers to the questionnaires will provide you with a preliminary SCID-D snapshot of your trauma response system. If you score a "mild" on all of the questionnaires, you can assume that your trauma response system is healthy and your dissociative symptoms are normal. If you rate a "moderate" or "severe" for any symptom, you would be well advised to see a therapist for a more complete evaluation. Identifying these symptoms in oneself and determining whether they are more than mild are crucial first steps for anyone in need of therapy and wanting the most effective care.

SCID-D Symptom Profiles of the Dissociative Disorders

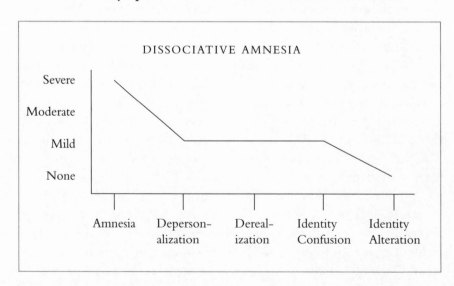

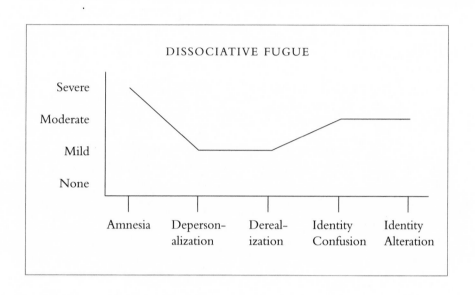

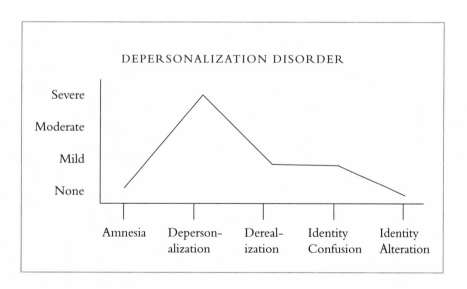

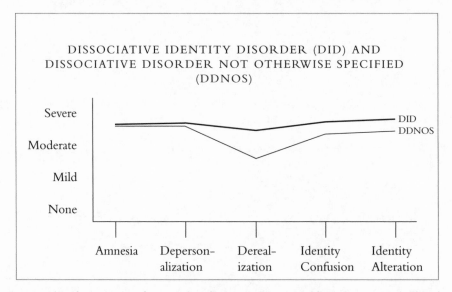

DISSOCIATIVE IDENTITY DISORDER (DID) AND
DISSOCIATIVE DISORDER NOT OTHERWISE SPECIFIED
(DDNOS)

Reprinted with permission from M. Steinberg. *Interviewer's Guide to the Structured Clinical Interview for DSM-IV Dissociative Disorders-Revised (SCID-D-R)*. Washington, DC: American Psychiatric Press, 1994.

SCID-D Symptom Profiles in Psychiatric Patients and Normal Controls.

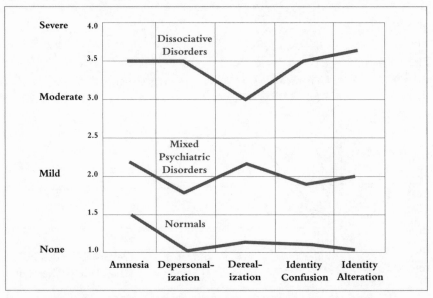

Data from M. Steinberg, B. Rounsaville, D. Cicchetti. The structured clinical interview of DSM-III-R dissociative disorders: preliminary report on a new diagnostic instrument. *American Journal of Pyschiatry* (1990) 147, 76–82.

Reprinted with permission from M. Steinberg. *Interviewer's Guide to the Structured Clinical Interview for DSM-IV Dissociative Disorders-Revised (SCID-D-R)*. Washington, DC: American Psychiatric Press, 1994.

5

THE BLACK HOLE OF LOST MEMORIES

Harry Connick, Jr., the popular singer and pianist, can laugh about it now, but at the time it happened it was a monumentally humbling moment. He was performing his act to a sell-out crowd in a large club, singing a song he'd done countless times before, when he spotted one of his most revered idols in the audience and promptly forgot the lines. His mind was a complete blank. Forced to improvise, he gallantly made a joke of it and managed to limp through the piece to the end.

This kind of blank spell associated with "performance anxiety" is a form of mild dissociative amnesia or memory loss that happens to almost all of us when we're under stress. Dissociative amnesia is different from the permanent loss of stored information, similar to the accidental erasure of a computer disk, that may occur in brain trauma. Amnesia in dissociation doesn't wipe out the memory; it displaces it from awareness to unawareness. In mild amnesia, the temporarily misplaced material can usually be retrieved after the stress has subsided.

There are many conditions in which amnesia is natural or even necessary. If the mind were constantly required to process all the data accessible to memory on a conscious level, the result would be an inconceivable stimulus overload. As Nietzsche once said, "Without forgetting it is quite impossible to *live at all.*"

MEMORY AND SELF-IMAGE

Memory can be considered the most essential part of human consciousness because we need to maintain a continuous memory of events before we can attach meaning to them. We can think of memory as the "language of identity" since our sense of self is typically constructed around a personal history. Our image of ourselves is dependent in large measure on how we remember our history of personal events, relationships, and beliefs, and on how we expect ourselves to respond to situations on the basis of past experience. Loss of memory or gaps in our personal history are often perceived as an assault on our sense of identity and can be worrisome or frightening. Since normal episodes of amnesia are widespread, it's important to be able to distinguish these from moderate amnesia, which can indicate a problem, and the severe amnesia that occurs with a shattered sense of self.

MILD AMNESIA

Occasional, brief forgetfulness is a mild form of dissociative amnesia or absence of memory that happens to almost all of us when we're under stress. The examples are legion. Who hasn't run up the stairs to get something and forgotten what it was? How often have we met up with an acquaintance whose name we know but can't recall, while it teasingly bounces around on the "tip of the tongue"? Someone asks us to recite the Pledge of Allegiance, and we forget the words in midstream. We're so preoccupied that we forget to show up for a doctor's appointment even though we had confirmed it earlier. Our mind wanders during a boring lecture or a run-on conversation, and we miss part of what is said.

One of the most familiar examples of normal dissociative memory loss is "highway hypnosis." It can happen in two different ways. The road we're driving on may be so familiar that we keep only part of our mind on it and arrive at our destination without remembering the ride. Or we can become so engrossed in other matters during the ride that we forget to take the right exit and "wake up" several exits past it, saying, "Where was my mind?"

Besides these widespread mild episodes of amnesia, there's the blank spell that the intense pressure of a test or a job interview can bring on. Julia, a computer specialist, recalls "screwing up" when she was interviewed for a job by a personnel director she found very intimidating. "It was like facing a detective in a police interrogation room," she says. "The man was like a block of ice. He shot questions at me and sat there stony-faced while I answered them. Then he asked me to solve a programming problem as a test of my skills. He left the room, but I was already so unnerved that I couldn't remember the most basic steps. Under other circumstances it would've been a piece of cake."

Alex, a twenty-nine-year-old graduate student who waits on tables part-time to help put himself through school, occasionally has the same kind of mild memory lapse. "The restaurant I work at is very trendy," says Alex, "and there are always a dozen specials you have to remember with different combinations of ingredients and fancy sauces. I can usually rattle them off with no problem. But every once in a while I'll get thrown off the track by the way someone at the table is staring at me, and my mind goes blank. It's very disconcerting. I have to stop and look at this little crib sheet I keep, and it kills the whole effect."

Many people are uncomfortable in the spotlight and are prone to stage fright, a common cause of a mild form of amnesia. For these people, giving a speech in public is as traumatic as a life-threatening event. Standing at the microphone with that sea of faces staring at them fills them with the dread of public humiliation. Instead of focusing on the content of the speech, they dissociate and draw a blank. Fortunately, training and practice in public speaking can help reduce the anxiety it provokes and lessen the likelihood of blanking out.

Time gaps are commonplace occurrences in dreaming. We may be in dream consciousness for hours and yet can usually remember only brief sequences from the dream. Candace, an advertising copywriter in her thirties, describes a typical experience of dream amnesia: "Sometimes I have these vivid dreams with all kinds of surprising twists and turns," she says, "and when I wake up I don't remember much of the dream at all. I know what it was about generally—let's say, being chased from car to car on a train when I'm having an anxiety dream about meeting a deadline—but I can't remember what led up to the chase or even who was chasing me. I'm left with more of a feeling about the dream than I am with a memory of what took place."

Normal time gaps also occur when we temporarily lose our recall of what we were doing at some point in the day or the week but are able to remember the events or activities with some intentional effort. The theory is that although we have immediate memory for some things, for others it's delayed. It can take a reminder of some kind—a ticket stub from a trip or another person's mentioning something that happened during that period—to "jog" a delayed memory out of hiding.

Ben, a forty-six-year-old accountant from Boston who enjoys traveling, experienced a delayed memory of a site he'd visited on a trip—an episode that happens to many of us on occasion. "My wife and I were having dinner with some friends who'd recently returned from a vacation in Santa Fe," he says, "and they were raving about a sculpture garden they'd seen on the way back from Taos. My wife said we'd seen it, too, when we were there, but I had no recollection of it. Then all of a sudden it came back to me when they started talking about the huge bronze animals that were there. It's the Shidoni Sculpture Gardens in Tesuque, and it was one of the places on our tour. I was impressed by it at the time, but it just slipped my mind."

These minor time gaps and brief memory blanks are widespread, generally benign, and no cause for concern. They can be annoying, but most of us accept the frustrations of this kind of everyday forgetfulness with good grace.

As a general rule, not remembering some of your childhood prior to age three is normal. Researchers tracing the development of ordinary amnesia have discovered that verbal memory for the first three years of life is fragmented. Infantile experiences are encoded in primitive prelinguistic form and can't be retrieved normally by an adult whose encoding state is mostly a more highly developed linguistic one. Hypnosis can return an adult to more primitive levels of consciousness and may be related to reported memories of experiences in infancy. But infants don't have the capacity to remember in the same way adults do. Amnesia, like all the dissociative symptoms, has its origins as a healthy defense against being psychologically overwhelmed.

MODERATE AMNESIA

When amnesia is moderate rather than mild, it can be disturbing to a significant section of the population. Moderate amnesia involves recurrent brief episodes of memory blanks not precipitated by stress, a few prolonged episodes of thirty minutes or more, or the occurrence of one or two brief blank spells in the course of a few hours. If the memory blanks occur often enough to make time seem discontinuous, they can cause distress. Moderate amnesia can be particularly disturbing to people whose occupational functioning is affected by it. A schoolteacher with a tendency to blank out briefly while she's teaching class has to worry about what her students were doing during that lost time.

Robert, now a practicing engineer, almost flunked out of graduate school because of moderate dissociative amnesia and difficulty in concentrating during exams. When I first saw Robert, he told me, "I have an excellent memory, but my mind sometimes goes blank when I'm taking an exam and I can't recall information I know by heart. I feel keyed up and tense and lightheaded, and the answers escape me."

Robert's SCID-D results showed that other than his moderate dissociative amnesia, his ratings for the other four symptoms were all mild and did not indicate the presence of a dissociative disorder. Though his moderate memory blanks caused distress and some dysfunction, they were related to his anxiety rather than to any history of trauma or abuse. Medication coupled with cognitive therapy and training in relaxation exercises proved to be the answer. Once Robert had tools for handling his anxiety, his amnesia during exams all but disappeared. Robert's case illustrates how the SCID-D rules out—or in other instances, rules *in*—a dissociative disorder.

SEVERE AMNESIA

In severe amnesia induced by trauma or abuse, forgetting takes a more alarming turn. Vince, a former professional wrestler who went into business with his wife's cousin after he retired, is a case in point. When the cousin got in trouble with the law for his shady business dealings and tried to blame them on Vince, the duplicity stirred up homicidal feelings of rage that Vince found unbearable. He collapsed, regressed into a childlike state at the age of forty-two, and woke up with no memory of his past at all except his three children and the family dog.

Vince had daily episodes of lost time—"trances," he called them—during which "dark people," shadowy figures of all sizes and shapes, accosted him. They held him down, stuck needles in him or tried to strangle him, and threatened to steal his soul. Their assaults impelled him to perform astonishing feats of athleticism that caused him pain, like doing five hundred sit-ups at a time or arching his back while he was standing on his head until he was standing on his *neck*.

Vince's psychiatrist referred him to me for an evaluation, and I diagnosed him with DID. In treatment with his therapist, Vince began to recall the trauma that originally brought on his amnesia. During his childhood he was sexually abused by priests in a Catholic school—the "dark people" in his trances. The homicidal rage he felt toward his wife's cousin set off a return of his dissociated rage during the abuse and accounted for his forgetting everyone in his past, including his wife. After five years in therapy, Vince is still working to recover his history.

How Trauma Affects Memory

Amnesia for traumatic memories is a case of memory interrupted. Traumatic memories are most likely "forgotten" because of faulty encoding or retrieving. A major mental process contributing to amnesia in dissociative disorders is known as state-dependent learning. According to this theory, information encoded in one mental state is most easily retrieved at a later time under that same state. If a person experiencing trauma dissociates into separate states of mind, different memories will become available to that person at different times. Data encoded in one state will not be available to a person who is in a different psychological state; it will only be available when the person returns to the same state he or she was in at the time when it was encoded. For example, Harris, a thirty-seven-year-old pharmacist who was sexually abused repeatedly throughout his childhood by an older cousin, developed a six-year-old alternate personality named Barney. Harris could not remember the abuse until an assault by an armed robber at the drugstore where he worked triggered Barney's return.

State-dependent learning theory explains the severe amnesia that occurs in DID. Experiences encoded in a psychological state of abuse can chain together into a complex and consistent personality if the abuse is sufficiently traumatic and persistent. These particular alter personalities may not remember facts that other alters remember. While the memories of overwhelming pain and fear are outside the person's conscious cognitive awareness, they live on in an alter personality and are still psychologically active and influential.

The "lost time" or memory "gaps" of someone with DID have preserved the person's sanity but have swallowed up a large chunk of his personal identity and past. Vince's history, for example, is like a badly edited film with too much of the story lost in the gaps. The future of someone with severe amnesia is compromised, too. The inability to integrate traumatic memories causes the person to fixate at the time of the trauma and impairs the integration of new experiences. When Barney resurfaced, Harris was unable to concentrate on his job as a pharmacist and fill prescriptions that were beyond the comprehension of a six-year-old child. For many people, traces of the painful memory tend to linger and intrude as flashbacks, obsessions, or reenactments of the trauma in self-mutilation or other self-destructive behavior, as in Vince's arching his back to the point of physical injury.

SELF-INJURY AND AMNESIA

Self-injury in all its forms, including accident-proneness or a tendency to be victimized again in abusive relationships, may actually constitute screen memories of abuse or symbolic memories that a person is using to keep explicit abuse memories out of consciousness. Repeatedly hurting oneself is a way of not having to remember the original hurt. Self-wounding may also be an unconscious repetition of past abuse in an attempt to make sense of a dim but haunting memory. The person is trying to knit the implicit remnant of the trauma memory into the fabric of a continuous mental narrative.

Some researchers have described cutting or burning one's own flesh as a short-term device for relieving the self-hate, guilt, and anxiety associated with childhood abuse and trauma. They note that the behavior is cyclical in many people, consisting of a repetitive pattern of self-injury, calm, and gradual escalation of psychic tension leading to another episode of violence directed against the self.

The amnesia that many self-injurers have for their destructive behavior may be related to the return of memories from which they have disconnected. Since the emotional pain of the returning memories is overwhelming, the person enters a trancelike state in an effort to keep them blocked. Self-injurers often say that they "find themselves" with cuts, scratches, or burns on their bodies in the same way that they find themselves in strange places without knowing how they got there. Self-wounding is a reality testing for abuse that the person, on some level, knows happened but has split off from consciousness. Injuring oneself can bring "forgotten" memories of abuse into awareness in several ways. The wounds themselves can reinforce the reality of past abuse, long disavowed by dissociation and the persistent denials of family members who maintain that the abuse never happened or was an expression of love. The pain of self-injury can test reality by restoring the feeling of being alive. Self-wounding can also reenact past abusive events symbolically, recalling them behaviorally, and reinforce the person's conviction that he or she was abused as a child. The fear of remembering what one was forbidden to remember may make amnesia a survival tactic once again.

Common Signs

Some examples of severe amnesia include:

- at least one prolonged gap in memory that results in serious dys-function
- finding oneself in a strange place without knowing how one got there
- inability to recall important personal information (address, tele-phone number, etc.)
- inability to remember months or years of one's adult life
- forgetting of a learned talent or skill
- experiencing of significant distress caused by memory problems

Precisely because amnesia is the negation of memory, people with severe amnesia may be unaware that something is missing from their recall; they may have amnesia for their amnesia. One woman with DID, who compares her amnesia to a broken TV, puts it this way: "There's just a blank there. Nothing. You have no recollection of existing at all. It's like turning on a TV, only the TV doesn't work, and there's just a blank screen." She goes on, "What makes it more confusing is my sense that even what I remember doesn't seem like I remember it. I'm not too connected to it. The memory is what I've been told is the memory. It's like people saying, 'Here, let's look at a movie of your life, and we'll help you fill in the blanks.' You watch the movie and that's your history there. You think it sort of looks like it, but you don't really remember."

Compensatory Techniques

Inventing information as a "cover" for a memory gap—known as confab-ulation—is a strategy that many people with chronic amnesia depend upon to maintain relationships, hold jobs, or stay in school. They often resort to confabulation when they sense that honest admissions of their amnesia will undermine important relationships. Some find that self-employment is the only answer to the disastrous impact of chronic mem-ory gaps on a job, but the gaps still get in the way. "I decided to become my own boss after my excuses weren't covering it anymore," says Jackie, a forty-three-year-old free-lance artist, of her severe amnesia related to

DID. "The only problem with that is, you do have clients who want so much done by such and such a time, and lost time can slow me down. I don't show up for appointments or they can't reach me, that kind of thing. I've lost a few dozen accounts because of it. But I can't be fired, so I'm lucky."

People often compensate for having a frighteningly unreliable memory by taking notes, keeping diaries, or enlisting friends and relatives to help them retrieve forgotten events or details. Openly admitting to memory problems in our "information age" can put a person on the wrong end of an uneven playing field professionally and otherwise. To get assistance from others and still conceal their plight, some people with serious amnesia demonstrate considerable ingenuity. Says one: "I'm pretty good at faking it. If I don't recognize somebody I think I should know or can't relate to what they're talking about, I just sort of keep my mouth shut and hope they'll say enough about themselves or the topic that something will click in."

DISTORTED SENSE OF TIME

Amnesia frequently involves a misperception of elapsed time. Time passes rapidly as a person goes "in and out" of time or is "transported" from the last moment of fully remembered consciousness to the present. Victoria, a forty-eight-year-old salesperson, recounts an episode of amnesia and fleeting time that is mild for most of us when we're daydreaming or engrossed in work but is severe for her, because it happens to her several times a week: "All of a sudden I'll find myself standing some place, maybe at the kitchen sink, and I think, 'What time is it?' I look at the clock, and then I go through a process of figuring out what time it was before I blanked out, what day it was. And then I start thinking, 'What happened? Where did the time go?' "

This distorted sense of the passage of time can extend to seasons of the year. "I get the months mixed up," says a thirty-year-old woman with severe amnesia. "I'm wearing a sleeveless outfit—it's eighty degrees out!— and I think it's January. I go into the mall to go shopping, walk by a sign that says, 'Summer Sizzling Sale,' and my reaction is, 'They should take that sign down, they've made a mistake, they shouldn't be advertising summer clothes in January. And then the message comes in, 'No, it's not January, dummy. It's July.' "

Paradoxically, people with dissociative disorders have amnesia for much of their childhood but can have an enhanced memory (hypermnesia) for the abuse under certain circumstances. Flashbacks, causing the traumatic memories to resurface with a searing realism, can be excruciatingly detailed and usually occur during stressful periods in later life—military service, academic exams, job loss—or when a sensory "trigger" abruptly activates them. A trace element of a past traumatic experience can cause a person to react dramatically to a seemingly innocuous object without any conscious awareness of the symbolic connection between the two.

Donna, a twenty-five-year-old secretary, described herself during her SCID-D interview as being "paranoid" about handkerchiefs and "scared to death" to touch one. She couldn't understand why until, in the process of being diagnosed with DID, she traced back over her history and suddenly stumbled upon a horrific hidden memory. "I guess I was four years old," she said, "and a baby-sitter used to gag me with a handkerchief, shove it down my throat, and rape me. No wonder I'm afraid of them, you know?" She went on to say, "I'm afraid of libraries, places with high bookshelves, because that's the room I was in. After a while you learn to remember things like that. I don't want to remember them, but in order to help myself I know I have to."

BLANK BUT NOT EMPTY

The time gaps that occur for people with a dissociative disorder are usually not really empty. In the most severe cases, as in DID, alter personalities typically emerge during these episodes, and the amnesia serves to separate one personality from the others. Some trauma survivors may reenact the abuse during lost time and awaken with self-inflicted wounds, having no awareness of their cause. Others may travel, sometimes arriving at a city in a different state with no recollection of how or why they are there, or commit violent crimes in a trance and not remember them afterward.

Self-destructive alter personalities may attempt to kill a person during a time gap, and the dominant personality may regain consciousness in the hospital without any memory of taking an overdose of pills or jumping off a bridge. In the distorted logic of a DID trance, one alter's wish to destroy the body that passively endured the original abuse is not always recognized by the person's healthier personalities as wanting the irreversible destruction of all of them. The amnesia that once banished overwhelmingly painful experiences from consciousness and helped the person survive has turned into a deadly threat.

The following questionnaire will help you identify what symptoms of amnesia you are experiencing and whether they are mild (normal), moderate, or severe.

Steinberg Amnesia Questionnaire

Instructions: Please check one box for each item to indicate the *greatest frequency* with which each experience occurs. If the experience occurs only with the use of drugs or alcohol, check the last box on the right.

	Never	Once or twice	Some- times	Many times	Almost all the time	Only with drugs or alcohol
	1	2	3	4	5	1
1. I have trouble recalling memories of my childhood prior to age 4.	☐	☐	☐	☐	☒	☐
2. When I look back at my life, it feels like a puzzle with pieces missing.	☐	☐	☒	☐	☐	☐
3. I have had trouble remembering my daily activities.	☒	☐	☐	☐	☐	☐
4. Before I give a presentation, I worry that I will forget something important.	☐	☐	☒	☐	☐	☐
5. I have felt that I was reliving the past.	☐	☐	☒	☐	☐	☐
6. I have forgotten personal infor- mation such as my name, age, address, or birth date.	☒	☐	☐	☐	☐	☐

	Never	Once or twice	Some-times	Many times	Almost all the time	Only with drugs or alcohol
	1	2	3	4	5	1
7. When driving a familiar route, I arrive at my destination and realize that I was not aware of the passage of time during the trip.	☐	☐	☐	☒	☐	☐
8. Hours or days may go by that I have no memory of.	☐	☒	☐	☐	☐	☐
9. I have found myself in unexpected places and have been unable to remember how or why I got there.	☒	☐	☐	☐	☐	☐
10. I forget where I put my keys, glasses, or other personal items.	☐	☐	☒	☐	☐	☐
11. I feel as if memories of my childhood are hidden away inside of me.	☐	☐	☐	☐	☒	☐
12. I find things in my house that belong to me, but I can't remember how or where I got them.	☒	☐	☐	☐	☐	☐
13. When I read a book or watch a movie, I lose track of time.	☐	☐	☐	☒	☐	☐
14. I have talents that I don't remember learning.	☒	☐	☐	☐	☐	☐

	Never	Once or twice	Some-times	Many times	Almost all the time	Only with drugs or alcohol
	1	2	3	4	5	1
15. I feel that I have "blackouts" in my memory (not related to alcohol).	☒	☐	☐	☐	☐	☐

If you have had any of the above experiences, answer the following:

	No	Yes
Did the experience(s) interfere with your relationships with friends, family, or coworkers?	☒	☐
Did it affect your ability to work?	☒	☐
Did it cause you discomfort or distress?	☐	☒

To Score Your Amnesia Questionnaire:

1. Assign a score of zero to the following items:
   Normal items: #1, 4, 7, 10, 13.

2. For all other items, assign a score ranging from 1 to 5 corresponding to the number on the top line above the box that you checked.

3. Now add up your score. Use the general guidelines below for under-tanding your score.

OVERALL AMNESIA SCORE

No Amnesia:	10
Mild Amnesia:	11–20 19
Moderate Amnesia:	21–30
Severe Amnesia:	31–50

If your total score falls in the range of *No* to *Mild Amnesia* (10–20), this is within the normal range, unless you have experienced Items #6 or 15 recurrently. If you have experienced these items several times, we recommend that you be evaluated by a professional who is trained in the administration of the full SCID-D interview.

If your total score falls in the range of *Moderate* to *Severe Amnesia* (21–50), we recommend that you be evaluated by a professional who is trained in the administration of the full SCID-D interview. If your amnesia has interfered with your relationships with friends, family, or coworkers or has affected your ability to work or has caused you distress, it is particularly important that you obtain a professional consultation.

Should an experienced clinician find that you have a dissociative disorder, you have a treatable illness with a very good prognosis for recovery. Your illness is widely shared by others who coped with trauma by using the self-protective defense of dissociation. With proper treatment, in time you will begin to access memories and feelings that you have mentally disconnected from because they have been overwhelming. Eventually, as you grow strong enough to reconnect with your hidden memories and feelings and accept them as your own, your amnesia will be reduced and you will become a more integrated and psychologically healthy person.

6

~

WATCHING YOURSELF
FROM A DISTANCE

THEY WERE PLAYING tennis, and Ray had just been beaten badly by a cocky younger man from his workplace who said smugly after the winning game, "I didn't even work up a sweat."

"After he made that remark," says Ray, "I said, 'Let's play one more time.' And I beat him six-love. I whipped his ass something terrible. It was like it really wasn't me. It was like I almost let someone else, within me, take over so I could rest. I was worried about my heart—he wasn't. He was about twenty years younger than me. And I'll never forget how fierce that imaginary guy beat him. And how I just focused on that person—it was very real—and the tennis ball. I didn't care how I hit the shots, I didn't care where they went. I just listened to the sound of the racket and knew that the guy I was playing couldn't possibly return the ball."

Ray's sensation of feeling detached from himself and letting an imaginary person within him perform while he looked on as an observer is a typical episode of *depersonalization* that is widespread in the normal population. This sense of detachment from oneself is commonly experienced as a feeling of strangeness of the self, a sense that one is observing oneself from the outside, and a flattening of emotional response.

Like Ray, we can have this experience at "crunch times" at play or at work when we rise to an extraordinary level of performance and feel as if we're watching someone else act automatically. Feeling detached from one's emotions lets us control our anxiety. And feeling physically separated from parts of one's body—Ray let his arm place the shots without giving any thought to how he made them—is what frees us up to rely on our natural abilities or instincts to see us through. Unencumbered by the fear of failure or anxiety about our performance, we do better than we would if we were not able to depersonalize this way.

Feeling detached from yourself can manifest itself in many forms:

- an out-of-body episode
- loss of feeling in parts of your body
- distorted perceptions of your body
- feeling of being invisible
- inability to recognize yourself in a mirror
- sense of detachment from your emotions
- impression of watching a movie of yourself
- feeling of being unreal or a robot
- sense of being split into an observer and a participant
- interactive dialogues with an imaginary person

There are many other variations. All of these experiences represent some kind of detachment from your sense of self or from your body or emotions and often occur simultaneously.

These manifestations increase across a continuum of severity, ranging from low intensity and frequency in normal people to high intensity and frequency in people with a dissociative disorder. *Intensity* refers to the severity of these episodes' interference with your personal well-being and your social relationships, the vividness of the episodes, and the degree to which you personify your internal dialogues as if you're talking to another individual.

Mild depersonalization at the low end of the spectrum—single or rare, brief episodes that are usually associated with stress or extreme danger—is normal. Moderate depersonalization in the median of the spectrum—recurrent episodes not precipitated by stress—is found in a number of different psychiatric conditions. At the upper end of the spectrum is the severe depersonalization found in people with dissociative disorders and posttraumatic stress disorder (PTSD). These experiences are not brought on by stress and are persistent, long-lasting, of high intensity, or some combination of these.

MILD DEPERSONALIZATION

As the accounts of people who've survived a traumatic event have shown, depersonalization is a normal, almost universal response to life-threatening danger. Victims of accidents or other traumatic incidents are able to function by numbing their emotions and operating on automatic pilot, feeling as if they're at a remove from themselves and going through the motions of virtual reality rather than real life.

"I heard myself screaming, and it sounded like someone else's voice coming out of my throat," recalls Janet, a college student who was able to escape being raped outside her apartment building by screaming loudly for help and fighting her attacker off while he held her on the ground. "I didn't know I was capable of making that much noise," she says. Sensing that her assailant was unarmed, she began kicking and punching him until he fled when a tenant came out of the building to help her. "I felt like it was only my body that was lying on the ground, and I was watching the body that I was supposed to be in from a distance," Janet remembers. "It gave me strength I didn't know I had."

Lionel, a firefighter, describes the feeling of depersonalization he had when he entered a blazing building and pulled people trapped inside to safety. "It's almost like you can't feel the heat or choke on the smoke because you're outside your body and totally numb inside," says Lionel. "You're watching yourself doing what you have to do like someone else is doing it. People said, 'Oh, you're so brave, you're such a hero.' But when you're in the zone like that, you're not even aware of the danger. Your body is doing the work, and you're just watching. I guess it's like those 'firewalkers' you hear about—they walk over burning coals on their bare feet and don't even get a blister."

Janet and Lionel are typical of normal people who have transient episodes of depersonalization in extremely dangerous circumstances. Lack of sleep, alcohol or drugs, meditation, or fatigue can also all bring on brief, mild episodes of depersonalization in normal people. Many of us also experience out-of-body episodes at times when we're not affected by sleeplessness or drugs or in a situation that may be very stressful but is not life-threatening. The stress we feel may make us want to disconnect from reality and watch ourselves from a distance. As long as these out-of-body episodes occur only a few times in a lifetime, they're still normal.

"The first time my boyfriend took me home to meet his family, I was very nervous," says Cynthia, a twenty-nine-year-old database manager. "I was afraid they wouldn't like me because I'd been warned that his folks could be somewhat critical." When her boyfriend introduced her to his family, Cynthia experienced an "eerie" feeling of depersonalization. "I felt that I was watching myself talking to his folks as if I'd known them all my life, and I thought, 'This person is winning them over. She's so poised and charming.' " Cynthia finds the feeling hard to describe: "I don't have the words for it, this going outside yourself. You become detached. You're outside the action, watching life happen. I guess it's something you have to feel to understand."

Warren, a forty-one-year-old architect who heads his own firm, describes his depersonalization episode during a career-making presentation to a prospective client: "I got this feeling that I was two different people. I felt as if I'd stepped out of my body—behind it or above it or next to it—and I was watching myself making the presentation. It was a weird feeling, like being some kind of ghost. It helped me control my nerves. I didn't feel anxious—I didn't feel anything, for that matter—because I wasn't the one involved. I was just watching."

INTERNAL DIALOGUES

A dialogue between the observing and the participating self may accompany an episode of depersonalization. The nature of the dialogue is a key distinguishing feature between normal people and those with a dissociative disorder.

Normal internal dialogue is the kind of conversation that takes place in the following situations:

Decision making: Usually, when we weigh the pros and cons of a decision, the dialogue is experienced as a metaphorical or symbolic conversation, and is not thought of as a conversation between oneself and another real person. We think of the "devil's advocate" as an imaginary proponent of an opposite position, not the embodiment of a separate human being capable of conducting an interactive dialogue with oneself.

Grieving: Normal people experiencing grief often feel detached and have a symbolic dialogue with a recently deceased loved one. This very common experience is a mild form of depersonalization. Instead of detaching from one's self and holding a conversation with an imaginary self, the mourner detaches from the intensely real memory of the deceased loved one and holds a conversation with that imaginary person. As the mourner completes the grieving process, this phenomenon usually fades.

Role playing: It's customary for normal people to have internal dialogues when they "role play" mentally, simulating anticipated interactions and reviewing past dialogues in fantasized situations. Someone getting ready for a date, for example, may rehearse possible conversational openers; or a student preparing for an oral examination may pose and answer a series of likely questions.

In contrast to these situations, when a person with a dissociative disorder has dialogues during a depersonalization episode, the conversations are distinctly personified as opposed to symbolic. They tend to last longer and occur more frequently, and they lack the purposeful quality of internal dialogues in normal people.

MODERATE DEPERSONALIZATION

The feeling of being an observer of oneself is prevalent in the normal population but can become troublesome for those who are prone to anxiety and depression. It might even indicate a dissociative basis for these problems. People describe it variously as a "chattering monkey" in their heads or "the critic" or "the nag" or a tendency to second-guess themselves. This critical observing self can be an annoying pest and, in some instances, can interfere with peak performance.

Evan, a talented violinist, says that he has "blown" a number of auditions because of his tendency to hover outside himself while he's playing and criticize his performance. "I'll be in the middle of a difficult passage," he says, "and I'll hear myself saying, 'You're rushing through this too fast' or 'Your movements look awkward' or 'I don't like the way this sounds.' It's a distraction that doesn't help. I'm better off when I leave myself alone and just play." This sensation of "watching" oneself hypervigilantly can cause some distress, but it doesn't rise to the level of severe depersonalization as long as the observer is perceived as symbolic and not personalized into a separate entity.

The transient or mild depersonalization that helps a person cope with anxiety in a life-threatening or stressful situation can itself become a cause of anxiety when it develops into a pattern. An anxiety-depersonalization-anxiety cycle is set up. Anxiety induces episodes of detachment from oneself or one's emotions that can stir up fears of loss of control and lead to increasing anxiety that results in panic attacks.

Gillian, an ambitious journalist whose fear of a committed relationship has kept her single for thirty-nine years, has episodes of depersonalization whenever a man gets too close. Her phobic anxiety about getting married, she says, stems from witnessing how her parents' tumultuous marriage destroyed her mother. Gillian remembers a depersonalization experience that led to a panic attack while she was on a vacation in Aruba with a man she was dating. "I had a feeling that he was going to ask me to marry him," she says, "and I was tense the whole time, waiting for him to pop the question. One night, before we went out to dinner, I looked in the mirror and saw myself staring back at me like another person. There were other times before when I had a sense of watching myself from the outside, but this one weirded me out. I kept looking at my reflection and seeing a total stranger, and I thought I was losing my mind."

PUTTING YOUR FEELINGS IN A BOX

One form of emotional numbing in depersonalization that is widespread in our competitive culture is the tendency to compartmentalize our emotions. Often reared to be more goal-oriented than women, men are more susceptible to moderate levels of this kind of emotional detachment, although it shows up in both sexes. Many success-oriented people, fearing that their personal feelings will impede their upward climb, learn *not* to feel when they think it will get in their way. Losing a job causes them emotional damage that is doubly devastating—not only is their sense of self dealt an ugly blow, but the loss also unleashes a flood of pent-up emotions with which they are ill equipped to deal, having so long held them at bay.

Carl had been a successful corporate executive for many years when he was fired at the age of forty-six. Married and the father of two children, he'd been involved in a serious affair with a woman for several years. Although he was much more compatible and passionate with the other woman than he was with his wife, Carl kept vacillating between the two, unable to end his mechanical, disagreeable marriage and allow himself to be with someone he could truly love. He was held back mostly by his fear of emotional confrontation and his detachment from his own feelings. If he left his wife, he would have to deal with her anger; if he let the other woman go, he would have to feel the emotional pain of losing her.

When Carl came to see me, he described himself as a "basket case on the edge of dysfunction." He said that he couldn't do a job at that point or have a relationship. He feared his life had peaked and he was on an irreversible downhill slide. He worried that "the emotions bottled up inside me will never be released and may, one day, explode."

The SCID-D showed that Carl had moderate depersonalization. Since he frequently felt detached from his emotions and numb inside and did not experience the other four core dissociative symptoms, I diagnosed him with depersonalization disorder. His detachment from his emotions was not surprising since depersonalization is the third most frequently reported problem among psychiatric patients, after anxiety and depression. Men exposed to a traditional "Boys don't cry" upbringing, as Carl and many men in our culture have been, are prone to this problem.

"I seem to put all my difficult emotions in a box, put them on a shelf, and try to forget about them," Carl said, describing his emotional detachment. "Anger, love, jealousy are all in boxes. I need the skills to be able to go to the shelf and open the boxes, but somehow I've either been born without them or lost them somewhere in my life, lost the instructions that came with my brain." He seemed perplexed by this deficiency in himself, musing, "Maybe emotion is like dancing class—I shy away from what I'm not good at. Or maybe my feelings really scare the hell out of me."

Men suffering from a dissociative disorder often separate their logical, intellectual self from their emotional self and have trouble with intimate relationships. Carl's therapy centered on identifying and understanding the emotions stored in his figurative boxes and beginning to comfort and express his feelings of anger, jealousy, and love. By expressing these emotions in therapy, he learned that he no longer needed to disconnect from them, reducing his need for depersonalization. Integrating his logical thinking with his emotions lessened his anxiety and played a big role in his ability to find new employment and gather the courage to end his loveless marriage.

SEVERE DEPERSONALIZATION

The anxiety-depersonalization-anxiety cycle, which is relatively widespread, can turn into a disturbing syndrome for someone with a dissociative disorder. This syndrome seems to be more common in women, typically starts in their late twenties, and is usually precipitated by pregnancy and childbirth or severe emotional trauma. The person's dissociative reaction to excessive anxiety triggers further fears of losing control and of being labeled crazy by others. These fears may in turn feed back into the cycle, setting off another episode of depersonalization and panic. It's a chicken-and-egg situation. If the panic attacks occur first, anxiety is the problem. If the episodes of depersonalization occur first, dissociation is the problem.

Kirstin, a thirty-six-year-old social worker who suffered from symptoms of anxiety, had been in treatment for obsessive-compulsive disorder for seven years when she came to me for an evaluation. She was diagnosed on the SCID-D as having a dissociative disorder and poignantly reported significant instances of depersonalization that she hadn't recognized before.

"It's happening all the time," said Kirstin during her SCID-D interview. "It's happening now, this feeling of being an observer, a witness; of being outside myself, taking global stock in what I've done with my life. I have the illness, and yet I have a witness who's very healthy, and very alive, and can see people my age going on, getting good jobs, buying their first house when I haven't. Even though I can communicate with my doctor in English, I can't communicate feelings, and what it's been like moment to moment, day to day, and the problems that it's caused in my personal life, in my professional life. And the saddest thing is that this witness knows that I'm a very good person. It makes me very sad. I feel like I've lost time that I can't make up."

People who experience severe depersonalization often recall that their first episode happened during past abuse, like the woman diagnosed with DID who remembered feeling the bottom half of her body rise to the ceiling while she was being raped. Others report that at times their arms or legs feel bigger or smaller than usual or feel disconnected from their bodies.

The sense of being invisible is another common sign of severe depersonalization. "I've been invisible ever since I was a child," says Paula, a realtor in her forties, who suffered severe emotional abuse and neglect as a child. "I had the feeling that the only part of me that existed was my eyes—that the rest of me was not there. That's something that happens to me many times, on an average stressful day or an unaverage one. I just become invisible. I think I'm not really here. I'm walking and walking, but nobody sees me."

Self-injurers have taught us that the emotional numbing in depersonalization, sometimes described as a feeling of being "dead," can become so terrifying that people may inflict pain on themselves to regain the feeling of being alive. "We were driving up Park Avenue," recalls Cheryl, a thirty-nine-year-old fashion designer, describing an episode that occurred after she had seen a play with her fiancé, "when all of a sudden everything was unreal, like a stage set. I struggled to get things back, but I couldn't. It was not working out well. This thing about being unreal kept on. And I went into the bathroom, and I found a razor, and I cut my wrist, and then things came back together. Things were real again. But I found that if things are unreal or if I start fragmenting, I can bring things back together if I cut. Then I'm whole again."

Unless you're aware that the emotional numbness you feel is a concomitant of depersonalization indicating a disturbance in your sense of self, you may mistake your feelings of being dead inside or detached from life around you as signs of depression. Here are some of the comments made by people who entered therapy complaining of depression and who were diagnosed with a dissociative disorder on the SCID-D:

> *I'm doing things, but it's as though I'm standing off from things, not involved—as though I'm not real.*

> *It's like watching a not very interesting, mildly amusing movie. It's not painful; it's just an absence of all feelings.*

> *I feel frozen and numb.*

You should also be aware that chronic depersonalization may not be distressing to you because you're so used to it that it feels as natural as breathing. You may even find that seeing yourself from a point outside your body is a calming experience. As a dissociative defense against anxiety, distancing yourself from yourself may help you function, but your functioning will be far from optimal. As Ira, a forty-seven-year-old mortgage processor who'd been "in and out of therapy since I was in college" and is now being treated for DID, says of his emotional detachment: "It's becoming increasingly stressful as I'm aware of it. It used to be just the way I was, and I dealt with it by avoiding any real intimacy. Now that I know what I've been doing and want to change, it's becoming stressful that I can't make connections when I want to."

FEELING FOGGY

Chronic depersonalization frequently occurs in people who have experienced recurrent trauma. One of the important differences between depersonalization experiences of normal people exposed to danger or reacting to stress and those of psychiatric outpatients is the matter of "mental clouding." The reports of accident victims' and normal people's reactions to stress show that they were fully alert to their circumstances at the time of their episodes of depersonalization. Psychiatric patients report more experiences of mental clouding. Instead of being sharper mentally, they experience a "dumbing down" when they detach from themselves. Says one patient, "It's not like watching something you have some control over. It's like watching something, and you know that what that person is doing is stupid, but there's not a thing you can do. You've got to sit there and watch them make a jerk of themselves."

The reason for this difference could be that a heightened state of arousal may not serve someone well when that person is helplessly and relentlessly subjected to chronic physical and sexual abuse, in many cases over several years. The quickening or slowing down of mental processes in response to trauma may represent a spectrum of helplessness associated with the overwhelming experiences. At each point along the continuum, there is some mixture of arousal and numbing. Arousal may predominate in reactions to transient traumatic experiences people feel they can escape, whereas numbing, like amnesia, may be more pronounced in high-helplessness reactions to chronic trauma, like those of a child sexually abused for years.

In addition, a child who suffers abuse at the hands of an emotionally significant adult may find mental clouding, again like amnesia, a more adaptive response than the hyperarousal people experience when they're exposed to extreme danger. There is something more painfully savage and intimately wounding about traumas inflicted intentionally by other human beings than there is about such impersonal life-threatening events as accidents or natural disasters. Studies of Holocaust survivors indicates that the mental and emotional numbing experienced by people in the death camps was connected to their knowing that they were victims of human malice and cruelty, not natural disasters or other "acts of God."

YOU AND YOUR SHADOW

The amount of powerlessness and loss of control you feel during episodes of depersonalization is an indication of their severity. "When it gets really bad and doesn't go away, I'm in a panic," says Lee of her severe episodes. "I get extremely dizzy, and the room begins to sway, or the sidewalk begins to go up and down. I actually begin to lose my sense of balance and feel as though I'm losing consciousness. I don't ever faint. Ever. But I'll get so dizzy that I feel myself slipping away. I'll go into the ladies' room, and I'll splash water on my face. That sense comes over me a lot."

Distortions in your perception of your body, as if you're looking at yourself in a funhouse mirror—your arms or legs look bigger or smaller than usual or you suddenly look like a size eighteen when you're a ten—may occur in severe depersonalization. Out-of-body experiences can range from a sense of strangeness ("This is not my face") to a sense of physical detachment from the body ("Where is my face?").

Someone with severe depersonalization even feels as if her head, limbs, or entire body has become foreign or disconnected. Bonnie, a survivor of childhood abuse, describes this sense of profound detachment from her body: "I feel that I do not belong in this body. It's the wrong body. I feel that I was not supposed to have been born into this body. Which body I was supposed to have, I don't know. It was not this one. I always felt I had the wrong face."

Severe depersonalization episodes often echo memories of repeated verbal abuse in childhood. The out-of-body experiences with internal dialogues between a person's active self and punitive observing self can have the sting of a caning. Darrell, a thirty-three-year-old man whose alcoholic father relentlessly tormented him in his childhood, describes such an episode. Fighting back tears, he recalls: "I'm just sitting there, but yet I'm drifting away. I look at myself, and my whole body feels unreal. I don't know if it's because of being called fat and ugly all the time when I was a kid, but I'm outside looking at my body like another person and yelling at it 'fat and ugly, fat and ugly' constantly. And I'm in tears, crying and crying and crying and crying."

Jerry, a feisty, funny construction worker in his thirties with a long history of alcohol abuse, describes how the continuous interactive dialogues a person with DID has with himself differ from the normal talking to themselves people do when they're debating the pros and cons of a decision or are role playing. Unlike the normal person who knows he's talking to himself, someone with DID has internal conversations with an alter personality in much the same way that he would interact with another person.

"He sees me sitting in that chair," says Jerry, "and he keeps asking me, 'Let me out; let me out.' And I tell him, 'Get out. Nobody's stopping you.' And he starts laughing at me. I actually see this guy for a couple of seconds. He's big, very big, with jet black hair and big green eyes staring at me. And he'll say, 'When are you gonna let me out, man?' And I tell him,

'Let yourself out, asshole! Leave! Nobody's holding you; you don't even pay rent anyway.' "

At its worst, habitual depersonalization can have a devastating effect on a person's ability to function, to engage in social relationships, and to enjoy life. The fear of losing control in the throes of feeling unreal and disconnected from oneself may prompt a withdrawal from social contact. Over time, the numbing of emotions can lead to an intractable depression. Not only is anxiety deadened, but so is the anesthetized soul itself. As one DID patient describes it: "I've been living in this dream. I just go from thing to thing, from here to here. I go to work, do whatever the stuff is I do. I don't even want to do what I'm doing, so I just do it. And then I may be going home, and I sleep. So it's like I go off, and then I just lose track, and all of a sudden I'm not sure what I'm doing or where I'm doing it or why."

For people who are detached from themselves, life becomes a joyless, "empty dream." They look at the world through a thick gray fog, feeling nothing inside except a cold deadness. Life as a walking suicide is the ultimate price to pay for distance from anxiety.

The following questionnaire will help you identify what symptoms of depersonalization you are experiencing and whether they are mild (normal), moderate, or severe.

Steinberg Depersonalization Questionnaire

	Never	Once or twice	Some-times	Many times	Almost all the time	Only with drugs or alcohol
	1	2	3	4	5	1
3 1. I have gone through the motions of living while the real me was far away from what was happen-ing to me.	☐	☐	☒	☐	☐	☐
2 2. I have felt that I was living in a dream.	☐	☒	☐	☐	☐	☐
4 3. I have been able to see myself from a distance, as if I were outside my body watching a movie of myself.	☐	☐	☐	☒	☐	☐
5 4. I feel that I can turn off or detach from my emotions.	☐	☐	☐	☐	☒	☐
1 5. My behavior has felt out of my control.	☒	☐	☐	☐	☐	☐
1 6. I have purposely hurt or cut myself so that I could feel pain or feel that I am real.	☒	☐	☐	☐	☐	☐

	Never	Once or twice	Some-times	Many times	Almost all the time	Only with drugs or alcohol
	1	2	3	4	5	1
7. I have gone through the motions of working while I felt that my mind was somewhere else.	☐	☐	☐	☒	☐	☐
8. I feel as if I am "spacey."	☐	☒	☐	☐	☐	☐
9. I have had the feeling that I was a stranger to myself or have not recognized myself in the mirror.	☒	☐	☐	☐	☐	☐
10. One part of me does things while an observing part talks to me about them.	☒	☐	☐	☐	☐	☐
11. I have felt as if parts of my body were disconnected from the rest of my body.	☒	☐	☐	☐	☐	☐
12. My whole body or parts of it have seemed unreal or foreign to me.	☒	☐	☐	☐	☐	☐
13. I have felt as if words flowed from my mouth but they were not in my control.	☐	☒	☐	☐	☐	☐

	Never	Once or twice	Some-times	Many times	Almost all the time	Only with drugs or alcohol
	1	2	3	4	5	1
5 14. I have felt that my emotions are not in my control.	☐	☐	☐	☐	☒	☐
5 15. I have felt invisible.	☐	☐	☐	☐	☒	☐

If you have had any of the above experiences, answer the following:

	No	Yes
Did the experience(s) interfere with your relationships with friends, family, or coworkers?	☐	☒
Did it affect your ability to work?	☒	☐
Did it cause you discomfort or distress?	☐	☒

To Score Your Depersonalization Questionnaire:

1. Assign a score of zero to the following items:
   Normal items: #7

2. For all other items, assign a score ranging from 1 to 5 corresponding to the number on the top line above the box that you checked.

3. Now add up your score. Use the general guidelines below for understanding your score.

OVERALL DEPERSONALIZATION SCORE
No Depersonalization:	14
Mild Depersonalization:	15-25
Moderate Depersonalization:	26-44 *34*
Severe Depersonalization:	45-70

If your total score falls in the range of *No* to *Mild Depersonalization* (14–25), this is within the normal range unless you have experienced item #3, 6, 11, or 12 recurrently. If you have experienced these items several times, we recommend that you be evaluated by a professional who is trained in the administration of the full SCID-D interview.

If your total score falls in the range of *Moderate* to *Severe Depersonalization* (26–70), we recommend that you be evaluated by a professional who is trained in the administration of the full SCID-D interview. If your depersonalization has interfered with your relationships with friends, family, or coworkers or has affected your ability to work or has caused you distress, it is particularly important that you obtain a professional consultation.

Should an experienced clinician find that you have a dissociative disorder, you have a treatable illness with a very good prognosis for recovery. Your illness is widely shared by others who coped with trauma by using the self-protective defense of dissociation. With proper treatment, in time you will no longer find it necessary to disconnect from yourself or your feelings. Eventually, as you grow strong enough to reconnect with your hidden memories and feelings and begin to accept them as your own, your depersonalization will be reduced and you will become a more integrated and psychologically healthy person.

———

7

A VISIT TO THE LAND OF OZ

A T   F I R S T   T H E   explosions sounded like fireworks to Pat Neville, fifteen, a sophomore at Columbine High School in Littleton, Colorado, who was outside the building in the soccer field that Tuesday morning. It was April 20, 1999, the fateful day when two students dressed in black trench coats went on a murderous rampage, killing twelve students and a teacher and wounding many others before turning their guns on themselves.

Pat thought it was a senior prank until he saw something whiz through the air and land on the school's roof. He heard a loud bang and saw a thick cloud of smoke billowing out of the building. Someone else with an assault rifle started spraying the ground, kicking up the earth outside the cafeteria. "Then a guy with a shotgun started walking toward us," Pat remembered, "across the field. Boom. I was just like, 'Oh, my God, is this happening?' It didn't even kick in."

The feeling that the world around you is unreal or that events are not really happening is called derealization. You may think of it as a kind of *jamais vu*. Instead of the *déjà vu* feeling that new places and people are familiar, you have the opposite feeling: that people or places that you should know very well are unfamiliar. You feel estranged or detached from the environment or have a sense that the environment is foreign to you or is not real.

For most people, derealization comes on when a traumatic event turns our everyday world upside down, as it did for the young student who suddenly found that the soccer field of his placid suburban high school had metamorphosed into a killing field. Combat, the loss of a loved one, and near-death experiences are times when normal people are prone to episodes of derealization.

You can recognize derealization by these signs:

- a feeling of detachment from the world
- a feeling that your home, workplace, or other customary environment is unknown or unfamiliar
- a sense that what is happening is not real
- a sense that your friends or relatives are strange, unfamiliar, or unreal
- changes in your visual perception of the environment—the sense that buildings, furniture, or other objects are changing in size or shape or that colors are becoming more or less intense

This last manifestation—disturbances in perceiving the environment—is more likely to happen in moderate or severe depersonalization than in the mild episodes experienced by normal people in an emergency. Not recognizing one's parents, home, and friends also mainly occurs in severe derealization and not in mild, brief episodes linked to stress.

DEREALIZATION AND OTHER SYMPTOMS

Cy, a lawyer, describes a typical brief episode of mild derealization brought on by stress. He became agitated while taking the bar exam and recalls: "It was very, very cold in the room, and I felt as if I was freezing to death. Maybe the cold got to me, I don't know. But I looked around and saw all these people bent over their exam books, scribbling furiously. I had this sensation of things' being very unreal, including myself. I was totally disconnected from the scene, like someone from another planet surrounded by all these strange earthlings. There was something ludicrous about it. I guess that put it in some kind of perspective, because I went back to the exam and finished it."

As Cy's brief episode shows, derealization commonly occurs in tandem with depersonalization—*he* felt unreal in that stressful situation, and so did everything around him. Although derealization rarely occurs alone, you can experience it separately. You might think of derealization as a wider form of depersonalization—the feeling of detachment from yourself, your body, and your emotions extended to your immediate environment or the larger world around you.

Amnesia can coexist with derealization and frequently does in recurrent episodes. People with severe derealization may find it difficult to recognize their home or their family members and friends while remaining aware of their own identity and family history. In amnesia, forgetting familiar people is absolute, whereas in derealization there is still some intellectual connection to the people who should be familiar but aren't. A woman knows that these people seated around the dinner table with her are her parents and siblings, for example, but she doesn't feel related to them. They seem like strangers. She knows that this is the house of her childhood, yet it doesn't seem like home. The landscape around her that she's seen every day of her life seems strange and foreign to her, because she has no sense of belonging there—or having ever belonged there—at all.

Amnesia and derealization are closely linked to anxiety. Since people with high levels of anxiety have a stronger need for some form of dissociative defense, those who are more anxious experience more severe derealization. It's not clear yet whether the anxiety precipitates the derealization or whether derealization produces the anxiety. What is known is that people with panic disorder who experience derealization are more severely anxious, obsessive, and depressed and have an earlier onset of panic attacks than those who don't experience it. This finding could be a clue that someone who has been diagnosed with panic disorder may have an unsuspected dissociative disorder that the SCID-D can reveal.

Derealization is a prominent feature in posttraumatic stress disorder (PTSD). People who experience flashbacks, whether they have PTSD or a dissociative disorder, relive the past as though it were occurring in the present. Superimposing a past reality onto the present makes current events seem unreal. Patients diagnosed with PTSD describe episodes of derealization on the SCID-D in the exact same terms as those used by people with dissociative disorders.

WHAT MAKES THE REAL WORLD SEEM UNREAL?

The feeling that "Mother (or whoever) is not real" reflects a disturbance in emotional memory. There's an awareness that a familiar emotion is lacking in the normal experience of Mother. The person recognizes Mother intellectually, but the emotion is withdrawn. The person is aware that the usual emotions associated with Mother—feelings of love, closeness, comfort, and security—are missing. How does someone know who Mother is, but perceive her as not mother at the same time?

A number of theories have been advanced to explain derealization. Cognitively, it can be seen as a disruption in the normal flow of experience. Consciousness breaks down under stress, and the person becomes aware of the components of a feeling of reality instead of automatically experiencing life as real. In a crisis, for example, a person's experience of the normal flow of time may break down into a perception that time has stopped. Similarly, the victim of childhood abuse may become aware of "behind-the-scenes" elements of consciousness and perceive a loss of a normal part of experience—the emotional bond with a loved one.

The cognitive theory of derealization implies a certain amount of voluntary control over it, similar to the way people achieve an altered state of consciousness when they meditate. Claims made by people in the SCID-D field study that they could control experiences of derealization or bring them on at will—"I can do it when I want to do it," as one woman said—may lend some support to this theory.

Most psychoanalytic theories consider derealization to be an ego defense against overpowering anxiety. One school of thought is that when the person splits into an observing self and a participating self, the participating self is thought of as separate from the real person and imaginary. As a result, all of the outside world is also thought of as imaginary and unreal.

Another theory that fits in with the close link between dissociative symptoms and severe childhood abuse is that the abused child withdraws emotional investment from internal images of the abusers and doesn't identify with them the same way anymore. This feeling of nonidentification carries over to other aspects of the outside world, making the familiar seem unreal.

All of these theories lead to the same conclusion: derealization is a dissociative symptom that severs a person's consciousness from familiar perceptions of the outside world and represents a loss of familiarity with someone previously invested with that familiarity. It's a coping strategy that helps people adjust to a traumatic event—a train wreck, a tornado, a shooting, a hostage situation—or it can occur as a childhood coping strategy for repeated abuse. However adaptive it may be when it is first experienced, if derealization persists and recurs frequently, as with all dissociative responses, it becomes maladaptive and causes difficulties with relationships, work, and inner serenity.

MILD DEREALIZATION

Normal, mild derealization—a few episodes in a lifetime that are usually not unpleasant—is common. Typically, it is brought on by stress, fatigue, hypnotic states, and alcohol or drug use.

Michael, a photographer in his thirties who uses marijuana to help him relax after a long day's shoot, describes a typical derealization episode induced by a mind-altering drug: "I get a dreamy buzz where nothing seems to matter anymore. I feel like I'm floating out in space. Whatever someone is saying to me gets lost in the buzz. I'm in a world where my senses are the only reality. Colors almost hurt my eyes, they stand out so much. Time hardly moves at all. Everything is so, so slow. I look at the clock, and it says nine. After an hour seems to have passed, I look at the clock again, and it says five after nine. I can't believe it. It's as if the real world doesn't apply to me. I'm living in a different dimension of time and space."

Any large-scale trauma, like the Columbine High School massacre, can trigger normal episodes of derealization in the members of the community affected by it. A personal shock, if it is sudden, is unexpected, and touches a sensitive area in someone's life, can trigger a brief episode of derealization, too, for people who are otherwise normal.

For example, Leonard, fifty-four, had been a bank manager with the same company for twenty-three years and thought he would coast along comfortably toward early retirement at sixty. The children were grown and on their own, and Leonard and his wife, an insurance claims adjuster, were building up enough savings to retire together and spend their "golden years" indulging their passion for traveling. Then, with a blow that was pitiless and final, the ax fell on their dreams.

"My boss called me into his office and told me to sit down," Leonard recalls. "Then he let me have it. He said the company was 'downsizing'—I hate that word!—and they were cutting my job out. They couldn't even offer me another position with the company or transfer me to a different branch. I felt that my life had been a failure, and I was going to die. It was like a rattlesnake had bitten me on the neck. How could they do this to me after I'd been there so long? Whatever happened to loyalty?"

Leonard describes how his feelings of humiliation, betrayal, and sudden loss of identity brought on an episode of derealization that is as fresh now as the day it happened six years ago: "I looked at my boss, and suddenly I didn't know him anymore. He didn't look real. The room looked strange and unreal, too—almost like being out of focus. And then everything came back into focus, very much sharper. My boss had this big, abstract painting on the wall behind his desk, and the reds in it started popping out. A highly vivid red. The objects didn't change size or shape or anything, but they were very bright. It distracted me. Other things just faded into the background, including my boss. I could hear his voice, but it was indistinct. I thought I was having a bad dream. All I wanted to do was get the hell out of there as fast as I could."

Feelings of shame, whether they're connected to a sense of failure and a sudden perceived loss of identity as an unemployed breadwinner or to transgressions of moral standards in sexual abuse, are a common trigger of depersonalization and derealization episodes. Problems in intimate relationships can be another trigger, particularly for women. They may feel that their identity is threatened by the actual or potential loss of the other person. Some feminist therapists believe that the way women are raised in our culture makes them prone to dissociation from their own experiences in love, because they are expected to defer to others' standards regarding their significant relationships. Symptoms like depersonalization and derealization are signs, among others, they suggest, of the loss of control and disconnection women feel in matters of the heart.

Rachel, a forty-four-year-old marketing coordinator who had been divorced for five years, remembers a derealization episode she had when her wealthy businessman boyfriend of two years suddenly announced that he was leaving her for a model who was half her age. "He took me out to lunch to give me the bad news in a restaurant, knowing that I wouldn't make a scene in a public place," she recalls. "That only made me more enraged at him. It was so typical of how calculating he was. After he told me, I had this roaring sound in my ears. I could hear the other people in the room talking and laughing and clinking tableware, but the sounds were muffled. Nothing around me seemed real. It was like a scene from a movie. I thought it *was* a movie, and I was just imagining it. I got up from the table and walked out in a daze."

Such transient episodes of derealization are normal if they occur on rare occasions as a response to trauma or a sudden shock to our sense of self and are not associated with amnesia or flashbacks. Rather than cause distress or dysfunction in our lives, they can help us get through the worst days of our lives in one piece.

People with moderate derealization have recurrent episodes that are not precipitated by stress and may involve disturbances in perceiving their family and home. Although many people are quite vocal about the unpleasantness of derealization, moderate episodes are not always disturbing.

Brooke, an artist, says that she finds creative inspiration in her episodes. "Spatial relationships become different," she explains. "Colors take on special qualities. It's almost like an intensifying and an abstraction, which give it an unreal quality." She squints her eyes, as if visualizing an imaginary room. "I am very aware of what's in front of me," she says. "It's a sofa, there, sitting in front of a fireplace, and there's this strange mauve color, with the canary yellow curtains and all that. But there's one way of looking at it up front, and there's another way of drawing back and seeing it differently."

Unlike normal episodes of derealization, a moderate episode can occur for a person's family or home. Libby, a fifty-three-year-old documentary filmmaker whose relationship with her impossible-to-please seventy-seven-year-old mother has always been full of hurt, has episodes when her mother does not seem real to her. "I'll be driving in the car with her, and after she has viciously attacked me, criticizing everything I've ever done," Libby says, "I'll sneak a sidelong glance at her, and she looks like a stranger to me, and I'll hear myself thinking, 'Who is this person? She's not my mother. *This person is not my mother.*'"

Survivors of a traumatic event who are living with the emotional aftereffects of fear and anxiety may have derealization experiences that are moderate if they don't recur frequently or interfere with their ability to function.

Terry, a police officer, was shot in the chest in the course of apprehending an armed robber. After a long recovery he retired from active duty. Although he was spared flashbacks of the shooting, Terry experienced an episode of depersonalization accompanied by derealization on occasion when he spotted someone dressed as his assailant had been.

One such episode occurred when Terry was walking down the street with his wife after seeing a movie. "We were walking to where my car was parked, and out of nowhere this guy pops up wearing an old army jacket and a gray wool knit cap pulled down low on his face," Terry recalls. "I thought it was the guy who almost killed me. 'He's back to finish the job,' I told myself. Everything around me got fuzzy, kind of blurred. I wasn't sure whether what was happening was real or I was still in the movies. It felt like I was in a surveillance car watching it happen. The guy took something out of his pocket, and I was sure it was a gun. I felt numb, like a stone, and yet I stepped in front of my wife to protect her. But the thing in his hand was just a remote to open his car. I watched him get into his car and drive away, and then things got real again. I could hear my wife saying, 'Are you all right?' "

Some trauma survivors, for instance, survivors of childhood abuse, have a tendency to overestimate the amount of danger in the world and may underestimate their own competency and worth. With relatively brief therapy Terry's fears of becoming the victim of a second violent crime lessened, and he was able to control his anxiety about being attacked again without experiencing depersonalization and derealization episodes.

SEVERE DEREALIZATION

Derealization episodes that are rated severe cause discomfort and dysfunction and are different from mild episodes because they involve parents, home, and friends. They recur more frequently than moderate episodes and are more persistent (twenty-four hours or longer). For people with a dissociative disorder, these disturbances in perceiving the environment are usually associated with amnesia, identity alteration, and flashbacks.

Derealization *without* depersonalization is a feature of the dissociative disorder called DDNOS (dissociative disorder not otherwise specified), a mild variation of DID or the other dissociative disorders. My research has shown that some people with this diagnosis are eventually found to have DID.

As a posttraumatic response to ongoing childhood abuse, derealization is often experienced in connection with the person who perpetrated the abuse. If you were an abused child, perceiving the mother or father who abused you as alien to you is an attempt to make sense of the incomprehensible without losing touch with reality. It's an emotional, but not intellectual, disconnect from your experiences of your parent as a caretaker, who was at the same time a source of crushing pain, neglect, or deprivation.

This illusory magic trick can be unsettling. "It's very scary," says a nineteen-year-old of the derealization episodes she experiences at home. "You feel like you've been dumped in the Twilight Zone. You're faced with knowing, obviously, that this is reality, but you don't know who these people are. Yet they're here, and you're in this house, and you're living with them. You wake up and come downstairs and this lady's serving you breakfast, and you don't even know who she is. It's, you know, your mother."

In some instances derealization can take on a surreal "Alice in Wonderland" quality. As a natural reaction to trauma, this heightened reality results from a simultaneous intensified alertness and a splitting off from awareness of overwhelming emotions. People, buildings, furniture, or other objects appear to be changing in size or shape; colors seem to become more or less intense. The net effect is to turn the environment into an abstraction or make the derealized person fade away.

Rosa, a thirty-one-year-old Hispanic woman with DID and a nineteen-year history of repeated sexual abuse, says, "I have a distancing thing that happens where I get very narrow like this"—she places her palms almost touching—"and this is all I can see. And then I lose vision altogether. My eyes close and at the same time I hear a roaring sound. I thought everybody had it."

An abuse survivor may project feelings of fear originating in childhood onto a person who serves as the abuser's stand-in—a boyfriend or girlfriend, employer or coworker who resembles the abuser or triggers memories of the trauma. Superimposing one familiar face onto another person known to the survivor, usually a friend or loved one, has the incongruous, surreal effect of making the second person appear unfamiliar. This is a common derealization experience associated with flashbacks.

Audrey, a thirty-seven-year-old abuse survivor, was referred to me for a SCID-D by her psychiatrist who was concerned about her severe dissociative symptoms. "Sometimes when I look at my doctor," Audrey told me during the interview, "I see the face of my father or my ex-husband, and I tell him about it right away. It's usually because I'm afraid he'll do the same thing to me that they have, even though there's no reason not to trust him. He's a very, very wonderful person, and he would never hurt me. When I was married, sometimes I'd look at my ex-husband and see my father's face."

A person's employment situation may trigger derealization of the workplace in flashbacks. If the atmosphere crackles with the heat of sexual harassment or a supervisor resembles a person's original abuser, an episode can be induced. Apart from personal interactions, many people report that episodes can be triggered by certain features in the physical environment of the workplace. Hypnotic patterns on computer screens, moving conveyor belts, flashing lights, reflective or mirrored surfaces can all stimulate the brain's information processing system and trigger flash-backs of the original traumatic incident.

What makes derealization experienced during flashbacks so intense is that the remembered event is much more than a memory. The fear-related experience that the brain has never processed properly bursts into aware-ness and is so arresting that it takes over the present and makes it very unreal. As a rape victim described her flashbacks during the SCID-D: "I'd be out on a date with a boyfriend and see a totally different guy—the guy who raped me. I'd be sitting there with my boyfriend, and then, oh my God, I'd go running out of the theater."

Faith, a woman who was sexually abused by her father, sums up the immediacy of flashbacks this way: "Flashbacks are not like snapshots that you can put in your album, and store in the back of the closet, and remember as part of your past. They're feeling the sensations that you would have felt then now."

Perpetrators of a crime can be as disconnected from what is happen-ing in the present as their victims. A rapist, for example, can dissociate himself from an awareness of the violence and pain he is inflicting on an utter stranger by imagining her to be some hateful, abusive female figure in his past. Even as the woman being raped floats out of her body and imagines that the crime is happening to someone else, derealization allows the rapist to act out his rage in this violent and brutal way.

The superimposition of another reality onto the present can also involve a fantasy. Derealization probably played an important role in the murderous rampage that Eric Harris and Dylan Klebold went on in April 1999, at Columbine High School, Littleton, Colorado. In the tragic after-math, a stunned nation wondered how these two young men, alienated as so many teenagers are yet seemingly "normal," turned into cold-blooded sociopaths, indifferently, gleefully snuffing out the lives of any student or teacher who crossed their path. How could they be so utterly soulless and devoid of pity, ignoring the pleas of their classmates to let them live or silencing anyone who cried or moaned with another shot?

One answer turned up in the violent video games the two were obsessed with playing. Graphic effects realistic enough to blur the line between fantasy and reality allow these kill-for-thrill games to be used to break down a person's aversion to killing. At the time of the massacre, Doom, the game favored by one of the mass murderers, was being adapted by the Marine Corps for its own training purposes. Survivors of the mas-sacre reported that Harris and Klebold seemed to be delightedly dis-patching flesh-and-blood real people as if they were animated cartoons.

Brooks Brown, a classmate who'd hung out with Harris and Klebold, claimed that when the two went on their killing spree, "they were living in the moment, like they were inside a video game." The Simon Wiesenthal Center, a tracker of Internet hate groups, discovered in its archives a copy of Harris's website with his customized version of Doom featuring two heavily armed shooters and their helpless prey. As an Internet investigator for the center put it, at Columbine the two killers were "playing out their game in God mode."

Harris and Klebold were pipe bombs waiting to explode in the grip of a derealization episode. Their addictive video game fantasies became their reality, and they superimposed that reality on the present when they took their revenge on the jocks and preppies who rejected and tormented them, unleashing their anger, hostility, and resentment in the bloody massacre. Feeling disconnected from their peers, they were also internally disconnected from their own humanity. It seems clear that violent video games can promote derealization in a susceptible person. For disaffected adolescents who may have undetected and untreated dissociative symptoms, spending hours and hours playing these games in isolation can be dangerous.

Despite Harris's website and other warning signs that he and Klebold were troubled, the two received no extensive psychiatric evaluation. Ironically, after participating in a community-service program and an anger management seminar as punishment for breaking into a van and stealing electronic equipment, Harris was declared "likely to succeed in life" and Klebold "intelligent enough to make any dream a reality." The psychiatrist who saw Harris sometime before the shooting recommended an antidepressant to alleviate his anger at the world. Klebold, a sensitive and caring person although shy and withdrawn, shocked everyone who knew him with his Jekyll and Hyde turnabout. Their fascination with neo-Nazism, death, and violent videos, along with their identity confusion and impulsivity, strongly suggests that these bright young men may have had dissociative symptoms underlying their anger and sadness. Had these symptoms been identified and treated in time, perhaps the missing links could have been filled in before their murderous fantasy overtook the real world.

Severing a person's emotions from familiar perceptions of the outside world may be an adaptive way to cope with the fear and anxiety aroused by intense trauma or repeated childhood abuse. When derealization becomes habitual and severe, its effect on relationships, work, and peace of mind can be devastating. The oppressive feeling of living in an out-of-joint personal world can cause an agony of inner confusion and turn the real people in that world into unreal ghosts.

The following questionnaire will help you identify what symptoms of derealization you are experiencing and whether they are mild (normal), moderate, or severe.

Steinberg Derealization Questionnaire

	Never	Once or twice	Some-times	Many times	Almost all the time	Only with drugs or alcohol
	1	2	3	4	5	1
1. People or places that I know have seemed as if they were unfamiliar.	☐	☐	☐	☐	☐	☐
2. I feel as if I am looking at the world through fogged glasses and people or things appear unclear or distant.	☐	☐	☐	☐	☐	☐
3. Friends, relatives, or my surroundings have felt strange or unreal.	☐	☐	☐	☐	☐	☐
4. I have felt as if people around me were just a dream.	☐	☐	☐	☐	☐	☐
5. I have felt as if things around me were changing in size or shape.	☐	☐	☐	☐	☐	☐
6. I have felt as if colors were changing in intensity.	☐	☐	☐	☐	☐	☐
7. People have appeared to change into someone else.	☐	☐	☐	☐	☐	☐

	Never	Once or twice	Some-times	Many times	Almost all the time	Only with drugs or alcohol
	1	2	3	4	5	1
8. Though I am intellectually aware of who my relatives are, I have felt as if they were not really related to me.	☐	☐	☐	☐	☑	☐
9. I have had difficulty recognizing friends, family, or my own home.	☐	☐	☐	☐	☐	☐
10. I have been puzzled about what is real and unreal around me.	☐	☐	☐	☐	☐	☐
11. People or places that I know have felt as if they were fading away or disappear-ing.	☐	☐	☐	☐	☐	☐
12. I have felt detached from other people.	☐	☐	☐	☐	☑	☐

If you have had any of the above experiences, answer the following:

	No	Yes
Did the experience(s) interfere with your relationships with friends, family, or coworkers?	☐	☑
Did it affect your ability to work?	☑	☐
Did it cause you discomfort or distress?	☐	☑

To Score Your Derealization Quesionnaire:

1. Assign a score ranging from 1 to 5 corresponding to the number on the top line above the box that you checked.

2. Now add up your score. Use the general guidelines below for understanding your score.

OVERALL DEREALIZATION SCORE

No Derealization:	12
Mild Derealization:	13–20 *2⁰*
Moderate Derealization:	21–40
Severe Derealization:	41–60

RECOMMENDATIONS

If your total score falls in the range of *No* to *Mild Derealization* (12–20), this is within the normal range unless you have experienced Items 9 or 10 recurrently. If you have experienced these items several times, we recommend that you be evaluated by a professional who is trained in the administration of the full SCID-D interview.

If your total score falls in the range of *Moderate* to *Severe Derealization* (21–60), we recommend that you be evaluated by a professional who is trained in the administration of the full SCID-D interview. If your derealization has interfered with your relationships with friends, family, or coworkers or has affected your ability to work or has caused you distress, it is particularly important that you obtain a professional consultation.

Should an experienced clinician find that you have a dissociative disorder, you have a treatable illness with a very good prognosis for recovery. Your illness is widely shared by others who coped with trauma by using the self-protective defense of dissociation. With proper treatment, in time, your need to disconnect from your surroundings and familiar people will diminish. Eventually, as you grow strong enough to reconnect with your hidden memories and feelings and accept them as your own, your derealization will be reduced and you will become a more integrated and psychologically healthy person.

8

WHEN YOU DON'T KNOW WHO YOU ARE

S TEVE WILLIS WAS making close to a million dollars a year as managing director at UBS, the Swiss financial conglomerate, when, still in his
late thirties, he walked away from Wall Street to open two restaurants in
Princeton, New Jersey, his hometown. Willis explained that although his
wife, Harriette, was "incredibly supportive," he got tired of a supposedly
glamorous job that wasn't much fun: getting up to catch the 6 A.M. train
from Princeton Junction to New York and riding home on the 8 P.M.;
spending 150 nights a year in hotel rooms around the world, chasing
potential clients and catching a glimpse of a restaurant here and a conference room there; getting calls on a Saturday night putting him on a plane
to Finland the next day, even when it was one of his kids' birthday; for
one five-year stretch missing every school play, every parent-teacher conference, and every sports match.

Willis was born with a corporate spoon in his mouth. His father was
a senior vice president at Gillette, and the younger Willis felt obliged to
try the executive route before concluding that more than money, he
wanted happiness. When he tires of the restaurants, he'll sell them and
move on to the next thing, maybe starting up an Internet investment
bank. Whatever the next step is, one thing is certain—Willis will never
again be riding the 6 A.M. train every day to the Wall Street world that
once defined his identity.

A SIGN OF OUR TIMES

Steve Willis is a dazzling example of how freedom of choice has made the traditional concept of identity as a consistent and coherent entity seem somewhat outdated. Reinventing oneself from an investment banker to a restaurateur to an Internet entrepreneur hardly fits in with the American Psychiatric Association's definition of identity as "the sense of self, providing a unity of personality over time." It also seems to challenge the teachings of Erik Erikson, the father of the psychosocial development theory of identity: that identity is a well-organized concept of the self made up of values, beliefs, and goals to which the individual is committed.

Although most people still subscribe to the idea of a core sense of self or basic nature that guides our choices and behavior, the flexibility of self-concept demonstrated by Willis is a sign of our times. Many people today have a "working" self-concept—one in control at any given moment—that gives their lives an unprecedented complexity. In his book *The Saturated Self: Dilemmas of Identity in Contemporary Life* (1991), sociologist Kenneth Gergen lists some situations he encountered within a span of several months:

- a neurologist, married to one woman, who spends Tuesday and Thursday nights with another woman, by whom he has a child

- a male lawyer who marries a female lawyer and invites both their former lovers—both of whom are women—to the wedding

- a woman who has switched careers four times in the past fifteen years, from working as a drama teacher to becoming a fund-raiser, then a stockbroker, then manager of her own antique business

"This pastiche personality is a social chameleon," Gergen says, "constantly borrowing bits and pieces of identity from whatever sources are available, and constructing them as useful or desirable in any given situation." This sensibility, according to Gergen, raises doubts about the need for personal coherence or consistency and makes us wonder why we need to be bound by "any traditional marker of identity—profession, gender, ethnicity, nationality."

Although no one decries freedom of choice, many people who are influenced by this "cafeteria mentality" end up feeling confused about their options, not really knowing who they are. This cornucopia of options, they feel, places pressures on their sense of identity and makes them question the existence of a "true" self. Our culture's emphasis on choice may be one reason why many people in the general population have a mild case of identity confusion, and those who are particularly vulnerable by reason of growing up in troubled families have a more severe degree of it.

The global economy is another reason for widespread identity confusion among normal people today. Corporate demands make it necessary for executives or professionals to uproot their families and relocate every so often or travel frequently throughout the country or abroad. As a result, many people have a shaky sense of geographical "place" or position. Add to that the uncertain nature of corporate life, with constant mergers and acquisitions and attendant layoffs and downsizings. Including the category of adjustment disorder in its 1994 *Diagnostic and Statistical Manual (DSM-IV)* is the American Psychiatric Association's recognition of how upsetting this particular form of contemporary stress can be to people affected by the strain of relocation or job loss.

Another fact of contemporary life, the speed and multiplicity of communications—faxes, e-mail, Instant Messenger, overnight express, and so on—can be wearing on anyone's internal center. We also have the mass media constantly bombarding our sense of identity with dramatic portrayals of "alternative" life-styles, gossip about celebrities, and information about different cultures around the world, along with a chaotic mass of conflicting expert opinion on everything from menopause to mutual funds. TV news and newsmagazine shows, CNBC, the tabloids, movies, home videos, CDs, talk radio, Internet chat rooms and message boards, magazines, and paperbacks have all combined into a maelstrom of uncertainty about the way we're living our lives.

And finally there is the sense of "systems overload" in people generated by the unending flow of random stimuli. People are increasingly expected to function in a "polyphasic" manner—that is, to divide their conscious attention among several different activities at the same time. An administrative aide, for example, may have to deal with people face to face, answer phones, respond to an intercom, and operate a word processor, all more or less simultaneously. Even during their free time, people who are used to polyphasic splitting of attention may "relax" by doing several things at once—driving while talking on the car phone, listening to a tape, or mentally planning a shopping list.

It may seem to be a giant leap from this kind of multilayered functioning to a dissociative disorder, but there is some evidence that modern technology is teaching the population as a whole to accept split or divided attentiveness as normal. Some theorists believe that polyphasic functioning can, over time, affect a person's sense of identity by making it harder to distinguish central concerns from peripheral ones. When life is made up of decisions, decisions, decisions, all requiring attention at the same time, where to eat lunch on a particular day may seem as important a question as, Do I believe in God? We can get to a point where the dailiness of life matters as much as the core elements of identity: one's fundamental beliefs, moral convictions, or close relationships.

HOW IDENTITY IS FORMED

Where does our identity come from in the first place? Choosing one theory of identity among the many that exist could itself be a cause of identity confusion. Theories of identity range across the entire map of human experience and can be grouped in four categories.

Learning theories: We acquire behavior in one of two ways: either we act in a certain way and experience the consequences ourselves, or we learn vicariously by watching how models' behavior is reinforced.

Cognitive theories: We construct reality, conceptions of ourselves, and our moral codes by exploring our environment in a series of age-related stages and by organizing information in order to solve problems.

Psychoanalytical theories: The psyche has three divisions—the superego, a partly conscious internalization of parental moral attitudes and society's rules, rewarding or punishing through conscience and guilt; the id, a completely unconscious grab bag of instinctual needs and drives that are a source of psychic energy; and the ego, the organized conscious mediator between the person and reality, in how the person both perceives reality and adapts to it. Conflicting mental processes, the unconscious mind, defense mechanisms, and mental representations of important others and patterns of relating formed in early childhood all shape current thought, feeling, and behavior.

Psychosocial theories: Like Erik Erikson's, these are essentially psychoanalytic but much more society- and culture-oriented. They set out a genetically predetermined unfolding of our identities in stages, each with its own theme, time period, and developmental task to be mastered. Our progress through each stage is linked to our success, or lack of it, in all the previous stages.

Erikson's theory is perhaps the one most relevant to identity confusion. The task of adolescence—stage five of his eight stages, beginning with puberty and ending around age eighteen or twenty—is to achieve ego identity and to avoid role confusion. To negotiate this stage successfully, we have to mold all we've learned about ourselves and life into a unified self-image that tells us who we are and how we fit into society. We must achieve a sense of identity in occupation, sex roles, politics, and religion.

Small children identify primarily with their parents, incorporating their beliefs, values, and behavior. As the child matures, identification extends to siblings, relatives, other significant adults, and peers. Erikson pointed out that these identifications undergo a continual process of selection and modification, making identity formation something like a kaleidoscope—an evolving configuration that is gradually established by syntheses and resyntheses of the ego.

Without adequate supports for this identity formation from adult role models, we succumb to role confusion—we're hounded by uncertainty about our basic nature, our ideals and philosophy of life, our purpose for being here, and our place in the world. Every subsequent developmental stage will carry the curse of this impairment. As Erikson put it, "Failure is cumulative."

IDENTITY DISTURBANCE

As a dissociative symptom, identity confusion is a subjective feeling of uncertainty, puzzlement, or conflict about one's sense of self. It involves difficulty understanding oneself and feelings of unhappiness resulting from internal strife. Hampered by a lack of self-knowledge, weak personal boundaries, and no coherent set of core beliefs and moral convictions, the sufferer feels an anguished "Who am I?" continually reverberating in his mind.

Many of us who thought we had that question resolved may have to revisit it and reinvent ourselves when life happens to us while we're busy making other plans. Faced with undertaking a major change—getting married or divorced, finding a new job, moving away—we get tossed into a state of "identity shock." Mercifully, this painful but mild identity confusion doesn't last very long, because we still have a core identity as a foundation to support the next step.

Some people are not so blessed. Something happened along the path to an identity that derailed them. And that something is a dysfunctional relationship with family members early in life. A common thread running through all of the personality theories is that a child's basic sense of identity depends in large measure on identification and interactions with empathetic family members who validate the child's feelings. Abusive or inadequate parents force a child to identify with negative traits or behavior or can force a negative identity as a family scapegoat or loser on a child. A child from an abusive environment can grow up with a distorted view of the world as a dangerous, threatening, unforgiving place with a severe scarcity of options. If the child's attempts to identify with an admired adult outside the family are criticized or thwarted by the parents, the child is a likely candidate for identity disturbances in adolescence and early adulthood.

Why are abusive parents so cruel? Some simply have poor impulse control and lash out physically when they feel angered or frustrated by the child's needs or demands. Others momentarily identify the child with a hated or feared parent or older sibling. They may "hear" the voice of their own authoritarian parents in their child's cries or whining and believe that the child deliberately tried to annoy them or generally "asked for it." Some abusive parents may "read" the child's facial expressions as a justification for abuse, misinterpreting a look as defiance or anger, and feel goaded to beat the child again. Obviously a child who is not only maltreated but verbally invalidated and accused of provoking the maltreatment is a candidate for some form of identity confusion.

The self-centeredness of parents who are blind to their children's emotional needs is another cause of identity disturbance. So many of my patients speak of their parents in such terms as "unbelievably narcissistic," "neglectful," "manipulative," "treated me like a slave," or "acted like I was invisible" that these descriptions have become a leitmotif in their life histories.

Another dimension of parental self-centeredness is the widespread assumption that children exist to gratify their parents' needs. This is the basic assumption underlying not only incestuous sexual abuse, but emotional abuse as well. Some parents push their children to pursue social prestige or measurable achievements—become a star athlete, win beauty contests, get into an Ivy League school—and other parents try to indoctrinate their children with certain moral standards or religious or political ideologies. If severe enough, these pressures might well create some identity confusion in children, who are uncertain about which goals or standards are their own and which have been imposed upon them by their parents.

Exploitative parents are often physically abusive, because they don't understand the normal human developmental timetable. They beat a child for failing to live up to their unrealistic expectations of the child's readiness for toilet training, self-feeding, and the like. As the child grows older, abusive parents are likely to continue piling on excessive and premature responsibilities—expecting a daughter to cook, clean house, and take care of younger siblings when she herself is only eight or nine. Children deprived of childhood acquire a painful sense of having no rights, only the obligation to serve the parent. Consequently they often develop impaired self-reference, an inability to know or experience their own needs or wishes apart from the reactions or demands of others.

Another form of adult exploitation of children is parental violation of the child's psychological boundaries. Many children may be prematurely drafted into the role of confidant or amateur therapist and are forced to listen to adult problems that are beyond their level of maturity. "I was thirteen when my parents split, and my mother kept crying to me about my Dad having an affair," a teenager recalls. "It made me feel all torn up inside. I remember writing in my diary, 'I'm so SCARED!' "

This untimely role reversal from protectee to protector puts a child at risk for identity confusion. A teenager compelled to become a "girlfriend" to a divorced mother when she is just starting to date herself feels threatened because too much is demanded of her. Having a parent who demonstrates this kind of self-centeredness or general lack of maturity disadvantages the adolescent who has to identify with that parent before moving on to forge her own identity.

Many compromised parents have been exposed to neglect or abuse themselves, and lack appropriate role models for parenting. With psychotherapy and parenting groups they can learn healthy parenting skills and end the cycle of abuse. Men are more likely than women to inflict sexual abuse on children, and substance abuse is the most common presenting problem among reported abusers. Treatment for their substance abuse is essential not only for their own recovery but for the protection of children in their care. Many of my patients describe parents who have a "Jekyll and Hyde" personality that fluctuates with their parents' alcohol or drug use and sobriety. Fortunately, some parents who were exposed to abuse themselves have vowed never to repeat their abuse on others. In fact, some abuse survivors, including people suffering from dissociation, are exceptionally good parents.

Some amount of identity confusion seems unavoidable in a world as complex as ours. The best insurance against it is to surround a child from infancy on with adults and siblings who exemplify a range of positive personality traits and provide a consistent and predictable source of love and support.

MILD IDENTITY CONFUSION

"When John and I got divorced, I felt as if I didn't know who I was anymore," says Glenda, a forty-six-year-old mother of two college-age children, talking about the identity confusion she experienced when she divorced her husband after twenty-two years of marriage. "We'd been married so long that I couldn't grasp the concept of myself as a single woman and not part of a couple. I knew money would be a problem if I didn't get a better job, but what was I trained to do? How could I quit without something else to go to? Should I go back to school?" She laughs ruefully and goes on, "It felt like the *Titanic*. You know, you're sailing along smoothly, and all of a sudden you hit that iceberg, and water is rushing in everywhere, and you start going down. I saw it coming, but I still didn't have a life raft. The kids tried to cheer me up with little pep talks like 'Come on, Mom, today is the first day of the rest of your life.' And I thought, 'Yes, but what am I going to *do* with the rest of it?' I didn't have a clue."

Mild identity confusion like this is common before or after a major life decision—deciding to marry or divorce, choosing a vocation, relocating geographically, going public about one's sexual orientation, et cetera. It's natural for these transitions to upset the internal equilibrium of someone who wants a stable sense of personal identity or has to decide among conflicting aspects of his or her identity.

Identity confusion during a period of adjustment, as in Glenda's case, is ordinarily transient, episodic, and related to a specific stressor. As we've seen, this kind of mild identity confusion is not unusual in today's age of rampant choices. It's especially likely to occur at defining points of transition in the adult life cycle, like graduation from college, marriage, midlife, aging, retirement, and a death in the family.

Trevor, a thirty-year-old art director in his father's advertising agency, went through a typical bout of mild identity confusion after his graduation from Parsons School of Design in New York. "I was uncertain about going into my father's business because I didn't know if it was what *I* wanted to do or what *he* wanted me to do," Trevor says. He goes on with a wry grin, "Besides, at that age I thought I had this magnificent talent that the world was just waiting to discover, so I went off to Italy to study art for a year. I met serious artists who were a helluva lot more talented and passionate about their work than I was," he confides, "and I realized that commercial art was actually more exciting for me. I came home and joined my father's agency because, in my heart, I knew that I really loved the work and was doing it for myself."

All of the transitions of psychosocial development involve their share of conflict and confusion. With the resolution of the crisis, the uncertainty gives way to a surer sense of comfort in one's own skin and one's place in the world.

MODERATE IDENTITY CONFUSION

When identity confusion advances beyond a transient episode related to a specific stressor and becomes a recurrent experience causing distress, it is moderate rather than mild. We can say that this kind of confusion is like a haunting melody that, for one reason or another, has become our theme song. Usually it revolves around some question about our identity that we have yet to answer.

People who are adopted often have this kind of confusion about their real identity. It's normal for them to question their identity even if they've been adopted into a healthy, loving family. No matter how close they are to their adoptive parents, they're still not related to them biologically—they might even belong to a different racial or ethnic group—and may wonder what their biological parents are like. What do they look like? Why did they give them up? Do these parents care about them at all? How are they like these parents? How are they different?

Aaron, a musician in his early thirties, was adopted in infancy by an affluent Jewish family. He loved his adoptive parents but had always felt a yearning to meet his biological mother and father. "There was a part of my life that was a mystery to me," Aaron says. "I was basically happy, but I didn't feel complete. There was something missing—a piece of my history that other people had for themselves and I didn't." With the help of an agency, Aaron tracked down his birth parents and found they were living in Ireland. "My girlfriend gave me the courage to write to my birth parents and see whether it was all right if I came to visit them," he recalls. "I was scared to death that they'd say no, but they didn't."

Aaron and his girlfriend took a trip to Ireland to meet his biological parents and discovered that they were sixties "flower children" living in a commune in upstate New York when they had him. His mother explained that the pregnancy was unplanned—she wasn't even married to his father then—and they were just too young to take on the responsibility of bringing up a child. As Catholics, they felt that abortion was out of the question and decided that giving Aaron up for adoption was the only alternative.

"Meeting them was a good experience for me," Aaron says. "They're two intelligent, decent people who got in a bind when they were young. I know they would've kept me if they'd been able to. I may never see them again—our lives are so different—but getting to know them finally gave me a feeling of being at peace with myself."

Aaron might have had a much more severe level of identity confusion had he been adopted into a dysfunctional family rather than a healthy one. A child sent to live with abusive foster parents or taken back from adoptive parents by a surrogate mother and given a different name could grow up with severe identity confusion and a predisposition toward DID.

Confusion about one's sexual identity or orientation frequently occurs following childhood sexual abuse or growing up in a dysfunctional family with parents who paraded their sexual activity in front of the child or aired their sexual conflicts openly. This confusion about one's own sexual nature is more serious than the mild identity confusion related to going public about one's sexual identity or orientation.

Valerie, a strikingly pretty thirty-seven-year-old biochemical engineer, has been struggling with confusion about her sexual orientation since late adolescence, when she first realized that she was attracted to members of her own sex. She grew up in a home where her father flaunted his mistresses in front of her mother, and her mother tore him down bitterly but stayed with him anyway. The nursemaid her mother hired for Valerie when she was little was a positive substitute identification figure. Losing her when her mother sent her away was deeply disturbing to Valerie. "My parents made it pretty hard for me to trust men or have a good opinion of them," she says. "I grew up thinking they were all pigs."

In her midtwenties Valerie had her first affair with a young woman her age. "I'd dated men, even enjoyed sex with some," says Valerie, "but the passion and depth of emotion I had with this woman were unlike anything I'd ever felt before."

Still, both Valerie and the other woman felt that they had to conform to parental and societal expectations and continued to have "public" relationships with men while secretly seeing each other. After four years of this double life, Valerie's lover broke off their relationship, because she wanted to marry her boyfriend and start a family. "I went to her wedding in an unbelievable state of turmoil," Valerie says. "I wanted to have a baby more than anything else in the world, but the question was, with whom? By that time I was deeply attached to another woman and was making us both miserable because I couldn't commit to her. I wasn't ready to give up on men entirely. My psychiatrist thought I was gay, but I didn't want to believe it. It didn't fit the picture in my mind of who I thought I should be. I didn't know who I was."

After twelve years of daily treatment with a psychiatrist, Valerie came to me for an evaluation. Her SCID-D showed that along with her confusion about her sexual orientation, she had a moderate level of depersonalization that had not been dealt with in her analysis. Her recurrent depersonalization needed to be addressed or she would stay immobilized forever. The discrepancy between her own sense of self and a mental representation based on others' opinions had created a deep sense of shame about her actual sexual orientation. By not recognizing and treating her depersonalization, her therapy was keeping her disconnected from her true sexual identity instead of helping her discover and accept it as a part of herself independent of others' reactions and opinions.

Valerie's predicament speaks to the so-called deselfing of women that is widespread in our society, even in healthier families. Female children are doubly at risk for loss of self in relationships, because early in life they are taught to put the demands of others first. The pervasive cultural assumption that women exist to meet the psychological and physical wishes of others exerts a negative influence on their identity development. Inability to finish graduate or professional training, anxiety related to promotion or success, and difficulties in establishing a clear sense of identity and a "life plan" are some manifestations of this influence.

As a result of the ongoing pressure to gratify others, many women grow up with a deep sense of unmet needs, anxiety about having those needs met, and a general lack of a healthy sense of entitlement. Recent studies have shown that female adolescents in general are troubled by a sense of invalidation and invisibility—of not being listened to or responded to empathetically—and feelings of "not being able to convey or even believe in one's own experience." Some researchers have hypothesized that the epidemic of eating disorders among American and Western European women is directly related to women's difficulties with selfhood and identity.

If mild or moderate identity confusion is prevalent among adults who grew up in relatively healthy families, this problem is enormously magnified for adults from abusive families, male as well as female. A clear sense of one's identity derives in part from knowledge and acceptance of one's gifts and interests. A boy or girl driven by fear of abusive family members and constantly on the lookout for signals of impending danger has little opportunity or energy left to define, explore, or gratify his or her own interests or desires. For this person identity confusion often rises to a higher level.

SEVERE IDENTITY CONFUSION

Identity confusion escalates into a persistent internal struggle tantamount to warfare in people who have suffered abuse in childhood. It involves recurrent episodes of dysfunction accompanied by strong feelings of unhappiness called dysphoria. You know your identity confusion is severe when it interferes with your interpersonal relationships or your ability to hold a job.

The magnitude of the disturbance to one's identity wrought by emotional, physical, and/or sexual abuse in childhood is understandable. How can children who were brought up with a malevolent disregard for their needs, rights, gifts, and interests, and were constantly reviled as "bad," "stupid," "worthless," or a "liar," develop a healthy self-image? Since their whole childhood was consumed by a struggle to avoid pain at the hands of those they loved, they cannot name or define who they are, what they believe, or what they want from life in any profound or coherent fashion. Identity confusion for them goes beyond the normal transient disorientation of adolescence or divorce or the death of a partner, or an adoptee's questioning of identity in adulthood. It widens into a deep, gaping chasm in their sense of self, driven into it by the sledgehammer of repeated abuse.

"It's this feeling of being split, like you're not part of your hand," says Bob, a thirty-six-year-old patient whose employment history reads like a cryptogram with too many blanks. "When you go through adolescence and you have an identity crisis, you know you're a whole person. You're just trying to put your values and your sense of self in place. But this is a feeling of being split, of not being whole. You feel so many different ways, you don't know who you are. You're a stranger to yourself."

Another patient, a middle-aged woman diagnosed with DID, gives this colorful description of the intensity of the daily internal struggle that puts her personal integrity at stake with every decision, even what to buy at the supermarket counter: "I feel like an amoeba with fifteen thousand different ideas about where it wants to go. And it's literally like being pulled in every direction possible until there's nothing left, and I feel split in half. There's a constant battle."

People with extreme identity confusion often experience the struggle over identity as a pitched battle or civil war waged inside themselves, even going so far as to include images of weapons and physical descriptions of the combatants. The anxiety they feel is related to fears of letting their abuse memories out and losing control over the self. "It's like a tug of war," says Jerry, the construction worker who earlier spoke of a huge man with jet black hair inside himself who yells "Let me out! Let me out!" during his depersonalization episodes. "Pulling, pulling the rope, pulling, you keep pulling and pulling," Jerry says, "and he pulls you back, and you pull it forward, and he pulls you back, and you pull it forward, and you want to say, 'Hey, man take the damn thing.' This guy wants to come out, and he must think I'm nuts if I'm gonna let him out. If I let him out, I'm never gonna get myself back in. And that's what scares me the most."

Rick, a thirty-four-year-old computer programmer who grew up in an alcoholic home where he suffered physical and emotional abuse from both parents, has a battle inside him that is familiar to many men and the women they love. Before he settled down and married, Rick had a history of brawling in bars and womanizing, flitting from one short-term relationship to another as soon as there was any mention of commitment. Now, although he is deeply in love with his wife and wants to be faithful to her, an untamed part of him that still wants to carouse and have casual sex—a part modeled after his father—is at war with his responsible side. "I have this struggle about who I really am," says Rick. "Am I just a total jerk or someone my wife wants to come home to and love and not be afraid that I'm going to leave her? Am I an intelligent, responsible adult, or do I just want to do what I want and take what I want when I want it?"

Rick goes on, obviously tortured by his identity confusion: "My wife wants to have children, but I don't know if I'm a family guy. At heart, I feel like a guy who could have a family and really care about my wife for the rest of my life, and make a nice, easy life together. Then I feel like a guy who doesn't care about anything or anybody, especially someone who loves me. And this guy keeps telling me that I should walk away from my wife and just have a bunch of noncommittal sexual relationships and be a big, noncaring stud."

SEXUAL ABUSE AND CONFUSION ABOUT SEXUALITY

Sexually abused children often develop problems with their sexuality. They commonly believe that the abuse would not have taken place if their sex had been different. A male survivor of his mother's incest, for example, may attribute the repugnant abuse to his being male and ask himself, "Why did I have to be born a disgusting boy?" Or a woman raped by her father may attribute the abuse to her vulnerability as a female and develop male alters to protect her from further victimization.

People with a dissociative disorder may have a generalized state of perplexity about their sexual orientation—like Valerie's, but more dominant and disruptive to their lives—or may question their entire sexual identity, not knowing whether they are male or female. Those with DID who have alter personalities of the other sex may experience the internal conflict as a literal "battle of the sexes." In a well-known instance of DID, for example, a man convicted of rape indicated that the personality who came out during the actual commission of the rapes was not only female but lesbian.

Another man I interviewed in my DID field study had been sexually abused as a child and had a blind woman inside him—typical of how powerful and metaphoric the images are. Although there was nothing wrong with his eyes, at times he couldn't see and would walk by marking steps with the aid of a cane. He also had a part inside that felt like a ballerina. He was so confused, in fact, that he had another woman inside him with whom he had an ongoing relationship. Sometimes his involvement with the woman inside him would conflict with his attending to a real woman in his life.

Some people with severe sexual identity confusion may express a desire for a surgical sex change. "I had many periods in which I felt I needed a sex change, debated if I was a homosexual," says Dan, a DID patient whose primary personality is male. He has pictures of himself in drag and some vague ideas of what Danielle his female alter, looks like. "I'm not sure Danielle's happy," he confides. "She's not happy with my genitalia, and I'm not so sure she's happy with my weight and bone structure. Danielle has her own agenda. She would like to see me dissolved from this person. I keep trying to tell her that if she comes out to my therapist and we work this out we'll be one person, but she doesn't want to be one person with Dan in charge."

IDENTITY CONFUSION IN THE WORKPLACE

SCID-D research shows that severe identity confusion is a significant factor in DID, when one personality creates an environment that conflicts with what an alternate personality expects. "It's like you come into work sometimes," says Edie, a forty-year-old personnel director, "and you don't know what you're supposed to do that day. I've walked into work wondering, Who the hell am I? Not knowing: What is my job? What is my title? What am I supposed to do? And then when you start asking for help, all of a sudden you know what you're doing there."

Another woman known as a crackerjack executive secretary found herself in a painful situation with a new employer because an alter personality who knew nothing about typing or dictation had unexpectedly emerged in the interim before she started the new job. "It's like my brain was damaged," she said during the SCID-D interview. "I told the company I had ten years' experience, but it didn't look like I had more than a week's experience to them. The vice president told me that I had no secretarial ability whatsoever, and yet I got straight A's and was told by all my previous employers that I had A-number-one performance. This executive said, 'I've been trying for ten years to get you to work for me.' I worked for him for a month and still couldn't perform anything, and he said, 'I can't believe what happened to you,' and started yelling at me. Right now I'm learning to type all over again."

We're all heir to some identity confusion by reason of inevitable conflicts between our different mental processes and representations of the self. Conflicts between who we are and who we would like to be or between what we want to do and think we should are bound to confuse us at critical junctures or transitional times in our lives. Still, most of us know that although our identity is continually evolving, it has an essentially solid core with consistent preferences, goals, and ideals. Someone with dissociative identity disorder, on the other hand, is constantly wrestling with separate, often adversarial identities that are engaged in a battle for control over that person's mind and body twenty-four hours a day.

The following questionnaire will help you identify what symptoms of identity confusion you are experiencing and whether they are mild (normal), moderate, or severe.

Steinberg Identity Confusion Questionnaire

	Never	Once or twice	Some-times	Many times	Almost all the time	Only with drugs or alcohol
	1	2	3	4	5	1
1. I feel that I need to find my true self.	☐	☐	☐	☐	☒	☐
2. I have a critical commentary in my head about things I do.	☐	☐	☐	☐	☒	☐
3. I have no idea what I stand for or believe in.	☐	☐	☒	☐	☐	☐
4. There is a struggle inside of me about who I really am.	☐	☐	☐	☐	☒	☐
5. It is difficult to juggle all the different roles and demands in my life.	☐	☐	☒	☐	☐	☐
6. Who I am can change from day to day.	☒	☐	☐	☐	☐	☐
7. Other people tell me that I have talents, but I don't understand what talents they think I have.	☐	☐	☐	☐	☒	☐
8. I feel confused as to who I really am.	☐	☐	☐	☐	☒	☐
9. I have felt as if I am two different people.	☒	☐	☐	☐	☐	☐

	Never	Once or twice	Some-times	Many times	Almost all the time	Only with drugs or alcohol
	1	2	3	4	5	1
10. I feel as if the real me is locked away inside me.	☐	☐	☐	☐	☒	☐
11. As a young child, I talked to imaginary friends.	☐	☐	☐	☐	☐	☐
12. I feel as if I have been possessed.	☒	☐	☐	☐	☐	☐
13. I have felt confused about my sexual identity.	☒	☐	☐	☐	☐	☐
14. There is a "Censor" inside me that prevents me from saying what I feel.	☐	☐	☐	☐	☒	☐
15. I feel as if there are different people inside me pulling me in different directions.	☒	☐	☐	☐	☐	☐

If you have had any of the above experiences, answer the following:

	No	Yes
Did the experience(s) interfere with your relationships with friends, family, or coworkers?	☐	☒
Did it affect your ability to work?	☒	☐
Did it cause you discomfort or distress?	☐	☒

To Score Your Identity Confusion Questionnaire:

1. Assign a score of zero to the following items:
   Normal items: #5, 11.

2. For all other items, assign a score ranging from 1 to 5 corresponding to the number on the top line above the box that you checked.

3. Now add up your score. Use the general guidelines below for understanding your score.

OVERALL IDENTITY CONFUSION SCORE

No Identity Confusion:	13
Mild Identity Confusion:	14–19
Moderate Identity Confusion:	20–44 *43*
Severe Identity Confusion:	45–65

RECOMMENDATIONS

If your total score falls in the range of *No* to *Mild Identity Confusion* (13–19), this is within the normal range unless you have experienced item #9, 13, or 15 recurrently. If you have experienced these items several times, we recommend that you be evaluated by a professional who is trained in the administration of the full SCID-D interview.

If your total score falls in the range of *Moderate* to *Severe Identity Confusion* (20–65), we recommend that you be evaluated by a professional who is trained in the administration of the full SCID-D interview. If your identity confusion has interfered with your relationships with friends, family, or coworkers or has affected your ability to work or has caused you distress, it is particularly important that you obtain a professional consultation.

Should an experienced clinician find that you have a dissociative disorder, you have a treatable illness with a very good prognosis for recovery. Your illness is widely shared by others who coped with trauma by using the self-protective defense of dissociation. With proper treatment, in time your confusion about who you are will diminish. Eventually, as you grow strong enough to reconnect with your hidden memories and feelings and accept them as your own, your identity confusion will be reduced and you will become a more integrated and psychologically healthy person.

9

⌇

ONE PERSON, MANY SELVES

"**I** HAVE TO wear so many hats around here that I feel like a quick-change artist," says Angelo, the overworked administrator of a government legal services agency. "When I'm with a client who wants me to take on a giant corporation, I have to play the tough guy. When I'm with a client who's going crazy in a custody battle, I have to play the shrink. When one of the other lawyers in the office comes to me with a question about a case, I'm the *jefe,* the supervisor. I guess I like being a supervisor better than dealing with clients, because there aren't any head fakes involved. I can wear just one hat all the time."

What Angelo is talking about is identity alteration in its mildest form—the donning of "different hats" or change of roles that most of us experience in the course of our work or personal lives. This kind of role playing and role switching is widespread in daily life—acting with buttoned-down propriety at work and turning into a party animal on the weekends; behaving like "mommy" or "daddy" with our young children and a peer with our friends. In these situations, we're usually conscious of the role performance or switching and feel that it's under our control.

SCID-D research has found that identity alteration, as with all the dissociative symptoms, occurs along a spectrum of intensity: mild levels of severity in the general population; mild to moderate levels in people with nondissociative psychiatric disorders, but also with dissociative disorder not otherwise specified (DDNOS); severe levels of identity alteration in people with such dissociative disorders as DID.

A person with moderate levels of identity alteration may act as if he or she is like two (or more) different people, but it's not clear whether these identity alterations assume complete control of the person's behavior or represent separate personalities. A normally shy person who gets drunk at a party, for example, may turn into a lampshade-on-the-head scene maker or an X-rated sexual provocateur, but may merely be disinhibited from constraints on his or her usual self rather than under the control of a distinct identity fragment.

Severe identity alteration, the sine qua non of DID, involves a person's shifting between distinct personality states that take control of his or her behavior and thought. These alter personalities are more clearly defined and distinctive than the personality fragments that characterize moderate levels of identity alteration. Each alter has its own name, memories, traits, and behavior patterns.

THE "BERMUDA TRIANGLE" OF IDENTITY DISTURBANCE

Identity alteration differs from identity confusion in that identity confusion represents the *internal* dimension of identity disturbance, whereas identity alteration represents the *external* diimension. A person with identity confusion, in other words, has thoughts and feelings of uncertainty and conflict related to his or her identity; a person with identity alteration manifests the uncertainty and conflict behaviorally.

It might be helpful to think of identity disturbance as a kind of psychiatric Bermuda Triangle with three dimensions—temporal, internal, and external (see accompanying diagram). The five core symptoms of dissociation make up the triangle's three planes. *Amnesia,* the fundamental symptom in relation to the other four, is the *temporal* or time line plane of disturbance at the base of the triangle. *Depersonalization* and *identity confusion* are the *internal* plane of subjective thoughts and feelings about oneself. *Derealization* and *identity alteration* are the *external* plane of relating to the environment and other people.

Amnesia can be thought of as a rupture in the temporal continuity of a person's identity. When someone can't remember large blocks of time, that person's sense of identity as a continuous life story with a narrative "shape" and a coherent sequence of events over time is compromised or lost. Depersonalization and identity confusion can be thought of as a person's loss of a coherent internal self-image with a reliable structure. And finally, derealization and identity alteration can be defined as disturbances in perceiving where one stands in the world and acting out of the loss of grip on one's stance in physical space. Fugue episodes of "sleepwalking" or traveling to another city or country in a state of dissociation, a frequent occurrence in DID and dissociative fugue, can be seen from this angle as a spatial expression of identity disturbance. Acting like a different person with others is another expression of this disturbance in the outside world.

The difference between this figurative Bermuda Triangle and the real one is that whatever disappears into the real Bermuda Triangle is never found again, whereas in identity disturbance the "lost" parts trapped in the figurative triangle can be reclaimed. Accurate diagnosis and appropriate treatment can help someone reconnect with the dissociated parts of the self and reintegrate them into a cohesive sense of identity.

MULTIPLICITY WITHIN THE MIND

As diverse as they are, the many theories of identity formation that have been advanced over the centuries have one aspect in common: none of

Fragmented Sense of Self: Three Dimensions of Identity Disturbance

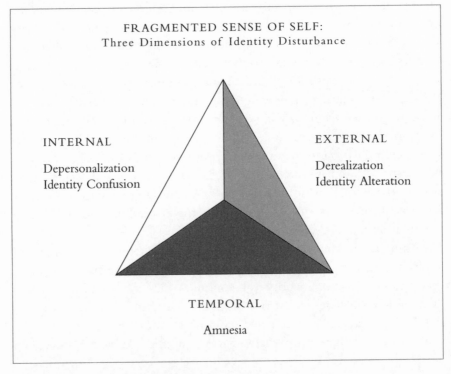

FRAGMENTED SENSE OF SELF:
Three Dimensions of Identity Disturbance

INTERNAL

Depersonalization
Identity Confusion

EXTERNAL

Derealization
Identity Alteration

TEMPORAL

Amnesia

the theorists understood human identity to be a monolithic given. All of the schools of thought were based on the assumption that identity is a *construct*, built up by the individual from a set of different elements, experiences, capacities, or components. In addition to different layers of consciousness, we have basic instinctual drives and a conscience; faculties of reason, emotion, will, and so on; capacities for analysis and logical thought in the left brain and intuitive, artistic, and musical capacities in the right; a predisposition toward introversion or extroversion; characteristics like agreeableness, sociability, conscientiousness, and ambition; and so on.

In the normal course of development, despite the glorious variety and complexity of all our parts, we are usually able to integrate our ongoing interactions and dialogue with our social surroundings into a coherent sense of self. We accomplish this principally by identifying with influential others and choosing qualities of theirs to incorporate into ourselves.

To some extent the early stages of DID in childhood can be understood as a disturbance of the normal process of identification. Many DID patients have alters who are essentially modeled after their original abusers. There is some evidence that an alter might also have started out as an imaginary playmate modeled after a real-life or fictional identification figure. Some researchers believe that being forced to identify with parents who have mutually contradictory personality traits—loving one minute, violent the next—coupled with the loss of a more positive identification figure, such as a grandparent or a caretaker, disturbs the normal identification pattern. Since it's impossible for the child who is developing DID to integrate incongruous loving versus abusive identifications with a parent, these identifications remain dissociated and form the nuclei of alter personalities.

Furthermore, once dissociative symptoms develop, the child may begin to behave in a way that either provokes additional maltreatment by the original abusers or makes it difficult to attract supportive attention from adults outside the immediate family who are better role models. Constantly accused of being "bad," an "airhead," or a "liar," the child continues to resort to dissociation as an accommodation to ongoing abuse, and the cycle continues. By the time an adult survivor manifests the symptoms of full-fledged DID, the level of identity confusion and identity alteration is usually far more severe than the milder forms of role switching common to most of us.

Belinda was tempted to bawl out the obnoxious passenger in seat 15C as she would have if one of her young nephews dared to come into her house and behave that way. The passenger was acting worse than a belligerent six-year-old. He'd obviously had too many martinis and was loudly shouting obscenities to someone across the aisle and had even thrown a roll from his dinner plate at him, narrowly missing the head of the woman in the next seat. As much as Belinda wanted to vent her anger, she knew she couldn't. Her job as a flight attendant demanded a courteous, pleasant demeanor and respectful attitudes toward everyone on board, no matter how a person tried her nerves. So, taking a deep breath, Belinda walked down the aisle to 15C and said in a firm but polite voice, "Sir, I'm going to have to ask you to show more consideration for the other passengers on this flight. Please lower your voice, watch your language, and do not throw anything else at anyone on the plane."

Belinda's awareness that her job required her to be more patient with obstreperous passengers than she would be with misbehaving visitors to her household led her to assume an "official" personality different from her nonwork personality. This deliberate kind of role switching in circumstances in which the person feels it is warranted typifies identity alteration at its mildest level. All of us, to some extent, have a public persona or face we present in formal situations and a private persona when we feel free to let our hair down. This conscious form of identity alteration that we perceive to be under our control is generally not associated with dysfunction or dysphoria and is not considered to be a problem or a sign of a disorder.

Actors engage in mild identity alteration every time they play a role. Other kinds of performers do, too. Stan, a "shock jock" radio talk show host in Miami, says, "Being bombastic and opinionated is part of the act. I couldn't get ratings without being outrageous. The listeners eat it up when I'm rude to certain callers and hang up on them. That's not something I would do in real life. I don't have it in me to be mean to people except when I'm on the air and putting on a show. Ask my wife and kids. They think I'm a pussycat."

There are times when a person might have to act like a professional with someone close. A doctor on duty in the ER, for example, might be called upon to treat a friend who's been injured in an accident. The doctor thinks, "This is my friend, but I have to deal with him like any other patient." The role switch is an intentional decision. Similarly, married or romantically involved couples who work together usually assume personalities with each other in the office that are quite different from their personalities as intimate partners at home.

Conscious role switching has become such a part of our lives today that not being able to switch when the situation demands it is a problem for some people. "I come home from making executive decisions and giving orders all day at the office," says Colette, a high-level manager at a pharmaceutical firm, "and it takes me a while to shift gears sometimes. My husband complains that I'm hyper and tells me to chill out, and my five-year-old daughter says, 'Mommy, why are you talking to me in your boss voice?' The trouble is, in my head I'm still at the office. I'm trying to make the trains run on time instead of just being a wife and mother."

The dissociation that our society demands of us in ordinary role switching is not always easy to bring off in the workplace. Most people have been socialized to keep personal matters separate from their work lives. Someone whose job performance begins to suffer because of preoccupation with family difficulties may be criticized or reprimanded by a supervisor. Even if that doesn't happen, the person may be concerned about an inability to compartmentalize the strong feelings that are intruding during work hours. Don, a mergers and acquisitions specialist who is going through acrimonious divorce proceedings, says: "My wife's lawyer is putting me through hell—she wants the moon—but I can't let my marital troubles interfere with my work. Unfortunately it's not that easy to separate the two. How can you put on a happy face when you're all torn up inside? But if you show you're weak at the office, you pay for it. You can get pushed around and find that the best deals are passing you by."

Whether or not we switch roles easily between our "work" personality and our "private" personality, most of us experience this mild form of identity alteration in the course of ordinary life. These transitions are usually made consciously and perceived as being under our control and are not ordinarily associated with amnesia or dysfunction.

MODERATE IDENTITY ALTERATION

Moderate identity alteration differs from its milder counterpart in that the alterations are not always under the person's control. Although these altered states may be perceived by the person as uncontrollable, they are not always manifestations of complete personalities as they are in someone who experiences severe identity alteration.

This middle level between mild and severe identity alteration may be characteristic of such nondissociative psychiatric disorders as manic-depression, or bipolar disorder, as it is now called. A person who has bipolar disorder often feels like "two different people," depending upon whether his mood is manic or depressed, and may attribute the moderate identity alteration that characterizes the illness to an uncontrollable temper.

"Sometimes I would just snap out for no reason at all," says Nick, a fifty-two-year-old automobile mechanic, of his behavior before he was diagnosed with bipolar disorder and stabilized on medication. "I lashed out at everybody when I was in a bad mood. It didn't matter who it was, I let 'em have it. It's just something that came over me. I felt like I was driving a car with no brakes, going ninety miles an hour, and couldn't stop. I never hit my wife or kids, but when I got mad I'd smash my fist through a wall. A lot of the time, though, I wasn't like that at all. I was quiet and pretty much kept to myself. There was no in-between with me. I was one way or the other, like two different people. My wife always said she didn't know who to expect when I came in the door."

Had Nick manifested the presence of the other four dissociative symptoms to a significant degree, his diagnosis would not have been bipolar disorder but DID. In that case his mood changes would not have been attributed to a bad temper; they would have been caused by the shift from one alternate personality to another.

People who've been diagnosed with borderline personality disorder also tend to fluctuate rapidly between radically different types of behavior and mood. If these moderate identity alterations coalesce around distinct personalities with different names, memories, preferences, ages, or amnesia for past events, the temper outbursts and other changes in mood and behavior could be the result of DID.

My SCID-D research has shown that people diagnosed with a dissociative disorder not otherwise specified (DDNOS), which might be considered a milder form or an early stage of DID, experience moderate levels of identity alteration. They may act like two or more different people, but it's not clear whether these alterations assume control of their behavior or represent complete personalities. When people with DDNOS experience a conflict between the person they usually are and some fragment of their identity, their personality fragments are less clearly defined and distinctive than those that characterize severe identity alteration in DID.

Vince, the former professional wrestler who was sent to me for a SCID-D after he developed severe amnesia and could remember nothing of his past except his three children and the family dog, first displayed only moderate identity alteration. In his dissociative states he saw shadowy "dark people" of all sizes and shapes—"tall, short, fat, skinny"—who held him down, strangled him, stuck needles in him, and threatened to take over his soul or kill him if he didn't do what they wanted. As menacing and scary as these "people" were, they were too vague and amorphous to be considered separate personalities. Since Vince's dissociative symptoms didn't meet the criteria for DID, he was originally diagnosed with DDNOS. It was not until Vince remembered being sexually abused by priests in Catholic school in his childhood that the "dark people" came into focus more clearly as distinct personalities modeled after his abusers, and the diagnosis of DID was made.

Substance abusers are another group of people who experience moderate levels of identity alteration when they are under the influence of drugs or alcohol. Says Carla, the wife of an alcoholic police officer who underwent a treatment program for his addiction and is now sober, "My husband was another person when he got drunk. He was a good-natured guy when he was sober, but when he was drunk—look out! He turned into a maniac. He screamed and cursed and threw things. The things he said, I couldn't believe they were coming out of his mouth. He didn't even look like the same person. After he sobered up, he'd say, 'It was the booze talking.' He'd be himself and everything would be fine—until the next time. It was like, what is this? I'm married to two different people."

These dramatic transformations are typical of many substance abusers who seem to be "another person" under the influence of drugs or alcohol. The danger here is that alcohol or drugs can mask a person's underlying dissociative disorder and cause the symptom of identity alteration to be written off. This is not unlike what occurs when a person with a shoulder injury thinks that the pain radiating down his arm is a result of his injury, although in fact it may be the precursor of a heart attack.

The same could be said of automobile drivers who are normally mild-mannered but assume a hostile and aggressive personality behind the wheel. Stressful traffic conditions coupled with the freedom of anonymity inside a car can remove normal constraints on a person's behavior, as "road rage" incidents show. Unless the person has other severe dissociative symptoms, the "driver" personality is probably not a separate, distinct personality fragment characteristic of the severe identity alteration in DID.

SEVERE IDENTITY ALTERATION

Unlike the person who is in control of a shift in roles, someone who has severe identity alteration experiences loss of control over his or her consciousness and behavior to a separate and distinctive alter personality. The person with severe identity alteration feels as if there are one or more different people inside who are capable of influencing or controlling his or her behavior. Each alter has its own name, memories, style of dress, speech pattern, handwriting, even physical ailments like headaches and allergies. When the alter emerges, the person may experience age regression as well as changes in voice, manner of speaking, dress style, body posture, and movements. Having an alter of a different sex may prompt the person to consider implementing a sex-change operation.

This shifting between distinct personality states that control a person's thoughts, memory, behavior, and emotion is the hallmark of DID. The "Ping-Pong" state of mind that we all experience when we're weighing pros and cons is a minor skirmish compared with the full-scale mental warfare experienced by someone with severe identity alteration. Having different alters arguing with each other or trying to seize control over the "host" personality makes a person's head feel like a "milkshake," as one of my DID patients said. This, I think, is an apt description of a fragmented sense of self bubbling and churning with contradiction and divisiveness.

Signs of severe identity alteration include

- referring to yourself by different names
- referring to yourself as "we"
- acting like a completely different person at times
- being told by others that you seem like a different person
- feeling possessed by demons or spirits
- finding items in your possession that you don't remember having purchased
- having marked differences in your memory recall
- experiencing a sudden loss of skills you previously had
- finding documents written by you in a different handwriting
- displaying knowledge of a subject or language you don't recall having studied
- acting as if you are still a child

Severe identity alteration is accompanied by marked distress or dysfunctionality and may cause job loss, troubled personal relationships, alcohol or drug abuse, or involvement with the criminal justice system.

Amazingly, many people with DID are able to hold down jobs and maintain stable relationships by walking a tightrope of wily compensatory tactics. Eventually some unexpected trigger trips them up, and they fall, dragging their tenuously held-together public persona and their internal house of cards down with them. That is why it is imperative for someone to recognize the signs of severe identity alteration and seek treatment for them as soon as possible with a therapist who can administer the full SCID-D and make a diagnosis.

Once it's been determined that a person does indeed have a dissociative disorder, the right therapy can bring about cooperation among the different personalities, so that they will not tear that person apart. Erika, a forty-two-year-old DID patient who has many alternate personalities, is managing to maintain a successful career in human resources with a large corporation by having a personality she calls the "Professional" take charge of her work life. Her primary personality held an internal conference and explained to her alters why it was important that they not come out while she and the Professional were on the job: "I sensed that all the personalities were there, so I had a talk with each one of them," says Erika. "We have a chart because there are so many. I explained to each one how I could lose my job if anyone except the Professional came to work. I said, 'You've got to promise to stay home tomorrow, and if you stay home and you're good, I will tell you what happened at work'—kind of how you talk to a child. And it worked. Since then, they've never come to to work."

Before she entered treatment, Erika felt that a "humongous" battle was going on inside her, a clashing of personalities that made her daily life a struggle for survival—both psychologically and on the job. Sometimes the energy consumed by this battle rendered her unable to talk. Erika, a tall, lovely-looking blond-haired woman who is dignified and composed though she had been sexually abused by her father throughout her childhood, recalls such a moment at work:

"I was about to walk into a meeting that I needed to attend, and the only chair that was available was between two men. I didn't turn around and walk out, but my body turned around and walked out. And I couldn't talk to save my soul because there was this battle going on about whether or not I should go into the meeting, and someone wanting some memory to come up and someone else suppressing it. I tried to walk into that meeting, but I couldn't do it."

In this one episode, Erika describes experiencing not only severe identity alteration ("someone wanting some memory to come up and someone else suppressing it"), but three other dissociative symptoms as well. Her identity confusion is expressed in terms of ambivalence about entering the room: the part of her that felt vulnerable about having to sit between two males in the meeting—possibly an alter personality with memories of the abuse—impelled her to perform an action that another part of her resisted. Her depersonalization is expressed in terms of "my body walked out," and her amnesia in terms of "suppressing" the memory that wanted to come up. This interdependence of symptoms is typical in DID.

The names people give their alters are sometimes the usual ones, like "Tommy," "Susan," "Joan," or "Joe," but they can also be symbolic names suggestive of split-off parts of their personalities or partially disowned capacities, like the "Commander," the "Nurse," the "Wise One," or Erika's the "Professional." Alters cover a wide age range, from infants to the elderly, often representing the person at different ages, including ages not yet attained. Some "guru" alters who represent internal helpers, guides, or counselors may be thought of as ageless or timeless rather than as having a specific age and may be modeled after religious figures who are not necessarily of the person's own faith. Many people can envision facial and other physical characteristics of their alters and delegate skills to one alter that the other alters or the primary personality doesn't share and can't perform when that alter isn't out. In addition, an alter in control may make friends without the person's awareness, so that he or she is unable to recognize the "friends" at a later time. The tendency of a multiple to refer to herself as "we," as Erika did, gives an indication of how it feels to have a group of markedly diverse individuals living in one body.

In some instances a person with DID will associate the different names of alters with particular actions or feelings. "Sally will have sex," says a law student, describing the different lives of Sally, Andrea, and Cindy, three of her four alters: "Sally eats. Sally grocery shops. Sally has friends at the law school. Sally has had a relationship, a friendship, with some junior professor from the law school. Andrea went to school, you know college. Cindy burned me with a cigarette lighter."

Switching personalities often occurs in a trancelike state. If the person is aware of it, the anxiety can be overwhelming. One woman, who refers to the childish parts of herself as her "kids," says that she has something like a "town meeting" with her alters from time to time to calm herself down after a disturbing switch. "If one of the kids mouthed off, say, or did something out of line, we'd all sit there and figure what we're going to do to repair the damage. Then we'd choose which personality was best to cope with the situation, and they'd go out and try to take care of it."

CIRCUMSTANTIAL EVIDENCE

As a result of the amnesia that often accompanies their dissociative episodes, multiples may find themselves with articles they don't remember purchasing and don't even like that were bought when one of their alters was out. "I have clothes in my closet that I wouldn't be caught dead in," says a young woman, bemused. "I have a ton of silver jewelry, and I hate silver. I like gold, and I have a lot of silver, like American Indian pieces and stuff like that. I have a china teacup collection, and I don't believe in collecting things; they collect dust. These things are all over. But I keep them. I can't get rid of them."

This unexplained possession of articles in DID is different from the nasty surprise that can be a feature of compulsive shopping. Shopaholics are essentially people who use shopping as a form of mood alteration. Many of them are surprised or shocked by the contents of their closets when some circumstance—usually the cancellation of their credit cards or confrontations with family members—forces them to recognize that they have a compulsive disorder. The surprise is caused by the number of objects they've purchased or the amount of money they've spent, not the nature of the items themselves. Although dissociative disorders and compulsive disorders overlap to some degree—a person can have an alter who is a shopaholic—the disorders are not identical. The person with bipolar disorder who goes on a buying spree during a manic phase doesn't have amnesia for the purchases, only a disregard for their cost.

Another sign of severe identity alteration that can startle someone is finding written evidence of some kind—letters, notebooks, diaries— attesting to the presence of alter personalities. These items can range from documents in a different handwriting to poetry or prose in a language the person doesn't remember studying. A woman who has never studied French, for example, may be mystified to find herself fluent in that language because an alter personality either studied it or picked it up from a French relative or friend without the woman's conscious awareness.

After suffering a miscarriage, a medical writer diagnosed with DID received a publication in the mail that she had written yet initially failed to recognize as hers. "An envelope came with copies of this pamphlet naming me as the author," she says, "and I didn't remember anything about having written this pamphlet. I was really upset. I read it, and sure enough it was my style. I had a chapter in there about miscarriage, and I know that when I wrote it I said, 'Hmm, I wonder if they're gonna think this is too intimate and toss it out.' And when I saw the word miscarriage in there I realized, yes, I did write this booklet."

FRIENDLY FEEDBACK

In most cases, a person experiencing severe identity alteration knows of this symptom primarily from reports from others. "Sarah is vicious and Terry is mean," says Randy, a twenty-seven-year-old dental technician diagnosed with DID. "Frank, my friend, told me, 'Just let me know when Sarah arrives. She has a black belt in karate, and I don't want to deal with it.' I feel really stupid about that. I mean, how can your friend tell you that you have a black belt, and I don't even know karate? I'm not very athletic either."

Although many people with DID experience only subtle vocal and behavioral changes when an alter personality emerges, when someone else notices these changes they can be embarrassing. Randy recalls being observed by a stranger when two of her alters got into a heated argument while she was driving her car. "I made a decision not to see the doctor because it was snowing, the roads were horrendous, trucks couldn't move. I went to a pay phone, called up and canceled my appointment, and got back into the car. Suddenly the one I call Sarah started yelling out loud that we had to go see the doctor. And I calmly told her, 'No, we don't have to go,' and then she started screaming again. There was a man in a truck or car who looked. And his eyes caught my eyes, and I realized that he could hear them."

People who are unaware of having alter personalities may believe that their friends or relatives are playing a very unfunny game with them and may react to the feedback with anger or annoyance. Cassie, a nineteen-year-old college student who was diagnosed with a dissociative disorder on the SCID-D, said during her interview, "You begin to wonder who your friends are. You think they're 'gaslighting' you. They'll say, 'Yesterday your name was Renee,' or whatever, and 'Your hair was done in a punk style.' It's freaky to me because it's like, 'What do you mean?' I didn't remember doing it. I had no idea that I was using different names or acting differently. It's like a big joke, a joke that I don't find amusing." Asked whether she thought her friends were teasing her, she replied, "Well, they are my friends, but I have two choices. I can either choose to believe they're pulling my leg or choose to believe I'm nuts."

TAKING THE CURE

Cassie's conclusion that someone with DID symptoms has to be "nuts" shows how badly we need to destigmatize dissociative disorders and counteract the defensiveness that is holding countless people back from getting the help they need. One young woman in the SCID-D study revealed how monumentally defensive a person can be when she spoke about the psychiatrist who originally diagnosed her with DID. "I thought he was getting extremely frustrated trying to explain the situation to me about multiple personalities," she said. "He's sitting there insisting that that was what my problem was and that unless you believe it or accept it, you can't be cured. It's like having a doctor tell you you're dying, but you feel perfectly well. Just because this guy is supposed to have a degree, and he has no obvious reason for telling me something that wouldn't be true, you don't have to accept it. And I choose not to."

When I corroborated her psychiatrist's diagnosis, she said, "You can sit there and tell me something about being—like having a split personality—and to me that's being totally imperfect. If I had to sit there and listen to you and believe you, then I couldn't survive. It's not something that I can accept or deal with."

What if this same patient had been told that she had pneumonia? Would her attitude have been the same? Knowing that her illness was treatable and that she had a good prognosis for recovery, would she have said, "If I had to accept or deal with this illness, I couldn't survive"? *Not if she wanted to survive.* If she did, she'd have accepted the diagnosis and done everything medically possible to help her recover. A dissociative disorder is no different from any other physical or psychiatric illness. With the willingness to accept the illness and get the proper treatment for it, patients have a good prognosis for recovery within three to five years. Conversely if the illness is undetected or is treated incorrectly, the person can go through many hospitalizations, spend years in treatment with no significant improvement, and suffer dire consequences.

Besides the depression and anxiety associated with an undetected or mistreated dissociative disorder, the impact on a person's employment and personal relationships can be ruinous. Antisocial acts committed in a state of severe identity alteration or dissociative fugue range from shoplifting and destruction of property to child abuse and homicide. At their worst hostile alters may thrust a person into debt, alienate the person's friends or intimate partners, place the person in a situation in which rape or physical assault at the hands of a stranger is likely, or impel the person to self-mutilate or attempt suicide.

In order to survive massive abuse in childhood, people with DID have had to carry dissociation to its outer limits, subdividing themselves into a number of separate personalities with isolated memories and feelings. Their secret inner world is plagued by all of the five symptoms. Parts of their past, even all of their growing-up years, have vanished into the black hole of lost memories, leaving them vulnerable to vivid flashbacks or puzzling gaps in memory that steal unaccountable stretches of time from their lives today. Some feel a profound disconnection from their bodies, floating outside them and observing themselves from a distance or experiencing parts of their bodies as changing shape or size. Others are so detached from their emotions that they feel as if they're walking through life like actors in a movie, distant and robotic, sometimes compulsively cutting their own flesh to relieve their terrifying anxiety and feelings of inner deadness. They may perceive the world around them as unreal or unknown—strangers in a strange land even when they're at home with their families. Some have feelings of confusion or conflict about who they are, even whether they are male or female. And finally there are those—the ones the TV talk shows love to exploit—whose identities have splintered off into a multilayered rabble of separate parts, each holding different fragments of the "host" and engaged in a harrowing tug-of-war within.

Even in these extreme cases, DID is highly amenable to treatment. The remarkable success that many patients have had in overcoming DID is an inspiration to everyone struggling to heal childhood wounds.

The following questionnaire will help you identify what symptoms of identity alteration you are experiencing and whether they are mild (normal), moderate, or severe.

Steinberg Identity Alteration Questionnaire

	Never	Once or twice	Some-times	Many times	Almost all the time	Only with drugs or alcohol
	1	2	3	4	5	1
3 1. I have mood changes that I can't control.	☐	☐	☒	☐	☐	☐
1 2. I have an image of someone inside me who is different from me.	☒	☐	☐	☐	☐	☐
○ 3. I act differently when I am with my parents than I do with my friends, or when I am at work (or in school).	☐	☐	☐	☐	☒	☐
3 4. I have temper outbursts that seem out of my control or out of propor-tion to the situation.	☐	☐	☒	☐	☐	☐
1 5. I have different names that I call myself or that other people have called me.	☒	☐	☐	☐	☐	☐
1 6. I don't recognize things that I have written.	☒	☐	☐	☐	☐	☐
4 7. I feel as if I am living a secret life and even my closest friends are unaware of what I am really like.	☐	☐	☐	☒	☐	☐

	Never	Once or twice	Some-times	Many times	Almost all the time	Only with drugs or alcohol
	1	2	3	4	5	1
8. I speak in a com-pletely different voice or style.	☒	☐	☐	☐	☐	☐
9. I feel as if I have a public persona and a personal persona.	☐	☐	☐	☐	☒	☐
10. People tell me that I have acted like a different person.	☒	☐	☐	☐	☐	☐
11. As an adult, I have had imaginary friends that I talk to.	☒	☐	☐	☐	☐	☐
12. I feel as if my "inner child" takes control of my behavior.	☒	☐	☐	☐	☐	☐
13. I feel as if there are different people inside me who influence my behavior or mood.	☒	☐	☐	☐	☐	☐

If you have had any of the above experiences, answer the following:

	No	Yes
Did the experience(s) interfere with your relationships with friends, family, or coworkers?	☐	☒
Did it affect your ability to work?	☒	☐
Did it cause you discomfort or distress?	☐	☒

To Score Your Identity Alteration Questionnaire:

1. Assign a score of zero to the following items:
   Normal items: #3, 9.

2. For all other items, assign a score ranging from 1 to 5 corresponding to the number on the top line above the box that you checked.

3. Now add up your score. Use the general guidelines below for
   understanding your score.

OVERALL IDENTITY ALTERATION SCORE

No Identity Alteration:	11
Mild Identity Alteration:	12–20 18
Moderate Identity Alteration:	21–35
Severe Identity Alteration:	36–55

RECOMMENDATIONS

If your total score falls in the range of *No* to *Mild Identity Alteration*
(11–20), this is within the normal range unless you have experienced item
#6 or 13 recurrently. If you have experienced these items several times,
we recommend that you be evaluated by a professional who is trained in
the administration of the full SCID-D interview.

    If your total score falls in the range of *Moderate* to *Severe Identity Alter-
ation* (21–55), we recommend that you be evaluated by a professional who
is trained in the administration of the full SCID-D interview. If your
identity alteration has interfered with your relationships with friends, family, or coworkers or has affected your ability to work or has caused you
distress, it is particularly important that you obtain a professional
consultation.

    Should an experienced clinician find that you have a dissociative dis-
order, you have a treatable illness with a very good prognosis for recovery.
Your illness is widely shared by others who coped with trauma by using
the self-protective defense of dissociation. With proper treatment, in time,
you will be able to integrate the memories and feelings of your separate
parts. Eventually, as you grow strong enough to reconnect with your hidden memories and feelings and accept them as your own, your identity
alteration will be reduced and you will become a more integrated and
psychologically healthy person.

10

~=~

MEN, ABUSE, AND
DISSOCIATIVE DISORDERS

ALTHOUGH FEWER MEN in our society may be sexually abused in childhood than women, the physical and emotional violence visited upon young males, even in middle-class or affluent families, is enormous. The psychological damage men suffer as a result of this mistreatment is aggravated by a fear of seeming weak if they talk openly about their internal wounds. Many men prefer to suffer in silence or express the turmoil inside them behaviorally in self-destructive or violent ways.

Men with dissociative disorders may be more likely to "act out" against society or engage in antisocial activity than women DID patients are. Actually, the sex ratio imbalance in DID diagnoses—nine females to one male—is often attributed to the fact that many men who have DID are diagnosed solely as substance abusers and are treated in rehabs or are sent to prison for antisocial behavior before they ever come to the attention of a therapist.

RED FLAGS

Explosive temper outbursts are a common symptom in men with an underlying dissociative disorder, and a man who experiences these outbursts needs to have them evaluated in the context of all five core dissociative symptoms. These symptoms are often masked in men whose anger is extreme. Rather than seek treatment for inner feelings of rage with a possible dissociative basis, many men self-medicate, using alcohol, cocaine, marijuana, heroin, or other substances to relieve their distress. The angry, sometimes filled with rage, out-of-character person they become under the influence may not be "the booze talking," but a dissociated part of themselves that is making itself heard. In some cases alcoholics (women as well as men) who have intermittent periods of remission and marked mood changes when they drink have a personality inside them who drinks, and one who doesn't. Since the one who drinks has amnesia for the one who doesn't, binges feel completely out of their control.

These are some of the more common symptoms or coexisting disorders experienced by men with an underlying dissociative disorder:

- depression
- anxiety, often experienced as constant terror or a feeling of always being on the edge
- substance abuse
- sudden outbursts of anger
- difficulty in concentrating, jumping from one thought to another, or similar symptoms of inattention or impulsiveness associated with attention-deficit hyperactivity disorder
- flashbacks and other symptoms associated with posttraumatic stress disorder
- social anxiety disorder (social phobia), characterized by an extreme fear of social or performance situations in which the person is exposed to unfamiliar people or to possible scrutiny by others, as in public speaking
- compulsive sex, a history of affairs, or sexual perversions
- violence, or engaging in sports that sanction violence, such as boxing or football

Jordan, the forty-nine-year-old general manager of a TV station in New York, exemplifies that the symptoms men present to a therapist often are not the whole story. Jordan's primary complaint was that he suffered from very severe anxiety, especially when meeting new people or speaking to an audience. He actually had a panic attack whenever he had to attend a social function with corporate clients or was called upon to address a community organization, an important part of public relations for the station. He was also troubled by masochistic fantasies of being beaten by a dominatrix and had a strange sexual obsession that was jeopardizing his marriage. Although he loved his wife and enjoyed sex with her, he felt compelled to visit topless bars and be hugged by anonymous naked women.

Jordan's previous therapist had diagnosed him as suffering from social anxiety disorder, but when I began working with him, I suspected that there might be a dissociative foundation lurking beneath the surface of his complaints. He revealed that as a young boy he was constantly terrorized by his physically abusive father and ran to his mother to be comforted after his father beat him. Although he didn't initially realize it, Jordan came to see that to him, love and sexual pleasure were associated with domination and beatings, because his father showed him love by being domineering and abusive. Seeking out women in topless bars to hug him was a reenactment of the pattern of his childhood—being beaten, then enfolded in his mother's arms. There was an adolescent part of Jordan that was getting gratification by means of this compulsion. Since Jordan was ashamed to admit to his wife that he was so needy, he was risking his marriage for the sake of an anonymous woman's hug.

It was this adolescent part of Jordan that felt terrorized by social situations or before public speaking engagements, because Jordan identified unfamiliar people or those in a position to judge him with his terroristic father. "Little Jordan," as he called this inner child, was not sufficiently independent or autonomous to constitute a separate personality but did represent the kind of moderate identity alteration found in DDNOS. Jordan is now learning to reduce his social anxiety, as well as lessen his sexual compulsivity, by calming Little Jordan in situations that are threatening reminders of the past.

THE WARRIOR PERSONALITY

DID explains the "warrior personality" that some men in combat have. They are able to shoot and kill and have no feelings for their victims. When they are no longer in a war zone, they may become dysfunctional. A combat veteran walking down a city street in civilian life, for example, may suddenly assault another man who innocently walks too close to him, because the veteran has a flashback to a combat situation and his dissociated warrior takes control. Since people with posttraumatic stress disorder often suffer from undetected dissociative symptoms, the dissociative basis of some cases of PTSD may not be recognized.

A dissociated warrior-type personality may also be found in men who are drawn to violent sports. Tom, a thirty-eight-year-old former professional boxer with a black belt in karate, came to see me after he had become an aerospace engineer and was in a relatively new, but troubled marriage. Joanna, his wife, had insisted that he seek treatment for his uncontrollable jealous rages and furious outbursts at any man who so much as looked at her or otherwise rubbed him the wrong way. Once, when Tom and Joanna were working out at a gym together, he called her a "slut" and a "whore" for chatting innocently with a man exercising next to her and had to be prevented from smashing the man's jaw. "They were just having a friendly conversation," Tom said, "but it seemed to me that they were having an affair right under my nose, and it set me off."

Another time Tom flew into a rage when a distracted driver almost knocked him down as he was getting out of his car. Before Tom knew it, he had grabbed hold of the man by the hair through his open car window and was about to beat him to within an inch of his life. "I didn't know where I was—maybe I thought I was back in a boxing ring. There was just me and this guy, and I was outside myself, watching the two of us. Then I looked up and saw the line of cars and a cop approaching, and that stopped me."

Tom told me that he had been severely beaten and emotionally abused by his father throughout his childhood and had taken up boxing and karate for self-protection and as an outlet for his feelings of rage. Tom's mother, powerless to protect her son from the overwhelming violence in the house, sought solace in extramarital affairs. One day when young Tom went home he found his father throwing his mother's clothes down the stairs, threatening to throw her out, too. "Slut! Whore!" his father was screaming at his mother, just as Tom screamed at his wife in the gym.

The incidents Tom described indicated that his rage might have had a dissociative basis. Derealization was manifested by his imposition of a past reality on the present. Confusing his mother's infidelity in the past with his faithful wife's current behavior prompted his explosiveness toward Joanna and the man in the gym. Tom's out-of-body experience when he reacted violently to a traffic mishap perceived as a personal attack was evidence of depersonalization. Within him there seemed to be a disconnected state of rage that could only express itself with Tom's fists, whether in the boxing ring or on the street. "I feel like I'm trying to keep the lid on a volcano," he said. "I have such a strong rage inside, and I don't know where it's coming from."

The SCID-D showed that Tom had moderate amnesia and severe levels of the other four dissociative symptoms. Since he also described having several well-developed personalities that took control of his angry behavior, my diagnosis was DID. There were three dissociated parts within himself that he was able to identify. Wild Tom, a nickname from his boxing days, was what he called the part that contained the memories and feelings related to his father's malevolent physical and emotional abuse. It was the repository of Tom's rage, and it came out appropriately in violent sports, and inappropriately in angry outbursts at people who offended him. Tommy was a spoiled, bratty little boy inside who felt all the hurt from Tom's painful childhood. He was mean and nasty to Joanna when Tom distrusted her or when she cried, something Tommy considered a sign of weakness. Dad, the most frightening part of himself, was critical and verbally abusive like his father and had a dark, totally destructive side that came out when Tom had too much to drink. "That's the part that makes me go 125 miles an hour on a highway after I've been to a bar," Tom said. "I think it's just trying to destroy me, piece by piece, the way my father did."

Since Tom is a very intelligent man as well as a gifted athlete, he is making extraordinarily fast progress in treatment today. He is learning how to calm his rage by using different strategies to help Wild Tom feel safe in the present. One technique that works for him is to carry a key chain with tiny boxing gloves on it. Whenever he feels Wild Tom taking control and is about to explode in rage, looking at the little boxing gloves reminds Tom that he is a grown man who has the strength to protect himself and doesn't need to beat people up.

It should be remembered that dissociative men who have temper outbursts are not necessarily violent. Some men (and women) with dissociative disorders have violent thoughts but never act on them. Others, having decided that they don't want to perpetuate the abuse they experienced, might eschew violence entirely and encapsulate their rageful feelings into a dissociative aspect of themselves that is nonviolent.

The case of Ross Cheit illustrates how men who have been sexually abused in childhood suffer the same deleterious repercussions as women. In 1992 Cheit, an associate professor of political science at Brown University and a happily married man, received a phone call informing him that his favorite nephew had been chosen to join the prestigious San Francisco Boys' Chorus and attend a special music camp. Cheit, who'd been a member of the same choir and a music camper in his youth, should have been elated, but instead he had a sickening feeling of alarm he couldn't understand.

Soon after the call Cheit dreamed of a man he hadn't seen since he was a thirteen-year-old boy at music camp—William Farmer, his most admired and trusted camp counselor. For the first time Cheit remembered in flashbacks how Farmer had entered his cabin each night, when the other boys were asleep, and sexually molested him. Determined to find out the truth, Cheit confronted the retired founder and director of the choir. She revealed that numerous incidents of sexual molestation were reported in the camp's history but were all hushed up and brushed off as inconsequential compared to the paramount importance of the choir's reputation.

With the help of a private detective Cheit finally tracked down Farmer, who confessed to the abuse in a tape-recorded phone conversation. Farmer also revealed that after being exposed and disgraced as a pedophile while working as a Methodist minister, he had become—unbelievably—a public school teacher. When Cheit went public with his history of sexual abuse at Farmer's hands, Farmer moved to another state and taught Bible school.

Criminal charges against Farmer failed because of a statute of limitations. To buttress a civil suit against Farmer, Cheit painstakingly garnered an archive of detailed, corroborated cases of recovered abuse memories and was eventually awarded $475,000 in damages. Michael Landsberg, who wrote about the Cheit case in *The Toronto Star* (March 4, 2000), was moved by the poignant letters male survivors sent him about feeling isolated and invisible after recovering memories of their abuse.

Male abuse survivors feel isolated for many of the same reasons that women do: being ashamed, feeling that they deserved it, not even realizing that they were abused, feeling that they are different from other people. Their isolation is compounded by the fact that since men are generally not as inclined to seek treatment as women, male abuse survivors receive less attention in the clinical literature and in the media.

Cheit's case showed that men who have been abused not only travel the same lonesome road as women survivors, but also may experience the return of verifiable abuse memories many years later. Even though men, like women, may have difficulty recalling the details of their abuse, they are at risk for developing a characteristic group of symptoms that underlie a dissociative disorder.

PART THREE

INSIDE STORIES

In the following chapters you'll meet three of the patients I've been treating in my private practice. You'll come to know them in all the richness of their interior worlds and the complexities of their personal lives. They've magnanimously given me permission to share their stories with you, and their names and other characteristics have been changed to protect their identities.

Even if your injuries seem small in comparison and your dissociative symptoms are mild, their case histories have much to tell you about your own sometimes mystifying feelings, thoughts, and actions. The skills they've learned in therapy apply not only to recovery from a dissociative disorder, but to psychological health in general, and are universally useful tools.

Nancy L. represents the neighbor next door, in the sense that she looks like, talks like, and acts like someone you know or would like to meet—she could be anyone's sister, friend, coworker, wife, or other familiar person. Like many others with DID, she has the surprising ability to function at a very high level, yet is suffering enormously internally. She also typifies how hard it is for someone with a dissociative disorder to find appropriate treatment: she was diagnosed and treated for attention deficit hyperactivity disorder for many years before her underlying illness was uncovered.

Linda A. is like the many other people who experience a life event that unleashes a flood of emotions they don't understand. She is an example of how an occurrence in one's adult life can trigger memories of an earlier childhood trauma, and how that earlier trauma can interfere with one's current life—in Linda's case, her relationship with her boyfriend.

Jean W. exemplifies a person's ability to survive the most extreme trauma imaginable, as well as a variety of other highly traumatic experiences, by using the creative defense of dissociation. She couldn't escape physically from the traumas in her life, but she was able to escape mentally and eventually rose above tragic circumstances to become an accomplished professional.

All of these people, in one way or another, inspire because of their remarkable progress. How they discovered their hidden parts and learned to connect with them constructively can serve as a traveler's guide for anyone on the journey toward an examined life. That even those whose sense of self has been most brutally shattered can learn to reunite the broken parts of themselves, and thereby heal, is a lesson that gives hope and wisdom to us all.

11

NANCY L.: THE "TROUBLEMAKER"

"I'M A GOOD GIRL"

I T STARTED OUT like any other day, routine and ordinary, with no ominous hint of what was to come. Nancy got up with her husband, Walter, fixed him breakfast; and saw him off for an early appointment. She stood in the doorway, waving good-bye as he drove away from their sprawling new hillside home in White Plains, New York, dubbed "the Glass House" for its shameless floor-to-ceiling sun-splashed windows on every side. Back in the kitchen she drank her morning coffee, scanned the headlines in the newspaper, and waited for Shawn and Chrissie, her teenage son and daughter, to come down. She fixed them some pancakes, then hurried upstairs to get dressed for work.

When she stepped out of the shower, Nancy could hear that Shawn was up to his usual hijinks, roughhousing with Chrissie before their ride came to take them to school. Their loud whooping and shouting got on her nerves.

"Hey! Cut it out down there!" Nancy called down to them. They were good kids, but she couldn't stand it when they fought, even if their scuffling was in fun. All that raucous noise and commotion drove her wild, filled her with an apprehension connected to some haunting memory of danger in the distant past. It was only eight o'clock in the morning, and already her head was spinning like the blade of a Cuisinart. "Take it easy," she muttered to herself. "They're normal teenagers. Let them do their thing."

She didn't have time to fight with the kids this morning anyway. If she didn't pick up the pace, she'd be late for work and spoil her record as the rehab facility's most dependable physical therapist, always on time, never missing a day in fifteen years. Her patients—fragile geriatric and volatile brain injury victims—depended on her. The thought of them lined up in the gym, waiting to be put through their paces, made the Cuisinart inside her head morph into a train, a high-speed line. She felt that old familiar locomotive, wind-at-her-back presssure going choo-choo-choo-choo-choo-choo-choo-choo, hounding her to hurry up and finish getting dressed.

Nancy quickly slipped into a pair of tan slacks and a chocolate-colored tailored shirt and rummaged through her closet for a blazer to go with them. To set off the outfit, she snatched the perfect scarf from her bureau drawer. After all, she had a reputation to keep up as a woman who could put on a potato sack and make it look like an Armani.

She dashed into the bathroom to find her blow dryer. It wasn't there—not on the shelf where she usually kept it, not in the cabinet under the vanity either. Could she have left it in the bedroom? She raced back into the bedroom. No, it wasn't on top of the bureau. Inside the night table drawer maybe? No, not there either. Where the hell was it? She glanced at the clock. Eight-thirty. She'd never get to her patients in time. The train noise in her head got louder and more insistent. *Come on, hurry up, let's go, let's go.* Could she have stuck the hair dryer in her closet? Ducking inside the walk-in closet again, she swept her hand along the top shelf.

The hair dryer came tumbling down, and along with it, her day planner, which she hadn't been able to find for days. What was wrong with her? Why was she so forgetful lately? She'd always misplaced things, but now she couldn't find anything she'd put away. She couldn't remember recipes either. She was from a family of gourmet cooks and could cook with her eyes closed but lately had trouble making brownies from a box. She'd even gotten lost going to her doctor's. It was a road she'd driven countless times, and yet several times this past month she'd forgotten which exit to take and wound up in some strange place, wondering, Where am I?

She glanced at her day planner, lying open on the floor. It was crammed with scribbled appointments—her work schedule, social engagements, soccer mom stuff, a grocery list with ingredients for a birthday cake she wanted to make for Walter, meetings with cabinetmakers and floor coverers and electricians to finish working on the house. Just looking at the book made her feel dizzy and nauseated. She picked it up and threw it in the trash.

Grabbing her hair dryer, she rushed back into the bathroom. She was standing at the mirror, drying her hair, feeling the heat on her scalp, hearing the whirring of the dryer mingled with the pounding noise in her head when suddenly she felt a thick wave of fatigue—a ponderous, all-encompassing world-weariness—wash over her. Every inch of her ached with physical and emotional exhaustion. She felt too tired to lift a finger, too tired to breathe, too tired to go on.

The dryer fell from Nancy's hand as she lost consciousness and collapsed on the floor. She felt herself float out of her body to the ceiling and look down on her other self lying there on the bathroom floor. "Get up, you lazy good-for-nothing fool; *get up!*" she urged her inert body in a mean-spirited, cruel, contemptuous voice that wasn't hers, but one she knew only too well.

Suddenly Nancy began crying like a child, completely regressed, sobbing and repeating over and over again in a broken, plaintive wail, *"I'm a good girl, I'm not a bad girl, I'm a good girl, I'm not a bad girl."*

Shawn went upstairs to say good-bye to his mother before leaving for school. He walked into the bathroom, gasped in shock, and dropped to his knees to help her. "Chrissie, there's something wrong with Mom! Call Daddy right away!" he yelled to his younger sister, who was already bounding up the stairs to say good-bye, too.

By the time Walter arrived, he found Nancy cowering on the floor in her closet, hiding under a pile of clothes. Sitting with her arms drawn around her chest, she was hugging herself, rocking back and forth. She gave no sign that she recognized him, saying only, *"I'm a good girl, I'm not a bad girl, I'm a good girl, I'm not a bad girl,"* over and over again in a pitiful childlike voice that he could not believe was his wife's.

THE LAST STRAW

This petite, pixieish, heart shape–faced woman sitting in my office is bright, stylish, and engagingly articulate. She looks a decade younger than her forty-two years. Outwardly she is every bit the "middle-aged white female professional," as she ironically describes the image she presents to the world. Although clearly frightened and worried, she seems remarkably poised for someone who'd been rushed to the emergency room after collapsing on her bathroom floor in a state of total decompensation two weeks earlier. She was on the verge of being hospitalized when fate intervened. The psychologist who'd been treating Nancy for the attention-deficit hyperactivity disorder she was diagnosed with nine years before called a psychiatrist to admit her. The psychiatrist had recently taken a SCID-D workshop of mine and, suspecting that Nancy was suffering from a dissociative disorder, referred her to me.

"I can't work at this point," she tells me. "I don't have control of my mind. Things frighten me—any kind of conflict. Whenever my children or my husband starts fighting in the house, I have to run away. If I've made someone sad or angry, it changes me into a scared little kid. My voice changes, my vocabulary changes, my mannerisms change. I cry like a little girl who's just lost her dog." She looks at me helplessly and goes on, "Or when I feel threatened, I turn into a mean, vicious, cursing bitch, yelling and screaming and criticizing my husband and the kids. I feel as if I have different behavior for different situations. The day before I unraveled, my husband got angry at me and was shutting me out big time, and I flew into a rage and almost tore his face off. It's a very instant kind of thing. I can feel the slide. I know it's happening, but I can't control it."

"Do you think your husband's anger at you was the trigger?" I ask.

"Yes. It felt like all the stuff I'd heard as a kid," she says. "My husband was going through a hard time and wasn't able to make decisions, and I perceived it as he didn't want to. He got very angry when I told him that he was dumping all the family decisions on me. He said that everything was my fault, and there was nothing wrong with him and to get a grip. That was deeply painful to me. I couldn't take the hurt. Someone that I trusted so much with my whole life and my whole being was again saying, to save a lot of words, 'You're full of shit.' Instantly I went into a rage. For the past year there's been this constant struggle in my head, and that was the straw that broke the camel's back."

"What kind of struggle have you been having?"

"I'd hear a part of me say, 'You stupid idiot, everybody's gonna leave you if you don't get control of yourself'; and then I'd say, 'I'll show 'em. I'll get better. Nothing's ever beat me before'; and then I'd come back with, 'Who're you kidding? You're a loser. It's never gonna change.' I tried whistling to drown out the thoughts until my lips cracked open and bled. Then I had a radio on all the time to distract me. But the thoughts started increasing and I kept saying inside myself, *Please somebody, help me; I'm sinking.* And nobody could hear me but me, so I would just get meaner."

I ask her whether she's been under any stress lately, and she tells me that her husband, a tall, handsome corporate executive who is deeply committed to her, lost his job six months ago. "We were about to move into our new home, this dream house we were building for our family, and we had no way to pay for it except to use all our savings," says Nancy. "The insecurity was very high. And then one of the contractors—we'd paid him an enormous amount of money—went bankrupt and disappeared. It was a very stressful period, horrendous."

When I question her about memory gaps during the SCID-D, she starts to relate an incident that happened when she was sixteen. "I had just failed my driver's test, and I went to my job after school at a Howard Johnson's. And then something happened, one of those things where I knew what I was doing, but I *didn't* know what I was doing." She pauses and asks, "Does that make sense?"

I nod yes. A perfect description of a state of dissociation.

"I was working behind the ice cream counter at the soda fountain," she goes on, "and I saw this shiny red Mustang in the parking lot that had the keys in it. I stepped outside in my white apron and hat, and I took the car. Took it. I stole a car." She leans forward and repeats emphatically, "*I stole a car*," as if to say, Can you believe it? "I drove it around for a while, and then I remember kind of like parking it somewhere, maybe back on the parking lot, and saying to myself, 'What the hell are you doing?' I got out and just went home."

"Did you ever have any other episodes like that?"

"Another time," Nancy answers, "was when I was in college in my dorm, an all-women's dorm. We were allowed to have men in until curfew time. One day the women across the hall who were good friends of mine came to me and said, 'Why did you do that last night?' And I said, 'What are you talking about?' And they said that I opened my door and took off all my clothes and stood in the door when there were lots of men there. At the time I thought they were just being cruel. Later, when I thought about that, I realized that they had no reason to be cruel. But I don't remember doing that. It was way out of character. The car thing I didn't know about, but did know about, but this I had no recollection of at all."

My sense is that the car had been stolen by Nancy in an episode of depersonalization without any loss of awareness, whereas it was possibly an alter personality who had disrobed, accompanied by Nancy's amnesia for the episode. "Can you recall any other time when you had memory blanks?" I ask.

She tells me this: "Several years ago I woke up about two in the morning and sat bolt upright in bed in a cold sweat and said, 'Oh, my God.'

There was such a vivid memory of sexual abuse from my paternal grand-father. It was unbelievable. He lived right next door to us when I was growing up, and I thought it was happening all over again, it was that real. I could feel it, not just the physical sensations, but the emotions, too—the fear, the shock, the shame."

"Was this the first time you had flashbacks like that?"

"Yes. I think the memories never surfaced before because the Ritalin I was taking for my attention-deficit hyperactivity disorder numbed every-thing. I was on a pretty heavy dose. The person who evaluated me said, 'I don't know how you got through school because you have one of the worst cases of ADHD that we've ever seen.' The clinic started me on Ritalin. Then I had my family physician regulate and manage it until it didn't work anymore."

"When was that?"

"About a year and a half ago. I was so edgy that someone could open their purse next to me and it would completely distract me. I couldn't work and go to the dentist on the same day. It was too confusing, so I'd forget to go to the dentist. I was unable to pay attention at work. At our team meetings I was like, 'What did you say? I'm sorry, I missed that.' I was alarmed. I told myself I can't let this happen, so I sought out a therapist. That's when I had the flashback."

"Did your therapist put you on any medication then?"

"No. He thought I didn't need it. He wanted to work through it without numbing everything again," Nancy says. "That went well, but—" She stops and shakes her head uncertainly. "Obviously, it didn't unmask all this other stuff."

Suddenly Nancy breaks into tears. "I don't want to be this way," she sobs. "At home I feel like a robot. I just do chores. There are windows of tenderness where my children are involved, but as soon as I walk in the door, all feelings just stop. When I feel threatened, either I act like a child and run into the closet and hide, or I turn into a raging bitch and say things that hurt people's soul. When we go to a party, if I can't hold it together, then I have to leave. I tell Walter, 'We have to go. Let's go,' almost to the point of being nasty. When I'm home and there's any fighting or arguing going on in the house, I feel that if I stay, I won't have any brain left, any mind left, that I'll lose it. Sometimes I'll just run out of the house and go for a ride, and that works to keep me kind of calm and not crazy."

Nancy looks at me imploringly. "You don't think I'm crazy, do you?" She squeezes her eyes shut and shudders, fearing the worst. "Please don't tell me that. *Please.*"

A dining-room chair hurtled through the air and landed like a smart bomb on a crystal vase. It was the opening salvo. The nightly war between her parents had begun.

"Stop it, you drunken sonofabitch!" her mother screamed. "Stop it!"

An ashtray and a candy dish flew by in quick succession and struck a lamp.

"Goddamn it, Barb, I know I'm drunk!" her father roared back. "Leave me alone!"

The sickening sound of breaking glass and the screaming and the swearing and the mean fury in her mother's voice made eight-year-old Nancy grab her younger brother, Keith, and run upstairs to the nearest closet for cover.

From the outside their house looked no different from the others on the quiet, tree-lined street in the quaint, peaceful suburb where Nancy grew up. It was a town where a boutique had a name like "Ye Olde Shoppe" and a drugstore was called the "Apothecary." The family home was a large stone-and-stucco house with black shutters, two white formal columns at the entrance, and a flower bed under a bay window filled with rose bushes, pink hydrangeas, and thick rhododendrons. A leafy maple tree spread its branches protectively over the front lawn. Someone walking by would have thought it was a home right out of serene tranquil *Pleasantville*. But inside it was more like *The War of the Roses*. Night after night the battle raged on.

Tonight it was worse than usual. Huddled together in her bedroom closet, Nancy and Keith hugged each other and waited for it to be over. They knew it wouldn't stop until her father broke every piece of furniture in the house. Poor Keith, Nancy thought, as she tried to comfort him. He was only thirteen months younger than Nancy, but he was crying so hard that she thought her mother would find them and punish them. It didn't matter that they hadn't done anything wrong. Nancy was terrified, too, but she didn't dare let herself cry. She had to stay alert and protect them.

Tramp! Tramp! Tramp! Oh, God, her father was coming up the steps. His voice sounded like a sonic boom. Her mother's was shrill as a siren.

"I told you, Barb, leave me the hell alone!"

"No, I won't, you stinking, sonofabitch drunk!"

More crashes, screaming, and swearing from her parents' bedroom. The noise howled through the upstairs, coming ever closer. Desperate,

Nancy jumped up, pulled her brother to his feet, and ran with him to the attic. They found refuge under an old desk.

Snap! It sounded like a branch crackling in a fire. *Snap! Snap! Crash!* Nancy stared in horror as a chair smashed though the attic door and her father entered the room, brandishing the chair like a sword. He looked over his shoulder, saw his wife approaching, and bellowed, "For Christ's sake, Barb, I told you, leave me the hell alone!"

And with that, not knowing that Nancy and Keith were hiding there, her father threw the chair at the desk, splintering it in half.

Open-mouthed, he stared at his children crouching together like two orphans shipwrecked in a turbulent sea. He was instantly remorseful. "I'm sorry, I'm sorry," he said, bending down and scooping them up in his arms.

But their mother was only concerned about the desk. She picked up a shard of wood from the floor and waved it at her husband reprovingly. "You drunken bastard," she said through clenched teeth. "Look what you've done."

THE BLAB BABY

Nancy enters the office dressed casually, but the eye-catching lapel pin on her jacket and the scarf folded into the open throat of her Oxford shirt hint at her artistic flair. She says that the antidepressant I prescribed to ease her bleak ruminations has helped but has not stopped the thoughts entirely.

"It's kind of like those old tapes still playing in my head," she tells me. "I can't get the dinner done, and I can't get the laundry done, and I can't work, and I can't look very nice. I can't hold my end of the bargain up. I must be a loser. I know where it comes from. As a child you were measured by what you could accomplish—the chores and tasks. Feelings and emotions that were negative or didn't suit my mother's needs were minimized and invalidated, and you were punished for them. My mother is so bossy and narcissistic, it's unbelievable. It's just ridiculous."

The scene Nancy paints of her childhood is like a Dickensian tale of a waif forced into indentured servitude. "My father came home drunk every night and had a violent temper and terrorized us," she says, "but he's been sober for years and has tried to make amends. Even then he was kind and loving and not half as bad as my mother. She just kept ranting and raving at him until she drove him wild, and she would torment and beat the shit out of my brother Keith and me, always finding fault and whipping us for it. Day and night she never stopped. She was brutal. Six years after Keith was born, my two younger brothers came along. My mom worked, and from three to five every day of my life, I had to hurry and get everything done before she got home. I wasn't very old, maybe eight or nine. And I'd be like, '5:05, my God, here she comes!' And if it wasn't all perfect—if dinner wasn't made and the table wasn't set and the boys weren't ready for dinner, and if I left one spoon in the sink after cooking dinner—she wouldn't talk to me. And then I'd have to keep trying to do nicer and nicer things so she'd talk to me again. Or she'd make me stand in the dining room with Keith without moving or speaking until she came in and would either beat us to a pulp or leave us alone. We never knew what to expect. The anticipation was awful."

I know how damaging an atmosphere of such chaotic violence coupled with thankless exploitation and cold, hard cruelty can be to the identity of a young child desperate for parental protection and approval. "Can you see any connection between that abuse and what is going on inside you today?" I ask.

"Yes, I'm on this goddamn rampage, like a tornado inside me," Nancy says, "a drivenness. I just have to keep moving, preparing for a war. It's like, 'Batten down the hatches!' I feel very tense, very threatened, and fearful. That's why I have to live in a house with so many big windows all around, so I can see my mother driving up the driveway and clean up and be ready. I never had any idea of what would come next."

Besides this exhausting hypervigilance, Nancy sees another effect of her mother's abusive treatment of her. She relates it to an uncontrollable part inside herself she calls the "Mean."

"I picture her kind of trailer park-y," she says, adding quickly, "I don't mean any economic slur, but I see her as a really tough, abrasive, tattooed, Harley Davidson kind of person, about my age. She only comes out when other people are around and tears into them viciously. She screams at Walter and the boys, and afterward I'll say, 'My God, what did I do? How could I hurt people's feelings that way?' And then I'll turn into this sad, helpless little girl who cries all the time. I don't know who I am. One minute I'm petrified of my mother, and the next minute I want to kill her. And then there's a part of me saying, 'Walter's such a loser, I told you you couldn't trust him,' and another part saying, 'That's not true.' Things feel very confusing. My head feels like an Olympic-size swimming pool with tons of people swimming in it. It's like a relay race in my head."

"If the child part of you could speak," I ask her, "what would she say about how she feels?"

"I don't know, I don't know," Nancy says. Shaking her head in confusion, she starts to cry. And then it happens. Abruptly, as if by sleight-of-hand, she changes into an anguished eight-year-old, her voice coarsening into the loud, keening sing-song of a child bawling her eyes out—the Child alter. With a little girl's exaggerated facial expressions and gestures, she slips into a grade school manner of speech, saying "skeered" for *scared* and "veery" for *very* when she answers:

"I'm skeered. I'm veery skeered. My dad's coming tomorrow. I like my dad, but I'm a-skeered my dad's gonna tell my mom something. Every time I try to be a good girl, my mom tells me I'm a bad girl. I try and I try and I try to be a good girl, and then I just be a bad girl again. I tell my mom something, and she doesn't believe it. She calls me a liar."

"Why does she do that?"

Nancy shrugs helplessly. *"I don't know. She's not a nice lady. I'm skeered of her a lot. She likes my baby brothers. She doesn't like me. I don't know why. I'm just a girl. It makes my heart veery sad."*

"It seems to me you are a good girl. Tell me, what do you like to do?"

"I like to paint. And I like to bake. My grammy made dough with me. I like the boys a lot. I like the house, but I don't like to fix it up. I don't like to move things. The Mom likes to do that." Nancy leans forward and cups her hand around her mouth confidentially. *"You know what the Wife just did?"* the Child asks.

"No. What?" The Wife, I take it, is another alternate personality inside Nancy besides the Mom and the Child.

"She was here a minute ago and—phhhht!—she went away. She wasn't gonna tell you anything, no siree bob. She's so skeered and sad."

Speaking of another alter, the Child goes on, *"The Sister died. I tried so hard to find her, but she's gone. I feel bad for her the worst. The Sister was a big girl. Veery nice. She's the only one that knew everything. Everything! She didn't tell me a lot, not at all. Her heart hurted too much and it breaked all up in a lot of pieces and she just died."*

"And the Wife who went away, what's she like?"

"She's a veery nice lady. She's the one who goes to work. I'm telling her, 'Come back.' But she won't come back. And I want her so bad, because I know it would make Walter so happy, too."

"Maybe it would be good to learn how to find her when you need her."

"Yeah, if I have to keep comin' here, she has to come here sometimes, too, right? Me and the Mom have to do all the work. That's not right. We're gettin' tired. The Mom falled on the floor in the bathroom, she was so tired. Bless her little heart."

"How long have you been inside Nancy?"

"I don't know. Do you know? Prob'ly a long time. I know all about her. She's a nice girl. She wouldn't tell anybody how she really feels. She gets a-skeered, so that's when I come. I gotta tell everybody. I can tell Walter when I don't like something. The Mom sews and cooks, never thinks she does enough. She's not like the Mean."

"She's not really mean," I say about Nancy's angry alter. "I think she's scared."

" 'Yeah, but she'll never, never tell you that. And she'll never ask for help. She justs gets real nasty and pushes everybody away. She gets mean to me, and you know what she says? She says, 'You're a blab baby.' "

"A blab baby?"

"That means you're a whiny crybaby."

"Did your mom call you that?"

"Yeah. She called me a blab baby. I'm not a blab baby. I'm not a liar. I'm not a tattletale. I'm a tattletale, but I'm not a bad tattletale. I don't tell bad things. I mean—' " The Child succumbs to a fresh burst of sobs.

"Are your memories the same as Nancy's?"

"No! They're not the same. They hurt my heart more. They'll hurt the Wife's so bad. They'll hurt the Mom's. The Mom's heart'll hurt for Chrissy and Shawn." Nancy looks embarrassed as the Child asks, *"You know what the Mean just said? 'I don't like you, Doctor. I don't want you, Doctor.' I told the Mean to take a nap. I don't want you to talk to the Mean. It's too hard. She's a veery strong girl. I'm veery tired of telling her all the time, 'Stop it! Don't be mean.' 'Cause when she's mean, then everybody's mad at me, too, and I don't like that.' "*

"Maybe you'll be able to help the Mean feel less scared and express herself in a different way. Then it'll be less tiring for you."

"I'll try. Later, not now. I'm too tired now," the Child sighs. *"It was hard for me to get the Mean to take a nap. The Mean wore me out. Can I go?"*

Nancy sits very still, draws a deep breath, and wipes her eyes and face with a tissue. She looks stunned. "Oh, God," she says quietly in her normal voice. "I don't understand this. I can't tell you how devastated I feel."

Her dark secret is out. The facade she so carefully built over many years has finally crumbled from the pressure of walled-in pain, exposing for the first time the separate parts of her that were hiding inside like a clan of noisy, quarrelsome squatters. The Child in control expressed with artless and primitive simplicity the feelings that Nancy had never talked about before. The sadness and deep hurt over her grandfather's incest and her mother's repudiation of her as a liar are embodied in the Child. Her rage and the fear of further abuse are carried by the Mean. And the mourning of something in her that died—unquestioning trust, per-haps?—is symbolized by the metaphor of the Sister's death from a broken heart. Could the Sister, the one who knew everything but would only tell so much, carry other memories of sexual abuse that seem to have disap-peared for good? Will they ever come back? It's too early to tell.

The completed SCID-D shows that Nancy has severe levels of four dissociative symptoms—amnesia, depersonalization, identity confusion, and identity alteration—making the diagnosis of DID a certainty. Partic-ularly telling are the continuous interactive dialogues that Nancy has when she depersonalizes and that her alters have with each other, each of whom is a distinctive personality with her own name, age, feelings, and memories.

The onset of Nancy's dissociative disorder, I surmise from the SCID-D, occurred when she was in the second or third grade. This was the time of Nancy's first depersonalization episode that she recalled dur-ing the interview. It was a warm day, she remembered, and she was stand-ing naked in the front doorway of her house, completely exposed to passersby, and she could see herself doing that.

When I give Nancy my diagnosis, she says numbly, "I knew what was happening after Walter found me in the closet. I just couldn't believe it. It's like those people you see on the news after floods or fires. They know their home is gone, but they don't want to believe it, because it's such hard work to rebuild your life. But when an expert tells you, you can't hide it anymore."

"You can get better," I assure her, aware of the dread and hopelessness she feels. "The depth of your pain does not have to continue." I explain to her why it is so important to end the isolation of the different parts, all living in the same house but divided against each other. "The Child is car-rying a huge burden of having to talk about a lot of your feelings. Try to listen to the Child's feelings and begin to express some of them so that the Child doesn't have to suffer alone anymore and take control as fully. It also would be helpful if you could try to find out how to calm the Mean because the Mean is still living with the terrors you had when you were a little girl. Right now she only knows how to get her feelings out in uncontrollable rage, sometimes at a person she's not even rageful at."

"What's the next step?" Nancy asks. "Where do we go from here?"

"I'd like you to think about the feelings these parts of you have—the Mean, the Mom, the Wife, the Child—and write down what you can do to comfort yourself when you have those feelings. How can you comfort the Child when she feels sad and deeply hurt by something someone has said or done? How can you calm the Mean's anger when she feels threatened and redirect her rageful feelings into constructive activities? Try to write it down."

"When I do some journal writing," Nancy objects, "I get so angry that it's really counterproductive."

"Then wait until you feel up to it," I encourage her. "You'll need a list of the different positive things you can use to comfort the Child's feelings and the Mean's feelings, so that when they want to come out, you can stay in control. You'll be able to go down that list and contact the Mom to help you do what needs to be done to calm that part down. Let your different parts know that you respect the feelings they're carrying. These parts that are inside you came around to help you during very difficult times, and they can help you now in your healing."

"I have to get better," Nancy says desperately. "I'm petrified that I'm going to wear my whole family out. They've been so good to me, I couldn't bear that."

"Once the different parts of you feel accepted and appreciated, they can start working together," I assure her, "and those outbursts won't occur so often anymore."

Nancy stares at the floor, looking downcast. "It's very lonely; that's all I know," she murmurs finally. "But I'll try."

GUILTY PLEASURE

The handknit blanket depicting a gorgeous sunset with brilliant bands of orange, red, purple, blue, and green dissolving into each other against a navy background looks professionally made.

"I'm making this for Walter; it's a present," Nancy tells me when she comes into our next session and holds the blanket up for me to see. "My grandmother—my mother's mother—used to make blankets for me. She had a restaurant and was a marvelous cook, too. She let me cook with her in her house, and when she was dying of cancer she came to my house and taught me everything so that I would remember how to do it after she was gone." Nancy casts a critical eye at her handiwork. "I don't think it's that good, do you?" she asks.

"Nancy, it's beautiful! You're very talented," I tell her, genuinely impressed with her craftsmanship. Like many people with a dissociative disorder, Nancy is a creative person who finds in artwork an outlet for self-expression that was ruthlessly stifled in childhood. I wonder what path she would have chosen in life had her artistic talents been supported early on.

She sits down and draws a yellow legal pad out of her handbag. "This is the list you asked me to make," she says. "Part of me thinks it's stupid to do this; part of me thinks I have to do this; and part of me thinks I'm not going to do this." She laughs apologetically. "I hope this is what you want."

"Let me hear it."

Not surprisingly, dealing with her mother is the number one item on her list. Her mother was skiing in Montreal when Nancy collapsed on the bathroom floor a month ago and, much to Nancy's relief, hasn't visited her yet.

"The most important thing for me to do is to not let my mother hurt me anymore," she starts off. "The incest that happened is a very small piece of the pie. Having her call me a liar and invalidate my feelings and punish me for them was worse. She still calls me a liar and takes great pleasure in belittling me. She's turned my two younger brothers against me, and I love them so much. I can't let my mother hurt me any more than she already has. If my father can't understand that, then he'll have to deal with those consequences."

Moving down the list, she goes on, "I have to learn to stop browbeating myself when I don't complete what I intended to do or don't do it perfectly. And I have to let Walter know the triggers that really make me anxious, like having him blow me off, and see if he can help me make a plan together to avoid those things."

She looks up at me and asks worriedly, "Am I doing this okay?"

"Yes, fine. Please go on."

"I have to be able to say no when I can't do something for Walter or the children, and that's really hard, because I'm afraid that they'll get angry at me and won't love me anymore, and they'll leave. That fear brings out the meanness in me. And when I'm feeling mean, I have to give that part of me compliments and let her know that she's not really vicious, that she's okay. Doing yard work or heavy cleaning calms that part down."

Nancy continues, "When the childlike part comes out, I need to sew and bake and paint. That makes her feel better. I loved to do those things when I was younger, but I wasn't allowed to make a mess in the house. I had to go outside and play instead. I just get such pleasure out of those things now, because I never did them. So when I'm feeling childlike," she concludes, looking up at me with a guilty smile, "I let myself have some fun."

"Does that little girl inside you know that she's free to have fun as much as she wants now?" I ask her. "Can you experience fun, too, even when you're not acting like a child?"

Startling me with the suddenness of her transformation, Nancy switches into the Child again, a frightened, agitated little girl. *"HELLO!"* she hollers in her uncanny eight-year-old voice. *"The Mom wants to leave and I have to yell for her to hear me,"* she explains. *"I have to hold the Mom back. She says she's only coming here because Walter wants her to, that this is silly and that nothing's going to get any better."*

Afraid to verbalize her doubts about therapy and her resistance to feeling entitled to have joy in her life, Nancy has let the Child speak out for her again.

I wait for her to return to herself and ask, "Why do you think the Child part of you, the part that feels sad, has to yell to be heard?"

"Because I couldn't tell anybody when I was sad as a child," Nancy says, adding quickly, "You couldn't tell. I don't remember why. I just know you couldn't tell. And they didn't care. So I don't know how to tell."

"That's something you can help this part of you learn how to do," I answer. "You can let her know it's safe now for her to tell, and you'll be listening. She shouldn't have to scream to make herself heard." I offer Nancy this hypothetical example: "Suppose you adopted an eight-year-old little girl who had a lot of stress before she came to you and she was sobbing and crying and wouldn't tell you what was wrong. What would you do?"

"I would pick her up and hold her and rock her and sing to her. I'd let her know that in our home our children are the most important things to us except our marriage. And that I'll listen to whatever she has to tell me."

"What would you tell her if she pushed you away and started sobbing again?"

"I don't know." Nancy becomes distraught, repeating, "I don't know. I don't know." Through tears she says, "I can tell you what I do with my children. When my children cry, I hug them and let them know that they're wonderful and please let Mom know whatever you need and I'll be there for you. We're always there for you. And there's no problem too big that we can't work on it together."

"You've been able to be very comforting to your children," I point out to her. "Do you think you can apply those same skills to yourself?"

"No, I can't. No," she sobs. "How can I do that if I can't figure out if I'm even worth comforting? It's like going through the motions."

"Maybe the first step is to acknowledge that you're worth it. The part of you that doesn't feel worthy of being comforted, why does it feel that way? What's the logic?"

"There's no logic, I know that," Nancy admits. "It's just that I've always believed that I've not measured up to anybody's expectations. It's been beaten into me over so many years. It's so ingrained, like Monday is Monday. It's like your curriculum vitae: Nancy L., defective and unworthy. Not nice words, and they've always been there."

"But it sounds to me that there are so many positive strengths that you do have. You just mentioned that you're able to give your children some things that you perhaps didn't receive."

Nancy makes a painful confession: "When I was pregnant I prayed so hard, so hard, you have no idea, that God didn't give me girls. But when I had Chrissie after Shawn, I was thrilled. And from the moment my children were born till now, the purpose that has kept me going is that the pattern will not repeat itself: they will not experience what I did. They'll know what love is and what choices are and that they're wonderful."

"You have to give yourself that same gift of undoing the pattern."

"On an objective level I get it. But when I interpret a situation, my emotions rule. I don't believe that I'm not bad; I believe that I *am* bad. I take some pride in my accomplishments, but those are not me; they're things that I did."

"But they are things you did because of who you are."

Nancy shrugs dismissively. "I'm so insecure now that I have to have physical proof that I'm not as bad as I think I am," she reveals. "Walter is so sweet. He said, 'Let's look at videos we've made of the kids over the years, and you'll see some of the wonderful things you've done.' At this point, it's impossible for me to have spontaneous positive thoughts about myself or feel entitled to do fun, comforting things."

Deep down, what's really stopping Nancy from committing herself to the work of comfort so crucial to her recovery is a fear of failure: "I don't want to try and try and get shoved all the way back down again," she says. "I don't know how to comfort myself. I don't even know how to begin." Nancy shakes her head, bemused by this admission, and asks, "Isn't it sad to be my age and not know how to do that?"

THE HOCKEY GAME

The parking lot at Valley View High School's ice hockey arena was filled with cars that night. Parents and children bundled up in hooded ski jackets, mufflers, and thick mittens to ward off the piercing chill in the air were streaming across the lot into the arena. The big game between Valley View's team and Saint Matthew's, their archrival, had drawn a sell-out crowd.

Nancy pulled her Jeep Grand Cherokee into the lot and drove slowly up and down the rows of station wagons and SUV's, looking for a spot. *"Hurry up, hurry up, hurry up,"* the Mean scolded her. *"You're always late. Why can't you ever get anywhere on time?"*

"Oh, shut up," she mumbled to herself as she finally found a place behind a few other cars parked on the grass bordering the lot. She stepped out of the truck into the cold night air and began striding toward the arena, her breath forming little white clouds of steam as she hurried along. She knew how important it was for her to be here for Shawn—her sixteen-year-old son was one of the team's stars. Walter was busy with his new job and couldn't make it, and Chrissie, her daughter, was home with a cold. She was tonight's cheerleader.

As she approached the arena, Nancy heard a roar from the crowd and assumed that the game had already begun. The Mean started in again. *"Damn you, hurry up, hurry up, keep moving, keep moving, keep moving."*

But then another voice stopped her dead in her tracks, shouting, *"Don't go in! Please don't! Please!"* It was the Child, crying out inside her.

Nancy entered the arena and started walking toward her seat, but the Child's voice held her back. *"No! You can't stay here! You have to leave!"* It was too full of anguish to be ignored. Abruptly, Nancy turned on her heel and ran out of the building as fast as she could.

BROTHERLY LOVE

"When you left the arena," I ask Nancy at our next session, "what were you feeling?"

"I panicked right inside the door and had to get away," Nancy answers. "I ran back to my Jeep and sat there, shaking and too upset to drive, until I got over it. And then it hit me. I found myself thinking about my two younger brothers. I taught both of them how to ice skate, and they became excellent hockey players when they were Shawn's age. My son looks just like Rory, my youngest brother. Going to the game reminded me of the horrible wedge my mother has driven between my brothers and me. She told them not to have anything to do with me, because I would just make trouble. They yes her to death, because it's easier that way, and I never see them anymore."

"Have you spoken to them about it?"

"No, they won't talk to me," she says unhappily.

"Maybe you could write a letter to your brothers, telling them how you feel."

"I should," Nancy agrees. "Alienating me from my brothers is one of the cruelest things my mother has done to me. I raised my two younger brothers. They were more my children than my mother's. And of course she takes all the credit. I think the reason they're half sane is that I raised them, not her. She raised Keith and me, and both of us are so screwed up. I remember thinking, 'No one will ever do anything to hurt these two boys' to the point where I would sleep in Rory's crib with him until he wasn't a baby anymore. I wanted to protect him."

"Do your brothers know that you have DID?"

"No, but my emotional state has interfered terribly with my relationship with them," Nancy replies. "About two years ago, I was in Arizona with my mother and my kids, and my brothers were down there, too. An incident happened—I can't even remember what it was—and the meanness in me kicked in and lasted a long time. Rory was appalled by it. In the middle of the night I put the kids in the car and drove back to New York, which is extremely irrational. I had no choice. I had to leave. I had to get out of there, because I was afraid that the Mean would come out again, and I'd say things that would be unforgivable."

"How did your family react to your leaving like that?"

"Rory wrote to me three weeks later and said, 'You're a different person. You are not my sister,' " Nancy answers. "And I was so pissed. I never pursued it, because since then my mother has taken advantage of this rift and has turned it into a massive triangulation between my brothers and me. And it's like, 'See, you really *are* nuts.' "

Nancy begins to sob bitterly. The simmering rage pent up in a childhood of silent suffering finally boils over. Her fury at her mother for inflicting emotional abuse more deeply wounding perhaps than even the incest she has suffered finds words. "I hate her!" Nancy shouts. "I *hate* her! I want to kill her!"

I tell Nancy that being able to express her feelings in the context of therapy is an important step toward integration of her separate selves. "You won't need the Mean to express anger for you inappropriately and have it come out at your husband and children," I explain, "when you reconnect with your rage and learn how to lessen its power."

"My brother Keith hates my mother, too," she tells me, "but he's too far gone to do anything about it."

"The one closest to you in age?"

"Yes. He's in a psychiatric hospital. He's been nonfunctional for years," Nancy reveals as if reluctantly peeling back the bandage over a raw wound. "Keith was on the Olympic track team, and he was a wonderful athlete and academic success. I was so proud of him! He came home one Christmas, and he had this big psychotic break, and he never recovered. Two weeks ago he jumped off a bridge. He never tried to kill himself before."

I sympathize with Nancy for this heart-breaking family tragedy and ask, "Were you and your brother close?"

"Very close; we took care of each other," Nancy replies. "I called him last week, and I've never heard him so depressed. I feel I need to go see him, as much for me as for him. He basically just sits in his room and holds his head. He was a senior in college when he had his first breakdown, and he's never worked. He's a wonderful person, and he's so trapped. It just kills me. I should never have lost contact with him. I just want to hug him and let him know how much we love him."

"Have you shared anything with him about yourself?"

"No, I don't know if he could handle that," Nancy answers. "For most of my life I didn't remember any of these memories of the sexual abuse. I don't think he knows about that. I don't think he was abused by my grandfather, but my mother was as awful to him as she was to me. His level of functioning is just too low to talk about the experiences we've gone through together, but there are glimpses of it."

Nancy begins to weep at the thought of how far her once-golden brother has fallen. "He didn't deserve this," she says brokenly. "I think I'm the only one who understands him." She smiles through her tears as she remembers her last time with Keith when he stayed at her home. "One night when we were sitting together in the den he looked at his fingers and said jokingly, 'Do you really think snakes come out of my hands or is that because I'm crazy?' We laughed together like two little kids."

Nancy wipes her eyes with the back of her hand. "The sad part of this is that Keith was the only one I could share this nightmare with," she says, "because my other brothers are so much younger than me. I was their mother, and they had a different childhood. Keith is the only one who knows."

Almost pleadingly, Nancy asks, "Is it okay if I go see him? I just want to sit with him and hug him."

"Yes," I answer, knowing how much it would mean to her to be with her brother at this terrible time in both their lives.

THE VISIT

Saturday Nancy awoke brimming with good intentions. This would be a perfect day to visit Keith. She drew back the bedroom drapes and looked out at the brilliant sunlight pouring through the crystalline coating of ice on the trees and grass, the residue of early morning dew. It would all burn off soon. The weather forecast was calling for "an unseasonably warm day with temperatures in the high forties." Walter was out jogging, and as soon as he got back they'd throw some clothes into an overnight bag and take off on the 150-mile ride to the hospital in northern Massachusetts. The kids had their own plans for the day, and she didn't think it would be a good idea for them to see Keith in that condition anyway. Her parents weren't due back from Arizona yet, so there was no likelihood of running into her mother at the hospital.

She was sitting at the kitchen table drinking her morning coffee when Shawn burst into the room and began rummaging through the cabinets. He was already dressed and looking for a quick breakfast before he ran off to be with his friends.

"Mom, don't we have any cornflakes?" Shawn asked.

It was an innocent question, but to Nancy it sounded like "Jesus Christ, why don't you ever take care of things in this house!" It stung her like an accusation, a casting of aspersions on her competence. Why didn't her family appreciate what she did for them? Why try to be nice when nobody cared?

Immediately the Mean sprang into action. *"Screw you, Shawn!"* she screamed. *"Why are you so helpless? Find something else if we don't have any goddamn cornflakes. I'm not your fucking slave!"* Nancy threw her coffee cup across the room and watched it shatter to pieces against the cabinet above Shawn's head.

"Hey, cut it out!" he yelled back at her, taken by surprise. "All I asked you was, 'Where's the cornflakes?'"

Now I've done it, she thought. He'll walk out the door and I'll never see him again. She felt her anxiety rising like a fever, her heart thumping loudly in her chest. The Child was frightened and didn't know what to do, and the Mom only wanted to bolt out of there and go someplace where nobody knew her.

Nancy couldn't wait for Walter to get home; she had to leave that minute. She rushed upstairs, threw on a pair of jeans and a sweater, flew downstairs to the hall closet, grabbed a ski jacket, and blew out of the house like a gust of wind.

She was tooling along Route 14 in White Plains in the Jeep Grand Cherokee when suddenly she noticed a sign that said she was approaching Foster Center. How did that happen? She couldn't have been on the road more than twenty minutes, and Foster Center was in Rhode Island, over a hundred miles from her home. She looked at the clock on the dashboard and was shocked to read 12:55. Her watch said the same thing. That meant she had to have been driving for at least two hours, and most of that time was a blank!

For the first time since she sped away from her house, Nancy became aware of her surroundings. It was a scenic countryside of fields and farms and orchards lined with curving fieldstone walls and shingled barns that looked centuries old interspersed with a few incongruous modern ranch and split-level homes. Foster Center itself was a bit of postcard Americana. Nestled between fairy tale pine forests, the town was composed of stately buildings dating back to the eighteenth century and a one-room red schoolhouse and bell tower that had been converted into the town library.

Nancy was tired and starting to get hungry, but the Mom didn't want to stop. She was pestering Nancy to go to Cepachet, an old stagecoach town famous for its antiques. The Mom loved antiques and was hoping she could find something for the house there. Since it was only another twelve miles or so, Nancy gave in and headed north through Rhode Island's apple orchard country to Cepachet.

All along the route Nancy spotted signs advertising different varieties of apples, apple pies, and cider. The Mom was dying to pick up some of those giant Japanese mutsu apples called crispins to take home and dip in caramel and chocolate sauce for the kids. She wanted to make it up to them for screaming at them so much when the Mean was out, but all of the farm shops were closed and wouldn't open until the season started in a few months.

Driving into Cepachet, Nancy felt that she'd entered a sepia-colored town in Montana or Wyoming in the cowboys and Indians days. Famished, she pulled up to Brown and Hopkins Country Store and bought a chunk of cheddar cheese and some crackers to hold her until dinner. Her next stop was Stone Mill Antiques, a former old stone mill now boasting a red, white, and blue flaglike sale sign in front and a nineteenth-century life-size white horse carved out of tree trunks near the entrance.

Browsing through the jumbled collection of furniture from days gone by, Nancy spotted a Shaker writing desk that struck a familiar chord. She felt her whole body tense, a chill rise up her spine. It was just like the desk in the attic that she and Keith were hiding under when they were little and their father burst in and smashed it in half with a chair during one of his drunken rampages.

"Don't be afraid, don't give into it, you need to be an adult," she told herself as she felt the childlike terror and helplessness of an abused and cornered eight-year-old begin to overwhelm her. But the Child wouldn't listen. *"I can't stay here!"* she cried.

Hurrying out of the building, Nancy jumped into her Jeep and drove away in a panic. Twenty minutes later she found herself pulling into the courtyard of a motel in Providence. She had no idea how she got there, but she knew she needed to check in, call Walter, and tell him to meet her there. She was afraid to make the rest of the trip to the hospital in Massachusetts alone. While she was waiting for Walter she could lie down and get some rest, and they could go back there and spend the night after they visited Keith.

It took every ounce of Nancy's energy to pull herself together and speak to the desk clerk like a reasonable, mature woman. She got a double-occupancy room and told the clerk, when he asked whether she had any luggage, that her husband would be bringing her overnight bag with him when he met her there later that afternoon.

"Nancy, are you all right?" Walter asked anxiously after he picked up the phone on the first ring and heard her say hello.

"I'm fine. I'm at—" She looked at the address on a book of matches and gave it to him. "I'm sorry I couldn't wait for you, but I got angry at Shawn and—" Feelings of shame for her behavior overcame her, and she dissolved into the Child, tearfully confiding, *"I was a bad girl, and Mom's mad at me, too, 'cause she wanted to get something nice for the house in a big place with lots of old tables and chairs. I told her it made me skeered in there, so she left. Mom's a nice girl. She called you to come stay with me and give me a hug and bring my 'jamas for when I go to bed."*

Walter told her he would pack a bag for her and be there as soon as he could. Relieved, Nancy lay down on the bed and slept until she was awakened by the ringing of the telephone. It was the desk clerk announcing that her husband had arrived, and Nancy said to send him up.

As soon as she saw Walter, Nancy threw her arms around him and embraced him as if they'd been away from each other for months. The Mean didn't trust him, but Nancy knew in the depths of her soul that Walter would never let her down.

When they pulled into the parking lot of the psychiatric hospital where Keith was a patient, Nancy took a deep breath to steel herself. She fished inside her handbag to make sure that she hadn't forgotten the little book of spiritual sayings she'd bought as a present for Keith and rubbed it for good luck.

Inside, the brick building looked like any other hospital except for the ominous locked door leading to Keith's wing. A nurse let Nancy and Walter in. They passed the lounge where a man in jeans and a plaid shirt was staring blankly at a ball game on the TV set and some visitors were talking to a young woman whose arms were covered with tiers of angry scars from self-inflicted cuts.

They found Keith looking more depressed than Nancy had ever seen him. His muscular body seemed shrunken, and the dark stubble on his gaunt face gave him a grungy look. He could barely muster a thin smile when Nancy kissed and hugged him hello and handed him his gift.

"You look wonderful," she lied. She was about to sit down on a chair next to Keith when she heard a sound that filled her with chilling alarm, like someone walking in the woods who hears the hiss of a rattlesnake. It was her mother's voice outside the doorway. Oh, my God, Nancy thought, what a cruel trick of fate! Either her parents had cut short their annual Arizona vacation or Nancy had been mistaken about the date of their return. It didn't matter. There was no way she could remain calm with them, not when she was this fragile.

Nancy wheeled around and screamed at her father as he was about to enter the room with her mother, "Get her out of here! Get her out! Get her OUT!"

Her father looked shocked, but he took his wife gently by the arm and said, "Come on, Barb, let's wait out here for a minute."

Nancy saw that she'd scared Keith half to death. She wanted to comfort him, but she knew that she had to flee immediately before she switched into the Child.

"I'm sorry, Keith. I've got to go," she said, bending down to kiss her brother good-bye. He pushed her away, frightened, so she blew him a kiss and left the room quickly. With Walter at her side, she brushed past her parents and strode down the hall to the exit without a backward glance.

THE WATCHER

"We were driving away from the hospital and Walter said, 'God did this on purpose so that your mother and father really can see the effect all this stuff has had on you over the years and that you're not bullshitting,' " Nancy recounts in my office at her next visit. "When we got home, we had a family meeting. We came up with signals for Walter and the kids to let me know that they don't hate me and won't leave me when something happens that makes me feel threatened or unappreciated. They've been wonderful about it, but the Mean is still coming out two or three times a day. Shawn provokes it the most. When he's a roughneck, he terrorizes me like my father."

Like many abuse victims, Nancy has to learn how to desensitize her hyperactive trauma response system so that she doesn't leap into full-scale protective mode at threats that are actually innocuous. Her trauma response system is stuck on permanent "alert" and will only get unstuck when she is able to access dissociated memories and feelings from the past and connect to them as an adult who is no longer a helpless victim.

Typical of DID patients who depersonalize, Nancy has a hypervigilant observing self that always expects the worst and constantly has to prepare for it. "There's this part of me, the Watcher, always on the lookout for trouble," she says. "She thinks my mother's coming any minute. The Watcher listens to the Mean—they're always together—but she doesn't say anything. She's too scared."

"You have to help her learn that nobody's going to hate you or hurt you or break anything or throw something at you if dinner isn't made or the house isn't perfect," I tell her. "She doesn't know that the house you're living in now is not the one you grew up in. You need to have the Mom explain that to the Mean and the Watcher and tell the Child that, too. The Child needs to know that she's no longer in any harm when she's around adults. She doesn't have to stoop down and be abused or run away because it's thirty-five years later now and you can have an independent life of your own. Remind them all of what year this is. I think they need to be oriented."

Nancy looks puzzled. "The thing that throws me is that I'm not afraid of getting physically hurt by the people I care deeply about; it's getting emotionally damaged," she says. "It's not a safety issue with me. That's why I could never quite figure out the hiding in the closet thing."

"A very important part of this phase of treatment is to begin to understand when something in the present triggers you into the past and causes you to have feelings of the past in the present, resulting in your behavior," I explain. "If you can identify when that's happening, communication and cooperation among these different sides of you will let you know that now it's safe. Being able to differentiate between the past, when it was very scary, and the present, when you're safe, is crucial at this juncture."

"I can recognize the triggers," Nancy says, "but my reactions are so automatic that I can't stop them."

"Comforting them is what stops them," I tell her. "If you try to squelch your different parts or drive them away, that will only make them angrier or more frightened and out of control. The idea is to be supportive of them and have these different sides of you begin to share memories and feelings with each other and ultimately work together. The Child can learn from the Mean that she can get angry and not just be scared and sad and hide in the closet anymore. And the Mean can learn from the Child to have sad feelings and also pleasurable feelings so that she just doesn't have to carry all the angry feelings and come out and be mean. And the Mom can learn from the Child that she needs to express herself honestly and not have to make the Mean or the Child do it for her."

Nancy nods her assent. "I've had it with all this crying," she sighs. She looks impatient and determined at the same time and says, "I want to go on with my life."

COMING OUT

After several months in therapy Nancy proudly reports that she was able to get through an entire week and the Mean had not come out once. "Shawn complained to me about my not coming to his hockey games," she relates, "and instead of turning into a screaming bitch, I recognized that he wasn't going to hate me or leave me. I just said, 'I'm sorry I can't do that, Shawn, but we can be together other times, and I can show how much I love you in other ways.' I'm more determined that this viciousness inside me has to end. I never felt so strong-willed about it before."

"Are you able to comfort yourself actively now?"

"I still feel that I'm not worth anything if I'm not productive all the time," Nancy replies, "so I approach comforting myself from the standpoint of doing what I enjoy. The Mean loves to paint, so I've been painting up a storm. The Mom likes to draw, and the Child loves it when I bake the honey buns my grandmother taught me how to make. For the first time I've started to believe that I didn't do anything wrong and that I don't have to be ashamed of the way I feel or behave."

I'm delighted with Nancy's progress and insights into her symptoms. She now understands that her symptoms previously attributed to ADHD—her difficulty sitting still or waiting, her distractibility, the trouble she has sustaining attention, her forgetfulness—have a dissociative core. She feels calmer and more hopeful about the future now that she is learning how to accept and nurture the different parts of herself underlying those symptoms. She realizes that she had tried to anesthetize her different parts with drugs like Ritalin that made her feel better short-term but delayed her recovery by not dealing with the root cause of her symptoms.

Nancy tells me that she has finally gotten around to writing a "respectful" letter to her two younger brothers and proceeds to read it:

> One morning last January, I seemed to run out of gas and could not maintain the cover that I have hidden behind for many years. I just unraveled, and there I was lying on the bathroom floor and behaving like a scared little kid. I lost recognition of time, and Walter found me hiding in the closet underneath my clothes, talking like a kid and not understanding any big words. I guess I still am partly a scared little kid. I ended up in Westchester Community Hospital's emergency room, but in the blink of an eye I was back to being a well-poised, middle-aged professional and fooled them quick enough to be able to go home.
>
> On the way home I turned into a mean, vicious, cursing bitch, yelling and screaming and criticizing Walter and Shawn and poor little Chrissie. It was pretty much surreal, and I was terrified that Walter and the kids would now think that they lived with a freak. Or worse, they would call me a liar and think that I was making all of this up. I've been called a liar all my life.
>
> I'm writing this letter for myself, because if I ever want to be healthy and happy again I must be honest about myself and my feelings and about the things that have happened to me. I will not go into any details with you about the incest nor do I ever intend to. It's a private, painful, and very sad affair. But I've confronted the truth and don't have to feel or be told that I'm a troublemaker and a liar anymore. Now I just have to learn to believe that I'm not.
>
> I have what they call dissociative identity disorder. I knew what was wrong with me years ago, but I was ashamed to tell anybody what was going on. Somehow I still held out the faint hope that I was a liar because at that time it was easier to be called a liar than dredge up all these awful memories.
>
> Now maybe that Arizona incident will make sense to you. I had to get out of that apartment, because if I had stayed in that situation I would have switched, and then all of you would've known the secret that I've kept for so, so long.

I'm keenly aware of the hard work that I have ahead of me and afraid that it may eventually exhaust Walter and the children. I'm very angry that I didn't do anything to cause this, yet I have to deal with all the consequences and all the very, very painful and gut-wrenching losses, one of them being the closeness we had. That was one of my true joys.

Two months ago I thought I lost everything as well as my mind. But now things are looking up. I'm gaining a little bit of control and I'm not going to quit this time. I will never have the same view of life or the world again, but at last I know that there's no need for me to hate myself. I am going to try my hardest to feel hope and joy again.

GRAMMY

Nancy loved being in Grammy's house, even on a hot, sticky day like this one. She didn't want to play outside and get all sweaty and thirsty when she could be with Grammy in her kitchen, baking dough and helping her make crab cakes for her big nightclub and restaurant downstairs. Grammy's nightclub was famous. People came there from all over, even movie stars who were in town on their way to somewhere else. Nancy would go into the dining room and hide behind the curtains on the stage and watch Dizzy Gillespie and Buddy Rich play. Sometimes Grammy let Nancy sit under the piano and listen to the music while the grownups danced. At home her mom kept the piano in the cellar and told Nancy, "Go to the basement if you want to practice." That wasn't very nice.

Grammy wasn't like her mom at all. She wouldn't let you get away with anything, but she was always fair. There wasn't one person Nancy ever knew who didn't think highly of her grandmom. The thing is, she never put on any airs. It didn't bother Grammy if she was a little fat. Even though she had good manners, she didn't always use 'em. She wore long pants like Katherine Hepburn in the movies. Grammy was very rich and could've had any fancy thing she wanted, but she gave away more than she ever kept. She didn't care about things; she cared about people.

That's what Nancy could never figure out. Her mom always had to have lots of things even when she was a little girl. Nancy saw a picture of her mom when she was eight or nine in a cute little skating suit that Grammy got her. It had a little white mink ruffle all around her skirt. And her mom's wedding, oh, my God! That was the biggest thing the town ever saw. Her mom didn't go without anything. So what happened to her along the way?

Her mom wasn't nice to people the way Grammy was. One Thanksgiving, when Nancy was in second grade, there was a table at the restaurant set for maybe fifty people. It was so much fun to get ready. Nancy sat down at the table and smelled something bad. She looked at the lady next to her, jumped up from the table, ran over to her grandmother, and whispered in her ear, "Grandmom, that lady over there smells." And Grammy said, "Be thankful you *don't*. That person has nowhere to spend Thanksgiving." Nancy found out later that the lady was somebody Grammy saw in church who looked very sad Thanksgiving morning, and she took her home with her. That was just the way she was. But it drove her mom nuts to think that she had to have someone at the table who wore smelly old clothes and didn't have anywhere else to go. "Oh, pshaw, pshaw!" she said. Nancy thought Grammy was right. What difference did it make as long as the lady was a nice person?

Grammy had ten brothers and sisters, and they all just loved her to death. She married a man who drank too much and was a pain in the butt. He barked at people and cursed all the time. Nancy's grandpa used to be a friend of Legs Diamond, the gangster, and run whiskey from Canada under the lumber trucks—bootleg whiskey, he called it. That's how he made all his money. He would never lay a hand on anyone, but one time he kicked Nancy's grandma in front of her. Nancy went right over to him and kicked him in the knee. She had a frying pan in her hand, and she said, "If you ever kick my grandma again, I'm gonna hit you with this pan!" He never kicked Grammy in front of Nancy anymore.

Nancy was never afraid of her grandpa. He drank too much and had a mean mouth, but he wasn't scary like her dad. He wasn't a break-every-thing-in-the-house kind of drunk. And he thought Nancy was the best little girl in the world. Nancy could chop someone's head off with an ax, and he'd say, "There must've been a reason." Her grandma was the same way.

Grammy's kitchen had a great big fan in it, bigger and taller than Nancy. It had fat gray blades that whirred and whirred and whirred and made a breeze that kept them cool. The honey buns they'd made from Grammy's own secret recipe were already baking in the oven. That sweet, buttery, cinnamon smell was so good that it made Nancy close her eyes and draw it up her nose when she breathed it in. Now Grammy was cooking chopped onions on the stove and pouring egg yolks from the mixer into a great big bowl of crab meat for the crab cakes. She called over her shoulder, "Nancy, bring me that bowl of mayonnaise, will you, sweetie?"

"Sure, Grammy." It made Nancy feel good when Grammy called her names like "Sweetie" and "Dear" and "Honey," not like the "Blab Baby" and "Liar" names her mom called her at home.

Nancy started carrying the bowl of mayonnaise toward Grammy when she lost her balance. She tried as hard as she could to hold on to the bowl, but it dropped out of her hands and hit the table. The mayonnaise flew up in the air and went right into the fan. *Splat! Splat! Splat!* It went everywhere.

"Oh, you naughty girl, you naughty girl," Grammy scolded.

But Nancy wasn't a naughty girl. She didn't do it on purpose. She bit her lip, trying not to cry.

Then Grammy wiped her hands on her apron and got a block of ice cream out of the freezer and cut it with a big knife. *Whack!*

Nancy was so scared. She'd never seen a knife that big.

"Now you go eat some ice cream," Grammy said. "You're not a naughty girl. The mayonnaise was too heavy for you." And she gave Nancy a hug.

Nancy ran off to eat her ice cream, knowing that Grammy still loved her a lot even when she did something bad. She knew that when her dad got mad at her, he still loved her a lot, too. But with her mom, it was different. Her mom didn't like her. Never liked her. Why was that?

Something must have happened for her mother not to like her own daughter. It never made any sense to Nancy at all. How do you match her mom up with a grandmom who was loved by everyone who knew her, who was looked up to by the whole town, who was good and fair to Nancy and loved her with all her heart? It was sort of like a jigsaw puzzle.

GRAMMY'S

We reach a point at which Nancy is talking about going back to work. Her ability to comfort the different parts of herself when she feels threatened has improved dramatically, and the Mean hardly comes out anymore.

"I found a little coffeehouse that I would just love to work in part-time," Nancy tells me. "I'd be making the honey buns and some of the pastries my grandmother taught me how to make. It would give me a focus and get me out of the house. You can't sit in the house every day when you've never done that. What do you think?"

"I think it's great for you to do things that you enjoy and get pleasure from," I tell her enthusiastically, "as long as you don't allow it to become too stressful."

"Oh, not like a steamroller; I'll never do that again," Nancy assures me. "And I don't want to go back to being a physical therapist again; it just isn't me," she says, expressing a newfound sense of her personal identity and her right to express it in her chosen work. "Therapy has given me my life back. Every day I keep asking, 'What do I need to give myself pleasure and joy?' "

Nancy's return to the workplace in her newly chosen field is like one of those meteoric success stories you read about in entrepreneurial magazines. In a short time her signature honey buns and other baked goods doubled her employer's business, and she began to think about striking out on her own. She decided to open a trendy little coffeehouse where she could serve and sell the pastries her grandmother taught her how to make, embellished with her own artistic designs. Always resourceful, she found space in a rundown vacant building virtually rent-free in exchange for rehabbing it. Nancy painted and decorated it herself and turned the shabby storefront into a warm and inviting little restaurant. She named it Grammy's.

After only a year in business Nancy happily reports that Grammy's is turning a profit and is moving to a location twice the size of the first place. Now the rehabbing has started all over again with an anticipated opening date in May, a month away.

"Forgive me for the way I look," Nancy apologizes, pointing to her paint-spattered jeans, when she comes in for her appointment. "I came straight from Grammy's and didn't have time to change."

"You look fine," I assure her. "How's it going?"

"Great!" Nancy says excitedly. "The invitations for the opening came today. I have to tell you that while I was designing them I kept writing out different styles of print in longhand first. The third time I wrote out 'Sunday, May 9,' and looked at it, I suddenly realized for the first time, That's my grandmother's birthday! It's so symbolic. Everything I am and know how to do I learned from my grandmom. I called Walter to tell him, and he said, 'See that? Your grandma is right there, helping you along the way.' "

AFRAID OF THE DARK

Nancy is very worried. It seems that her fears of wearing her family out might be coming to pass. Shawn has tired of "walking on eggshells" around her and has moved out of the house to live in an apartment with two friends. And Walter is depressed. Although he's happy for her success, he feels neglected and makes snide remarks about her cooking for everyone else except him and not entertaining their friends at home anymore. She almost thinks he'd like her to go back to being a martyr again now that the Mom is stronger.

"He's withdrawn and sits by himself in the dark a lot after he comes home from work," Nancy says. "I won't go with him to anyplace where people are drinking heavily, so he's been going out with his friends a couple of nights a week and coming home late with beer on his breath. I hate that smell!"

"Maybe there are other fun things you can do together that don't involve drinking. Have you suggested any?"

"He'd like to go to the movies, but I won't do that," Nancy says emphatically. "I can't go to the movies. It's too dark in there. I can't see if anybody's coming."

The panicky note in her voice catches me by surprise. "When you're with Walter next to you, do you realize you're safe?"

Nancy fidgets in her chair and feels her forehead. "My face is hot," she murmurs. She seems agitated. "My face is hot. Does my face look red to you?" She reaches for a glass of water and gulps it down.

"What are you feeling?" I ask.

"I don't know. My face is hot," she repeats. She cringes and looks terrified.

"Nancy, why are you frightened? Who's feeling frightened at the movies?"

"Me," the Child says, speaking out as Nancy is caught in the grip of uncontrollable fear. *"I don't like to be in the dark. I'm telling you right now. Nossir."*

"What are you afraid might happen?"

"Somebody might get me in the dark. I can't see them coming in the movies. They're coming from the back."

"Did anyone ever get you in the movies before?"

"I don't think so, but in the dark—" The Child's voice trails off. Then she says, *"That's why you can't sleep with your back to a door. You can't ever do that. And you have to sleep on the edge of the bed. And you can't sleep without a blanket tucked inside the bed."* Nancy feels her forehead again. *"I don't like it when my face is hot."*

"What is that related to when your face gets hot?"

"I had a bad thing that I remembered this week, something I never remembered before, and I had a really, really hard time but I didn't get—I mean, I didn't tell anybody, and I think that could be some of what's wrong."

"Do you want to talk about it?"

"I don't want to talk about it, but I think I have to."

"You can talk about it as much or as little as you want, and you can stop at any time. You can realize that talking about your memories isn't the same as being there."

"I know that," the Child says, sounding like a precocious elementary school student. *"Once I talk about it and say it out loud, then I don't have to ball it up in my head."*

She starts to tell me what happened. *"The other night I went to bed before Walter, and I was in my bed, and all of a sudden I was crawling way down to the bottom of the bed. I used to hide at the bottom of the bed a lot. I sleep on the side of the bed closest to the door with my face to the door so I can always see who's coming. But that night I got in the other way. I don't know why—I never do that—and I got so skeered and my heart started going da-dum, da-dum, da-dum because I knew I couldn't see who was coming. I knew something bad was starting to come up in my head, and I didn't like it. Usually I say, 'Go back down!' and I didn't say that. I don't know why. And I was very sad for a long time. And I remembered when I was—"*

The Child hesitates. *"I don't know if I should—"* She pauses, possibly to confer with the other alters or to get her own nerve up. *"Okay, I remembered when we were in our old house,"* she goes on, *"and we had pink bedspreads and I was a little girl. I had feet on my 'jamas, and I was in kindergarten or first or second grade. My dad was a drinking man—I told you about that, I believe, maybe not—and—and"*— it's obvious how hard this is for her to say— *"lots of times he would come up in my room and he would do naughty things. And I didn't remember that until the other day, and that was very hard on my heart to remember that."*

"What kind of things did he do?"

"Not very nice things. I turned over the other way real quick."

"And then what happened?"

"I remembered those things that happened, and that was enough for my head. I just pushed everything back to that dresser drawer in my head and closed the drawer because it was too much for my head all at one time."

"And were you able to go to sleep?"

"Yeah. I said that I know I'm in the house that we made ourselves and that Walter was downstairs watching TV and nobody could get in the house and hurt me now. What happened was a long time ago. I almost called you; that's how scared I was. But it was late. I never called you in the nighttime before. The Mean was saying, 'You better call that doctor. You better call that doctor.' "

"So the Mean was trying to be helpful?"

"I think so, yeah. She came out to protect me. And then the Mom said, 'If I don't feel any better and I can't calm myself down, then I'll call the doctor. I'm not gonna jump the gun.' The Mom was worried. She wasn't sure that any of us could take care of ourselves, but she wasn't going to give up. She just kept telling me nobody could hurt me, and she made me go away quick. She wasn't mean or pushy or bossy about it. She just said, 'I'm coming here, so you don't have to worry about being by yourself.'"

"That's good that she protected you like that," I tell her. "Now you know that you can reach out to her the next time you have anything worrisome and ask for comfort from within yourself again. The more experience you get with this, the more it will become like second nature."

"It scared me that the next day I forgot all about it—I didn't even remember that I remembered," the Child says, describing how frightening amnesia can be. *"That's never happened before. It scared me when it came back into my head today because even though I didn't remember it happening, I really did remember it happening."*

"And what makes you think you remembered it even though you didn't?"

The Child explains the delayed recall of a traumatic memory in this simple, affecting way: *"It's like maybe you went to Disney World when you were a little tiny girl, and maybe you didn't go back for twenty years. You didn't remember going as a tiny little girl, but you somehow knew about it."*

"Something about it felt familiar. Was the feeling of sadness familiar, too?"

"The sad part was remembering that my dad did that," the Child answers. *"I felt that somebody else did me dirty and then lied to me for a long time. That's the bad part. Not even what happened. It's the lie."* Nancy's face contorts, and she begins to cry. *"Anybody can do almost anything, and I'll forgive them, but don't lie to me,"* she sobs. *"Everyone always lied to me. That's what was wrong more than anything else."*

In the stillness of the room punctuated only by the sounds of traffic and an occasional ambulance siren coming from outside, Nancy slowly returns to herself. I tell her how proud I am of her that she was able to comfort herself so effectively when the memory of her father's incest returned after so many years.

"The Sister came back, too," she tells me. "Isn't that amazing? I thought she was dead for sure. She's only come out twice in the whole time I've known her. The first time was when I had the flashback of my grandfather's sexual abuse, and she was like a wild animal, very scary. This time she spoke in a robotic voice without any inflection. She wouldn't talk to me or any of the others inside, only to Walter. She kept saying, 'I know you. I've seen you before.' She's the one who knows everything, but she won't talk to anyone, and nobody talks to her. It's like there's a wall."

As I earlier thought she might, the Sister represents the part of Nancy where all of the sexual abuse memories are buried. The wall is there to protect Nancy from total decompensation should more memories come back at a given time than she can handle.

"It's very significant that you were able to put the memories of your father's sexual abuse back in the 'drawer' in your mind when you felt that they were becoming overwhelming," I tell Nancy. "The fact that they're surfacing now is a sign that you're getting stronger and are better able to deal with them. When you feel up to it, try to communicate more with the Sister and help relieve her from bearing all of those memories alone. Communication and sharing will help bring that wall down so that you can integrate the memories and feelings from the past that are still hidden."

Nancy recalls how much worse it was when she had the first flashbacks of her paternal grandfather's sexual abuse. "I freaked out so badly that Walter called my parents. They believed me right away. My mother even told me that my dad's father tried to *attack her* once when my dad was away, and she had to run out the back door. She admitted to me that he had a reputation for molesting young women." Nancy frowns uncomprehendingly. "So why didn't my mother believe me when I first told her? Why did she say I was lying? Why did she deny it about my father, too?"

"I've found that a parent who has a blind spot toward a child's sexual abuse may have had her own problems growing up," I tell her, "and is unconsciously allowing other problems to reoccur. If she has dissociated her own traumas, she has to block out her child's too, and is unable to hear about it. There are many different reasons people have trouble believing children."

Nancy continues, "There was never any physical or sexual abuse of the children in my grandma's house. She would never tolerate that."

"Then what was your mother's relationship with her own mother like?"

"My mom worshiped her mother, loved her dearly," Nancy replies. "And my grandmom doted on my mother—she was her only daughter. My mom was a figure skater. She was beautiful, absolutely gorgeous. She was the prom queen, and my dad was the prom king. He was the handsome quarterback on the football team. My mom went to college and quit after two months and came home and told my grandmother she was getting married. And that was it."

"But your mother seems to have tremendous unresolved anger from her own childhood," I remark. "Something must have angered her."

Nancy tells me that she has thought about this a lot, and this is her supposition: "When I was born, my grandma shifted all of the attention that she gave my mother to me and never stopped. My mom couldn't stand it. I had much more in common with my grandmother than my mother did, and my mom was very jealous. The other thing was that my mom's family was very wealthy and powerful, and my dad was a roofer's son who didn't have a dime. He made money later, but he was just starting out then. So my mom went from being a privileged only daughter adored by the town to a roofer's way of life and a marriage to a raging alcoholic. She felt that everything had been snatched away from her, and she took it out on me."

So that's the missing piece of the jigsaw puzzle: not nearly as monstrous as sexual abuse, but a precipitous fall from grace that left a gaping hole in her sense of self. "She lost her place in the sun," I remark, "and by shaming you, she tried to make herself feel better."

"But if you ask my mother, she'll tell you that she never did anything wrong," Nancy says bitterly. "She thinks she's been a marvelous *Better Homes and Gardens* mother because she always had a better home and garden. She has no insights."

"Obsessing about her home was her way of coping with issues she didn't want to face," I tell Nancy, "an ineffective way of trying to maintain control. Here was a woman who was emotionally incapable of dealing with her husband's drinking or taking care of her children or protecting her daughter from sexual abuse. By focusing on something superficial and relatively benign, like keeping the house spotless, she was able to distract herself from her deeper problems and appear high-functioning to the rest of the world. Acquiring things was a substitute for the emptiness she may have felt inside."

"Isn't that sad?" Nancy says wistfully. "The nicest thing anyone will ever be able to say about my mother is, 'She had a beautiful home.' "

A NEW VOICE IS HEARD

Nancy has obtained financing for a factory, she tells me proudly, and her baked goods are about to be distributed nationwide. Her star continues to rise now that she has found the perfect outlet for her artistic talents and business acumen inherited from her beloved grandmother. Her relationship with Walter has improved, too. She has faithfully stuck to the plan we worked out for her to take off at least two days a week for pure rest and relaxation and has become more available to Walter for fun they can have together. Even though Shawn has moved out of the house, he still calls her every day, and their relationship is better than ever.

"You've made a tremendous amount of progress in the three years that you've been in treatment," I tell her. "Not only that, you've done wonderful things."

"I've done a lot in a little amount of time," Nancy concedes modestly, "but emotionally charged situations are still difficult for me. If I ran into my mother at a trade show somewhere, I'd be okay—I'd just blow her off. But seeing her at Shawn's graduation from high school this summer might be something I won't be able to handle."

"When the professional side of you—the Wife—is in control, that part has the skills not to let your mother hurt you," I point out. "But in emotionally charged situations another part of you—the Child—is in control and doesn't have those skills. She's just a bundle of emotional memories and is still frightened."

"The Wife has those memories, too," Nancy says, "but they don't weigh her down so much. The professional side of me is able to be more objective, logical, and rational when I react to things."

"So it's not that you can't acquire those skills; it's that you need to have the side of you that has them teach them to the side that doesn't. Then you'll be aware that you don't have to be frightened of your mother in any situation."

Nancy agrees to have further communication and cooperation between the Wife and the Child. Then she tells me about another problem she's been having with a part of herself she calls the Heckler. "It makes fun of me and frightens me, and it's coming more often now that I'm getting better. It's different from the Mean. It's this inner voice saying to me all the time, 'Well, you think you're so wonderful. I'll fix you.' It punishes me with flashbacks of the sexual abuse. I hear that voice, 'I'll fix your ass,' and—bam!—there's a flashback. They're more frequent, more vivid, more clear. It's like watching a rerun. Why is there a part of me that wants to punish me?"

"But you're stronger now and can handle the flashbacks, right?"

"Yes, I have enough control over them not to let them push me over the edge again, the way the first one did. They're not comfortable, but they're not frightening anymore. Even the Sister's not frightened of them. It's a brief intrusion in my day, over in seconds or minutes. But I still can't understand why some part of me has to kick me back down a step. It's a demeaning, degrading kind of feeling."

"You've always had that part, haven't you?"

"I have," Nancy admits. "Anything I ever did that I felt was pretty spectacular, I was convinced that I didn't do it. Now I've finally gotten to the point where I can own the good things about myself, so then the derogatory part comes in. I know it's very much like my mother, but why would I develop an alter like that if a dissociative disorder is a protective device?"

"This part of you is there to maintain the misperception that you're no good and don't deserve to be happy because that's something you learned," I answer. "That part of you is identified with what you were taught."

"My mother literally hit me in the head with hairbrushes all the time," Nancy reveals. "Now the Heckler is doing that in a way, too."

"That's what you're familiar with. You learned that people who are supposed to love you punish and demean you."

"And that there was always an ulterior motive and that they really *didn't* love you," Nancy adds.

"How much longer do you have to allow that part of you to maintain these misperceptions that you've been taught?" I ask. "Perhaps the Heckler could talk to me about why she's always giving you a hard time. Is that the only way she knows how to express herself?"

"There's no other way. All that part knows how to say to me is that I'm a lazy good-for-nothing and full of shit." Nancy's becoming vehement. "I'm sick of it! I want it to stop! I want it to go!"

"Try having conversations with that part or writing a letter to her or having some of the other parts of you counter these negative things that you were always told and let that part know that they're wrong."

Suddenly a voice I have never before heard from Nancy speaks up. It's the Heckler, a sullen adolescent girl with a truculent "show me" attitude.

"How do you know they were wrong?" she scoffs. *"You weren't there. You don't know."*

"Because I've heard what Nancy told me," I reply, "and I know that as a child she was trying her hardest and her best to please her mom. You were told things that are untrue. You're not a bad person, and you no longer have to make Nancy feel as if she's bad."

"Why?" the Heckler demands to know. *"Why? Why?"*

"Because she's worked really hard to be good, but her mom wasn't able to appreciate her because of her own problems. But now you can begin to acknowledge how good and how talented Nancy is and what a good person she was back then even though her mom couldn't appreciate her."

"*I know Nancy's not a liar, but that's the only thing I know that's not true,*" the Heckler allows, sounding less confrontational but not entirely convinced. "*Nancy got punished a lot. She would stand in the dining room, and her mom would scream at her, 'You lazy good-for-nothing little bitch' and slap her face hard over and over, and that's when I would come.*"

"Nancy did nothing to deserve that. It's time to correct—"

A loud, distraught voice interrupts me, shouting, "*I want to go home now! I'm uncomfortable now!*" It's the Child calling out in fear. "*That girl never talks. She never talks to anybody but me. I don't know why she talked to you. She just left.*"

"Maybe she's trying to get therapy," I suggest. "It's okay. It's fine."

"*Was she nice to you? Did she swear at you?*" the Child asks anxiously. Since amnesia in DID functions to separate or distinguish the personalities, the Child is aware only that the Heckler spoke, but has no memory of what she said. "*She didn't swear at you, right? She swears at me.*"

"No, she didn't swear at me."

"*I only heard her talk inside my head. I never heard her talk outside. That was a scary thing. I feel like I'm sweating now.*" Nancy holds her head, overwhelmed by the fright and shame of having an alter known only to oneself come out publicly for the first time. "*Oooh, oooh, it's like vacuuming in my head.*"

"Take some nice deep breaths."

In a moment Nancy is back to herself. She looks at me questioningly. "What happened?"

I fill Nancy in on what took place during the time gap that often occurs while an alter is out. "You should continue to have conversations with the Heckler alone or in therapy," I tell her, "and try to have all the parts of you work together to give you positive feedback so that you won't accept these critical thoughts any longer."

"That takes a lot of energy."

"I know, but you've made solid progress, and you're not going to go backward," I assure her. "It's like learning to swim. First you learn how to breathe with your head in the water, then you learn how to move your arms, then you learn how to move your legs, and then suddenly one day it all comes together."

Nancy's proficiency at comforting her separate parts and having them work together has reached a desirable point. No curve ball that gets thrown at her in life is likely to shove her all the way down to that place on the bathroom floor where she lost control completely. The skills she has acquired will continue to propel her forward, but rapid progress in therapy is not without its speed bumps.

"I got angry at Walter and Chris last week because they still hadn't taken the Christmas tree lights off out front, but I was not mean," she reports proudly. "I was just, 'Hello, it's March, I'm not doing it, and I don't want to be looking at those lights a week from now.' " She goes on, "That punitive voice inside me still goes full tilt sometimes, but the rational part of me refutes it, so it doesn't get me down as much as before. The only time I get panicky now, ever, is when I go to Shawn's hockey games. I can't stay longer than a period. I have to run out of that building. It's overwhelming."

"That started when your brother Rory stopped talking to you," I observe, "but you're on speaking terms with him now, aren't you?"

"Yes, but when I go to a game, it's Shawn I keep thinking about," Nancy replies, "and how he left home too soon." Her voice breaking, she says, "It wasn't supposed to end this way. We miss him terribly."

"But he hasn't really left; he keeps in touch every day," I remind her. "Maybe he felt he needed to do this for his own independence."

"He's doing very well on his own, working part-time to support himself, but he gets terrible marks in school, and I feel responsible for that."

"You shouldn't," I counter. "Living with someone who has DID can be difficult, but you have a tendency to personalize things. I think you're blaming yourself for Shawn's academic difficulties more than you should."

"Last weekend I couldn't bring myself to go to his hockey game, and I was disappointed that I didn't have more control," Nancy recounts. "Shawn was supposed to receive a trophy for most valuable player, and Walter said, 'Would you just come for me? I don't want to go alone.' And I still couldn't do it. Then I thought, I have to do this for Shawn. It took enormous physical energy, but I just put one foot in front of the other and got myself there. And I'm so glad I did."

"It went well?"

Nancy smiles, remembering the event. "All of the moms recognized me when I walked in and presented me with a lovely bouquet of roses for Shawn. After the game he gave me a big hug and said, 'Mom, I love you with all my heart.' And I said, 'I know you do, Shawn.' It was very important for both of us."

"That was a big step for you to get yourself there and stay in control of your memories and emotions so well."

"It was," Nancy agrees. "I went to bed that night bone tired, and I thought, Why did I have to go through such an exhausting struggle to do something that should have been a pleasure for me? It didn't seem fair. But getting through that struggle also showed me that I've made a lot of progress." Tears well up in Nancy's eyes—tears of gratitude. "I'm traveling a hard road," she says softly, "but look how far I've come."

12

~

LINDA A.: WOUNDED PASSION

Under Arrest

Later she would remember that Jennifer Lopez's "If You Had My Love" was playing on her car radio on that cold, clear winter night when she went to pick up Julie, her seven-year-old daughter, at a friend's house. The brilliantly sunny day after a heavy snow had left the narrow, hilly road slick with ice and the side of the road piled high with snowy embankments starting to freeze over.

Linda noticed that a state trooper had been following her fairly closely in his cruiser for a mile or so, but his flashing lights weren't on, so she thought nothing of it. Her eyes were fixed on a slippery patch of glare ice glinting ahead of her. She tried to navigate it carefully, but the wheels of her red Saturn spun around and made her veer to the right into an embankment. Now the trooper was parked right behind her, and his flashing lights were on, casting rotating red and blue shadows on her dashboard. Through her rear-view mirror, she watched him get out of his cruiser and walk over to her car.

"Evening, ma'am, where're you headed?" the officer asked.

He seemed pleasant enough, although Linda sensed a certain cockiness about him. Even with his wide-brimmed hat partially obscuring his face, he looked young, no more than twenty-five, she guessed.

"I'm going to pick up my daughter about five minutes from here," Linda said.

"Have you had any alcohol tonight?"

The question caught Linda off guard. She'd never been drunk in her life. "Yes, I had a glass of wine with dinner," she replied. "That was about an hour ago."

"Let me see your license and registration."

"Sure." Linda was beginning to feel worried. Had she done anything wrong? She fished through her handbag for her wallet, pulled out her license and registration, and handed them to him.

The trooper shone a flashlight on her license photo card and saw the name Linda Alvarez under the picture of the pretty thirty-three-year-old woman with the big, luminous brown eyes; creamy olive skin; blondish brown hair; and full, sensuous lips.

"I didn't know that there were any spics living around here," the trooper snickered as he read Linda's name.

Linda bristled, but she kept her composure. In her work as a teacher of emotionally disturbed children she was used to kids' calling each other names, but she didn't expect that kind of racial epithet from a police officer. Still, she thought it best to ignore the slur rather than stir up trouble.

"Step out of the car," the officer said brusquely. The veneer of politeness was gone.

Even before she was out of the car, the trooper asked Linda to recite the alphabet, starting with the letter G. It occurred to her that starting with G instead of A was supposed to rattle someone who was already disoriented from having too much to drink.

She recited the alphabet and got out of the car.

"Take your coat off," the officer said.

Linda hesitated. She thought that was a strange request. Did he think she was carrying a concealed gun? Was he going to frisk her?

"Take it off," the officer said testily.

She was wearing a heavy ankle-length suede coat with a sheepskin lining—warm and protective. Linda was loath to take off the coat in such cold weather, but she complied.

"Okay, now I want you to do a heel-to-toe," the officer said.

"What's that?"

The officer did a few steps, demonstrating how he wanted her to walk, alternating between the heel and toe of each foot.

"I'm cold," Linda complained, shivering. "Could you please give me my coat back first?"

"Uh-uh," the officer said, shaking his head. "Do the heel-to-toe."

Linda took a few steps, but she realized that they would be going down a steep, slippery hill. "Could we do it up the hill?" she asked.

"Okay, turn around and do it."

He watched while Linda took a couple of tentative, rocky heel-to-toe steps, struggling to keep her balance on the icy road.

Unexpectedly the trooper reached out and grabbed Linda by the arm.

"What are you doing?" Linda exclaimed shrilly. It terrified her to be alone with a strange man on a deserted road at night even if he was a police officer. First he made her take her coat off. Now he was grabbing her arm. What next?

"You're under arrest," the trooper told her. He took out a pair of handcuffs and pulled her along to the front of the cruiser.

Linda came unglued. Unstoppably a flood tide of rage, fear, and indignation surged through her and deluged her with uncontrollable panic. "Get your hands off me!" she screamed. "Let me go! Under arrest? What for?" Like a trapped animal, she tried to wrest herself free of the trooper and began crying hysterically.

The officer said nothing. Poker-faced, he grabbed Linda by the neck and pushed her facedown onto the hood of the cruiser. She felt something stab her in the neck and saw blood dripping onto the front of her sweater. She knew the officer was about to handcuff her behind her back.

"No! Stop it!" Linda screamed wildly. "Leave me alone! You can't do this to me!" She lifted herself off the car and fell backward against the trooper.

"You're resisting arrest!" he told her sharply and radioed for a backup.

Within minutes another officer was there. "Looks like you have your hands full," he said when he saw the frenzied state Linda was in.

"We gotta put her down," the first officer told him. Together the two men pushed Linda down onto the icy snow of the embankment. "Please don't handcuff me," Linda pleaded. "Don't handcuff me. Please! If you have to handcuff me, do it in the front where I can see you, not the back."

They ignored her pleas. Linda heard a metallic click and felt the handcuffs pressing rudely into her spine with a rigid finality.

The first trooper opened the door to the back seat of the cruiser, made Linda get in, and slammed the door shut. Linda began kicking the window repeatedly, trying to get out.

The officer opened the door. "If you don't stop it," he warned her, "I'm gonna Mace you!" He went to get her coat lying on the ground beside her car, carried the coat back, and threw it on top of her. Then he shut the door and got in the front seat to drive Linda to the police barracks with the second officer following them in his car.

Linda lay down on her side. She couldn't stop screaming and crying. The utter helplessness of riding in this car alone with this man with her hands handcuffed behind her back reduced her to feeling like a terrified child. She began praying in Spanish as she used to when she was a little girl and her mother took her to a Latino church on Sundays in Philadelphia, where she grew up. She thought she had forgotten those prayers, but they came to her lips automatically.

When they got to the state police barracks, the trooper took her inside and took her to a room with a long table and some chairs.

"Can I make a phone call?" Linda asked. "I need to call Ted, my fiancé, and tell him where I am. My seven-year-old daughter is waiting for me at her friend's house. She'll be frightened if nobody comes for her."

"You're not going to get a call," the officer told her. "We're not going to let you get cute with anybody."

"But I need to call my fiancé. Let him at least know I'm here," Linda begged. "I'm entitled to a phone call."

"Forget it," the officer said stolidly.

Linda's coat pockets had been emptied of their contents, and there were a few ballpoint pens lying on the table. The officer unlocked Linda's handcuffs, picked up one of the pens, and told her to sign some papers.

The powerlessness she felt enraged Linda again. "I'm not going to do it!" she yelled. She grabbed one of the pens and began banging the table with it, hammering the table with the pen over and over again, like a four-year-old having a screaming temper tantrum, all the while yelling, "I'm not gonna do it; I'm not gonna do it! I'm not gonna do it until my fiancé knows where I am!"

Without another word the officer dragged Linda over to an iron ring bolted into the wall and attached her to it by one of her handcuffs, hanging her from it like a side of beef in a butcher shop. Then he sprayed Mace in her face.

The Mace stung her eyes viciously, and she could feel mucus dripping down the back of her throat. She crumpled against the wall, blinded and dazed. "Could I have some water, please?" she asked.

"What for?" the officer asked snidely. "You want to drown somebody with it?"

Another officer appeared on the scene. She couldn't see him, but Linda heard him asking her whether she wanted some wet napkins to soothe the irritation in her eyes. He sounded kind.

"Yes, please," she told him, and he kept handing her the napkins for her eyes.

Finally, the trooper who had arrested her asked, "What's your fiancé's phone number?"

Linda gave it to him, and he called Ted.

In less than an hour Ted arrived at the police barracks with Linda's daughter, Julie. He'd gone to her friend's house first and had to wake her up to take her with him. Ted asked for Linda and was told that she wasn't there yet; that they were still in the process of transporting her.

When Linda heard Ted's voice and realized that they weren't allowing him to see her, she started screaming hysterically again. The trooper who had arrested her closed the door to the room.

"Let me go to her," Ted said. "I know her. Once I'm there, she'll be okay."

"Let her calm down," the trooper said.

When Ted was finally allowed into the room, he found Linda lying on the floor in a fetal position. "My God, what have they done to you?" he asked as he got down beside her and helped her to her feet. He confronted the trooper, eyes blazing, silently demanding an explanation.

The trooper regarded Ted closely, taking the measure of this man with the trim body of a marathon runner and Irish good looks—clean features, wavy auburn hair. He could tell that this was an intelligent guy, a nice guy maybe, but one who knew the score. "It's a good thing we wear these," the trooper said, pointing to his bulletproof vest. "She tried to stab me in the chest with that broken pen over there."

Linda knew that wasn't true. If she'd hurt the officer at all, it certainly hadn't been intentional. But she wasn't about to argue with him. All she wanted to do was to get out of that place as quickly as possible and leave this nightmare behind her.

"Why did you arrest her?" Ted asked.

"OUI—operating under the influence."

"Did you do a Breathalyzer test?"

"No, she refused one," the trooper said. "She was doing sixty-five miles an hour in a thirty-five-mile-an-hour zone and swerving in and out until she plowed into an embankment. I was going westbound, and she was coming eastbound, and I clocked her with my radar gun. She resisted arrest and cursed me and used obscene language. She said plenty more in Spanish that I didn't understand. And after we got her here, like I said, she assaulted me with the sharp edge of a broken pen."

Lies, lies, lies, Linda thought angrily. He was building the case against her bigger than it was because he wanted to destroy her credibility if she ever reported that he'd called her a "spic." But she had to admit that there were some parts of the incident that she couldn't remember—she might have blanked out here and there.

"If you were going in one direction, and she was going in the other," Ted began, "how were you able to make a turn, grab your radar gun, and—"

"Honey, let's wait for my day in court," Linda cut in, tugging at Ted's sleeve. She'd had enough of tangling with this trooper for one night. "They towed my car, so I'm going home with you and Julie. Let's leave, okay?"

When Linda walked out with Ted into the reception area, Julie was devastated by the way her mother looked—the swollen red eyes, the bloody neck, the hair matted from lying in the snow, the disheveled clothes.

"Did they hurt you, Mommy?" Julie asked, running to her mother.

Linda stooped down and hugged and kissed her. "No, it's okay," she said. But it wasn't.

"Don't Touch Me"

"I felt so violated, so attacked, and so ashamed to have been arrested in that way," Linda tells me when she comes in for her first visit, looking ultrafeminine and professional at the same time in a soft charcoal gray wool jersey dress and a leather belt with a decorative buckle accentuating her narrow waist. "For a week I was in shock," she says. "I just limboed around, saying, 'I can't believe this happened.' It felt like a really bad dream. And then it hit me that it *did* happen. And I am just so totally paranoid from this thing. All I do is think and think and think and think about that night and relive the moment. I live in fear of that officer coming after me and hurting me to keep me quiet. My panic attacks have gotten so bad that I think I might have to be hospitalized at some point. That's why I'm here."

"Have you ever had panic attacks like this before?" I ask.

"Oh, yes, I started having them when I was in my late teens," Linda replies. "I became agoraphobic for a while after that and was afraid to leave the house. I've been in therapy on and off for the past five years."

"Are you seeing anyone now?"

"No, it's been about a year since I stopped therapy, but I'm still on medication for my anxiety."

She shows me the pills she's taking, and the dosage seems appropriate. "When you get these panic attacks," I ask, "what exactly are you feeling?"

"I had one about four o'clock this morning that was so intense it woke me up from my sleep. It started with chest pains that went down my arm. My heart was beating fast. My hands were sweaty. My face was flushed, and I felt dizzy. I thought I was having a heart attack. My fiancé woke up and asked, 'What's wrong?' We've been living together for six months, but we've known each other for two years and he's very attuned to me. I almost felt like saying, 'Ted, call an ambulance.' "

"But you didn't?"

"No. I knew from experience that this would probably last only about twenty minutes. I asked Ted to use some guided imagery to put me back to sleep. We do a lot of sailing on his boat in the summer, so he started talking about sailing and being out in the calm ocean and the gentle rocking of the boat and feeling at peace. I closed my eyes, and eventually I felt a little better. But I'm afraid that's not going to work anymore."

"Why not?"

"I'm under too much stress. They suspended my driver's license, and that means I have to drive without a license to go to work. I'm terrified of being stopped again. That officer charged me with assault and battery. I went to court the next day and got out on a twenty-five-dollar bail. They could throw me in jail if I get stopped this time. In retrospect I think, 'Why did you have to overreact like that? Why couldn't you have gone quietly, yada, yada, yada?' But then I tell myself, 'You can't think about those things. It's a done deal.' "

"When can you get your license back?"

"It's been suspended for 120 days—they have a right to do that if you refuse a Breathalyzer test," Linda tells me, "although I don't remember refusing one. Ted took some pictures the night of the arrest, and the prosecutor was taken aback when my lawyer showed them to her. She agreed to meet with my lawyer in a couple of weeks to discuss the situation."

"Ted sounds very supportive."

"He *is!*" Linda says feelingly. "He's one of the best men that I've had in my life. When I got cleaned up I realized that the cut on my neck came from one of the earrings Ted gave me for Valentine's Day. I was wearing them that night, and this one was missing. It was a beautiful Florentine gold heart with a diamond in the middle. I felt it dig into my neck when the officer grabbed me and pushed me down on the hood of his cruiser. It must have fallen off some time after that. I started crying because that earring meant so much to me and I wanted it back."

"I can understand why."

"The next day we took my daughter with us and went to the embankment where they threw me down," Linda continues. "Even though it was dark I knew the exact spot. My body print was still in the ice on top of the embankment. We kept looking for the earring, but we couldn't find it. I gave up and said, 'It's not here. Maybe somebody walked by and found it.' Ted said a little prayer for it to turn up. And as soon as he started praying, he found the earring. He said, 'Oh, my God. Here it is!' It was bent, but we got it fixed."

"You were lucky."

"Ted and I were supposed to get married this August when we're both on vacation," Linda says. She speaks glowingly of her fiancé. "Ted recently took a job as an administrator in the mental health system. He went from counseling to administration because he wants to provide a better life-style for me and Julie. He's such a caring person. He cooks dinner and has it waiting for me on the nights when I come home late from work. And he keeps telling me how much he loves me and that I'm more beautiful now than when he first met me." Linda bites her lip and seems on the verge of tears. "But I don't know—I—I asked Ted to postpone the wedding for a year," she stammers.

"Why? What's wrong?"

"I think that maybe we should take a little break from each other for a while. Ted gets very upset when I say that and starts to cry. It makes me feel awful."

"Why do you think you need some time apart?"

"It's hard for me to be intimate with him now," Linda says in a low voice, looking away in embarrassment. "I just don't want Ted to touch me," she continues. "I get very angry when he touches me. He's having a hard time because we're not intimate, and I don't know what to do."

"How long has this been going on?"

"About a month," Linda says tearfully. "It started right after the police incident. I guess I'm still raw around the edges. Ted can touch me, and I get angry. Or he can touch me, and I don't feel it. I don't know if I just shut down or what. I just don't feel connected with him or to myself. I have a numb feeling inside of not desiring, not wanting to be close, not wanting to be touched."

"Earlier in your relationship were there times when he touched you and you didn't feel angry and you were responsive?"

"In the beginning it was fine," Linda says. "But after the police incident, I started setting boundaries: 'Please don't touch my breasts in the middle of the night. Please don't touch me in the morning when you wake up.' I felt I had to control the situation. Now I think I've shut myself down completely. I don't even give him a chance. I mean, Ted has his needs; and early in the morning the first thing he does is hug me, and I can feel his erection, and I—I just can't stand it. Instead of feeling flattered I get very angry, filled with rage. I don't say anything to him because I don't want to hurt him."

"So you detach yourself and don't feel anything?"

"I try to work myself up and think of all the good things about this man, not connect him to anything else just because he has a penis. It doesn't work." Linda begins to cry softly, confused and torn apart by a deep contradiction within herself. "More and more I keep saying, 'Oh, God, I have to move out and be on my own. But I'm fighting it. I don't understand myself sometimes. I love Ted and want to make a life with him. It's like—everything I've always dreamed of, but I just never imagined—I mean, I thought I could *never* get anybody like that. And I *do* have somebody like that. I have somebody who's a good man and wants to be with me and doesn't want anybody else and has a master's degree and a wonderful job and wants to help me raise my child in a beautiful home and take me sailing and go to the finest restaurants and—and I'm pushing him away."

I wonder whether this trouble with intimacy is a pattern with Linda or whether it's peculiar to her relationship with Ted. "Have you ever had this trouble with men before?" I ask.

"I think I've always mistrusted men," Linda says, "and at the same time I never expected much from them. My standards were very low. Before Ted, the men I became involved with were all needy people who depended on me to take care of them. I was drawn to men who were not very aggressive—not pushy with me, but not ambitious either. They all took advantage of me in one way or another and tore me down."

"Was that what happened with your husband?"

"Rafael, my husband, was kind and gentle and patient with me, like Ted," Linda answers, "but he used me. He was an artist who didn't earn very much, and I had to support us on my salary. That would've been okay if he didn't spend most of the money on drugs. He died in a motorcycle accident when Julie was only three."

"How did you cope with that?"

"I just closed down and went into a shell," Linda answers. "I don't know what it is. It seems so surreal, this mechanism within me that clicks in and says, 'You've had enough, and this is as far as you're gonna go.' It's something that protects me." Linda goes on in a tremulous voice, "Two years after my husband died I met Ted. And now I'm shutting down with *him,* and he hasn't done anything to deserve it." She looks at me searchingly. "Why? What's wrong with me?"

It's obvious to me that Linda's protective mechanism of "shutting down" is a form of depersonalization related to posttraumatic stress. This dissociative symptom is the mechanism that "clicked in" when she couldn't deal with her husband's death. Now she is experiencing it again in the wake of her unseemly arrest. The detachment from her fiancé and from herself when he touches her, the sense of emptiness inside, the surreal feeling of living inside a shell that she speaks of are all common descriptions of depersonalization.

Apparently the police officer's treatment of Linda triggered emotional memories laden with rage and fear that, in turn, are being triggered irrationally by her fiancé's loving advances. But what was it that caused her to react with such inordinate terror and rage when the trooper first grabbed her by the shoulder? Why did she become hysterical when he wanted to handcuff her behind her back? What made the ride in the cruiser alone with this man so terrifying that she regressed into reciting her childhood prayers? It seems to me that the arrest flipped her back into some malevolent, horrifying event in her youth. What was it?

"The police incident seems to be affecting your relationship with Ted," I tell Linda, "and may have stirred up thoughts and feelings related to some past event."

Linda nods understandingly.

"Can you see any connection between the rageful feelings you had toward the police officer and that you now have with Ted," I ask her, "and something that happened to you earlier in your life?"

"Yes, I can," Linda says quietly. "It happened when I was fourteen years old."

At Knife Point

Linda's mother was adamant. She was not going to allow her fourteen-year-old daughter to go visit her boyfriend, Miguel, at his house that night. "You just saw him last night," Consuela said. "Why do you have to go see him again tonight?"

"I just wanna see him," Linda said. Why couldn't her mother trust her? This was just going to be a friendly visit. She was a good girl, a virgin, and she wasn't going to do anything to get herself in trouble.

"Mama, it's New Year's Day," Linda said, trying to be persuasive. "It's a holiday. I know I was out with him last night, but I came home early, didn't I? He's not expecting me. I just want to surprise him and say, 'Happy New Year.' "

"Talk to him on the phone," Consuela said.

"Oh, Mama, it's not the same thing," Linda remonstrated. "It's only seven o'clock. I'll be home by nine." She looked beseechingly at her mother. "Can't I go?" she begged. "Please, Mama, please."

But Consuela wouldn't hear of it. She was a deeply religious woman who knew the trouble young girls Linda's age could get into when they started going out with boys. No daughter of hers was going to get pregnant by some teenage boy and have to drop out of school in the ninth grade. Miguel was a decent boy, but he lived close to the projects. It was a dangerous neighborhood. She'd heard about the drug dealing going on there and the night shootings that rang out like the backfirings of cars.

"No, Linda, I don't want you going to Miguel's," Consuela said firmly. "It's not good to be in that neighborhood when it's dark out. It's not safe. I want you to stay home tonight." She saw the crestfallen look on Linda's face and relented. "Look, if you want to go out tonight, go see your friend Annina up the street. Just make sure you're back by nine. Tomorrow is a school day."

"Okay, I'll go see Annina," Linda said, grateful for the compromise. Anything to get out of the house. Ever since her parents got divorced when Linda was nine, religion had become her mother's whole life. Linda missed her father so much. She was heartbroken when he remarried and moved away to teach music at a college in Miami. She'd be starting high school next year—at the school where he used to teach—and he wouldn't be there. Linda's mother was determined to raise her children right even without a father, but the home once overflowing with laughter and warmth and Latino music was now as solemn and cheerless as a rectory.

It was raw outside, bitter cold with the feel of oncoming snow. The wind whipped Linda's face and sent discarded candy wrappers and cigarette butts scudding across the pavement. The red and green Christmas streamers strung between the light poles swayed in the wind, too. Linda started out toward Annina's house, but midway up the street the thought occurred to her that no one would be the wiser if instead she went to Miguel's, a couple of miles away. As long as she was home in time, her mother would have no reason to call her at Annina's. And just to be safe, as soon as she got to Miguel's she would call Annina herself and tell her to cover for her in case her mother needed to reach her there.

Linda continued walking toward Annina's house, but instead of going up the steps to her home she walked to the corner of the street and turned left toward the twelve-story projects looming up in the distance. She went down narrow streets crowded with row houses and entered a section that was beginning to show signs of deterioration. She passed an empty playground littered with rubble. On the corner there was an abandoned boarded-up factory.

Turning the corner, she passed an empty, run-down garage next to a small building with a cyclone fence around it. Then more blocks of row houses. The streets were deserted, and that was fine with Linda. She couldn't wait to get to Miguel's. Defying her mother gave her a tingly feeling of nervous excitement—it was something obedient, responsible Linda rarely did.

She rounded another corner and walked past the projects. Next came a lonely little stretch of ground, a vacant lot. Miguel's house was only a few minutes away. Linda quickened her pace, her head down against the wind. Out of the corner of her eye, she spotted a lone car parked on the lot. It was a black car, and a man was standing next to it—a large African American man who looked to be in his forties. What was he doing there? Linda wondered. Was he waiting for someone? *For her?*

Linda could hear her heart begin to pound loudly against the wall of her chest. Don't look at him, she told herself. Just keep going and you'll be okay.

"Miss, do you have a match?" the man asked as she drew near him.

"No," she said, and kept on walking.

Linda felt a sharp pain as the man's fingers closed around her arm with an iron grip. She twisted around and froze when she saw the long, sharp knife in his other hand gleaming evilly at her.

"Unh—unh—" Linda tried to scream, but the sound died in her throat.

"Get in the car," the man said, pushing her into the back seat. "I'm not gonna hurt you; I'm not gonna hurt you," he kept telling her, trying to make her feel safe even as he brandished his knife. "All I want you to do is make a telephone call to my wife's sister," he said incredibly, "and all I'm doing is, I'm trying to find a telephone booth."

But they never got to a telephone booth. The man drove and drove and drove. Linda lay down on her side in the back seat of the car, frozen with terror, her mind fixated on the knife that was never far from the man's side.

Finally he drove down a street of row houses, and at the fourth house on the right-hand side—Linda was counting—he pulled into the driveway and entered the garage. Standing behind her with the knife at her back, he led Linda up two flights of steps to the third floor of what she guessed was a duplex. They entered a small one-bedroom apartment, very clean, well-furnished, with homey accents showing a woman's touch. The family photographs made it obvious that the man was married. His wife was probably out of town for the holidays, Linda surmised.

A telephone on a table in the living room caught Linda's eye. She was trying to commit the number to memory, hoping she'd be able to report the man, but he told her to go into the bedroom and get undressed. He followed her into the bedroom, slammed the knife down on top of the dresser just to remind her, and left.

Linda was still dressed when the man returned. She was sitting on the bed, immobilized with fear. He walked over to her and pushed her down on the bed with his hand. Then he took her jeans off, pulled down her panties, and raped her. The pain was unbearable, unlike anything Linda had ever experienced in her young life, but she neither struggled nor cried out. She was in shock. This big, powerfully built man was relentlessly, ruthlessly thrusting himself inside her again and again like a promethean machine while she lay there, an automaton, numbly allowing it. All that was going through her mind was "God, please let me get out of this alive."

When he was through, he left Linda alone to get dressed. Dazed, she washed herself off in the bathroom, put her clothes back on, and went out into the living room. The man told her he would drive her wherever she wanted to go.

In the car he tried to talk to her, but Linda pretended that she spoke only Spanish. If he knew she spoke English, she thought, he would have to kill her to prevent her from reporting him to the police. So many horrible things happened in the city that you heard about all the time, and she didn't want to be one of those statistics.

"Just tell me where I can drive you to—at least a side street," the man said.

Linda gave him the name of the street where Miguel lived and had him drop her off at the end of the block where no one would see her get out of the car.

"God bless you," the man said as she left, and he handed her a ten-dollar bill.

You pig, how could you mention God's name? Linda thought. She tore up the bill and threw the pieces into the gutter before she went to her boyfriend's house to wish him a happy new year.

"He stole my soul, but he let me live," Linda says of her rapist when she has finished telling me her story, "and sometimes I wonder, 'What's worse?' "

"When you went to your boyfriend's house, did you say anything about what happened?"

"Nothing," Linda answers. "I stayed there a little while, and then he walked me home."

"After you got home, did you tell your mother about it?"

"No. I felt that I deserved it, because I had defied my mother. I was supposed to be at a friend's house, but I went to my boyfriend's instead. My mom was very religious. She instilled in us that when you do bad things, bad things happen to you. The Devil gets you. I don't believe in all that now, but that's the way I was brought up. To this day I carry a sense of guilt—you know, if I'd gone to my friend's house, this wouldn't have happened."

"So you didn't tell anyone about the rape at all?"

"I would talk to people as though it happened to somebody else," Linda says. "I'd say to my teenage friends, 'You're not gonna believe what happened to this girl I know.' I'd make up a fictitious name, and then I'd tell them the whole story. And they'd gasp and say, 'My God!' And I'd say, 'Yeah, she coulda got killed! He had a knife!' I was too ashamed to admit that it happened to me," Linda explains, "but talking about it in the third person helped a little. At least I got some vicarious sympathy."

"When was the first time you spoke of it as something that happened to you?"

"About four years ago. I told my friend Nora because I just felt the need. Nora has a degree in psychology, and I felt safe talking about it with her. She was very supportive. She referred me to a women's center where I did group therapy for about twelve weeks. It was a positive experience. After that I was able to talk to my mother about the rape, and she was understanding."

"What about Ted? Have you talked to him about it?"

"I've been very open with Ted about it, more so than with anybody else. He's been unbelievably supportive—very sensitive and very angry, too. He's cried with me about it, and then he'll say, 'How could someone do that? How could the world be so ugly?' Now I feel as if I'm kicking him in the butt. I share all this with him, and then I say, 'Now keep away from me. Don't touch me.' "

"How do you feel when you say, 'Don't touch me'?"

"Childish. Very childish. Not like a full-fledged woman."

"What effect do you think the rape has had on you?"

"I think I've suffered depression ever since then, even though I couldn't acknowledge it or voice it," Linda answers. "I started having these black moods where everything seemed so dark and gray even though it was sunny outside. For the most part, though, I kept what happened under the rug and didn't really think about it until I became an adult. Then I had a revelation like, 'Wow! This was really a violation! This was a really awful thing that happened to you! You've never told anybody; you've never dealt with it; you've lived this lie!' That's when I told Nora."

"And did your panic attacks and anxiety start after the rape?"

"Yes, in high school," Linda replies. "I always felt that there wasn't a hole big enough for me to crawl into. Sometimes I would go into the closet and hide, because the world seemed so big. It was really scary to me. I decided that I had to get out of Philadelphia and go to college some-where else. I chose the Massachusetts area, because my uncle was getting his doctorate at Boston University and invited me to stay with him and his family while I went to school."

Linda recalls how her fear of being attacked made college a nightmare for her: "It was horrible with all those other students all over the place. I'd be walking through the campus and see students—strangers—everywhere and think, 'Oh, my God, how am I gonna do this? I can't do this. I've gotta get home.' And I just stuck it out, stuck it out, stuck it out. I wanted my degree, and I made up my mind that I wasn't going to let this thing get the best of me."

"When you got married, did the anxiety and panic attacks persist?"

"They got worse," Linda says. "I would go grocery shopping and leave the grocery cart in the middle of a long aisle and have to go back later because I thought everybody was staring at me. I'd be in line at the bank, and my heart would start beating so hard that I thought it would just come out. If I was driving the car and got stuck in the middle of traffic, I had to close my eyes and listen to soothing music and start saying affir-mations to keep myself from going berserk. It was just this awful feeling. Unbelievable. I thought that I was going crazy—losing my mind."

Linda shakes her head at a recollection that would be comical if it weren't so painful. "I remember one day when Julie was a few months old, and she was sleeping with her arm tucked under her. I could only see one arm, and in my mind, she didn't have an arm. And I freaked out. I thought that her arm came off or something. I didn't dare look, just felt to see whether her arm was still there. Things like that would start an incredible panic attack, and that went on for several years. It got so bad that I was afraid to go out of the house."

"How did your husband react to that?"

"My mother told him that I had these *attaques de nervos*—her expression for panic attacks—and he accepted it," Linda says. "When we were first married and we'd go to Philadelphia to see my mother, Rafael would be driving, and I'd be in the back seat, lying down. I was always afraid that something inside me was going to tell me to jump out of the car."

"So even though it was your husband who was driving you back to Philadelphia and you were safe," I comment, "you felt in danger. What did you think might happen?"

"I guess I was afraid of being abducted again, because I was going back to where it happened. I felt as if I *had* been abducted. I felt trapped."

"Do you have any thoughts of how your encounter with the state trooper might be connected to that feeling of being trapped that you had before?"

"When I was describing how I was abducted to you—being grabbed by the arm," Linda answers, "I thought about the state trooper grabbing my arm to handcuff me. I could see the connection and why the arrest was so traumatic for me. My lawyer told me last week that the other officer said that he had never seen an arrest like that before in history. That I was totally, just totally—out of control. I know now that I can be very volatile in situations where I feel cornered, and that's scary."

"What do you remember happening in terms of your resisting?"

"I remember not wanting to be touched, not wanting to be handcuffed. I remember being put in the back seat of the car and kicking the door and desperately wanting to get out. And I kept telling him, begging him to let me out, let me out, let me go, let me go. And afterward, I thought about it, and I'm like, 'Why didn't I just go? Why didn't I just follow along and go?' "

"And what did you conclude?"

"I was out of my mind," Linda answers simply. "I had the same trapped feeling that I did when I was a fourteen-year-old girl being abducted at knife point. If I'd been in my right mind, I wouldn't have kicked the door. I wouldn't have begged him to let me go. There was no way for him to let me go. If he had to make an arrest, he had to make it."

"It sounds as if some of those feelings of being trapped when you were fourteen were trying to come out when you felt trapped again at thirty-three."

"I know," Linda says. "I remember praying in Spanish, but the police report says that I was also talking to the officer in Spanish when I was in the car. I thought that was really strange because I knew that he didn't speak Spanish. Then I realized that I'd spoken Spanish with the rapist, too. So it was as if I had traveled back in time."

"What other connections do you see between the rape and the arrest?"

"There are a lot of similarities," Linda says. She ticks them off: "An isolated area with nobody around. Alone with a strange man. Being taken by the arm. Being forced to turn around with him standing behind me. Being told to take off my coat. The darkness, the coldness of a winter night. Being restrained—the officer used handcuffs, the rapist, a knife. Being forced into the back seat of the car. Lying down on my side behind the passenger's seat. Being scared to death. Feeling violated."

"The similarities between the two incidents triggered a lot of emotions that came out inappropriately," I tell Linda, "because you've kept them inside your shell for a long time. You need to identify some of those feelings and express them in an appropriate way. Then you can learn how to handle them so they don't turn into a panic attack or make you chase Ted away when he wants to be loving and close."

Linda utters a deep sigh. "God, I would really like that," she says longingly. "It would almost be like a rebirth. I feel that I live in this nonexistent world. I'm here, and I'm not here, and I pinch myself really hard sometimes, and it doesn't hurt. I wonder, do I have a heart? Is it beating? Am I really alive? I don't feel that I'm out of body, but sometimes that I'm smoke inside—*whoosh*—the shallowness and emptiness of that. People think I'm strong, because I've been able to go through some very difficult times in my life without showing any emotion. They don't know that I'm eating myself up inside. There's nothing left but this blankness. I feel I've missed out on so much, and my life is whizzing right by and through me."

Linda recalls her first visit to a psychiatrist. "After my husband died, I made up my mind that I wasn't going to let my panic attacks keep me cooped up in the house and make me dependent on anybody," she says. "I went to see a psychiatrist, and he frightened me, and I never went back. He told me, 'You have a locked Pandora's Box inside you, and when that Pandora's Box opens—watch out! You're going to get worse before you get better.' And I said, 'No way! I'm not ready to go through this,' because to me to get worse meant to actually lose my sanity. I think I'm still afraid of that."

"Therapy will teach you how to comfort yourself when those feelings come out so they won't be so frightening," I reassure Linda. "What I'd like you to do is to write a letter to the man who raped you. It doesn't have to be mailed. It's just something to help get your feelings out. You can bring the letter in, and we could discuss it."

"It won't be very pretty," Linda says, chuckling.

"I don't expect it to be pretty," I tell her, letting her know that I won't be offended. "And then I'd like you to write a letter to the fourteen-year-old girl inside you who is still traumatized and very frightened, because she hasn't been comforted enough. It's that child who's rejecting Ted."

"But it's an assertive child who can say, 'I don't want to be touched,' " Linda counters. "A child sometimes has a hard time realizing that she can establish her boundaries."

"But does the child who's setting those boundaries know that nineteen years have passed since she was abducted and raped, and that she can feel safe now because you're able to protect her?"

"I don't know; this is all so totally new to me," Linda says wonderingly, "having to rediscover this child and write to her. What good do you think it will do?"

"Once that childish part of you is comforted sufficiently, I think you'll be able to be close to Ted," I tell Linda. "Right now this child part feels that it has to be present as a kind of alert watchdog when Ted touches you. If you can get her to relax and allow the adult part of you to be in control of your sexuality, you won't feel angry and you can let yourself get close and enjoy sexual intimacy fully."

"Dear Rapist"

It takes several sessions for Linda to grasp the concept of communicating with the traumatized little girl within. One of her biggest problems, she says, is Ted.

"I need my space to sit alone and write, and Ted doesn't give it to me," she complains. "When I start writing, he'll come over and say, 'I'll support you in any way you need.' What I want him to do is to please leave me alone. He starts asking me questions, wanting to help; and I get annoyed with him, very angry, the same as I do when he touches me. I feel that he violates me. I want my writing to be personal."

"Maybe you need to schedule some private time for yourself to do your writing," I suggest.

"I did," Linda says. "Saturday I took a walk with my Rolf, my Great

Dane, for protection. I sat down in a woodsy area alongside a tree and wrote in my journal."

She shows me her letter to the fourteen-year-old within her:

Dearest Linda,

You have been silent too long, half-asleep, and stuck inside a shell. I'm writing to you because I want to help you break your silence and get out. I know what a heavy burden you've been carrying on your back of fear, guilt, and shame. It's time for you to let go of your pain, embrace yourself, and be good to you.

I want you to know that you don't have to live in fear for your life anymore. You can stop reliving the moment over and over again. It happened, and it's done. It won't happen again because I will keep you safe, my darling.

Please understand that this was not a punishment from God. What kind of God would have been so cruel to you for lying to your mother about where you were going? This was a random act by a sick man that could have happened to anyone. Your only crime was being young and fearless. That awful man robbed you of your tender soul, and I will get it back for you.

I wish I could turn back the clock to when you were a carefree, happy child and change those terrible moments into a positive experience to cherish for the rest of your life. The truth is that I can't. For this I am truly sorry. But I can help you cherish all the positive experiences you have had and can have now. Please do your part to help me help you get strong.

You are a good little girl. You must never forget how much joy you brought to people. You're special, you're beautiful, you're kind. And no one can take this away from you. I love you unconditionally. Please, for God's sake, let's live, love, and be one.

"That's a very comforting letter," I tell Linda. "How did it make you feel when you were writing it?"

"I had a mixed bag of feelings. I felt like a mother, very loving; and at times, I would feel helpless and hopeless and start crying; and then I'd feel powerful, depending on what I wrote and what I was thinking. That's so typical of my moods. I can be fine one minute and crying the next. I used to think I was bipolar, but that didn't seem to be the case."

"What were you crying about when you wrote this letter?"

"I felt sad, because I wished I could be what I once was—the happy-go-lucky person that everyone liked and seemed to admire, the one who was full of life and happy to wake up in the morning. I haven't felt that way in such a long time."

"I think the child part of you has a lot of sadness to deal with, so the more you can reach out to her, communicate with her, and provide her with comfort and support, the sooner she'll feel happy again."

"I want to go on writing to her; there's so much more to say," Linda asserts. "It's like I've been running away from myself for years, and now I want to give the part of me closed off inside a shell a chance to catch up. I feel like I paved a road."

I ask whether she was able to do any writing to the man who raped her, too.

She shakes her head no. "Every time I tried to write to him, I tore it up," she tells me. "I couldn't bear the anger. I hate him, and I don't even know who I'm hating; and I don't like hating anyone." Linda's face contorts with emotion, and tears spring to her eyes. "He's like a ghost, this—this"—she takes a deep breath and clenches her teeth—"this *thing* that's part of me and just doesn't go away. It doesn't leave me alone. And I think that's the emptiness I feel inside, because he's not supposed to be there—he should never have been there. At first, I felt repulsed whenever I saw an African American man on the street. And then I started realizing how unfair that was. His color had nothing to do with it. He was an evil man. And sometimes I wonder, 'Am I turned off by men?' Maybe I cringe when Ted touches me, because I don't want to deal with *any* man. I don't want to see a penis ever in my life again."

"What you're saying is that because this particular man was evil, you're not allowed to enjoy sex with a decent man. Can't you be with someone who's good?

"Ted is *that*," Linda agrees.

"Then you need to get your anger out at the person who deserves it," I tell her, "and exorcise the ghost."

Several sessions later Linda comes in with her handwritten letter to the man who abducted and raped her when she was fourteen.

"I started to write 'Dear Rapist,' " she tells me, giggling, "and then I realized how ridiculous it was for me to be polite. So this is what I wrote."

Dear Rapist,

   Why did you do it? How could you have kidnapped a fourteen-year-old girl in Philadelphia, stuck a knife in her

back, and forced her to have sex with you? You're disgusting—
a demented, narcissistic asshole. You lied to that poor girl and
terrified her and violated her and stole her virginity, you ani-
mal! I don't know how you can live with yourself.

You talked about God. Do you think He will forgive you
for raping an innocent child? Do you know how much devas-
tation you have caused in her life? You made her grow up wish-
ing she didn't have sex organs and feeling dirty and ashamed
of her own body. People like you make me sick!

If only you could cross my path now! I am the person you
did this to. I have suffered unbearable pain and mental anguish
because of you. I wish I could meet you, so I could tell you
how I felt, how I feel, what I have gone through. You continue
to haunt me. You're like a snake, poisoning my insides with
your venom. I wish you were a visible snake that I could chop
to pieces with a knife like the one you had. I hate you, mister,
I hate you!!

By the time she finishes reading me her letter, Linda is sobbing bitterly. After a moment she says, "I'm so angry to think that he might still
be walking around."

"What would you do if you saw him again?"

"I used to fantasize about that all the time," she admits. "I even took
a friend of mine to look for his house years later, but the neighborhood
was different. I have no idea where he lives. My first thought was to take
this man hostage and torture him and let him know that I'm that fourteen-year-old girl and I'm back. And as time went by, I stopped thinking
about revenge. Now I just want to ask him why. I want him to see my face
and hear how much he hurt me. And I want him to apologize, show some
remorse, take some responsibility, feel some of the pain that I've felt
throughout the years."

"You want this man to know that you're a real person who has feelings and a soul and suffered because of him; but since he can't apologize
and ask to be forgiven, Linda, I think you have to forgive yourself," I tell
her. "And you know, as much as you want to be seen for who you are, so
does Ted. When he touches you, who do you think he is?"

"I know he's Ted."

"You know that intellectually, but emotionally do you react to him as
though it's Ted? Or do you react as though it's someone else that you once
were afraid of?"

"I just know that I don't want to be touched. I don't want to be talked to. I want him to leave me alone."

"Has Ted ever done anything when he's touched you or talked to you that has been hurtful or destructive to your relationship?"

"No."

"So is there any logical reason why you would be so upset when he touches you or wants to talk to you?"

"No."

"So if it's not logical for you to repel Ted's advances, what situation comes into your mind from the past that makes you do that?"

"I guess on a subconscious level I'm relating to Ted as though he were the rapist," Linda concedes, "but it's so hard to back out of that reaction. Once I'm caught up in it, I hate what's going on. I can't stand it. Even if he takes my hand in a gentle way to hold me, I snap at him and get furious." She starts to cry again, this time in anguished sorrow. "Ted's pain is so bad that it makes my pain that much worse. I keep thinking he could be happy with someone else who doesn't have these problems. But then the thought of losing him frightens me, and I think, 'How long will he put up with this before he leaves?' "

TROUBLED WATERS

They were both excited about the weekend. It was perfect sailing weather—clear skies, generous sun, a balmy springtime breeze. Ted needed to get away even more than Linda did. He couldn't contain his feelings as she could. He felt frazzled and distracted at work because his concerns about the way things were going at home were always on his mind. For her, it was the opposite. Work was her safe haven. Her job was where she went to escape. She could immerse herself in the problems of her young clients and forget about her own—lock them away as if they didn't exist.

At one point Ted had been so discouraged that he wasn't going to put the boat into the water this summer at all. "This isn't gonna work out," he told her when she flared up at him the week before. But he got over it and was as loving as ever. She knew he'd be lost without sailing—he'd done it for so many years—so she told him she wanted to go.

Now here they were in Old Lyme, where Ted's boat, *Tranquility,* was docked in the marina. They were having dinner Saturday night at the Bee and Thistle Inn, a charming old mansion in the historic district. Nestled on a wide expanse of lawn spreading down to the Connecticut River, the inn provided an oldtime sense of space and graciousness along with skill-fully prepared dishes like rack of lamb and lobster pot pie. That night they'd sleep on *Tranquility*. Linda was looking forward to the soothing feeling it gave her to stand on the boat and gaze at the moon glimmering on the rippling waves—a sight that made even the most reluctant lover vulnerable to the mystical allure of romance.

They were sipping their cocktails, and Ted was gazing at Linda with frank desire. He wants me, she thought, and that made her feel nervous, but she told herself to stop worrying and enjoy the moment.

She smiled affectionately at him, and he took her hand and held it. "You know, Linda, you're the world to me," he said. "I love how warm and outgoing and passionate you are about things. You have a wonderful personality."

"That's so sweet," Linda said, thinking to herself, *What personality? I don't have one. What are you talking about, Ted? Maybe I should have been up front and told you I don't have a personality before.*

He leaned toward her. "All I want is to take care of you and protect you as much as I can."

Yes, and that's the last thing I want, she thought. *I don't need you to take care of me and protect me. I can do that myself.* But all she said was, "I know you do, Ted."

She wished he would leave it there, but he went on, "You know how I feel about what happened to you, and I want you to tell me what I can do to help you heal."

Jesus, God, I don't want your sympathy! I shared it with you just so you would know. Can't you get that? She said nothing.

"I'm trying to understand what you're going through," Ted continued earnestly. "Maybe it would help if you let me read what you're writing in your journal."

Linda felt her spine stiffen. Did he think she was writing something about him? "It doesn't have anything to do with you, Ted," she said, trying not to sound huffy. "It's just that I have these thoughts in my mind and I want to write them down. I'm not sure if it would help you understand."

"But I feel that you're leaving me out of the loop," he persisted. "Do you mind if I read it?"

"I *do* mind," she said. Now she was getting angry. "Look, what I write in that journal is part of my therapy. I don't feel comfortable sharing it, and I don't want to feel that I have to hide it. I want to be able to put it somewhere at home where it's safe and it's not read. Is that clear?"

"Okay, okay, I won't read it; you have my promise," Ted said, pulling his hand away. He looked around uncomfortably, afraid that they were making a scene. "There's no need for you to raise your voice about it. I'm not deaf, you know."

"But you act as if you're deaf," she said. Her voice rose in spite of him. "That's why I have to scream. I keep hoping that maybe you'll hear."

"That's not true. I do everything in my power to be sensitive to you, and all you do is push me away." The frustration and hurt on Ted's face were like an accusation. "I wish you'd stop acting so childish and talk to me like one adult to another."

"I can't talk to you; you invade me!" Linda snapped. She saw the tears forming in Ted's eyes. He was making her feel guilty and angrier at the same time. She wished he wouldn't be so mushy. She thought, *Why do I have to deal with your hurt? Am I sinking you down with me? I can't stand this! I have to get away.*

The other people in the room were staring at them now. Linda saw the waiter walking toward their table, and she stood up abruptly.

"I'm sorry, Ted, I have to leave," she said. Feeling everyone's eyes boring into her back, Linda rushed blindly out of the dining room and left the inn.

Outside she realized that she had only a vague notion of how to get back to the boat. If she wasn't careful, she could fall into the river and drown. She knew enough to walk toward the intersection, three houses down from the Bee and Thistle.

When she got to the intersection, she was at Hall's Road. If she turned left, that would take her farther into the historic section, away from the marina; so she turned right, passing a shopping center and an A&P and a gas station, and headed toward the bridge. To get to the marina she had to walk the entire length of Hall's Road, but she was so overwrought that the half-hour it took flew by.

At the end of the road Linda turned right and walked toward the marina at the base of the Connecticut River. As she approached the marina, she began to panic. In the darkness it was hard to pick out *Tranquility* from all the other boats that were docked there. She was terrified of losing her footing and ending up in the water. Her heart began hammering its familiar drumbeat of alarm.

Hurrying along the dock, Linda peered at the names on the boats—an alphabet soup of idiosyncratic vanity plates bobbing in the water. Despite the cool breeze, she felt flushed and clammy. Perspiration broke out on her forehead. Her head began to spin, and she felt that she was on a carousel.

Tranquility! Linda had to look twice to make sure it was really there and not an illusion. Relief surged through her as she clambered aboard. She stumbled over some tools Ted had left spread out on a dropcloth and almost fell into the open bilge hatch before she made her way into the B berth and sank down on the bed.

About an hour later Ted walked in, looking distraught. "Oh, thank God, you're here," he said. "I thought you'd be waiting outside, and I spent a half-hour searching for you in the gardens around the inn before I came back here. Are you all right?"

"I'm okay," Linda mumbled.

He looked at her reproachfully. "You scared the life out of me. Please don't ever run away like that again," he said, sitting down on the bed beside her. "Do you want to talk?"

"No!" Linda shouted. She pulled the blanket over her head.

Ted tried to take the blanket away.

"No, please don't take it off!" Even muffled by the blanket, there was no mistaking the fear in Linda's voice. She began crying hysterically. She didn't want to see Ted or talk to him. She just wanted to be underneath the blanket, safe and secure.

Ted stood up. "My God, Linda, what did I do to you?"

"Please, Ted, leave me alone," Linda sobbed. "We'll talk about it in the morning."

Ted slept somewhere else on the boat that night.

Linda awoke in the morning filled with remorse. When she looked in the mirror and saw her drawn face and red, puffy eyes, she asked herself, "Who is this person?" She tried to stare herself out of it, but it was too scary. She put the mirror away, washed and dressed quickly, and went to find Ted.

"I'm so sorry for the way I acted last night," she said contritely. "None of this has anything to do with you. It's all related to my past."

Again Linda suggested that they take a break from each other while she worked out her problems in therapy. "I'm not going to walk out on you," she told Ted. "I just think it might be easier for both of us if we could be apart for a little while."

"No, no, I don't want that," Ted said firmly. "I still love you, and I'm going to hang in for as long as it takes."

He spent the day working on the boat while she sat on the top deck, writing in her journal. It was a pleasant, peaceful Sunday free of disturbance, but the romance implicit in the weekend had been tossed overboard and swept out to sea.

"Why do I have to be suffering when I know I don't have to be suffering?" Linda asks me disconsolately after she tells me about her weekend on *Tranquility*.

"You say you did some writing on the boat. What did you write?"

"I wrote another letter to the fourteen-year-old part of me. I tried to think what I would say as a teacher speaking to one of my teenage students who was upset, but it didn't come out that way."

Linda's letter says:

> I need to let you come out of your shell, but it seems that it's too hard a shell to crack. Am I not trying hard enough? Am I holding back? What is it that I need to do to get you out? Am I too weak or too blind? Do I need to sacrifice myself? I've done that already.
>
> I have, as you can see, a lot of questions. I just can't find the answers. But I do know that you want to be free; I realize this. I am so good at solving problems for others, and I can't do it for you. You are the most important person to me; you are my life. So what is wrong? How difficult can this be?
>
> Linda, you must help me. This has to be a team effort here. You and me, kid, you and me. I'm sick and tired of being a stranger to myself and having my life pass me by. I want to start feeling the air, smelling the grass, feeling the love. But no. Sometimes I feel stone-cold. It's like the lines from that song by Madonna: "You're frozen when your heart's not open. . . . You waste your time with hate and regret. . . . If I lose you, my heart will be broken. . . . Love is a bird, she needs to fly. . . . Let all the hurt inside of you die."
>
> I know and understand the problem. Why can't I solve it? Why?

"It's so frustrating being frozen in time, frozen in feelings," Linda says angrily, making fists of her hands. "Sometimes I want to take this part of me in the shell physically and shake it and say, 'Get out!' "

"Is that a respectful way to try to connect with that part?" I ask her. "You know that there are a lot of reasons why that part has been driven into the shell and is afraid to come out. And it's not going to come out unless it's made to feel safe."

"How can I make that part feel safe when I don't feel safe?" Linda asks. It's the same question I hear from all my patients who don't know how to comfort themselves, because they've either been systematically abused or, as in Linda's case, subjected to a severe trauma that has kept them frozen in time, reliving the event.

"But your adult part is able to overcome those feelings and perform well on the job, working with other children," I counter. "You were on the right track when you tried to assume your professional role as a counselor with your own child frozen inside the shell, but you let your impatience get in the way. You need to put your frustration aside and focus on respecting that part's feelings and being empathetic toward them and welcoming them into your life."

"I'd better do *something* or the situation with Ted will keep on getting worse and worse," Linda says morosely. "This is the same thing that happened with Ted's ex-wife. She stopped having sex with him six months after they were married. Maybe she had a history of sexual abuse, too."

"Could be."

Linda makes a disgusted face. "Pulling the blanket over my head—my God, that was so childish."

"But that's the problem, isn't it? You feel more like a child whenever he wants intimacy."

"Yes, and being caught in that feeling of immaturity and having this man try to make love to you when you're like that is very—it's—" Linda struggles for the word and finally says, "At that moment I think it's sick, like, 'For God's sake, what's he doing?' "

"I think you should be comforting the part of you that has the feelings of a child on a regular basis," I suggest. "Don't wait until you're already in a potentially sexual situation, and your fears and anger are overwhelming." I recommend a paperback called *The Woman's Comfort Book* by Jennfier Louden. "Obviously, it's not appropriate for a child to be involved sexually," I continue, "so you need to let that part know that the adult part of you will be there and in control and won't be abandoning the child then. You need to communicate that to the child so that the child can—"

"Go to sleep," Linda finishes for me.

SEALED OFF BUT NOT SEPARATE

After a review of Linda's SCID-D, the diagnosis I come up with is DDNOS, or dissociative disorder not otherwise specified. This is a category for people who have dissociative symptoms that don't meet the criteria for the other dissociative disorders. Survivors of extreme trauma, hostages, members of cults, and victims of torture or terrorism are all people who may develop dissociative symptoms of this nature. As a survivor of a single highly traumatic event, Linda has developed a milder form of DID that falls within the DDNOS category. In some people DDNOS is actually an early stage of DID. For the most part, the symptoms are similar but less severe, and some are absent, for example, amnesia for important personal information or the presence of two or more distinct personalities.

Linda does not have amnesia for her child part, which is not sufficiently distinct to qualify as a full personality. The traumatized fourteen-year-old girl within Linda is not a completely separate personality with her own name, memories, traits, manner of speaking, handwriting, and other characteristics. Although some of Linda's feelings are sealed off in this child part of herself, Linda doesn't have a sharply defined visual image of that part or have internal interactive dialogues with it. In circumstances that evoke the traumatic event that befell her when she was fourteen—being taken hostage and raped—her indistinct child personality state takes over her consciousness and behavior and causes her to act in an immature and emotionally overwrought manner. Her volatile mood swings, panic attacks, and sexual dysfunction with her fiancé all stem from this dissociative basis.

The dissociative symptom that Linda experiences most severely is depersonalization, particularly feeling disconnected from her emotions. She speaks of this in all the familiar ways—her feelings are frozen or locked inside a shell; she has an emptiness or blankness inside; she feels like a stranger to herself; she doesn't recognize herself in the mirror at times; she feels that she is going through the motions of living while life is passing her by. Although this symptom has negatively affected her relationship with her fiancé, it has not impaired her ability to function on the job. Ironically Linda claims that compartmentalizing her feelings has helped her job performance because it allows her to immerse herself fully in work and not have to think about her disconnection from herself and fear of intimacy. But she is in therapy, because she knows that running away from her problems has only made them worse.

Besides depersonalization, Linda experiences a moderate amount of the other dissociative symptoms. During her panic attacks she may occasionally "space out" and have some memory loss. Her derealization or distorted perception of her surroundings occurs when she reacts to Ted as though he were her rapist although she doesn't actually see her rapist's face when she looks at him. She also has identity confusion vis-à-vis her attitude toward men. On the one hand, she wants a loving relationship with her fiancé, and on the other, she wishes he would go away and leave her alone. Part of her feels unwomanly when she refuses to have sex, and another part thinks she never wants to see a penis again.

When I tell Linda that she has DDNOS, she accepts the diagnosis with grace. "I know this is going to be hard work," she says with a deep sigh, "but I feel I'm headed in the right direction. This therapy is different. For the first time, I'm able to do more than just talk and leave. I'm crying a lot more, and it feels good to cry." She chuckles at the incongruity. "Digging deep is painful and scary," she explains, "but connecting to all those buried feelings and accepting them are very helpful. I don't want to be crying forever, though," Linda adds. "I'd like to be crying because I'm happy."

A Close Call

Oh, my God, not again! Linda thought. She was driving to work in the morning when a police cruiser passed by her. There was no other car going in the same direction as he was. When she looked in her rear-view mirror, she saw him behind her with the flashing lights going. He'd turned around! He'd recognized her! The state laws for driving without a license, she'd found out on the Internet, were very stiff. She could be thrown into jail for that—especially since she was already out on bail for drunken driving, resisting arrest, and assault and battery on a police officer. Could she handle another arrest? Panic was rising in her like a fever. One question pounded in her head: *What am I going to do?* She thought of the plan she'd rehearsed over and over in her mind. She'd go quietly and not make a fuss. If it was the same guy, she'd lock the doors and ask to wait for another officer, a female, to come.

The road curved, and a turn came up on her left. Escape! As she drove onto a side road, she could see that the officer actually had turned around as if to follow her. Would he follow her now, too? No, thank God, he kept on going straight ahead on the main road. Maybe he couldn't see that she'd gone onto a side road, because it went up a hill. Or maybe she wasn't the one he was after. He could've turned around because he got a call, and started flashing his lights so she'd move over and let him pass. But that was close, *too* close.

Linda was due at work at nine o'clock. Her nerves were so frayed that she sat in the car, crying, for close to an hour before she took off. And then she got lost. The roads were unfamiliar to her, full of head-swimming twists and turns. It took her another hour of wandering around until she finally found her way back to the turnpike. She showed up for work two hours late.

The next morning Ted couldn't get her out of bed. "Linda, c'mon, you have to get up and get ready to go to work," he said, gently shaking her.

"Leave me alone," she muttered, her face turned into the pillow. "I'm not going in today."

Linda couldn't face one more day of driving an hour to work and an hour back, terrified that she'd be stopped and arrested. The turnpike was under construction, and state troopers were buzzing around it like bees around a honeycomb. How could one of them not recognize her? She was sure her picture was in every state police barracks. And that scene she'd made in the barracks could not have been unnoticed by the other troopers around. They were bound to remember her when they saw her again on the road. As ridiculous as it seemed, she felt like a criminal—a marked woman.

"Mommy, get up," Julie said when she saw Linda still lying in bed. "You have to drive me to school. It's almost eight o'clock."

Linda grunted disgustedly.

"What's wrong, Mommy? Are you okay?"

Linda saw the worried look on Julie's face as she sat up in bed. "Yeah, baby, I'm okay; I just overslept, that's all," she said. She felt a stab of remorse. It wasn't fair to Julie to make her late for school. The last thing Linda wanted was another black mark on her conscience. She dragged herself out of bed and dressed.

Once she'd dropped off Julie at school, Linda decided that she might as well go to work. Okay, I'll take the risk one more time, she told herself, but I can't go on like this. She tried to think of other options. She could take the bus, but it left an hour too late in the morning to get her to work on time. Ted couldn't drive her because he had to be at work at seven-thirty. The hearing to get her license back was a month away. She could quit her job, but she loved her job and would rather go to jail than sit home and go crazy—at least in jail she'd have someone to talk to. Her only choice, she concluded, was to gut it out for another month until the hearing.

Heather, her lawyer, said that if the judge found Linda guilty at the hearing, her license could be suspended for another forty-five days and she'd have to take some very expensive classes for drunk drivers. She could even get jail time for the assault and battery charges. Heather didn't want to go to court at all. She suggested a plea bargain: a ninety-day suspended sentence and a year on probation. Linda balked. She didn't want a stain on her record—what would happen to her career as a teacher if that ever came out? And besides, she didn't think she was guilty. Her lawyer didn't know that Linda was a rape survivor who was being treated by a psychiatrist for a posttraumatic dissociative disorder. Linda kept quiet about about her illness, because she was afraid of being labeled or stigmatized. People knew about panic attacks, but they were still in the dark about dissociation.

It was Ted who told Heather. She called him to ask him some questions, and he filled her in. Linda wasn't angry when she found out; she was relieved. It turned out that Heather had worked at the Disability Law Center before and knew about posttraumatic disorders. Many of her previous clients had been victims of sexual abuse. Heather agreed that they should go to court. She was confident that no reasonable judge would find Linda criminally responsible for the charges against her once her medical condition became known. She would be vindicated. It was only a matter of time.

THE FIRE

"I think it's done," Linda said, sticking a fork into a sizzling piece of chicken Ted was barbequing on the grill.

They were home, having a family cookout on their deck Saturday night, because Ted had to work that weekend. It was a simple summertime meal—barbequed chicken, corn on the cob, and a tossed salad. Later they went inside and watched the video of *Mulan* with Julie.

After Julie was in bed, Linda noticed that Ted was unusually quiet. "Is something wrong?" she asked.

"No, not really."

"Yes there is. What is it?"

Ted reluctantly confided that he was starting to feel guilty, because he wasn't as productive on the job as he thought he should be.

"Then maybe you should go back to counseling if you're not happy," Linda said. She wanted him to know that he was more important to her than the job. "Really, Ted, it's a great position, but I don't like what it's doing to you. It's not worth the extra money if it's driving you crazy."

"It *is* worth it," Ted said. "It's $25,000 more a year, and I like the job; I just don't like the half-assed way I'm doing it."

The forlorn look on his face made Linda feel a surge of compassion for him. "Ted, I see you walking around, lost in space, not enjoying your job as much as you should, and I feel responsible for it," she told him.

"Don't be silly, Linda. Why should you feel responsible?"

"Because I'm the reason your work is suffering. You think it's your fault that I don't want to make love, and you go into work feeling guilty about it. Then you can't do your job right, and you feel guilty about that. Your whole life right now is guilt, guilt, guilt—and I'm to blame."

"Oh, Linda, you're not to blame for anything," Ted said. "Nothing is your fault. Don't you know that?"

He gave her a hug, and Linda resisted the urge to push him away. *He's not going to hurt you,* she told herself, calming the part of herself that felt a stab of alarm. *He just wants to be comforted the way you do.* She allowed herself to feel safe in his arms, and they cuddled together affectionately for a while before they grew sleepy and went to bed.

In the middle of the night Ted got up to go to the bathroom and saw that the deck was all lit up. He thought he must have forgotten to turn off the outside lights, but when he flicked the switch, the light outside didn't go off. He couldn't understand why until he looked out the window and saw that the deck was in flames. One of the charcoal briquettes must have fallen from the grill and started a fire. Quickly Ted filled a bucket with water, rushed outside, and doused the flames. When he got back into bed, Linda was still sound asleep.

"Good God, Ted, what happened to the deck?" Linda asked when she got up in the morning and saw the huge hole the fire had made the night before.

"You slept through the whole thing. The deck caught on fire from some embers that fell from the grill."

Linda looked shocked, then mystified. "That's strange," she said. "I had this dream last night about a burnt hockey puck and kept wondering how it got that way. I probably dreamed it right before the fire broke out."

"That really is strange," Ted said.

They chalked it up to synchronicity.

The Charred Man

Several days after the fire Linda comes in for her therapy session and recounts a dream she had last night—this one about a charred man. How much the metaphor was inspired by the fire on the deck I don't know, but the dream itself is very significant for what it says about Linda's fear of intimacy.

"There was this man who was all charred from being burnt and had scorched skin that was like a black crust," Linda says. "He asked me to go into this house that was almost burning. And I was very hesitant. I said, 'I don't want to go in there.' But he was very persuasive, and he convinced me to go into the house. It was a big house, and there were spits of fire here and there, and I kept saying, 'I want to get out of here; I want to go back.' And he said, 'Trust me; nothing's going to happen to you. Come with me. It'll be okay.' Then he grabbed me and had me kiss him, and he was all yecchy, really gross. But I felt I was stuck and had to do it to be safe. It was very dark and dungeony in the house. We kept walking and walking, and then as we started going into a path, it seemed brighter and more pleasant. Whatever it was that was on him was slowly peeling off and coming loose. When it all fell away, I could see that he was just a regular man. And I was so thankful that I did go with him because I felt love—ultimate love. And I told him how foolish I was to be so scared to go with him, and he said, 'I was testing you to see if you would come, and you did.' "

"Can you relate that dream to anything?" I ask her.

"I think it's related to Ted, and the way he's trying to help me through the process of differentiating him from the rapist, and I'm so resistant," Linda answers. "I just don't let go—don't let him feel good about what he's trying to do for me and let myself feel good. I was crying throughout the dream, but when I woke up I was happy, because it didn't turn out to be what I had expected."

"What did you expect?"

"I was terrified because he was so ugly, and everything else I saw was distorted and ugly; and that's how my life had always seemed," Linda answers. "I think the dream is about being able to trust. It's about knowing that on the other side there can be beauty and a wonderful man. I felt very happy and safe when all of that charred stuff peeled off him, but when I woke up, I was disappointed." Linda breaks out laughing. "I wanted to go back to sleep again, so I could pick up where I left off."

"In the dream you felt happy and safe with Ted, but not in real life. Why?"

"There's a part of me that won't allow me to receive Ted and accept and appreciate all his kindness and affection. I keep thinking, 'What can I bring to him? Nothing but pain and misery.' "

"I'm sure Ted doesn't think that."

"No, he keeps telling me how happy he is with me, and I say, 'How *can* you be?' " Linda replies. "Why is it that I can feel anger and fear and sadness so easily," she asks, her voice cracking, "but I can't feel joy?"

"Why do you think? Is it safe for you to feel joy?"

Linda thinks for a moment. "No, I guess not," she answers slowly. "I'm afraid that if I do feel any joy, it's going to be taken away from me. That's why I keep my defenses up. I'm always waiting for the other shoe to drop."

"That's learned behavior that you will have to relearn," I tell her. "Joy doesn't have to be taken away and joy doesn't have to be associated with pain. You adopted that defensive behavior as a teenager in order to survive. But you're not fighting for your survival now, and that behavior isn't adaptive anymore. In your present situation you're with someone who is loving and safe and isn't going to hurt you, and that's very different from the past. The part of you that was able to get to know Ted and be close with him has to teach the part that's still scared and angry that this is a different moment in time and this man is safe."

"It's funny, but when I met Ted, I was like a kid, all happy and excited to be with such a great guy," Linda recalls. "But when he began catering to me and buying me jewelry and sending me these wonderful e-mails and showering me with compliments all the time, I felt uncomfortable. I wasn't used to it, and I didn't feel I deserved all that nurturing. Could it be that I'm trying to sabotage the relationship, because I'm used to being a giver and not a receiver, and it's too hard for me to embrace being loved?"

"Are you saying that you don't feel entitled to have a good life; that you have to continue the way your life has been in the past?"

"I don't know what it is," Nancy says with tears of frustration in her eyes. "I was strong enough to conquer my agoraphobia, but when it comes to having real intimacy with a caring, responsible, competent man who is really there for me—the first one who ever was—I don't know if I can do it."

"You can do it," I assure her. "What would you tell one of your troubled adolescent students who was raped the way you were and believed that it was her fault? Would you tell her that she was to blame and that she'll have to protect herself for the rest of her life by locking up her feelings and throwing away the key? Would you tell her that any man who tries to get close to her is invading her space and trapping her and that she has to push him away?"

"No, I'd tell her that she had no control over what happened, no way to protect herself then, but now she does," Linda answers like the supportive surrogate parent that she is to many of her students. "She can use good judgment. Don't take foolish risks, but don't push away someone who really does love her and is good to her."

"Exactly. You see, that ugly charred second skin on the man in your dream is made up of your own cognitive distortions of reality. By continuing to communicate and connect with and comfort the frightened child within your woman's body, you'll be able to lay those distortions to rest. You're the one who has to peel that second skin away, so that Ted isn't frightening to you anymore and you can embrace him and experience the love you had in your dream in your waking life."

A SHOOTING STAR

As their week of vacation drew closer, Linda became more and more apprehensive. How will I get through this, she wondered, being together with Ted on the boat in close quarters for so many hours? In preparation she began talking quietly to herself, assuring her child part that there was nothing to fear. The day before they were to leave, she busied herself packing and cooking. She made pasta and rice dishes to accompany the fish or meat they'd grill on the hibachi when *Tranquility* was out on the ocean, all the while repeating her little mantra, "We're gonna go, and we're gonna have a good time."

The first night in Old Lyme they had lobsters for dinner at The Hideaway Pub near the marina and went dancing. Ted wasn't a good dancer, but he was funny about it. Linda knew he was enjoying himself, and she felt good dancing with him.

They held hands walking back to the boat. When they got to the dock, neither of them noticed that a board was missing.

"Watch your step," Ted said. "It's dark out."

His warning came too late. Linda's foot went through the hole in the dock and—*plunk!*—she was in the water.

"I really have to take care of you, don't I?" Ted said, laughing affectionately, as he pulled her back onto the dock.

Linda had to laugh, too, in spite of her minor scratches and bruises. She felt silly and grown-up at the same time, able to have fun and freely give and receive affection, while keeping her frightened child out of a relationship that only an adult should be involved in.

The next day Ted took *Tranquility* out into the ocean. Linda reveled in the fresh, salty smell of the air and the beauty of the gently waving jade green water all around them. Just before they were ready to turn back, they threw the carnations and roses they'd taken with them into the sea in memory of John F. Kennedy, Jr.

That night in the dark passageway between the master stateroom and the B berth, Linda took Ted's hand and said, "I feel like I want to be close to you." She was happy that she'd gotten herself ready to be able to say that.

When they made love on the bed in the master stateroom, Linda knew that this man was different from the others before him. He was not a stranger who only wanted to gratify his animal lust with her or a man who would break her heart in the end. He was a good man. It was safe to love him. He was never going to hurt her.

Both Linda and Ted wished that the vacation would never end. Not once did Linda issue angry "Leave me alone" or "Don't touch me" directives. She realized how unfair she'd been to Ted when she was trying to protect her space from what she perceived as an invasion. Now she could see that Ted's attempts to get close to her because of love and affection were different from the events when her space really was invaded in the past.

Her need to go to such protective extremes had also lessened, because Ted was learning how to give her the space she needed. He used to be so overprotective that he wanted to be there all the time like some little angel on her shoulder everywhere she went. He found a support group on the Internet for women survivors of sexual abuse and logged onto it, hoping to get a better understanding of Linda's illness. And the women kept sending him letters of encouragement: "Linda is feeling some real pain; she needs space; give her space," and "She really does love you; she's still with you; give her time."

Whenever Linda felt an urge to sabotage the intimacy she was experiencing with Ted on the boat, she took out her journal and wrote notes to herself to alleviate her fears. "This closeness is the ideal thing that should happen between a man and a woman," she wrote one day. "You thought you weren't cut out to have it after the rape, and so you've always protected your hurt feelings. Either you didn't expect to be nurtured by a man or you pushed warm love away, afraid that hurt would follow. But love doesn't mean you get hurt. The love you have now is beautiful and sweet. Stay strong and let yourself grow into it."

Sometimes Ted would tease her when they were acting playful with each other and say, "Is this you or the kid in you?"

Instead of getting defensive and retorting, "That is not something to joke about," Linda started laughing along with him. She knew that he wasn't making fun of her in a disrespectful way; he was just trying to give some humor to the situation. He had to lighten up, and Linda did, too. There were times when they'd gone for days without laughing, because they'd been so sucked into the pain. Now Linda's wounds were not so fresh that she couldn't let laughter help.

"Hey, Linda, look, a shooting star!" Ted exclaimed one night when they were sitting together on the upper deck of *Tranquility*.

"Make a wish," she said.

She closed her eyes and made her own wish silently, and Ted made his. Without asking, Linda knew that Ted's wish was the same as hers: "Please, God, let us continue to be this happy together." And she knew that they had it in them to make their wish come true.

HER DAY IN COURT

"I have this feeling of impending doom," Linda tells me, speaking of her day in court tomorrow. "The scariest thing for me is that I have to see that trooper again. I'm afraid that seeing him and being badgered by the prosecutor will give me a panic attack, and I won't be able to talk. I know I need to think and act like an adult and not come across as this scared little person, but I'm not sure I've gotten a grip yet."

"But you did get a grip, Linda, on your vacation with Ted," I remind her, "when you were able to have the child part of you feel safe, and the adult part of you stay in control. Now you need to be aware of whatever you did then and utilize those same strategies and skills over and over again with Ted and in other situations that might be triggers of your past trauma, like the trial tomorrow."

"But to see that trooper in his uniform with a gun strapped on him—it's a form of intimidation," Linda insists. "It's the same as if I would ever see my rapist again in a way, the same inner feelings."

"Yes, but the feelings you had when you were raped shouldn't be put onto this trial any more than they should've been projected onto Ted," I point out, "because the situations are not the same. You need to comfort those emotions by telling yourself that this is not the same as if you saw your rapist again and felt alone with a predator and helpless. Today you're a capable adult, and you've created a support system around you, and you're safe there. You have a lawyer whose job it is to try to protect you. I will be there giving my opinion on your behalf. You will be able to speak for yourself, too. And Ted will be there so that you're not alone."

"I have to tell myself that this trial is an adult's business; it's not a fourteen-year-old's business to have to take care of," Linda says. "If I can get myself in that mode, I know I can do fine. I have to sit there and feel confident and remind myself that I have the ability to do that."

Linda gets a resolute look on her face. "I have to do this, not just for me, but for Ted," she says. "He had a dream the other night that he was picked up by a couple of police officers who told him he was being questioned for raping a little boy the night before. And he said, 'How could that be? I was with my wife, and she can testify to that.' And they said, 'Don't even try it. We know your wife is gonna cover for you.' Then he woke up, and he was sick over it. He said, 'Can you believe in my dream I was being charged with raping a child?' It was so sad. All of this is really getting to him—my rape, the police incident, my going to court, his going to court. This has to end."

I show Linda some stones with affirmative words like *trust, forgiveness, truth,* and *hope* written on them. "Do any words on these stones capture some meaning that you think you should focus on today and tomorrow?" I ask.

"Trust," Linda says. "I have to trust the people who will be there to support me and trust myself that I'll be all right."

She picks up the stone with *hope* written on it and turns it over slowly in her hand. "I have to remember never to give up hope for a better future," she says softly. "I hope that tomorrow is going to be the last awful thing in my life." Then she asks, "Is it okay if I keep this one with me? I'll give it back to you after the trial."

"Of course."

The next day I sit in the courtroom, anxiously awaiting the judge's decision after providing expert testimony about Linda's posttraumatic dissociative symptoms and how they influenced her behavior on the night of her arrest. I am proud of the way Linda has spoken up for herself, maintaining her composure and dignity under difficult circumstances.

Finally the judge renders his opinion. He acquits Linda of the charges against her, reinstates her license, and mandates continuing psychotherapy.

Linda hugs her lawyer and rushes over to Ted to embrace him. She turns around and gives me a broad smile, raising her arm in a kind of victory salute with the stone that says *hope* held tightly between her fingers.

13

JEAN W.: NIGHTMARE VISIONS

THE GREEN LIGHT

We ARE DOING the initial interview when Jean quietly and matter-of-factly starts talking about that fateful night some thirty years ago when her mother killed her father. She recounts this singularly traumatic event with a gifted storyteller's eye for detail and a daughter's indelible memories of horror and profound loss. Now, at forty, married and the mother of two young children, she is a junior in college pursuing a B.A. in sociology, a remarkable accomplishment in light of her hardscrabble family history filled with trauma and grief. She tells her story in the strangely subdued manner of an abuse victim who has had to detach herself from her emotions in order to survive. Here, culled from several sessions, is her narrative of an impoverished childhood and an unforgettable night that left her fatherless at the age of nine.

My father was a violent man, and that's how he died—violently. He'd lost his business by then, and we were living in an old farmhouse in the foothills of the Adirondacks near the Canadian border. Our house was high up in the thick woods, and it was so dilapidated that my mother once fell through the kitchen floor. Whatever money my father earned in the lumber mills he drank away. He was often too sick to work. There were five children in our family, and we rarely had anything to eat. We had no electricity most of the time, no indoor toilet, no central heat, no hot running water. Our frozen outdoor latrine was the strangest washroom ever: a chamber pot cracked from ice, a wash basin with no pipes, a claw foot tub, tilted from a missing leg and stained greenish brown. The living room was bare except for a worn-out wood stove, a sofa, a card table, a kerosene lamp, and an old red armchair where I used to sit in my father's arms. I still remember that sweet smell of tobacco and port wine.

Our community was very small, isolated, and poor. No one lived within sight. Our closest neighbors were about three-quarters of a mile away. When we played outside, all we could see for miles and miles around was one lush green mountain after another, like the Emerald City in *The Wizard of Oz*. It was breathtakingly beautiful, and it's the only part of my childhood that I wouldn't change.

I don't remember very much of the years before six except for one thing: I remember violence. My father brutally beat the older children in the family, especially my brother Eddie, the middle child. He was the scapegoat, the battered boy. How he was treated was unforgivable. I can still see him running from my father with his arms twisted about his head and hear the sound of leather across his back. My sister Betty and I spooned together in her bed, squeezing our eyes shut and humming and thumping our feet to drown out the noise of my brother's screams.

I called what happened at home every night the "Circle Game" because our house was constructed like a big loop. My father would chase after Eddie, and my other brother, Gavin, who loved a fight, would run after them. Then my mother would come. And there'd be all this punching and screaming and swearing and banging doors and throwing things. They would chase round and round and round. And I can't remember who won—and I can never forget—the Circle Game.

I was the youngest child and my father's favorite, so I was able to escape direct beatings. For the most part, if I laid low, I was invisible. When my father was drunk, he was the meanest man in the world, and I can't remember ever seeing him when he wasn't drunk. He fought with my mother constantly and abused her physically, sexually, and mentally. My relationship with him was bittersweet. One minute he would hold me in his arms and hum to me and call me his "little blackberry" and be very loving, and the next minute he was punching my mother in the face. He wasn't physically or sexually abusive to me—not that I can remember—but just witnessing the violence in our household was mental abuse enough.

The first memory I have of my mother was an incident that happened when I must have been three or four years old. I was sitting on the kitchen floor, and she was ironing and having a fight with my father. He walked out the door, probably going to the bar to drink. And my mother yanked the iron out of the plug in the wall and threw it out the window at him. The cord ripped off and slapped the wall next to my face. I was sitting right under the window, and all the glass came slamming down on me. My mother ran out the door after my father, yelling at him, and she never turned around to see whether I was okay. That gave me an inkling of how hot her temper was, but who could foresee where that would lead?

All of the children in our family went to school at a three-room schoolhouse that held grades one through six. What I remember most about school was that they had free breakfast and lunch. It was great to get food. The school nurse diagnosed us with malnutrition three different times, and the women in the cafeteria were very good to us. It was the one place in the community that was able to provide us with some kind of charity. My parents resisted charity, because they were ashamed. They were striving so hard to be working-class, so they tried to cover up the abuse and neglect by denying it and pretending to be what we weren't.

The community was not all that willing to help. Most of the people looked down on us. We were the lowest of the low, the poorest of the poor. A minister from a neighboring town once tried to intervene on my brother Eddie's behalf, but my father physically attacked him. Then there was a schoolteacher, Mrs. Alden, who tried to talk, woman to woman, with my mother, but there was a moral implication in her "friendly" visits. She was a middle-class lady coming into the home of an impoverished one, trying to tell her how to do it right. My mother would go out of her mind. She would scream and cry that they were implying that she was an unworthy person. It played into all of her fears about Judgment or God. My mother was a lapsed Catholic. She often told me, "There is no God for women."

Both my mother and my father were hopeless romantics who had trouble distinguishing reality from fantasy. They were impressed with the image of Camelot projected by the Kennedys and had dreams of power, grace, and beauty. They didn't understand the difference between Camelot and hell.

It's hard to explain my mother. She was an unskilled woman, an empty woman who didn't have any daily living skills. She didn't know how to keep a house, didn't know how to raise her kids, and didn't know how to cook, all of which was really odd for a woman at that time. My mother didn't value her children. She was emotionally unavailable to us, and she hit us and neglected us to the point of cruelty. But she was bright. She was a reader and a writer. She wrote love stories and tried to get them published a few times, but they were rejected. Denial was all she knew. She felt powerless to change things, so she worried about how things looked. She made up rules—say "bahth" for bath, stand up straight, sit down straight, sit with your legs crossed, don't swear, don't speak unless you're spoken to, don't put your elbows on the table when you eat—as if a Boston accent and good manners could erase the chronic alcoholism, violence, poverty, and dependency that our lives were all about.

My early childhood went by without any notice of the usual developmental markers or milestone events. There were no logs of when I first sat up, took my first step, or got my first tooth; no home movies of my first bike ride or my first day of school. There was little nurturing in my family. It was mostly a matter of survival. I didn't have a bicycle, and I really don't remember any children's books in the house. The sickness of our parents bled down into our relationships as siblings. At times a brother or a sister could be far more dangerous than a parent. You learned to watch everything closely. Nonverbal communication was all-telling in our family. The look on a face or a tone of voice could tip you off about someone's intentions and forewarn you that trouble was ahead. My brothers and sisters tortured me and were violent to me and to each other. They got a big kick out of hanging me tied up in a chair from a clothesline strung across the kitchen and forcing me to drink homemade vile concoctions. In our house conflict resolution simply meant the meanest won.

We were taught not to kill, steal, lie, or cheat, but our values didn't stretch into our community. I mean, they were all racist rednecks, to be honest. The adult world was so corrupted, and the boundaries were really loose. It was not uncommon to be hit by your neighbors' parents—or worse. At school during recess there was a game called "got you." The boys would chase the girls around, and if they caught a girl they would throw her to the ground and stick their hands down her pants. But there was an age limit: you had to be in at least the third grade. This "game" took place as the teachers stood around talking to each other. The girls at school were being sexually assaulted right under the teachers' noses, and they paid no attention to it. They had the "Boys will be boys" and "Girls will be victims" philosophy.

Another game I used to play at school, with one friend in particular, was "reading." At recess we would take a book and pretend to read it. She did most of the "reading," and all her stories were about bondage, rape, fathers and sons having sex with mother and daughters. This girl was out of school a lot and finally ended up at a burn center because one of her brothers lit her on fire. This was our community.

My father's death was the end of my childhood. It happened one night when he came home drunk as usual, and my mother started fighting with him in the kitchen. I remember everything about that night like a videotape, oddly enough, because there's so much of my life that I don't remember. My brothers, Gavin and Eddie, and my oldest sister, Ginny, weren't home. My sister Betty and I were playing cards at the table in the dining room. While we sat there, the fighting in the kitchen got louder and uglier. My mother was screaming at my father to stop hitting her, but the blows went on and on. All we could hear were my mother's screams and the sickening sound of my father's hand pummeling her mouth and his knuckles smashing into the bridge of her nose. Flesh against words and bone against bone.

Suddenly it got very quiet, and we thought that my father had finally passed out. But then my mother came into the dining room clutching a serrated paring knife dripping with blood and told us that my father had committed suicide.

"You saw what happened, didn't you?" my mother asked. It was a leading question. "You saw him plunge this knife into his chest, right? You could hear me yelling at him not to do it, couldn't you?"

My sister, who was eleven, ran to the Comlys', our nearest neighbor, to get help—we were so poor that we didn't have a telephone to call 911. I started screaming, jumping around, and wiggling my hands, and I kept running back and forth from the kitchen into the living room, back and forth. My mother was on the floor with my father, and she yelled at me to stop it. I came back into the kitchen and must have been there for at least half an hour, and it's just all blank. I don't remember anything except the blood. It was everywhere. It was gushing from a hole in my father's chest, just pouring out. He'd been stabbed clear through the heart. The floor was covered with blood, the stove was streaked with it, and it was dripping down our old round-topped refrigerator. I guess my father slumped against the stove first, staggered to his feet, and fell backward and slid down the refrigerator to the floor. There's a lot of blood in the human body—a lotta, lotta blood—and I think it all came out.

My mother sent me to the Comlys' to stay there for the night while she waited for the police to come. When Mrs. Comly saw me in my blood-soaked clothes, she said, "Oh, poor Jeanie, you come right upstairs and take a nice bath, and we'll find something clean for you to wear."

After my bath I went downstairs in a pair of pajamas and a bathrobe that belonged to one of the Comly girls. The clothes must have been freshly laundered because they smelled of soap. Mrs. Comly thought that some warm milk would help me sleep, and she gave me a glass. I was standing at the kitchen window sipping the milk and staring out into the pitch-dark when I saw this bright green light, all aglow, coming down the path in the woods toward the house. It looked like an asteroid that had fallen from the sky. I thought it was my father.

I began shouting to the people in the house, "Look out the window! Look! It's Daddy! It's Daddy! He's coming down the path in a green light." My neighbors shushed me and said that it was only my imagination and that maybe I should lie down and try to get some sleep. But to me, that light was my father, the last bit of connection. It was silent, but for some reason it gave me the courage and will to go on. I called the light Knowledge. It became my strength, and it's with me still.

CAVE GIRL

Jean is here in the first place because she has symptoms of anxiety that recently landed her in the emergency room. Her anxiety is related to her fear that she won't succeed in school. She desperately needs her sociology degree so that she can get out of her marriage to a nonsupportive man who cheats on her, spends most of his $50,000-a-year salary on lottery tickets and pot, and has left the rearing of their two children, five and nine, largely to Jean. One semester she's an outstanding student with an A in Spanish, and the next semester she's handing in late papers and flunking Spanish, the kind of rapid, inexplicable change in abilities or loss of skills that smacks of dissociative amnesia.

What an unspeakable trauma for a nine-year-old girl to go through, I think, after hearing Jean's story at our first session: her mother stabbing her father to death while she was in the next room.

"Did you actually see your mother stab your father?" I ask.

"No," Jean answers, "but the way she coerced my sister and me to lie and say we saw him kill himself made it obvious that that's not what happened. Later the autopsies and other evidence showed that he was killed." She recalls how *she* lied about the killing to protect her mother when she testified in court. "They asked me about a glass of port wine that my mother was drinking that night. I told them that she *wasn't* drinking it— that she poured it on my father's wounds and tried to save his life. I think I watched too many cowboy movies," she laughs, "and they knew I was lying."

"What happened to your mother? Was she found guilty?"

"She was indicted for my father's murder, but the case was dismissed for lack of sufficient evidence," Jean informs me. "Actually it was thrown out on a legality because it wasn't listed on the court docket in time to be tried, so they let it go." She recalls the unfortunate publicity: "When it happened, the local newspapers splashed it all over the front pages in huge headlines: 'Mother of Five Denies Murdering Her Husband' and 'Father of Five Killed by Wife.' When I went to school, the kids picked on me a lot about my mom killing my dad. They said my mother was a murderer."

I commiserate with her about the cruelty she suffered from her peers and ask, "How did you feel about your father's death?"

"There was this sense of relief," Jean admits. "I really loved my father, but by the time he died he was so sick and so mean from the drinking that all I could feel was, 'Oh, thank God, it's over.' It didn't matter how or why it happened, just that it did."

"Did you stay with your mother after he died?"

"No, my mom went away for a while, and Betty and I went to live with the Comlys. My brothers were staying with different people in town, and my oldest sister, Ginny, was married and on her own. Five months later we were all living together again, except for Ginny. Things didn't get any better at home. When I was eleven, my mother was diagnosed with breast cancer. It was too far gone to save her. She died two years, two months, and two days after my father. Neither of them lived to see fifty."

"How did you react to your mother's death?"

"I started to develop strange symptoms. Nothing around me seemed real. And I couldn't feel anything. I became very emotionally detached from my life. When I was twelve, I was taken to a mental health clinic for a psychiatric evaluation. They diagnosed me with severe depression."

"So your emotional detachment started when your mother died?"

"No, it started the night my father died," Jean says. "I didn't feel any kind of terror when they took my mother away, or in the days after. She was lost by then. We never talked about the beatings and what it was like for her. We never talked about the reality of the stabbing; only about what she wanted me to say about it. We never really talked at all. I'm upset that she threw her life away in a rage, but I just couldn't feel anything for her. I was numb inside. I guess I was in a state of posttraumatic shock. I blocked my feelings out then, and I'm still doing it now."

"How?"

"I have this noise inside my head—a kind of shrieking, squeaking, screaming noise—and I turn the volume up whenever I feel anxious or hurt," Jean reveals. "It stops anything from having any impact on me, or if there is an impact, it stops me from feeling it."

"When did you first start having this noise?"

"I think I set it up originally as a defense system so that I could hide from the violence around me and shut it out. I would hide somewhere and rock myself and listen to the noise and not feel so afraid. I remember making that noise the night my father died—I don't know whether it was audible or not—or when anything else terrible happened in my life."

"When do you hear the noise in your current life?"

"I'm hearing it right now," Jean says surprisingly, "because I'm nervous about what you're going to ask me. I hear it during supervision at school to keep from being hurt by criticism. And I hear the noise at home when I'm with my husband. That's what makes it possible for me to stay with him." Jean frowns and adds uncomfortably, "But listening to the noise is becoming more painful than what's going on outside."

"The noise is not only painful, it's no longer necessary," I tell her. "You developed it to protect you from feelings that arose from being in a violent and very dangerous situation in the past. Your current life isn't filled with violence and you don't have to get into or stay in situations that aren't safe, so you don't have to block out your feelings anymore."

"Yeah, but if the noise doesn't stay there, if you don't keep your guard up," Jean objects, "then you don't know what's going to happen."

"Do you still want to cope with life by not allowing yourself to feel?"

"No," Jean answers quietly. "Being emotionally detached from myself all the time feels very bizarre. I have to struggle to stay connected. When I answer intelligently in class, I think, 'This person is bright and articulate.' But afterward I couldn't even rephrase what that person just said. I'm aware that I said it and that people are responding to me, but it just feels weird, like, 'Where did *that* come from?'" She goes on, seeming somewhat confused, "Sometimes my husband doesn't seem real to me. He's like a complete stranger I should know but don't. And when I look back on my life, I don't feel very connected to my experiences. It feels like someone else's story. I don't own my life, and I'd like to be able to."

The noise Jean hears in her head has become a double-edged sword. She used it to detach herself from her feelings and from her environment as a terrified little girl. Now these once-useful coping devices—depersonalization and derealization—are working against her, keeping her disconnected from her feelings and memories and stuck in a degrading marriage. That's the insidious thing about habitual dissociation—some people find that detaching themselves from disturbing situations and their feelings about them enables them to go on with their daily lives, but at the same time it prevents them from addressing their worsening problems.

Elaborating further about depersonalization, or "this void of feelings," as Jean calls it, she says: "Now when I connect emotionally to my daily experiences, because I never really did that before, I get bombarded by feelings sometimes. When I'm really upset, like when I found out that my husband was cheating on me, I get a whole barrage of feelings that have nothing to do with what's going on. So I have a panic attack and hyperventilate."

"Is that what happened a couple of weeks ago when you ended up in the ER?"

"Yes, but it was about another man, not my husband," Jean replies. "I had a friendly relationship at school with Drew, my statistics professor. It started becoming very provocative and strange for me, and I was feeling really overwhelmed. The feelings Drew aroused all of a sudden connected me to a lot of other feelings about my sexuality that had nothing to do with Drew." Jean laughs self-consciously. "I know I might sound kind of Sybil-like, but I'm becoming aware of different levels of my sexuality and different aspects of myself for the first time, and it's very overwhelming."

I suspect that these different "levels" or "aspects" of herself that Jean has become aware of are separate fragments of her identity. Like many people with a dissociative disorder, she does not think of them as distinct personalities.

"Can you connect the feelings that Drew aroused to anything that happened in the past?"

Jean seems reluctant to answer. Finally, she says, "From the time I was six until my mother died, I was sexually abused by my brother Gavin. I don't remember much about it at all, but lately I've been having flashbacks about his hands. When my relationship with Drew started getting more intimate, it somehow triggered those memories." She pauses and adds, "And then I remembered Troy, too."

"Who was Troy?"

"My brother-in-law," Jean answers. "My sister Betty and I went to live with our oldest sister, Ginny, in New Hampshire after our mother died. Ginny was married to Troy, and they had a baby. Life in New Hampshire was very different."

"How so?"

"We lived in a nice house, we had family meals with a lot of food, and we had clothes," Jean recalls. "It was the first time in my life that all my clothes matched from head to toe when I went to school in the morning and I hadn't witnessed violence, verbal abuse, sickness, or death before I got on the bus. I entered junior high school virtually illiterate and way below grade level. I was a poor student, but I was starting to develop some reading and writing skills. And then it was all ripped apart in less than a year."

"What happened?"

"Troy, my sister's husband, started molesting me sexually, and one night he forced me to have oral sex with him," Jean reveals. "It was at the point where I was afraid he was going to rape me. I told my sister, and she slapped me across the face and said that I was sick. Eventually, she divorced Troy, but she couldn't believe that he would do anything like that then. She packed up her stuff and took the baby to stay with a friend for a week, leaving me with Troy. I made it through a very scary week physically unharmed, but mentally angrier than I'd ever been. Six months later my brother Eddie was killed in a car accident. It was too much! I started to experience some of the old symptoms. Four months after Eddie's death I was living on the streets. I was sixteen."

"What happened then?"

"I fell into the drug culture of the seventies and became promiscuous and got involved in sexually abusive relationships," Jean answers. "I discovered very fast that drugs alleviated many of the symptoms of depression. I was a heavy user of pot, heroin, cocaine, prescription drugs, or anything else I could get my hands on until I was eighteen. After that I turned to alcohol. I drank for nine years until I was arrested on a DWI charge and thrown in jail. That cured me. I went through a thirty-day program and six months in a halfway house, and I've been sober for as long as I drank."

With so much emotional pain bearing down on her, Jean, like many substance abusers, resorted to mood-altering drugs to self-medicate or distance her consciousness from symptoms like depression and anxiety. She may also have used alcohol and drugs to escape from her dissociative symptoms, particularly the feeling of disconnection from her life. Although alcohol and drugs may induce such dissociative symptoms as depersonalization and memory "blackouts" in people who don't have DID, substance abuse can also exacerbate dissociative symptoms in people who do. When dissociative symptoms precede substance abuse, as in Jean's case, they can't be written off as a function of drinking or drugging.

"I think I was going in a direction with Drew that stirred up a lot of memories of sexual abuse and my own self-destructive behavior," Jean says, "even though our relationship is nothing like that. I didn't realize what was happening and just became so panicky that I ended up in the hospital."

"You'll learn how to recognize triggers like that and realize that you're in control of your sexuality now and don't have to be a victim," I reassure her; "and that will keep you out of the ER the next time you're in a similar situation."

"I have this image of my sexuality as three different women," Jean reveals. "There's this tough, promiscuous, flirtatious 'bad girl,' who invited sexual abuse in my nonsober period, and this loving, caring 'good girl,' whose passion is tied into being a wife and mother. The third woman is a mute survivor of rape and incest and other sexual abuse, who sort of stands back and watches the two without saying anything."

This compartmentalization is typical of many sexual abuse survivors who dissociate during sexual abuse in childhood and develop a split-off part of their sexuality that can be reckless and aggressive about sex later in life as an expression of intense rage. People who've been sexually abused as children are very susceptible to abuse in other relationships, because the only love they know is associated with abuse. It's familiar to them, and they tend to reenact it with the partners they pick. They may also believe on some level that they brought the abuse on themselves or should have been able to extricate themselves from it and don't deserve anyone other than an abuser. Conversely some women who've been sexually abused as children pick out men who are completely the opposite of their abusers or may be so traumatized that they can't trust any man and undermine or shun relationships altogether. Finally, like Jean, an abuse victim who thinks that part of her sexuality is "bad" may want to express the "good" part in marriage and motherhood but picks an unfaithful and irresponsible husband to prove just how "good" she can be.

"There's another part of myself I call Cave Girl," Jean reveals. "I can't talk or write about her, so I started drawing pictures of her."

"How old is she?"

"She's young, maybe five or six," Jean answers; she adds, "At first she was a very dirty little girl, unkempt, neglected, completely isolated in the cave. I cleaned her up, and I'd put flowers next to the cave to try to draw her out into the sunshine or a campfire to bring her out at night. And suddenly, there was this other girl, older and not as dirty or messed up. I drew the older girl, Jeanie, so the little girl in the cave would know she's not alone. But Jeanie is never next to the little girl; she's always apart. I've never been able to get Cave Girl out of hiding."

"Can you communicate with Cave Girl?"

"No. She's too far back and unreachable and unmanageable. When I want to reach out to her I'm too scared."

"Can the little girl communicate with me?"

"No, I don't think so. She can only communicate anger to me. That makes me uncomfortable."

In some ways, the Cave Girl image is an apt way to describe that inaccessible part of Jean that is beginning to emerge from hiding. When Jean describes Cave Girl, there is always a sense of innocence and gentleness associated with Cave Girl. Jean wears no makeup to illuminate her cover-girl complexion and dresses in simple yet fashionable clothes, often in black or dark brown. Her radiant brown-green eyes and wavy russet hair tumbles loosely to her shoulders. I am impressed with Jean's ability to nurture this side of herself that has contained much fear and sorrow. Her descriptions of Jeanie visiting the cave symbolize Cave Girl's reawakening.

"When did the little girl in the cave first come around?" I ask her.

"She started when I was eleven, right before my mom died."

"How does she feel?"

"She feels nervous about my coming to therapy. She's anxious about being revealed, being discovered. She's anxious about her anger, not staying in control."

Jean has the normal anxieties about drawing her hidden Cave Girl out into the open after so many years in the dark: Am I crazy? Will you think I'm crazy? Will I get worse and not be able to function? I try to reassure her. If Jean is to recover, we need to find out what secrets the little girl in the cave is keeping.

BARNYARD GAMES

Summer days like this made the mountains and woods surrounding the old farmhouse in the foothills of the Adirondacks a thing of surpassing beauty. The majestic geometry of a forest of pine trees thrusting skyward toward the fiery red-orange circle of the sun was a magnificent sight.

"One, two, three, four." The game of hide and seek with her brothers and sisters had started, and six-year-old Jean ran through the kitchen to the wood pit outside, lay down on her stomach, and dangled her legs over the edge. Her hands searched for a ledge somewhere and found it. She dug her fingers into the rough wood floor, shimmied three feet to the left, and with a desperate grab, reached out and snared the old rusty tractor chain. The chain buckled around her fingers as she swung, praying not to fall, and dropped herself down to the top of the fieldstone foundation.

As she let the chain go, Jean saw white pinch marks on her fingers.

She arched backward to the ground and landed smack on her rear end. Quickly jumping to her feet, she spotted a convenient hole in the wall and slipped through it into the garage under the kitchen. Jean stopped and held her breath. Was her sister Betty still counting? She couldn't hear. I'll hide under the horse sleigh, she thought, but decided she'd be found too easily. No, go on, she told herself; get to the barn. God knows what would happen if she lost the game.

Jean climbed up into the odd crawl space that had no room above it. Cobwebs full of dirt hung down all over. Maybe she should stay here. No one would look. But she couldn't. It was too narrow and scary. She crawled out the hole at the end of the crawl space and into the barn.

There were no animals in the deserted barn, and everything had fallen into disrepair. The air was still thick with the pungent odor of cow dung mingled with the tangy molasses smell of silage, earth, dust, and old hay. Jean pushed the water trough, and to her surprise, water gushed out—the one sign of life in the spooky old barn. She pushed it again, and the pipes banged with the pressure. A dead giveaway! Where to hide? Jean was scared. Everywhere she looked she saw spiders crawling on their spindly legs, and she hated spiders! She wished she didn't have to play the game, but she didn't want to be called a chicken—or, worse still, a *baby*.

Jean walked slowly down the aisle, listened, but heard nothing. The ladder that led to the next floor had mostly broken rungs. The second rung was intact, but when Jean reached for the next whole one, she heard a thump above her. Her heart began to pound wildly, making it hard for her to swallow. Carefully she put her foot on the stump of one of the rotted rungs and pushed up. Her hands reached for the first floor, and she began to pull herself through the trapdoor. What if they step on my fingers before I can get through, she wondered, or kick me in the face as my head pops up? No, no one is around. It's just my imagination, she assured herself, trying to calm her fears. She pulled herself through the door and sat on the edge. One more flight and she would be in the hayloft. No one would look for her there. They'd all think she'd be too afraid to go there by herself.

The stairs to the hayloft were still in good shape. She poked her head through. Oooh! Hay ticks! There must have been millions up there. But the smell of warm fermenting hay was luscious. She decided to hide over by the hay door and keep watch. She was gazing at the three wooden beams saddled with burlap and bailing twine when—

"BOO!"

Someone's hands were around her throat, and she was slammed backward to the floor. God! Oh, God. Terrified, she stared at the boy pinning her down and looming over her. It was Gavin, her twelve-year-old brother.

"Get off!" she yelled, kicking futilely at him.

"Crybaby!" Gavin jeered. "I followed you." His lips curled in a snide smile. "Pretty brave today up here in this old hayloft with the spiders and ticks, aren't you?"

"Yes, I—I—I'm a big girl," Jean quavered.

"I'll wait with you, 'big girl.' "

Gavin got up and slumped into a pile of hay. He lay back and watched Jean without saying a word.

Jean sat with her back to him and could feel his eyes boring into her.

"Want to play a game?" Gavin asked.

What game? Jean wondered. A knife game? Ghost? Werewolf? What?

Jean just wanted to please her big brother. She wanted to be liked.

"Okay," she said and turned.

He was exposed.

"I showed you mine; now you show me yours," he said. His eyes glinted at her, right through her. "Come on, I'll help you."

Her brother came toward her. Before she knew it, he had her pants off and was lying on top of her, covering her with his body.

NO! NO! NO! Oh, God! Oh, please! Please don't. Please. Please. Please.

Dizzy, dizzy, dizzy, dizzy, dizzy, dizzy, dizzy. Blank. BLACK.

Cave Girl in College

At our next session Jean tells me that she has been having more detailed memories of her brother Gavin's sexual abuse. This is the first time that she has ever talked to anyone about the incest. She finds it easier to jot down her thoughts and memories, and I discover what a talented writer Jean is when she shows me something she has written called "Shadow Memories." It reads in part:

> I think about these shadow memories, these secret visions,
> sacred fears that make brothers and sisters, mothers and
> fathers act like some villains in a bad, bad movie. I'm that
> removed . . . but the main character.
> I think about abuse, sibling torture, mother's neglect.

And barnyard molestation. Who were the animals? Was it me?

What about the whip game with the father of four kids up the road?

What about the schoolyard game? Chase and violate. Only third grade and up can play!

Tied to a chair. Suspended. "Here, drink this." Aagh! "Don't move or you'll fall down and smash your head wide open. Ha, ha." Where did everyone go? God, don't leave me here like this. Please! My stomach hurts. I'm going to be sick.

"Good!" my mother says when she hears that Jack, an older guy who hangs around all the time, has a girl-friend. "Now maybe he'll leave my daughters alone." You knew!?

Turn out all the lights. Cover all the windows. Black-out horror. Every day gets pushed down more and more and more.

I have only the opening scenes, the first bad lines of a horror picture.

I'm trying to figure out how to live.

What an indictment of her childhood! It amazes me that Jean was able to survive such victimization without being chronically institutionalized. The trauma of being a virtual bystander to her father's death by her mother's hand would have been enough, in and of itself, to leave her with a severe posttraumatic stress disorder. Added to that, the continual domestic violence she witnessed and the parental neglect, mercurial volatility of her parents' personalities, sibling torture, incest, and other sexual abuse she suffered would have been impossible to survive, I conclude, without her starting to dissociate at an early age. Her academic difficulties, panic attacks, and relationship problems are certainly understandable, given what we know about how trauma and abuse in childhood can alter the brain's chemical processes in ways that inhibit learning, concentration, and attachment, among other aftereffects.

Jean's SCID-D clearly shows that everything she has endured has left her with a hyperactive and fixed response to perceived dangers. Only after she has responded in an extreme manner by dissociating can she return to rational thought and logically evaluate any perceived threat. She has moderate to severe levels of all five of the dissociative symptoms—amnesia for whole parts of her past and for subjects she is learning in school now;

depersonalization and derealization on a daily basis in any situation that makes her feel anxious or hurt, such as having supervision at school or confronting her husband in their troubled marital relationship; identity confusion experienced as a conflict between different "aspects" of herself; and identity alteration, as shown by the existence of her different parts: Knowledge, Cave Girl, Jeanie, and her compartmentalized Sexuality.

When I tell Jean that I have diagnosed her with DID, she becomes defensive. "I know I'm not as integrated as I should be and maybe I feel a real sense of denial," she says, "but this sounds like just another one of those big tricks. I came here because I had a panic attack and wanted help with my anxiety about not doing well in school. Why can't you just treat my anxiety?"

"I'll prescribe antianxiety medication for you," I tell her, "but the SCID-D shows that your symptom of panic about not doing well in school has an underlying dissociative basis. That means I need to work with you in a different way than I would with someone who simply has 'performance anxiety,' for example. We also have to work in a more advanced way than viewing Cave Girl as a kind of generic 'inner child.' Your child part appears to be a *separate* part of your personality, and it's more extreme than the conventional inner child. It takes control and comes out inappropriately and causes dysfunction, acting in current situations as if you were back in the past."

Jean looks intrigued. "Are you saying that Cave Girl is a part of me that doesn't know what's going on in school, and when that part takes control, I forget everything I've learned in Spanish?"

"That's right," I reply. "Cave Girl represents a lot of your childhood trauma. She carries the memories of your abuse. If you walked around every day having those memories, you couldn't function. That's why you have Knowledge. That part of you can be free of those memories and concentrate on your schoolwork. When Cave Girl, a part of you that doesn't have the memory of what goes on in school, comes out, that's when you don't do well, and that's where the problem lies. What was once an adaptive defense that helped you survive the abuse has become a problem now that you're no longer being sexually abused and have to go to school."

"How can I stop that part of me from coming out?"

"You don't need to stop her," I answer. "You need to have Knowledge communicate with her and help comfort her."

Even as I say this, I recall the story of Knowledge's genesis—nine-year-old Jean's father's returning to her in a green light the night he died.

I marvel at how this pitifully neglected and traumatized little girl was able to find a source of inspiration in her drunken, abusive, mostly unemployed father, who forced his family to live in abject poverty. By dissociating, young Jean could cope with her father's nightmarish death and preserve the moments of tenderness she had with him in a healthy part of herself that she gave the name Knowledge. It also seems to me that the green light she envisioned could be taken literally: the cessation of the daily furious violence in her home, so noisy and corrosive that it didn't allow the mind to think, that recruited from her father's death had given her the "green light" to move ahead and try to better herself.

"When Knowledge goes to school," I go on, "you need to have Knowledge share with Cave Girl so that Cave Girl can listen and learn and have the memories over time that Knowledge has, so she won't have to be banished to the cave and only come out under stress. Then you won't find yourself switching from high functioning to low functioning anymore."

"How can I make that happen?" Jean asks dubiously. "The little girl in the cave doesn't want to be reached. She wants to be left alone."

"You might want to try writing a letter to the little girl in the cave, comforting her so that she doesn't have to continue to relive old abuses today," I suggest. "Maybe have Jeanie, the part of you that you created to be her friend, write to her."

"There are other silent aspects of me that are full of anger and fear," Jean reveals, "but they're on my 'other side.' I'm not unconscious of the other side; it's just that I can't access it. It can come over, but I don't go the other way."

Jean has trouble communicating with her separate parts because she thinks of them mainly as mute. Her episodes of depersonalization are occasionally accompanied by interactive internal dialogues—one of the distinguishing features of DID—but most of the time she hears hidden parts as noises in her head or sees them in flashbacks. Except Cave Girl and Jeanie, who are very real to her, Jean experiences each of her other separate parts mainly as an intrusive, inchoate jumble of fear, anger, and sadness.

Knowing that she's typical of many people who've been forced into silence about the trauma they've suffered in childhood and find creative expression in artwork, I encourage Jean to use her ability to draw therapeutically. "Try drawing some more pictures of Cave Girl and draw the parts of yourself that you envision on the other side. Write down your thoughts about what each of them represents—the important feelings and memories they have—so that you can begin to reclaim them and connect them to yourself."

"It's hard," Jean says, "because I actually think that the other side is much more powerful than this one."

"Then that's all the more reason for you to get to know it," I tell her, "and help both sides share their strengths and feelings and memories and comfort each other and eventually become one."

FACES OF A MUTE SURVIVOR

The hand-drawn pictures Jean brings in depicting the parts of herself as she envisions them are astonishing in their power, stark symbolism, and raw emotion. Most of the drawings are in black and white, and the set bears the simple title "Aspects."

Jean's first picture is of Sexuality, a Janus-like figure with two opposite faces and a third face between them. On the right is the face of an innocent-looking young woman with her hair pulled back in a pony tail. She represents the "Good" or healthy part of Jean's sexuality—appropriate passion related to marriage and motherhood—that came into being after Jean went through rehab and became sober. In the center is the "Mute Survivor," a close-mouthed, stony-faced woman with hooded eyes who represents the observer part of Jean's sexuality. On the left is a hard-looking, sullen young woman with long eyelashes and shadows indicating heavy makeup. She represents the "Bad" or unhealthy part of Jean's sexuality that came along in puberty; survived sexual abuse by her brother, brother-in-law, and others; and is associated with her nonsober sexual behavior.

"The bad part has trouble with boundaries," Jean says.

"Yes, and I think it may have cropped up in your seductive relationship with Drew, your professor at school," I tell her, "and that triggered the flood of memories and emotions that sent you to the ER."

The pictures of Sexuality show how Jean's internal barometer was totally skewed toward abusive relationships for a long time as a result of the abuse she suffered in childhood. Now that she has achieved sobriety and is getting healthier, she can realize that her current marital relationship is also abusive. She's at the stage at which her barometer—the "Mute Survivor"—is motivating her to leave her chronically unfaithful husband and not become involved in an inappropriate sexual relationship with the professor.

Knowledge is a pretty, clear-eyed, confident-looking young woman

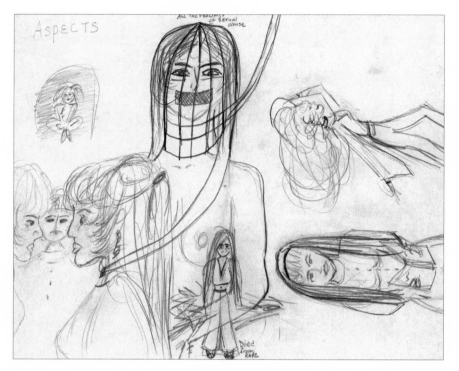

Aspects of Myself

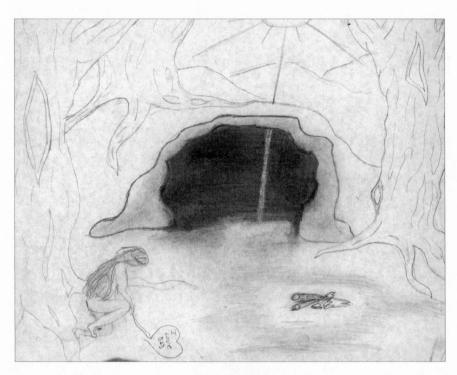

Cavegirl

Depression

Drowning in Alcohol from a Broken Heart / Hope After Rehab

The Wailing Woman

Family Tree

Anger

Wisdom

with long, straight hair (all of the images Jean draws, even Cave Girl, have the same loosely flowing hair as hers). Inspirational words like *wisdom, happiness, imagination, liberation, hope*, and *spirituality* are inscribed around her.

Cave Girl sits naked and cross legged in her dark cave—an isolated, forlorn little figure. Sometimes she is so far back in the cave as to be invisible. Outside trees surround the cave, the sun is shining, there are campfire logs on the ground, and a sorrowful teenage girl, Jeanie, is drawing a heart in the earth with the words "I love Daddy" inside, indicating that she shares Cave Girl's feelings of loss for their father.

In several "family portraits" of all of the figures together, Jeanie is always pictured near Jean's heart. "She's stuck," says Jean. "She's lost and scared and neglected and abused, but she's the part of me that really wants to be helped. She's not like the other little girl, who just wants to stay in a cave and be by herself."

One of the most striking pictures Jean has drawn is of someone from her hidden other side. She's a naked long-haired woman with a forbidding muzzle across her mouth and a rope around her neck like a hangman's noose. "This is the feeling I have of being caged," Jean says. "She came into being when I was living on the streets. She's the icon for all of the bottled-up feelings of pain and suffering and oppression I have about the sexual abuse and the killing of my dad that I've been silent about. Not being able to talk started when I was seventeen and lasted really severely for two years."

"How did you function during that time?"

"I could answer general questions with a 'yes' or 'no,' but that was it."

"Why does the woman have that yoke around her neck?"

"When I feel trapped, the halter around my neck holds my head up and keeps me from being connected to my body."

What a powerful symbol for depersonalization, I think. I notice what might be a hopeful sign that therapy is having a positive effect: in another picture the muzzle around the woman's mouth is gone and she has a mouth, indicating that she's no longer mute.

"This person came to be when I was twenty-one," Jean says, pointing to a drawing of a nude, muzzled woman in a coffin with bars on it. "I think she's the one who makes that weird noise and causes me to self-mutilate sometimes. She's how I feel about my painful memories—trapped and dead inside. Not only is it a coffin, but it's a caged-in coffin. She can't speak, and she's completely naked."

The one picture done with vivid color is of a horrified young girl peering out the barred window of a jail cell. Two bright red rivulets of blood are flowing like tears through the prison bars and down the iron door of her cell. "No matter how I try to clean her up I can't get rid of the blood," Jean says, "and I can't stop her screaming. She's nine years old and represents the fear, anger, and grief I've carried in me since the night my father was killed."

"This looks as if it was drawn by two different people," I remark as I unfold a large picture of the nine-year-old girl on one side and a unicorn on the other. The sharp contrast in styles is evidence of different personalities' taking control when Jean drew them. The girl is sitting on a stool inside a Beck's beer bottle with a blood-tipped knife going through her chest and is drawn in the simple, plain style of a young person. The huge unicorn with a golden horn and a tiny stick figure of Cave Girl outside her cave surrounded by green pine trees are done in the more complex and mature style of an older artist.

"I drew the unicorn to represent a magical, hopeful part of me that emerged after I came out of rehab," Jean explains.

The most intriguingly artistic drawing of all is of the little girl sitting in front of her cave with a gnarled tree behind her. The faces of Jean's identity fragments are subtly embedded in the trunk and branches of the tree and in the smoke swirling from the campfire in the foreground. One face merges with another, and it all has a "Now you see it, now you don't" quality. The picture imaginatively depicts the separateness of Jean's parts and at the same time their interconnectedness.

And, finally, there is Anger, a tough, hollow-eyed, alienated young woman with a cigarette dangling from her mouth, who started in Jean's teenage years when she got caught up in the drug culture and represents her nonsober years. In one picture Anger has a cage over her face and a gag over her mouth and tears running down her cheeks. There is a heart drawn around her with the names of Jean's daughters inside.

"Anger thinks it's really stupid that she can't say anything," Jean says. "We all know that if she did say something, I might feel better. I wrote my daughters' names in there because she doesn't know about my kids. If I really get into her mind-set I could kill myself."

"Because she's so depressed," I say. "Maybe as you begin to communicate more with the different parts of yourself and learn how to comfort them and have them share memories and feelings, Anger won't have to feel only pain and pain and pain."

"I've had healthy use of her lately for the first time, I think," Jean tells me, smiling. "I put my foot down with Drew and told him that I don't want to become sexually involved with anyone now. And I laid the law down with my husband, Clay, too. It's like a business agreement. I told Clay that he's free to go out and be with whoever he wants to be with, but don't bring her home."

"Is he physically abusive?"

"No, not to me or the children," she answers. "He's just not able to experience any kind of fidelity. His value system is different from mine. We're in different places from each other. Clay knows I've been to see a lawyer about a divorce, but of course he's in denial about it. His way of dealing with the world is not to deal with it."

I ask Jean how she is doing in school, and she says, "I think the antianxiety medication you prescribed has improved my concentration."

"Have you been trying to comfort Cave Girl when you feel nervous or upset?"

Jean shakes her head no. "There seems to be some—internal trust issue—that's stopping me," she says hesitantly, searching for the words to explain the resistance she has. "When I drew the pictures, I was finally able to give a face and shape to these different parts of me that have their own ages and memories and fears and angry feelings. I guess you could call them personalities, although I never thought of them that way, but I'm uncomfortable reaching out to them. When I tried to give Cave Girl a pep talk or write a letter to her or comfort the parts of me on the other side, I began to understand an internal conflict that I have."

"You don't trust yourself to do it?"

"That's right," Jean says. "It stems from the fact that I made a lot of bad decisions when I was younger. Those decisions hurt me, and even worse, they hurt others, maybe so badly that I can't trust my reasoning. So now when I try to communicate or open the door to my internal children, there's no adult person they can trust. I can't say, 'Please trust me, little girls,' when on so many occasions I've failed to make decisions and choices that were good for them. It's like asking the chickens in the hen house to trust the fox. Or an abused child to blindly trust her abuser."

"But there's a part of you that has grown up and can be trusted. You've shown that by being a very responsible mother to your own children."

"That's true," Jean concedes, "but the parts of me that've grown up are really traumatized themselves and don't have any faith in my ability to make good decisions. I think that has a lot to do with why I don't kick Clay out of the house."

"You're not giving yourself credit for the good decisions you *have* made," I answer. "You made a wise decision to go back to school, and you've made the decision to divorce Clay, but you have normal fears about not being able to support your children. So you *can* make good decisions. It's the part of you that doesn't believe that you can that's the problem. That part has to realize that you're a different person from the one you were when you weren't sober."

"I'm not the person you think I am either," Jean says cryptically. "I don't want to come off to be somebody I'm not. There are things about me that you don't know."

"Do you want to talk about that?"

"I can't," she says firmly. "I know I have to, but I don't think I can."

I wonder, after all Jean has told me about her "secret visions" and "sacred fears," what this haunting, fearful secret is that she is not yet able to reveal.

A Study in Contrasts

After several months of therapy Jean's resistance to doing the comforting exercises I've asked her to do begins to recede. She finds that having sympathetic internal dialogues with Cave Girl and writing encouraging letters to her and other frightened and angry parts of herself have significantly reduced her anxiety about failing Spanish. She is still struggling but has managed to stay out of the ER and is doing well in all of her other courses at school. She is also receiving high praise from the staff at a battered woman's residence where she does volunteer work and has been promised a practicum for her senior year.

Although Jean's switches from one personality state to another are subtle in another person's presence, the switch manifests itself more dramatically when she draws or writes to her separate parts. The dramatic difference between the following excerpts from two letters written by Jean shows that they were composed in two different personality states. The first letter is to Cave Girl from Jeanie, the semiliterate part of Jean that originated in her early teens. The second letter is to Jeanie from Jean herself when she is not in a dissociative state.

DEAR LITTLE CAVE GIRL,

WHAT CAN I DO TO HELP YOU? THE PEOPLE YOU ARE SO ANGERY WITH ARE DEAD AND GONE. I KNOW THE FEAR, ANGER, AND BRUATTALLITY YOU FEEL ABOUT THE WAY YOUR DAD DIED. HOW CAN I MAKE YOU UNDERSTAND HOW SICK YOUR MOM AND DAD WERE? MAYBE WE COULD CREAT A MAKE-BELEAVE PICTURE OF

THEM LOVING YOU THE WAY YOU WOULD HAVE LIKED. FIRST YOU MUST UNDER-STAND THAT YOUR DAD DRANK BECUASE HE MAY NOT HAVE KNOW THAT HE COULD, WITH ALOT OF HELP, STOPED. HE DRANK SO MUCH THAT IT MADE HIS MIND SICK. NOW IF HE KNEW HOW TO GET BETTER, HE WOULD HAVE BEEN THE LOVING WARM DADDY YOU WANTED. REMEMBER HIM HOLDING YOU IN THE BIG RED ARMCHAIR AND DANCING YOU AROUND ON HIS FEET? I'M TRYING TO SHOW YOU THAT HE WAS A GOOD MAN WHO WAS VERY SICK. SO IN OUR MAKE-BELEAVE PICTURE TRY TO SEE YOUR DAD NOT DRINKING.

IN MANY WAYS YOUR MOM WAS SICKER THAN YOUR DAD. SHE DIDN'T KNOW HOW TO DO THINGS FOR HERSELF. YOUR MOM AND YOUR DAD BELEAVED IN THIS VERY STRONG, WERLWIND KIND OF LOVE. SO WHEN YOUR MOM MET YOUR DAD, HE WAS NOT DRINKING, AND SHE THOUGHT HE WOULD TAKE CARE OF HER AND THEY FELL DEEP DEEP IN LOVE AND GOT MARRIED. THEN YOUR FATHER STARTED TO DRINK ALOT, AND YOUR MOM DIDN'T KNOW HOW TO LEAVE YOUR DAD WHEN HE STARTED TO HURT EVERYONE. SHE DIDN'T KNOW HOW TO GET A JOB OR A PLACE FOR EVERYONE TO STAY. SHE WAS RAISED BY A VERY STRICKED MAN WHO BELEAVED THAT WOMAN WEREN'T AS GOOD AS MEN AND SHOULD ALWAYS DO WHAT THE MAN SAID. YOUR DAD WAS THE SAME WAY AND YOUR MOM LIVED BY THAT HER HOLE LIFE. SHE BEGAN TO SEE THE TRUTH ABOUT HER LIFE ABOUT A YEAR OR SO BEFOR YOUR DAD DIED AND SHE BECAME VERY ANGERY AND BITTER AND SHE BLAMED YOUR DAD.

SO NOW IS THE HARDEST THING TO EXPLANE TO YOU. WHEN YOU MOMMY KILLED YOUR DADDY, IT WAS THIS ONE AND ONLY STAND SHE HAD EVER MADE. I'M NOT SAYING IT WAS THE RIGHT ONE BUT TO HER IT MUST HAVE SEEMED LIKE THE ONLY ONE. SHE PUT AN END TO THE YEARS OF HELL SHE LIVED WITH. I KNOW YOU DIDN'T FEEL LOVED BY HER, BUT DO REMEMBER THE TIME YOU WERE TWERLING A STICK OF WOOD LIKE A BITON? REMEMBER YOUR MOM SAID TO YOUR DAD "LOOK TOM MAYBE WE HAVE SOMETHING HERE" AND EVERYONE WATCHED YOU. YOU MOM WOULD HAVE PAYED ALOT OF ATTENTION TO YOU IF SHE THOUGHT THAT WOMAN WERE WERTHWILE PEOPLE.

SO YOU SEE WHAT HAPENED TO YOU WAS NOT YOUR FALT. YOU DAD HAD A DESEACE THAT MADE HIM SICK, AND YOUR MOM WAS NEVER TAUGHT TO BELEAVE IN HERSELF. SO FOR OUR MAKE–BELEAVE PICTURE TRY TO REMEMBER YOUR DAD NOT DRINKING AND YOUR MOM BELEAVES IN HERSELF AND THEY ARE BOTH LOVING YOU THE WAY THEY COULD HAVE. REMEMBER YOU ARE A LOVED CHILD, YOU WERE A LOVED CHILD, YOUR MOMMY AND DADDY JUST WERE TO SICK TO SHOW YOU. I CAN FEEL YOUR LOSING CONSINTRATION SO WE WILL STOP NOW.

LOVE YOU VERY VERY MUCH,

JEANIE

Dear Jeanie,

I am surprised to find you. I guess you were so close to me that I didn't feel your presence. I'm really sorry for not getting in touch with you sooner, but I am so happy that we found each other. Dr. Steinberg is helping me to discover ways to calm you, comfort you, and nurture you. I have part of your memory, so I can effectively tell you how things are today.

I know that you absorbed a lot of negative words and actions regarding your intelligence and ability to learn. But that was a long time ago. Today you are going to college with me, and whenever the path seems clear, you step out. You still carry the fears from a terrible time in the past when you were neglected and abused and not doing well in school. You may not be aware that today we are nearly a straight A student. We get along really well with all of our teachers and other students and are liked and respected by them.

Do you remember the Light that we got the night Dad died? Well, that light grew up a lot and became what I call Knowledge. She has learned most of what everyone else didn't have a chance to learn because you were all busy fighting the abuse. Knowledge is really quite bright and eager to learn.

What you need to do is let Knowledge go to school and finish getting a college education—even if that means she might fail Spanish. She could handle it. She is grown up enough to know that we can't be the best at everything. But if we show confidence in her and give her our support, I think she can get us through class without your suffering even more pain. Please don't be scared about Spanish anymore. Just relax and let Knowledge take over. You should not be expected to handle all of the failure while Knowledge experiences success. Remember, you are not alone and unprotected anymore. I will always be here for you, and I will never let anyone harm you again.

Love,
Jean

THE UNSPEAKABLE

A year has gone by, and Jean is a senior now, doing beautifully in school. The people at the battered women's center where she is doing her practicum love her. Jean is another familiar example of a troubled person drawn to the helping professions by the lodestar of private pain. Her empathy for those she serves is not unnoticed. She has come up with the innovative idea of a weekly "Ethnic Night" celebrating the food and culture of the different ethnic groups of the people in residence at the center. One night they prepare Hispanic foods and sing Hispanic songs and perform Hispanic dances; another night, Russian; and so on.

Jean tells me that Drew, her former statistics professor who made sexual overtures to her, called her for the first time in a long time. "He said he's been really, really sick," she reports, "and that he'd like it for us to start talking to each other again. I don't have a problem with that, but I don't need any more complications in my life. I'm just struggling so much with my mental health. I'm starting to see that the way I'm dealing with my divorce is not good for my kids, and I feel that I go in big circles."

"In what way?"

"I still perceive things as so unreal most of the time that I'm never sure of how valid anything I'm saying is," Jean answers. "It's been very hard putting the pieces of my life together because there's so much of it I don't remember. I fight month to month really hard to remember my children when they were younger, and I can't. It really bothers me."

"That's what happens when people split off their emotions," I remind her. "That defense is there to protect you, but when it continues after you may not need it, it gets in the way when you should remember what's happening in your life."

"I woke up this morning and nothing felt real. I didn't feel connected. I had this feeling of being outside myself, behind myself. I felt detached, like watching a movie in slow motion."

"Who was in control of you at that time?" I ask Jean, trying to pinpoint what brought on this most recent episode of depersonalization that she has so accurately described.

"I'm not sure," she answers. "I had this feeling of dread, of apprehension. It was a mixture of feeling that what I'm doing in therapy is positive and the fear that what I'm doing will blow up in my face."

"Did you try to comfort whoever was in control and let yourself know that you are safe in therapy?"

"Safety is a foreign feeling for me," Jean responds. "I can't picture it. Safety is not something that I've ever experienced. Not after what happened to my father and my mother's cancer and my brother Eddie getting killed. There's self-abuse that's going on that makes me feel unsafe. When I'm trying to feel safe, the self-abuse interrupts it."

"What's the self-abuse about?"

For the first time in the two years that she has been in therapy, Jean begins to cry.

"What are the tears about? What are you feeling?"

"I'm confused—I'm all mixed up in my head," Jean sobs. "The thought of expressing these really awful things—I'm uncomfortable; I can't share it. That makes me cry."

"The things that you lived through were awful, but that doesn't mean that you're awful. You're a very special person who has lived through awful stuff."

"That's not exactly true. I lived through a lot of awful stuff, but I did worse stuff."

"But you were a child. You were a victim."

"No, I wasn't."

"You're not responsible for the things you were exposed to when you grew up."

"No, I'm not talking about this person who grew up as a victim," Jean answers. "I'm a person who *victimized*."

"Well, sometimes that happens to people who have been victims," I offer.

But Jean doesn't want to hear any explanations. "I've done things that are unforgivable, unthinkable," she says. "When I'm in touch with what I've done, I experience a mental self-abuse that possesses me and enslaves me with self-hate."

I wait as Jean gathers the courage to tell me her awful secret. "I was eighteen," she begins, "and I killed a man."

FATAL JUNCTION

She wasn't in love with Bobby, but she felt comfortable with him. He was gentle and kind and intuitively sensitive—not bright or good at verbalizing his feelings, but tender and caring all the same. If it hadn't been for Bobby, Jean didn't know how she would have survived her brother Eddie's death two years earlier. She was sixteen then and living on the streets near the town where she grew up. Bobby used to hang out with Eddie and his best friend, Luke, a heavy drinker. Bobby wasn't with them the night of the accident. Luke was driving Eddie to his job at a gas station when he veered off the road and slammed into a telephone pole. Eddie went flying through the windshield and died instantly. He was twenty-one.

Jean turned to Bobby for solace after Eddie's death. She felt as if the accident had split her in two. Half of her was in shock, a void, like a vacuum or a wind tunnel that sucked feelings in and enveloped them in emptiness. The other half was like a rock, not as hard, but very battered and enraged and hurt, always prepared for violence from a stranger on the street—violence to be taken as a victim without fighting back.

At first Bobby was only a friend, someone who smoked pot with Jean while she lifted herself out of her pain for an evening. They drifted apart for more than a year. When they caught up with each other again, Bobby was a man with a dream. For someone so passive, he was surprisingly persuasive. They hadn't been seeing each other very long when he talked Jean into leaving town with him and going to Wisconsin.

"There's nothing here for us, Jean, except bad memories," Bobby said. "We both need a change of scene, a fresh start somewhere. I grew up in a town near Racine. My cousin has a landscape business there, and I could get a job with him. You'll find something there, too. There's gotta be more opportunity than what we have here."

Bobby was right, Jean thought. Everyone in town still remembered the scandal surrounding her father's death and treated her as a pariah. Whenever she drove past the road where Eddie was killed, it was a fresh reminder—a sharp knife in her own heart like the one that killed her dad. The pain was unbearable, and she was tired of stumbling around in a fog to escape it. There were periods when she just ceased to be at all. Living in communes, crash pads, or her car was growing stale. She loved working with kids, but not in the school system here, corrupt as it was. Maybe if she found work with kids in a decent environment somewhere else, she'd have the incentive to get off drugs and straighten out her life.

"Let's do it," she said.

Jean couldn't believe how quickly she'd landed a job at a day care center after they moved. The kids were underprivileged but unspoiled, and she had fun playing games with them and teaching them how to draw.

"Hi, honey, want to meet me at Pasquale's tonight on your way home?" Bobby said when he called Jean at work that day.

Pasquale's was a popular bar in the area, and this was their last night before the owner closed it down and retired.

"Sure, why not?" Jean said. The apartment she was living in with Bobby was little more than a shack and had no heat. That was all they could afford. They'd be better off getting a pizza at Pasquale's and hanging out for a couple of hours than spending the night in a dreary, cold apartment.

Pasquale's was noisy, crowded, smoky, and throbbing with loud music. Bobby and Jean shared a pizza, and each had a couple of beers—neither of them was much of a drinker and they'd spent all they had. They sat around at the bar, laughing and talking with friends. After a while the noise, smoke, and beer all combined to make Jean feel woozy and tired. Her head ached and her throat felt scratchy. Cold as their apartment was, she wanted nothing more than to go home and curl up in bed.

"Bobby, I'm really beat," Jean said. "Could we go now?"

"Yeah, I'm ready to split, too," Bobby said. "Let me pay the bill, and I'll walk you to your car."

Outside in the parking lot, standing in a drizzly fog, Bobby gave Jean directions home. Jean had been living there less than a month, and it was still unfamiliar to her. They kissed good night and got into their separate cars.

The ride home reminded Jean of flying in an airplane through thick clouds. She wasn't sure whether the murky fog was outside the car or inside her skull. Nothing around her looked familiar. In the darkness and mist no signs were visible to help her. She could make out none of the landmarks Bobby had mentioned. The road she was on looked deserted except for one low-slung building with metal shutters that she passed, probably a factory or a warehouse. Where was the highway Bobby told her to take? Had she made a wrong turn somewhere? A swirling uneasiness was beginning to build inside her.

Peering through the windshield, she saw red taillights cutting through the fog in the distance. The highway! Ah, back to civilization again. As Jean approached the highway, all at once she came to a hanging red traffic light at a junction that cut the road in half. There were three lanes headed east and two lanes headed west. Jean turned left toward the town where they lived. She went all the way over to the guide rails and continued up the road.

A man in a parking lot at the side of the road was waving his arms at her. Poor guy, what a night to have car trouble, Jean thought. If it hadn't been so late she might have stopped to help him, but not at this hour. In her rear-view mirror she saw flashing yellow lights and thought that was strange but kept on driving up the highway another two miles.

Oh, my God! Blinding lights coming straight at her! A blaring, screaming horn! The sickening sound of screeching brakes. She hadn't seen that the two lanes on the other side of the guide rails were going in the opposite direction. She was headed west in oncoming traffic going east.

The collision felt like a bomb exploding inside her body: the loud, visceral boom of the impact; shards of glass tearing into her flesh; the taste of blood on her lips; the smell of burning metal; the crushing pain. The last thought she had before she lost consciousness was, What have I done?

Jean woke up in the hospital to find one of her legs suspended in traction. It had literally been broken in half and was held together only by tissue. One of her arms had been broken, too. She had a head injury and multiple lacerations on her face and a row of stitches alongside her mouth where her tongue had protruded through the skin.

When a lawyer entered the room to question her about the accident, there was something about the solemn expression on his face that made her insides lurch with a stricken, abysmal feeling.

"What about the other driver?" Jean asked tremulously. "Is he okay?"

The lawyer took a long time before answering. "No," he said finally. "I'm afraid he's dead."

THE WAILING WOMAN

"He was just a man going about his business," Jean says, sobbing, "and I killed him. His name was Jason Mansfield, and he was only twenty-seven. When I think about that man's mother and his father, his brothers and sisters, friends, and how I took that away from them—it's unthinkable and there's nothing I can do. The most hideous thing that anybody can ever do is kill somebody—and I did."

"You didn't intend to do that or plan to do that, Jean," I remind her. Now I know where the jagged scar on the side of her mouth came from and what she meant by her relentless mental self-abuse.

"That doesn't matter. It doesn't change it," she says in a low, heartbroken voice. "I can't ever feel as awful and horrible as his friends and family must feel. I can never, ever hurt enough. I wish I died. I really do."

"Did you ever try to contact his family?"

"No, I was too ashamed. And I got very sick mentally, really insane, hearing all these voices and noises and conversations inside my head. I was very suicidal. I couldn't eat. They kept me in the hospital for seven weeks. Then I was out for a week and fell down a flight of stairs and broke my leg and went back in the hospital for another week."

"Did you have any psychiatric treatment?"

"The court sent me to a mental health center for suicide intervention. At first the therapist thought I might be schizophrenic because of all the voices and noises in my head. But then he told me that he was from upstate New York, too, and had read in the newspaper about my mother's killing my father. He was the first person to approach me about multiple personalities and asked whether he could hypnotize me. He tried to take me back to the night of the killing, but he was pushing me too hard, going too fast. It terrified me. I left and never went back."

"Did the court mandate any alcohol treatment for you?"

"No, I wasn't drunk when I had my accident," Jean answers. "I didn't start drinking until some time after that. I was originally charged with driving while impaired, but that charge was dropped because my alcohol level wasn't high enough." Jean sounds sorry that the court let her off: "I got charged with negligent vehicular homicide, and the lawyer went into court and said that I was all messed up. His argument was: 'Look where she came from, look what she went through, poor her.' It was like I had a horrible life, so I should be forgiven for this horrible event. And they let me go."

"Did you talk to anyone about the accident?"

"No, I completely blocked it out. Every time I started to think about it I tried to cut myself. But I couldn't do it, so I scratched myself instead."

Typically Jean's attempts at self-mutilation were both a way of dissociating herself from thoughts and feelings about the accident and a form of punishing herself for causing it and reenacting the pain.

"How about your family?" I ask. "Were they of any help?"

"My family didn't come to see me in the hospital and didn't want to have anything to do with me."

"Why?"

"Because I killed someone," Jean says bleakly. "I didn't speak to anyone in my family for a couple of years after that, and we still don't talk about the accident."

"Did you talk to Bobby about it?"

"I couldn't. He was a mess after the accident. He felt responsible for it, because I didn't know the way home, and he thought his directions weren't good enough."

"That junction sounds like a very dangerous place."

"There were five people who made the same mistake before I did, and three of those accidents were fatal," Jean informs me. "A lot of people were very angry about it, but the town didn't want to fix the highway because they didn't know how to do it without overpassing the town. I don't know if they ever resolved it. I moved away."

"So if you didn't talk about your grief to anyone, how did you deal with it?"

"I kept on trying to die and stay alive at the same time," Jean says tonelessly. "And I still feel that there's no rationalizing it or justifying it or coming to grips with it or forgiving it or letting it go. That's why I have the Wailing Woman."

"The Wailing Woman? Who is that?"

"That's an ageless part of me that has to be always mourning, always, always. If I stop mourning, then I have not lived up to what I was supposed to do. I can't ever forgive or forget, because if I do, that makes it really awful, even more awful than it was. It's a way of punishing me and not forgetting Jason Mansfield, not letting go of him."

"How can you comfort the Wailing Woman?"

"I don't dare comfort her," Jean answers swiftly, "because she's like a tombstone, a grave marker—something you don't disrupt in respect for whoever died."

"If you comforted her, does that mean that you're not being respectful to what she feels?"

"No, it means that I'm not being respectful to Jason Mansfield," Jean insists. "I can only honor his memory by keeping it with me and not letting it go away. Do you understand that I have to stay in grief?"

"I understand that's the way you feel," I counter, "but I don't agree that you have to be constantly in grief and never forgive yourself. I think you can remember what you did and feel responsible for what you did and feel terrible for what happened, but you can also begin to forgive yourself for what happened. You can stop punishing yourself constantly and honor the memory of Jason in a more constructive way."

"I keep thinking that I'll do something someday that will make up for the horrible thing I did, and there's no making up for it no matter what," Jean says. She begins weeping inconsolably. "I could sit here month after month, year after year, crying like this every single week, and I could just never stop. Anything that comes close to any kind of forgiveness gets me angry, and it gets me scared. The Wailing Woman allows me to live. As long as there's something that's in pain and suffering and sad and shrieking in my head, then I can keep going." Sounding confused and helpless, she sobs, "I can't figure out what the right thing to do is. I can't figure it out."

The Wailing Woman illustrates how strong the need for self-punishment is in abuse survivors. Although they didn't deserve and couldn't escape the abuse or trauma they suffered as children, adult survivors continue to punish themselves if they're not perfect. Having identified with their abusers, they can't accept or forgive any mistakes they make. At the same time people who relied on dissociation to cope with childhood abuse may continue to dissociate from traumatic events in their adult lives and deal with them in an irrational, compartmentalized way.

In Jean's case the only emotion she allows herself to feel is grief for Jason Mansfield. She has no sympathy for herself and only mute anger at her parents and siblings for all of the unthinkable things they did to her. She ignores the facts of the accident—she wasn't legally drunk; visibility was poor; five other people had accidents previously at the same hazardous junction—and focuses only on blaming herself. She can't integrate this experience and find a meaningful way to atone for it because she has a dissociated part of herself, the Wailing Woman, whose punitive purpose is to mourn perpetually and never let her forget or forgive.

This raises the whole issue of forgiveness, about which we hear so much today. Ideally it can be beneficial both emotionally and physiologically for an abuse survivor or a victim of a crime to forgive the offender. Forgiveness can dissipate anger, help relieve depression, and be useful in treating anger-related illnesses, but recent writings have shown that forgiveness is not always an essential element in recovery. It may not be realistic to expect total forgiveness of an abuser, given the horrific nature of the abuse in some situations. It has been argued that forgiveness covers up hatred and self-hatred rather than resolving them. Patients like Jean may also find it difficult to resolve the guilty feelings they don't deserve to have if they are told to forgive their parents for abusing them with their destructive actions. For many abuse survivors, forgiveness for themselves is a bigger issue.

I try to find a way to help Jean see that she is harder on herself than she would be on others in the same situation. "If somebody you cared about experienced the same thing and came to you for counseling or comfort, what would you say to that person?"

"That actually happened to me," Jean replies. "Luke, the guy who was high on drugs and drove the car off the road in the accident that killed my brother Eddie, came to me at Eddie's funeral and begged my forgiveness. We decided not to press charges. I was really more angry at my mother and father for Eddie's life as a battered child than I was at Luke for the way Eddie died. Some of the grief I feel for Jason Mansfield is connected to my brother's death. They were both so young, and the accidents happened within two years of each other."

"So you were able not to blame Luke and direct your anger more appropriately toward your parents. Why can't you apply those same skills of forgiveness to yourself?"

"Because I should have known better," Jean answers. "I should've been more careful. I knew what happens when you drive recklessly or drunk. I knew. I had all of the information, and I didn't use it."

"But you weren't drunk, and you weren't reckless. You made a mistake. Does the Wailing Woman know what you grew up with? Does she know that you may have been quite depressed and emotionally impaired at the time? Why can't you trust yourself now that you're sober to take responsibility without having to punish yourself with guilt?"

"Because there always has to be a part of me that doesn't excuse what I did," Jean insists, "and won't allow a cop-out. It's always easier to say, 'Oh, look what happened to you; you were such a victim,' or 'Look where you came from and how well you've done, your schoolwork, raising your kids, blah, blah, blah.' That's a cheap rationalization. When I had my car accident, I stopped being a victim and became a victimizer."

"Is it one or the other?"

"Yeah."

"How does someone stop being a victim if that person has had certain life experiences in which he or she was victimized? Were those experiences erased by the fact that you had an accident?"

"Yes, the accident changed the world," Jean says. "I can never feel the same way about myself again." She begins to cry again. "There's just no way to undo what happened, so I'm always, always sad about it. I'm so sad."

"That's a natural feeling to have, Jean," I tell her, "and you need to share those feelings of grief with the Wailing Woman and comfort her. What do you think would happen to you if you comforted her?"

"It's not safe," Jean answers. "When I come into contact with this part of myself, I become self-abusive and suicidal, because that's what she's about—the self-hate."

"You become self-abusive and suicidal precisely because you're not comforting her," I counter. "She's your designated mourner. But you're strong enough now that you don't need to have one part of you do all the grieving by herself and punish you with guilt and self-hate when she takes control. Trying to contain the grief is what makes you feel caged in and stuck." I try to help Jean see how her punitive attitude toward herself is impeding her recovery. "At the same time that you're not allowing the Wailing Woman to forget," I point out, "you're also preventing the memory of Jason Mansfield's death from ever becoming integrated with the other parts of yourself."

"What do you want me to do?"

"Try to comfort the Wailing Woman so that you can get beyond remembering and make something positive come out of this."

ATONEMENT

At the next session Jean has a drawing she has made of the Wailing Woman. Draped in a shroud, she is an ancient-looking, skeletal crone sitting on the ground in front of a large dark globe representing the weight of the world. A puddle of tears lies at her feet. There is a flower sprouting in the puddle. An inscription reads, "I am born new from your sorrow."

Jean tells me that she wanted to visit Jason Mansfield's grave but has no idea where he is buried and can't locate his family. Nonetheless she has written a letter to his family and friends, expressing her feelings about his death. In part it reads:

> *There is no justice in this situation. If I go to jail for life, I still survive and Jason does not. How can I tell you how deeply I love him, too? No other thing has so profoundly cut my soul. I will forever have him inside me and feel the sharpness of this disaster.*
>
> *Not only do I feel the pain of Jason's death, but I also live in deep sorrow for all of you who loved him. I know that the death of one person creates partial deaths in the spirit of those who loved him. I see myself as responsible for the darkening of your spirits and will dedicate my life to making amends for this in any way that I can.*
>
> *I pray that you are strong and healthy people and are able to pick yourselves up from this catastrophe and move forward. I hope that you find ways to hold on to your love for Jason and through that love keep him alive.*

I'm encouraged that Jean's letter ends on the same hopeful note as the inscription on her drawing of the Wailing Woman. "What did you mean," I ask, "when you wrote, 'I am born new from your sorrow'?"

"I've given what you said about moving past grieving and taking positive action a lot of thought," she replies. "I called the township where I had my accident and found out that they finally put up a decent traffic light and warning signs to make that junction safer. At least, Jason's death may have prevented other innocent people from getting killed. That got me thinking about ways that I could work in the community with regard to giving something back—you know, pay some kind of tribute to Jason Mansfield and show some respect for his life. I came to the conclusion that one of the biggest things I could do was to try to help people who've been injured through trauma and alcoholism and all those kinds of things—somehow to educate them and give them tools so that they won't hurt themselves or anybody else. I could talk to them about what happened to me and tell them what tools I've used to try to get better."

"Isn't that what you're doing at the battered women's shelter?"

"Yes, but I felt I wanted to extend that to a larger population—reach more people, change more lives—and I came up with an idea," Jean says excitedly. "I'd like to set up a local support group for people who've accidentally caused the death of an innocent person. If there had been a support group like that for me to turn to when I had my accident, maybe I wouldn't have become an alcoholic for nine years. I'm just lucky that I didn't kill someone else while I was drinking. Who knows how many lives that kind of support group could save?"

"That's a great idea, Jean!"

My praise is genuine. This is a big step Jean has taken toward integrating her dissociated traumatic memories of the accident, so long stuck in the past and mired in self-punishment, into her current state of being. Not only will her network comfort the Wailing Woman grieving for the man Jean killed, but by comforting others similarly traumatized, she will have found a uniquely appropriate way to honor the memory of Jason Mansfield.

WAKE-UP CALL

She was in the kitchen making a salad for dinner when the telephone rang.

"Is Jay there?" the man asked. He sounded upset.

"I'm sorry, you have the wrong number," Jean answered. "There's no Jay—" She stopped when it occurred to her that maybe the man with the shaky voice had the right man but the wrong name. "Do you mean Clay?" she asked.

"Clay, oh, that must be it, *Clay,* I'm sorry," the man said apologetically. "Are you his wife?"

"Yes. Clay isn't here right now. May I ask who's calling?"

"This is Hank Watson, Patty Watson's husband," the man said. He drew his breath in sharply and blurted, "Your husband is having an affair with my wife."

Jean could hear the hurt, anger, humiliation, and pain of betrayal in the man's voice. The poor guy probably just found out, she thought. She remembered her own shock and rage when she went home unexpectedly early from school one afternoon and found Clay in bed with Patty, his old girlfriend. Jean searched her mind for something to say to Patty's husband but couldn't think of anything that didn't sound insipid.

"Hello, hello?" Hank said. He thought she'd hung up.

"I'm here," Jean said. She decided to be straightforward. "Look, I've known about this for some time now, Hank, and I think you should know that my husband and I are getting a divorce. I feel truly sorry for my husband's behavior, but I'm not responsible for it." Jean tried to be compassionate. "I know how painful this must be for you. I wish there was something I could do to help."

Hank sounded on the verge of tears. "I can't believe she would do something like this. I thought we had a good marriage; we have children."

Improbably the conversation turned into a "hotline" call—Hank Watson pouring his heart out and Jean offering as much sympathy and support as she could. By the time she hung up, she felt so much anger and disgust toward Clay that her mind was filled with an intrusive stream of verbal lashings. She listened to herself screaming and hollering at Clay and at the same time screaming and hollering at herself.

She should have thrown Clay out months ago when she found pot in his bureau drawer. Before they were married, he gave her his solemn word: clean and sober and no drugs in the house. That was her one ground rule, and he'd broken it. She wanted to see whether he'd lie about the stash in his drawer after she found it, so she asked him whether the rumor going around that he was smoking pot again was true.

"That's bullshit!" he said vehemently. "I've been sober for twelve years, and I don't believe anybody would say that about me."

Clay went into his whole indignant, self-righteous posture until Jean couldn't stand it anymore. She took him into the bedroom, got the pot out of his dresser, and waved it in front of his nose. He began to cry and act helpless. This is his pattern, Jean thought: he does something wrong; I question him; he denies it; I call him on it; he whines and cries and carries on. She decided then and there that she'd had enough.

Now Jean had to tell him about the phone call from Patty's husband. She didn't hit him with it right away when he returned home, but after dinner she asked to talk to him in her study. They went in and sat down.

"Clay, I got a phone call from Hank," Jean said quietly.

"Hank who?"

"Patty's Hank. He found out about your affair and called asking for you, and I talked to him."

Clay's body became rigid, and his face flushed with anger. "Why did you talk to him?" he demanded. "Do you have any idea what you've done? How could you do that? That was horrible of you!"

Jean looked at him incredulously. "What do you mean that was horrible of me? You're the one who's having an affair. I haven't done anything."

Clay jumped up from his chair and glared at her. "You mean to tell me that you're not going to take responsibility for what you've just done?"

"Clay, you've got to go," Jean said firmly. "This is it. This is the final thing. You have got to go."

"I'm not going anywhere!" Clay shouted. "I paid for this home! It's mine."

Jean got up and strode toward the doorway of her study where Clay was standing. "Clay, I'm going right now," she said, "and I'm gonna take the kids with me."

"You're not taking those kids anywhere."

"Oh, yes I am," Jean said, pushing past him.

Clay followed her and stood in front of her again, and Jean yelled out, "Girls, get your stuff together. You're coming with me."

Without being aware of how she did it, Jean hustled the two girls into the car.

"But, Mommy, what about my hat?" Thea, the younger girl, kept asking.

Jean ran back into the house for Thea's hat and got into the car again.

"But what about my mittens?" Thea asked.

Jean could see how startled and upset Thea was by having to leave so quickly, so she told the girls to go back into the house. She followed them in and found Clay in the kitchen thumbing through the phone book.

"Clay, you've gotta get out of this house," she said.

Without even looking up at her, he answered, "This is my house, and I'm not going anywhere. You've messed things up enough already."

Suddenly Jean started having flashbacks of the night her father died—the same feelings of anger, terror, and oppression overwhelmed her. The flashbacks ceased as abruptly as they'd come on. Afterward, when she looked at Clay, she didn't recognize him. He was a stranger, yet she knew all about him. He was repulsive to her. He was a mean man, a controlling and manipulative man, a man with no conscience. What was this sadistic person doing here? Who was he to tell her that she'd messed up?

Jean's sense of derealization, of knowing Clay, yet not knowing him as her husband, made her feel disoriented and dizzy. She put her hand down on the counter top and leaned against it to steady herself, and her fingers caught in the bowl of leftover cucumber salad she'd made for dinner that night. The bowl flipped off the counter and landed on the floor near Clay's feet.

"What are you, nuts?" Clay said to her, thinking she'd thrown the bowl at him. "You're acting like an idiot."

That did it. Enraged, Jean hauled off and shoved Clay against the refrigerator with all of her might. "I hate you!" she screamed. "I wish you were dead!"

"Get your hands off me!" he shouted. "You're sick!"

"I want you out of here! I never want to see you again!"

"I'm not leaving! This is my house!"

Clay's intransigence frightened Jean. She knew he had rifles in the house—disassembled, but there. Feeling that she had no alternative, she reached for the phone and called the police.

UNCAGED

" 'Go ahead, go!' the cop said," Jean tells me in her therapy session, recounting what happened after her fight with Clay. "He told me to get the children out of there and that he'd be over right away. I took the kids to my sister's, and while I was gone, the cop confiscated Clay's guns. Clay told him that I became violent and was pushing him and throwing things at him, and he got some kind of restraining order against me. When I called the police station from my sister's, the officer told me that I could go home, but I couldn't say or do anything threatening to Clay."

"Did you go back?"

"No, we stayed at my sister's for the weekend. I didn't want to be in the house with Clay there, but eventually I had to get stuff for the kids, so we all went back home Sunday night. Monday morning I got up early and went to work and didn't get home from school until late at night. I was frightened leaving the kids alone with Clay, worried that he might run off and take them away somewhere, but they were there when I got home. I can't stand living with him. I hate him, and it's very hard for me to feel that way. It causes this rage in my head that I can't shut up."

"How long will it take for the divorce to come through?"

"I could have it now if I let him walk out with everything and leave me with no money for food and two little kids to raise. He'll pay support when the divorce comes through, but I have no money. He leaves, I'm done for. There's a part of me that says, 'Just let him take whatever he's gonna take, forget about it, and move on.' That's the way I've always been with people before. But there's another part of me that gets pissed off and says, 'Screw that! Let the sonofabitch stay in the house and pay the bills, and don't let him off the hook.' " Jean's voice quavers. "I'm so confused," she says, starting to cry. "I never wanted to see what a conniving game player he is."

"I think you're getting more and more empowered," I tell her. "You're beginning to realize that no part of you needs to be a victim anymore."

"But these thoughts that are going through my head at such a loud volume are scaring me," she protests. "And what happens is that instead of trying to get out of this situation, I try to exist within it."

"Maybe those thoughts are trying to protect you," I tell her. "This is an unhealthy situation for you to be in. The sooner you can get your husband out of the house, the better. I don't see why you can't get some interim money to tide you over until the divorce comes through. What does your lawyer say?"

"I don't have my own lawyer. We went to one jointly because Clay said we could save money that way. The lawyer can't help me because Clay's paying him." Jean shakes her head sadly. "What a fool I was. Now I realize how Clay was manipulating me so that I wouldn't get any of his money. When I told him I needed my own lawyer, he got angry and accused me of being paranoid because I didn't trust him."

Jean's vulnerability to exploitation by her husband is yet another familiar story of how easy it is for an abuse victim to be revictimized. The only love she has ever known has been associated with abuse, so she thinks that abuse is love and that suffering is her lot in life.

"Jean, you need to get your own lawyer," I urge her. "You can get one from legal services if you can't afford a private attorney. The law is on your side. It's just a matter of when you're ready to free yourself of any remnants of being a victim."

"I know that's what I have to do," Jean says reluctantly, "but I feel really bad fighting Clay. This is such a different thing for me to do—standing up for myself; I've done that before—but I, I," she struggles to find words for her feelings of doubt.

"What do you think it would be like if you weren't involved in an oppressive relationship and you could be free of that?"

"I don't know," Jean murmurs uncertainly. "When I left here after I talked about my accident and the Wailing Woman for the first time, I went home and cried for hours and hours. I was afraid I would never stop." She begins to cry again and goes on haltingly, "There's some kind of connection between realizing that these parts of myself serve a huge function, and realizing how oppressive Clay has been, and realizing how oppressive I am to myself. And I guess there's some kind of connection about lifting myself above oppression and worrying whether I can really experience—I don't know . . . it's just a very, very overwhelming feeling."

"Of what?"

"Of being uncaged," she says finally.

A Walk in the Woods

"I'm graduating magna cum laude," Jean informs me, adding with a little laugh, "I missed summa cum laude by three-tenths of a point. I guess that's not bad, considering what a hard time I've been having remembering things."

"What have you been forgetting?"

"Oh, a whole series of things," Jean answers. "First, I ran into a woman who's in one of my classes, and she started talking to me about how fantastic my presentation was on battered women. And I realized I didn't remember the presentation at all. I felt panicky and kept trying to change the subject, because I didn't want her to know that I didn't remember it. Then the next day my professor came up to me outside, and the same thing happened. She said, 'Jean, you had no idea of the impact you were having on the class when you made your presentation.' I was worried that she knew I was dissociating, but she thought I was being humble. Then she asked me a question about a point I made, and I couldn't answer it. And on the weekend, something happened with my daughter Thea. I wanted to take her to see *Fantasia,* and she told me we'd already seen it. She showed me a toy character from the movie, and I still couldn't remember watching it with her. And finally, I went to write a check for something, and I noticed that there were three checks that had been written out of the checkbook that I couldn't account for. I called the bank and found out that they were for small amounts, but I have absolutely no idea what I bought with them."

Jean's memory gaps are typical of the dissociative amnesia that occurs during flashbacks or when a separate personality has taken over. It was probably Knowledge, for example, who gave the presentation on battered women, a subject that may have triggered too many painful memories for Jean to stay in control.

"Graduation is only a few weeks away," I observe. "Do you think the stress of that has something to do with your memory problems?"

"Definitely," Jean answers. "I've been flapping through this last mile because it's scary. A lot of things are ending at once. I'm ending school. Clay is moving out. I'm in a big shift: going from school to work and going from living with Clay and being dependent to not living with him and being independent. I worry, What kind of job will I get? Will I do well in it? And I can feel myself starting to lose it."

"Who is in control when you feel overwhelmed by these thoughts?"

"I guess it's Jeanie, a frightened, needy little girl in her teens."

Jean proceeds to tell me about her awareness of Jeanie as a separate part of herself during a depersonalization episode and internal dialogue she had last week:

"I live on a small country road, and it was a beautiful day and I decided to go for a walk. About a mile from home I started to get this feeling that there was something behind me—the same heightened awareness I had when I would go into the woods as a child and was afraid of being raped. I kept on walking, but I couldn't get a grip on myself and just lost control. I felt very disoriented and scared and began walking in circles. I was upset about somebody leaving. Somehow I realized that the state of consciousness I was in at that time was not really who I am. I started crying, and I kept on saying, 'I don't want you to leave. I don't want you to leave.' I visualized the person I was talking to sitting in a chair. And the person sitting in the chair was me. I ended up interpreting the whole thing to mean that there's a part of me who's frightened that when I graduate, the part of me that went to school is going to go away. There was this feeling of abandonment, so I cried. And then I just did some self-comforting. I said to myself that I couldn't leave because the part of me that went to school is always going to be there. I didn't have to be scared because I was always going to have that kind of control, ambition, and drive, and my life was not going to go back to not having any kind of direction. And it worked. By the time I got home, I was feeling better."

"That's wonderful, Jean, that you were able to comfort the frightened part of yourself that way," I commend her.

"Yes, but I don't seem able to do that very often," Jean says. "I think that visualizing Knowledge sitting calmly in a chair helped."

"Perhaps we can try a little exercise here. Are you open to something new?"

"Yeah, I'm curious," Jean says.

I carry a folding chair and open it up close to her. "I'd like you to imagine that Knowledge is sitting in that chair," I instruct her, "and you are sitting where you are now, talking to Knowledge about some of your concerns. Then I would like you to sit in the folding chair as Knowledge and respond to your concerns."

"Okay, I'll try it," Jean says. "If Knowledge is sitting there, I would tell her that it's really important for her not to leave. I need her to learn and remember things."

"What about her sharing them with you?" I ask.

"Yeah, that would be good," Jean says. Her voice wavers and becomes soft and tearful. "I would really like her to be in control more because when she leaves me, I get confused and scared. I like her and she makes me feel safe."

"Why are you crying, Jean?"

"It's awful when she's not here, just really scary. I'm terrified all the time because anything can happen at any time, and when she's here, there's a sense of control."

"A lot of terrifying things have happened to you in your life. Does the side of yourself sitting in your chair carry those memories?"

"Some of them," she answers. "I think I'm Jeanie. I'm always afraid of being raped."

"Do you want to sit in this other chair and put on Knowledge's hat and respond to Jeanie? What would you tell her?"

Jean takes the other seat, clears her throat, and adopts the same kind of calm, empathetic tone of voice that I imagine she uses with battered women in the shelter: "I'd tell her that she doesn't have to feel terrified anymore because there is control today where there was no control before," she says, "and we don't have to lose that control just because I'm leaving school."

"Is there anything else you could tell Jeanie that would help her feel safe and stop the terror quickly?"

"Yes, I'd remind her that Knowledge is very responsible," Jean answers, showing how much her sense of self has improved. "I know every reason why Jeanie is scared to death and I don't blame her, but I want her to know that she's in good hands. I haven't done anything in the last twelve years to put myself or my children in harm's way. I haven't had liquor. I haven't drugged. I haven't slept around. I haven't been foolish with money. I have been very clear-headed and disciplined and have gotten a lot done and have climbed over some huge mountains. She can trust me."

When we finish the exercise, we talk about how therapy has given Jean a new way of organizing and controlling what was once a chaos of roaring noises in her head and a tempest of fear. "Now that you're graduating from school and becoming independent," I tell her, "it's important for you to stay connected to the abilities and information you gained in school. Jeanie has to know that she can immediately reach out to Knowledge and be comforted when she's terrified, the way she did on your walk. Her intense fear is an automatic and irrational response to events in the past triggered by current stress. If all the different parts of you work together like a community, family, or partnership in which you care for one another, you can stay in control."

"What happens when everybody's scared at once?" Jean asks.

"You'll need to do some grounding exercises to remind yourself instantly that you're living in the present and not the past," I tell her. "Write down the year it is and your name and your age and list all the things you've done that have shown stability and competence. Then ask the most grounded part of you to do the comforting."

I hand Jean a little book, *Wonderful Ways to Love a Child* by Judy Ford. "I think you'll find some excellent ideas in here that will help you understand Jeanie and how to comfort her when she's scared or hurt."

"I like this book," Jean says, leafing through it. "I think I used to get so freaked out before I started coming here because the terror I felt was completely mysterious. And now when I feel myself starting to slip away and turn into panic, I can see that two different parts of myself can be there at the same time, and there's a way to get help from inside. Having one talk to the other makes me aware of their separateness, but also makes me feel more together. I'm starting to be less possessed by fear."

GRADUATION

Jean surprises me when she walks in for her session wearing white slacks and a becoming emerald green shirt. She has been in therapy for two years now, and this is the first time that I have ever seen her out of the funereal-colored clothes that signified her internal state of mourning. The bright green seems symbolic of springtime and the renewal of hope after a long, dark, gloomy winter within. Out of her dark clothes Jean seems much more attractive to me, softer, more relaxed and vibrant. I wonder whether her green shirt might also symbolize the rebirth of Knowledge—the wisdom and strength that came to her in a green light the night her father died—associated with her graduation.

"How was graduation?" I ask.

"Just perfect," she says. "I was in my body the whole time. I wasn't floating; I wasn't watching from someplace else. I was fully present, and it was really nice. Very unusual for me."

"What did being fully present feel like?"

"I wasn't frightened. I wasn't hypervigilant. I was relaxed. I was able to follow what was happening. I just was *there*. Internally I was very content. And happy. I was *really* happy. It's what I need."

"Was your family there?"

"All of them—my sisters and my brother and his wife and my nephews and nieces. They were all happy, and there wasn't any family tension. I'm the only one of my siblings to graduate from college. I came down the stairs after getting my degree, and my sister Ginny was standing there. She was crying. She wrapped her arms around me, and we hugged. Then my brother hugged me. I was starting to go back into the procession when my nephew stepped out with this huge bouquet of flowers in the school colors—roses, long bow and everything—I was so moved. I loved it."

"That's a very great accomplishment that you did so well in school and were able to be there during the graduation and have your family so supportive."

"What I'm really excited about is that the battered women's residence where I did my practicum offered me a position on the staff," Jean informs me. "With my salary and the increase in support money my lawyer managed to get from Clay, I think I'll be okay financially. The job is exactly what I want to do. I'll be doing treatment plans and counseling women who've been traumatized and have addiction issues, and both of those things," she adds, laughing, "are something I know a lot about."

When I think of the promising new life opening up before Jean like the roses unfolding in her graduation bouquet, I'm reminded of her professor's comments on the "Self Reflection Paper" she wrote for one of her courses. The A paper is a gripping chronicle of Jean's life in the "culture of poverty," as she calls it, and her recovery from her traumatic childhood and years of substance abuse. On the cover there is a touching picture of Jean's mother and father on their wedding day, and on the last page the teacher has written:

Jean,

> *This is a truly profound story and I thank you for sharing it in such a beautiful manner. You are very gifted, as a writer, student, and as a human being. I recognize the courage it took to write this and hope that in some small way it was helpful.*

PART FOUR

BEFRIENDING THE STRANGER

14

~

A DIFFERENT APPROACH: THE FOUR C'S

For whatever reason we enter into psychotherapy, our goal is the same: to gain better control over our thoughts, feelings, and actions so that we can achieve a relatively peaceful and genuinely healthy internal state and lead a more productive life. What we usually find is that for some reason we have adopted certain automatic ways of regarding ourselves and responding to the world around us that are unhealthy and need to be reorganized. This is true whether we're depressed, anxious, bipolar, obsessive-compulsive, attention-impaired, or dissociative.

For people with a dissociative disorder, the process of regroupment is intrinsically more complicated because they have more than one internal state in need of reorganization. They may not even be aware of the separate parts of themselves—"hidden" parts, as I've called them—that are not under their control. All they know is that at times a "mood" comes over them or some inner "demon" makes them act in an angry, panicky, or childish manner that seems completely out of character.

At their worst, these angry outbursts, panic attacks, and childish regressions can make them dysfunctional, as the case histories you've just read have shown. Jean, an A student, became so panicky in Spanish class that she got F's when Cave Girl, a hidden part that developed in childhood to protect her from violence and sexual abuse, came out in college. Linda, who loved her fiancé, was overcome by an aversion to intimacy and wouldn't let him touch her when the traumatized fourteen-year-old rape victim inside her took control. When Nancy's hidden parts were in control, this model wife, mother, and professional lashed out at her family in uncontrollable rage and became too childlike to be able to work.

Unlike these people, you may have dissociative symptoms that are all mild, but you could still have qualities that are not within your control as much as you would like them to be. They're not separate personalities, but they can be unruly emotions or types of behavior that are working against you in your personal life or on the job—troublemakers like angry outbursts or runaway anxiety or childish neediness or relentless self-criticism or unwarranted feelings of gloom and doom. You'll find that the method of treatment that I use for people with a dissociative disorder can readily be applied to helping you achieve greater mastery over any of these errant tendencies.

SURFACE VERSUS HIDDEN SYMPTOMS

Now that you're familiar with the five core symptoms and the ways they manifest themselves, it's important to remember that whatever symptoms you may have—depression, panic attacks, substance abuse, mood swings, et cetera—may be external manifestations of an underlying dissociative problem. Unless that deeper problem is detected and treated appropriately, you will not recover fully.

The accompanying figure of a circle within a larger circle shows that your symptoms may be external or surface manifestations of internal or deeper symptoms of dissociation—the five core symptoms. If a symptom in the outer circle is treated without regard to the symptoms in the inner circle, the external symptom may get better, but it will recur, or another external symptom will develop. When internal core symptoms are detected and treated properly, external symptoms will diminish significantly or be eliminated entirely.

The link between the symptoms in the inner circle and those in the outer one can be made only by having the full SCID-D done. Substance abuse, for example, may be related to a person's trying to self-medicate inner feelings of detachment from himself or his emotions—symptoms of depersonalization. Similarly, someone who has regressed to a childlike state and finds himself in a situation he doesn't understand may experience panic attacks. He may complain of panic, but the panic is related to identity alteration—the fears of a childlike part that has suddenly taken

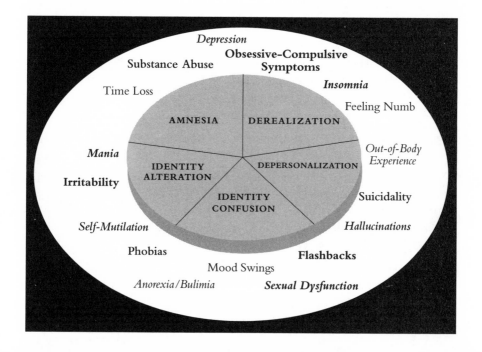

Depression

Obsessive-Compulsive Symptoms

Substance Abuse

Insomnia

Time Loss

Feeling Numb

AMNESIA   DEREALIZATION

Mania

Out-of-Body Experience

IDENTITY ALTERATION   DEPERSONALIZATION

Irritability

IDENTITY CONFUSION

Suicidality

Self-Mutilation

Hallucinations

Phobias

Flashbacks

Mood Swings

Anorexia/Bulimia   Sexual Dysfunction

Reprinted with permission from M. Steinberg, *Handbook for the Assessment of Dissociation: A Clinical Guide.* Washington, DC: American Psychiatric Press, 1995.

control. Since any treatment's successful outcome is critically dependent on an accurate diagnosis, having a clinician make the connection between surface symptoms and deeper ones is essential.

THE FOUR C'S AND HOW THEY WORK

What differentiates treatment for dissociation from the usual talk therapy is that it gives you a new way of relating to yourself on a deeply nurturant level. Its strategies help you to accept and respect the different sides of yourself by communicating directly with them in a comforting way and encouraging them to cooperate with each other and connect into a functioning whole rather than remain in conflict. The four C's on which this therapy is based—*comfort, communication, cooperation,* and *connection*—are especially helpful for people with a traumatic past who have dissociated from it in order to survive. Even if your history was much less traumatic than those described here, this process can help you accept your past while maintaining control over your emotional responses to your memories.

Therapy for people with DID is designed to gently bring down the walls of amnesia that keep their different parts hidden from themselves and each other. Most experts agree that the key to treating dissociation lies in the connection, or integration, of memories, feelings, and behaviors. The process is like connecting the dots in a child's coloring book. The dots are the person's different parts, and the connections are the memory links that have to be built. Once the person feels safe enough to accept the memories, the amnesia, as well as the other dissociative symptoms, is reduced, and the person becomes connected just as the picture in the coloring book becomes whole.

Some people with a dissociative disorder are able to integrate their separate parts into a single, congruent self-image. Others may fear that integration means the "death" of their alternate personalities and may not want to give them up. They may continue to have separate parts but can achieve "functional cooperation" between them, which is a giant step on the path toward healing and recovery. Nancy may retain aspects of the Child, for example, but she has built an increasingly positive source of identity in the Mom. Now she is able to monitor her internal states and marshal her inner resources in times of stress, as she did when she had flashbacks of her father's sexual abuse. Cooperation between her separate parts has also enabled her to regulate her emotions more effectively so that her misdirected rage at her abusive mother embodied in the Mean rarely comes out anymore. Now she can maintain her inner equilibrium when she interacts with family members who trigger memories of her mother's cruel treatment of her or the frightening violence of her childhood alcoholic household.

Studies have shown that this kind of specialized treatment for people who have a dissociative disorder, when combined with medication for such symptoms as mood swings, depression, anxiety, and obsessive-compulsive behavior, is highly effective. Richard P. Kluft, M.D., reported that 81 percent of 184 DID patients he treated achieved "stable fusion," meaning that all signs of DID and related symptoms were absent for at least twenty-seven months. Regular follow-up visits for as long as two to ten years after treatment ended showed that these patients maintained a complete absence of clinical signs of a dissociative disorder. For a large subgroup of these patients who were high-functioning before they were diagnosed with DID, their treatment averaged two and a half years of a minimum of two forty-five- to fifty-minute sessions a week. Most patients who achieved integration discontinued treatment and remained essentially well during the follow-up period. Recent research indicates that length of treatment varies, three to five years being the average.

THE FIRST STEP

There is a process of discovery that needs to take place before the actual work of therapy can begin. During this process you explore whether or not you have detached from your identity, your surroundings, or your memories, and, if you have, what are the different parts that exist within you. Do you have a Cave Girl or a Wailing Woman, as Jean did? If your dissociation is less severe than Jean's, you may just be aware of acting differently from the way you normally do at times—behaving like a child, throwing temper tantrums, saying things that are uncharacteristic of you in verbal outbursts, or behaving in other ways that are not in your control.

These hidden parts are likely to emerge when you're under stress. You may be able to cope when things are going smoothly, but when you're in the midst of a conflict or a stressful situation, you might start acting in ways that are out of character or have an out-of-body experience and not recognize yourself in the mirror, or feel that you're removed from what's going on. It's as if you've hidden away your feelings in a closet, and the closet is full. Then one day something stressful happens, and once again you stuff your uncomfortable feelings into the same closet. Since there's no more room, the feelings from twenty years ago come tumbling out, and you respond to the present situation in an uncharacteristic manner. In Linda's case, for example, her overreaction to being arrested by the police officer was fueled by unresolved feelings of anger at her rapist that had been hidden away since she was in her teens. Once those angry feelings were out of the closet, they took over whenever her fiancé tried to become intimate with her.

If you have hidden parts of yourself that are disrupting your life, unless you identify them, you can never get better. These parts have been hidden essentially for safekeeping. They need to emerge and be acknowledged and accepted in order for you to heal from the abuse or trauma that caused you to shelve them in the first place. By answering the questionnaires on each of the dissociative symptoms adapted from the SCID-D in the previous chapters, you've taken the first step in this process of identification. At least you are now aware of what the symptoms are and how they manifest themselves, so that you can knowledgeably describe them to a therapist. Your test scores are only a preliminary indication of whether your symptoms are serious or not. *The administration of the full SCID-D by a trained clinician is what will allow you to gauge the severity of your actual symptoms and identify whatever hidden parts you may have.*

Although I present the four C's of treatment in a particular order, they are all somewhat intertwined. Comfort generally does come first, but communication occurs simultaneously and is also involved in the work of cooperation. There is an element of connection, the last stage, in that first phase of comfort. As a person works through all these phases—identifying the dissociated parts, comforting them, communicating with them, enlisting their cooperation with each other, and connecting to them in the sense of owning their emotional memories so the abuse or trauma is no longer perceived as having happened to someone else—integration is a natural by-product. With the flow and sharing of memories, knowledge, and feelings back and forth, the barriers erected by amnesia gradually erode over time, and each fragmented part enters the mainstream of the person's identity.

COMFORT

To make yourself feel safe enough to bring dissociated memories and feelings out of hiding, you need two sources of comfort: internal (within yourself) and external (environmental).

External Comforting

The most obvious forms of external comforting are making your home a comforting place and connecting to people who can be supportive. On a more profound level, you need to take measures to reduce and eventually eliminate stress from abusive or destructive relationships. Nancy's decision to minimize contact with her still emotionally abusive mother was a big step in this direction, as was Jean's initiation of divorce proceedings to end her demeaning and exploitative marriage.

Since all dissociatives have been taught that their emotions must be either invalidated or denied in order to survive, learning to trust your emotions sufficiently to make these decisions is a process that therapy can help you address. Building supportive relationships and a stress-free zone within therapy and outside ensures that healing and recovery will not be impeded by the continuing bombardment of external poison arrows.

SELF-COMFORTING STRATEGIES

Internal comforting is a huge problem for people who have been exposed to any kind of abuse or trauma. They are terribly deprived of self-comforting skills because appropriate comfort has not been role modeled to them. They were raised by people who have violated their trust or their boundaries, have betrayed or neglected them, or have been too remote from them to be relied upon for emotional support. Since comforting themselves is a foreign concept to them, they doubt their ability to do it. They also need to learn that they're worth comforting, as Nancy said, and that's a difficult task for someone who was so invalidated in childhood as not even to feel real, let alone worthwhile.

People who have disconnected from their emotions because they're frightened of them often perceive the dissociated part of themselves as destructive and want to get rid of it rather than comfort and respect it. Nancy, for example, was initially desperate to get rid of the Mean. Attempting to get rid of any dissociated part is not going to work, because that part has served a valuable function in the person's life and is holding important memories that need to be accessed and accepted.

Wonderful Ways to Love a Child by Judy Ford is a concise little guide to parenting a child and can also be used to learn various ways of accepting yourself and giving yourself love. It offers such suggestions as Listen from Your Heart, Speak Kindly, Try to Understand, Ask Their Opinions, Allow Them to Love Themselves, Honor Their Noes, and Celebrate Mistakes. One suggestion, Let Them Cry, is particularly meaningful for dissociatives. They're often afraid that once they start crying over the painful memories and feelings they've buried away in a hidden part of themselves they'll never be able to stop. That's where the work of comfort comes in. When people are able to comfort their hidden parts sufficiently, two things happen: they don't have to keep them under wraps anymore and they don't become dysfunctional with them out. Comfort gives people the strength to stop hiding their tears and to stop crying after they've shed them.

The Woman's Comfort Book by Jennifer Louden, a book clearly not written for the dissociative population but for everyone, is filled with detailed and explicit strategies for comforting every disturbing feeling you might have—afraid to be alone, angry, burned-out, can't sleep, confused, depressed, emptiness, exhausted, feeling fat and ugly, had an awful day, inadequate, lonely, needy, nervous, scared, self-loathing, trapped, temper tantrums, and so on. The strategies range from Your Nurturing Voice and Creating a Comfort Network to Nutritional Music and A Forgiveness Ritual.

Reading Children's Books

One of the strategies in *The Woman's Comfort Book,* Reading as a Child, is introduced this way: "Reading children's books is a simple but very effective way to comfort ourselves. We can reconnect with innocence, magic, and hope. . . . Reconnect with wonder, and comfort the part of yourself that is still a child." I have found that children's books address self-comforting issues in a very simple but powerful manner that relates to people of all ages.

The purpose of using children's books in therapy is to help people understand the comforting process and develop a language for it. Loving, caring parents read comforting stories to their children and act in a consistently nurturing manner, employing a rich repertoire of supportive techniques for their children to experience and replicate. By contrast, abused children may not have had exposure to comforting books and have not had sufficient experiences in real life to strengthen their self-comforting abilities. For these children self-comfort may exist only in fiction, in their fantasies, or not at all. By reading children's books and learning how loving parents care for their children, people can learn to apply these basic approaches not only to their own children, but to themselves.

Part of the pleasure we derive from reading to a child is that the soothing message of the book soothes the reader as well as the listener. As an adult you may find reading a child's book strange or silly, but it can be very effective. Reading children's books that deal with comfort and safety or rereading your favorite childhood books can help you recognize the need for comfort and compensate for some of the comforting that was unavailable to you when you were growing up. When you read these books, try to think about the basic ingredients of comfort—which strategies you were exposed to and which were lacking. If you feel foolish reading these books, try reading them to a child. As you do, be aware that you can both share in the lessons of these stories. The idea is to begin to develop a supply of comforting skills that will enable you to withstand life's stressors, including painful memories from the past or ongoing pressures today.

Besides being a useful tool for anyone, child or adult, who has ever had trouble falling asleep (an extremely common problem amongst abuse survivors), Martin Waddell and Barbara Firth's *Can't You Sleep, Little Bear?* helps the reader learn about the range of comforting techniques available in general. As the title suggests, Little Bear cannot fall asleep because he is afraid of the dark. Using the cub's father, Big Bear, as a guide, the book takes the reader through a number of ways in which an adult can attempt to relax a child. At first, Big Bear thinks Little Bear is afraid of the darkness in his room, so he hooks a lantern over the young cub's bed. When Little Bear is still afraid, Big Bear brings him a book. When Little Bear still can't fall asleep, Big Bear hooks a bigger lantern over the bed, then an even bigger lantern, then The Biggest Lantern of Them All. Finally, Big Bear realizes it's not the darkness inside that frightens Little Bear, but rather the darkness outside. So he takes the cub outside of the cave, lifts him up, cuddles him, and tells him to look up at the dark. Big Bear shows Little Bear the moon and the stars until the cub finally falls asleep, feeling warm and safe inside his father's arms. Similarly, adults who fear the terrors of the night as children do, or are haunted by other fears, can comfort themselves with light and love. Just as Big Bear comforted Little Bear, we, too, can remind ourselves that the darkness that makes us afraid also holds the moon and the stars.

Mordicai Gerstein's *The Wild Boy* explored the power of love and comfort on a boy who was found living alone under harsh conditions in the woods of Aveyron. Raised by himself, the boy's life was filled with physical violence and basic survival. Unresponsive to any human contact, he was evaluated at the Institute for Deaf-Mutes in Paris, where he was befriended by Dr. Itard. Itard immediately recognized the classic symptoms of "a boy who had never been held or sung to or played with," and "who had never learned to be a child." After naming the boy Victor, Itard decided to raise him himself. As Itard showers him with consistent love, a new home, and much-needed attention, Victor gradually begins to respond and express feelings of joy, sadness, comfort, and safety. After reading this book, those who are confronting their own inner "wild child" may likewise find themselves accepting that aspect of their personality, rather than disrespecting it for its lack of control and civility. They may finally be ready to befriend the stranger within.

Basically what abuse survivors need to do is learn how to parent themselves. If they've been a good parent to their children or kind to friends, they have these skills. They just haven't applied them to themselves. They would rush to comfort a screaming son or daughter, yet they ignore the parts of themselves that have been screaming in pain for years. Jean was willing to let the Wailing Woman cry forever rather than comfort her pain over unintentionally killing a man and redirect her grief into a positive act. Similarly the horrified little girl locked up in prison or screaming at the table the night Jean's father was stabbed to death would go on screaming and screaming, frozen in time, compartmentalized forever if Jean hadn't reached out to comfort her. By making the little girl feel loved and safe, Jean was able to begin the process of unfreezing her and gradually accepting her into her life today.

Dissociates who've survived abusive childhoods are often able to be excellent parents, never wanting to do to their children what was done to them. Parenting is a constant struggle for them because of all of the inner turmoil they're experiencing. Many of them have children who've been diagnosed with attention deficit hyperactivity disorder (ADHD), as were Nancy's son and daughter, Linda's daughter, and Jean's two daughters. Dissociation is much less commonly identified by child psychiatrists, so it's possible that a child identified with ADHD could have an underlying dissociative basis for the ADHD symptoms or a coexisting dissociative disorder. A characteristic feature of ADHD is inattention—essentially, memory problems—and loss of memory is also a core feature. Another is the fluctuation between high functioning and low functioning or scattered performance—a child gets an A and an F in the same semester. ADHD might be one explanation for that; another might be that the child has different parts of herself, like Jean, who had Knowledge and could get all A's, and Cave Girl, who couldn't be in school at all.

"Grounding" or Reorienting Techniques

One strategy for self-comfort when you feel disconnected is to make physical contact with objects in the immediate environment—press your shoulders against the back of the chair you're sitting in, for example—and state your name, location, and safe circumstances to yourself. Jean was able to ground herself to the present time, for example, by saying, "I'm Jean W.; I'm in school now; and no one is going to hurt me here." You might remember how Tom, the former boxer who had a warrior-type personality within him named Wild Tom (Chapter 9), used a grounding technique to help himself stay centered in the present. Whenever he felt on the verge of exploding in rage, he looked at the miniature boxing gloves on his key chain, a symbol of comfort and safety, and reoriented himself to the present time. He realized that he was not in the boxing ring with a dangerous opponent or fighting for his life with his father, and didn't need to protect himself by savagely beating up someone. Tom used a verbal grounding technique as well. To prevent himself from flying into a jealous rage when he saw his wife talking to another man, he told himself: "My wife loves me. She is having a harmless conversation with an acquaintance, and this is not a dangerous situation." Such grounding techniques are quick ways of stopping an automatic flip back into the past when some trigger sets it off.

Distraction Techniques

Another strategy for coping with dissociative episodes is to turn to an absorbing *external* activity that you enjoy. Reading, handicraft work, exercising, conversing with others, and so on, can interrupt the cycle of escalating thoughts and feelings that lead to a sense of disconnection from yourself or your body or a feeling of unreality.

Creative Visualization

The technique that Ted used with Linda to calm her panic attack—helping her visualize that they were out sailing on a calm sea—can also be an effective way to manage a depersonalization episode. Visualizing a safe place or a sanctuary; recalling pleasant memories, particularly of supportive adults from your past; and using religious or spiritual imagery that is meaningful to you can all help to rein in your galloping overreaction to triggers in your environment or in your intimate relationships.

Triggers of depersonalization abound in intimate relationships for people who have survived abuse or trauma. Many people experience depersonalization in the presence of family members who have abused them. Others experience the symptom in the presence of romantic partners or spouses who trigger memories of their original abusers. Linda's fiancé reminded her of her rapist, for example, and Jean's seductive professor brought to mind her brother's sexual abuse. Still others experience these episodes whenever any of their significant relationships breaks up or appears to be in jeopardy. It's as if they feel that their fragile sense of identity cannot withstand the loss of the other person who has been the glue holding it together. It was Nancy's fight with her husband and her fear that she might lose him that precipitated her shocking episode of depersonalization and regression into a childlike state.

Experience in the use of creative visualization and the other self-comforting techniques can offset the kind of severe depersonalization episode that might land a person in a hospital emergency room. Jean, Linda, and Nancy all managed to stay *out* of the ER once they had developed a number of strategies for comforting themselves.

A Self-Comforting Schedule

Comforting oneself is something that everyone needs to do on a daily basis, and most people naturally gravitate toward this by regularly going to the gym, listening to music, meditating, pursuing a hobby, reading, watching a movie, going out to dinner with friends, jogging, or doing whatever suits them. Dissociatives have to make an effort in the early phase of treatment to think about comforting and build a lengthy repertoire of comforting skills. I ask people to make a checklist with the days of the week and a listing of things that they can do that comfort them. I recommend that they do something comforting every day and that they take the list into therapy so that I can see where they've checked off what they've done on each day.

COMMUNICATION

One of the most important comforting skills that you can have is the ability to conduct positive dialogues with yourself—so important, in fact, that acquiring this skill can be considered a separate phase of treatment in itself. The goal is to build an inner voice that can respond effectively to the voice of fear, rage, sadness, or disparagement within yourself that resulted from trauma or abuse.

YOUR PERSONALIZED MISSION STATEMENT(S)

Just as many corporations have a "mission statement" that conveys in a few short sentences what the company is all about, it is useful to draft a mission statement that offers guidance for each separate part of yourself. In a sense this mission statement is like an affirmation, except it is individualized to address the issues of whatever part of yourself needs to be comforted.

Jean's mission statement for the Wailing Woman was "I respect and care about your sadness and want you to know that you no longer have to carry this burden all alone. You can depend on me to help you with your tears and find a way to ease your suffering. I am here for you."

For Cave Girl, Jean had a different mission statement to address her fear of coming out of the cave and having to deal with people: "Now it's safe outside, and you can come out and see the light of day and begin to walk freely. You are no longer alone. I will be with you." Because the "I" was the adult Jean or Knowledge, this was not only a mission statement, but the start of connection between Cave Girl and the other parts.

In Linda's case, she had her own positive mission statement when she was with Ted that helped to ground her: "This is today, and I'm in a safe home. This is my home; there are no rapists here. I am with a man who loves me, and love doesn't mean I'll get hurt. There is no need to push him away."

Nancy's mission statement for the Mean was "I appreciate your keeping my anger safe for me. Please let me know why you're so angry and what I can do to comfort your anger." For the Child her mission statement was "I understand how frightened and sad you are, but there is nobody here who will hurt you or leave you if you're not perfect. You are a good child. You are safe now. I will protect you."

The theme of all of these personalized mission statements is the sense of responsibility that dissociatives have for their different parts and how they need to work together to end the state of being detached and bring about wholeness. The coordinator is the primary self—the one who is present or in control most of the time. In our business analogy, the primary self is like the CEO or chairman of the board of the corporation who sets the course of building connections among the different parts and having them pull together to reach the goal of integration.

Everyone can benefit from a personalized mission statement directed toward achieving an inner life of health, balance, and wholeness. Even if you're not aware of a completely separate part of yourself, you could have a side that needs a message of encouragement and hope from you or from your external support system under certain circumstances. You may have an angry side that prompts you to have temper tantrums or an abandoned, lonely "inner child" that makes you abuse alcohol or become overly needy in relationships or feel frightened in front of new people. Your mission statement should put into words what you need to build in your life both within yourself and in your environment that will result in comforting that side.

If your goal is to have fewer angry outbursts, for example, Nancy's handling of the Mean is instructive. You need to comfort your anger from within by communicating with it, learning what that anger is about, respecting it, and beginning to accept it. The rational side of you that is not so angry has to communicate with your angry side, comfort it when it's provoked, and help it respond to the situation more appropriately than with a temper tantrum. Externally to the best of your ability you want to reduce or eliminate environmental triggers of that angry side, whether it's a nerve-jangling environment or exposure to abuse from a loved one, boss, or friend.

CORRECTING DISTORTED THOUGHTS

When strong emotions are triggered by essentially innocuous things, that can be a sign of some dissociated memory that needs to be addressed in therapy. The color red might trigger a memory of being raped, because you were wearing red on the day you were raped. Since you've developed the distorted thought that "red means I will be raped," a therapist can help you disprove that distorted thought and challenge it effectively when you communicate with yourself about it. Nancy's fear of the dark, Linda's fear of intimacy, and Jean's fear of abandonment are all examples of fears related to distorted thoughts that people learned how to correct in therapy.

Cognitive distortion takes several forms, including overgeneralization, self-hatred, perfectionism, and gender negation.

Overgeneralization: This involves drawing a broad, sweeping conclusion from the particular abuse or trauma. Since Nancy's father would steal into her bedroom at night and sexually abuse her, for example, she thought that she could never be safe in the dark. Having been raped by a man, Linda thought that all men were bad or that intimacy meant getting hurt. As a result of the violence and abuse in Jean's childhood, she believed that no adult could be trusted, not even the adult part of herself.

Self-hatred: This results when the victim of abuse or trauma believes that his or her "bad" behavior caused that abuse. Survivors typically feel that they deserved the abuse. Nancy assumed that she was "a bad girl" because her mother mistreated her; Linda thought she deserved the rape because she disobeyed her mother; Jean thought she was a hateful person who deserved the cruelties of her childhood and should be punished forever when she accidentally killed a man.

Perfectionism: The assumption that "if only I had been perfect, I could have prevented this" is another form of distorted thinking. Nancy, Linda, and Jean were all given to painful ruminations about what they could have done differently to prevent the abuse or trauma. This habit persisted into adulthood and would not allow them to forgive themselves for any mistakes they made, predisposing them to depression and disowning of their own strengths and talents.

Gender negation: This is the belief that one sex is better than another and is the sole cause of one's problems. Meredith, a patient of mine who developed a male alternate personality, was taught by her mother that in order to lead an independent life you had to be a boy. Rather than believe that her mother was wrong, Meredith crippled her independence while she allowed her boy alter to enjoy what she thought she couldn't do.

What causes these cognitive distortions? People develop this way of thinking about undeserved abuse or trauma in order to survive. In her book *Betrayal Trauma: The Logic of Forgetting Childhood Abuse,* Jennifer J. Frye coined the term "betrayal blindness" to explain how survivors develop amnesia for abuse as well as cognitive distortions about it. She defines betrayal blindness as "the lack of conscious awareness or memory of the betrayal" and says that it must occur under certain conditions of extensive betrayal of necessary trust. "The degree of betrayal by another person affects the victim's cognitive encoding of the experience of the trauma. We are equipped to detect betrayal and escape it. However, for children who need their parents to survive, it is dangerous . . . to detect it and try to escape. It could mean more abuse and little or no love and care. It is more beneficial to be blind to the trauma."

Part of that blindness is to believe that the abusing parent was right and the child was wrong. As abuse survivors get healthier, they can begin to acknowledge that bad things can indeed happen to good people—it was the way their parents attempted to show them love that was destructive; they did not deserve the abuse.

There are touches of this blindness in everyone. To some extent we all have to integrate the fact that our parents were supposed to love us, yet they treated us at times in a manner that was not loving. Children of critical or rejecting parents or parents who saddled them with excessively high expectations may have had to blind themselves to this form of abuse, because if they saw it, they wouldn't have had any parent who they thought was loving. Since they couldn't survive without a parent, they had to believe that their parents did love them, but they weren't good enough. As a result, their whole lives became a driven pursuit to disprove this cognitive distortion.

In a perverse way parental rejection is a spur toward accomplishment, but the price tag is often enormous anxiety. Milton, a physics professor, would get so frightened at times when he was teaching class that he was unable to talk. One time he actually fainted when he was going to give a presentation. In therapy he revealed that his extremely critical father was very physically abusive and would take him down to the cellar, where he would ritualistically have him walk around in a circle and beat him. Milton grew up with chronic terror that he carried around inside him into his fifties. He couldn't say no to his superiors and had to take on more and more projects because he was afraid of disappointing them. Like Linda, who thought that all men were potential rapists, Milton believed that his students and his superiors were all his surrogate father, who would punish him brutally if he didn't live up to their expectations.

A physician put Milton on medication for his anxiety as a teenager when he was a very successful athlete in school and suffered terrible anxiety on the field. From then on he medicated himself with barbiturates, and he entered psychotherapy for the first time only when his wife divorced him, complaining of his unavailability to her. In therapy I was able to reduce his medication and also the constant pressure he put on himself to be perfect. He reexamined his cognitive distortions and learned how to comfort the terrorized child within him. Another happy result was unexpected—his wife remarried him. Their relationship improved dramatically as Milton became able to share his feelings of anxiety and vulnerability with her.

DIALOGUING

Having internal dialogues with the hidden parts of oneself is an important part of communication, whether it's done silently, out loud, or in writing. I find that writing letters is the most practical way to have the inner dialogues. The goal is to become aware of inner dialoguing and strengthen ongoing communication among the different parts. Jean's letters to Jeanie and Jeanie's to Cave Girl, a study in startling contrasts, set up a network of communication almost like a supportive message board or chat room on the Internet. Not only did it provide comfort for the different parts, but it also laid the groundwork for cooperating with each other in the next phase of treatment.

The letters are a way of building on and implementing the personalized mission statements and can be modeled after what you would write to a child of your own or an adopted child in need of comfort. You need to schedule regular time for these dialogues in your appointment book, making an appointment with yourself, in effect, rather than do them in a haphazard fashion. Like Linda, you may need to do your letter writing outside your home in a peaceful, quiet place safe from intrusion, such as a park or a library. Establishing a pattern of dialogues is absolutely essential; otherwise the hidden part of yourself from which you've disconnected— the part that is screaming or crying in fear or anger—will continue to cause problems in your life. A repetitive pattern of comforting dialoguing is what will eventually stop inappropriate fear or anger from erupting at work or jeopardizing, perhaps even breaking up, a close relationship.

Internal dialoguing is a powerful tool for clearing up cognitive distortions about love—"Love means getting hurt," for one—that can keep you stuck in a destructive relationship or, like Linda, make you try to protect yourself by sabotaging a positive one. Your dialogue should help the frightened, lonely part of yourself distinguish the present from the past when you were forced to be with caretakers who abused you, because you were not mature enough to be independent. That needy, self-hating part needs to be told that it doesn't deserve abuse and that it's possible to invest in a supportive relationship and not get hurt. The more encouragement and hope you can give that part through your dialogues, the less likely you are to stay stuck.

COOPERATION

Since the language of the "inner child" has become part of our culture, you can probably identify with this concept. You may not be disconnected from the feelings you had as a child or have them compartmentalized in a separate part of yourself, but you may not always be aware of how those feelings are influencing your behavior as an adult. Reconnecting yourself to those feelings and joining with them to bring about greater health are the tasks of cooperation. What are the feelings of your inner child? Is that child frightened, sad, alone? If those are the feelings that you've identified by communicating with that child, the adult part of you has to befriend that inner child now and help heal those feelings. The adult part that functions well in the world, that is capable and responsible and has talents, has to lift the burden from that child of harboring all those feelings of loneliness and isolation.

Cooperation occurs as a result of communication—discovering rituals or routines that you can do so that your inner child no longer feels so lonely, frightened, or sad. Jean, a talented artist, helped to ease Cave Girl's isolation by drawing pictures of an older girl outside the cave to keep her company. You might develop some other creative, physical, or social routines that will help your scared inner child feel less lonely and afraid.

If you've identified a child part that is isolated by barriers of amnesia, the first step is to make that part aware that there are other parts, that the child isn't alone. The feelings and memories held inside can come out and be shared. Sharing what's inside them breaks the conspiracy of silence that has kept the parts disconnected from one another; now they can begin to cooperate with each other on a consistent basis. The adult part—some might say, the rational or professional part—begins to meld logic and reasoning with the emotional part, and the emotional part begins to emerge more freely in creativity or in the enrichment of personal relationships. It was this cooperation that helped Jean get her college degree, that enabled Linda to unfreeze the emotions that the rape trapped inside her shell, and that allowed Nancy to rediscover joy in her life through the exercise of her creative talents.

CONNECTION

All of the preceding phases culminate in the development of an inner team. This connection of a person's separate parts is the unity that ultimately cures the disconnection of dissociation.

INNER TEAMWORK

For both dissociatives and nondissociatives connection between one's intellectual side and one's emotional side is a major issue. The corporate world, to some extent, promotes the compartmentalization of emotions, and work becomes the "safe haven" where people can disconnect from their emotions, as Linda did. People with this tendency function at a high level when they're at work and can store their emotions in a box temporarily. When they're not at work and their jack-in-the-box emotions spring out and confront them, they can fall apart.

With the inner teamwork that connection brings about, the intellectual side can share logic and reason with the emotional side that's frozen in time as a traumatized child. The rational side can begin to challenge distorted thoughts and misperceptions that keep a dissociated part trapped in an automatic response. When Jean began to depersonalize on her walk in the woods, for example, her thinking self challenged the irrational assumption of the abandoned child within her that graduation meant the disappearance of the talents that got her through college.

The process of connection actually begins in the preliminary phase of identifying who the team players are. One might be a responsible professional; another, a self-destructive loose cannon; yet another, a lazy foot-dragger who doesn't like to work; or there could be a stubborn, angry holdout who doesn't want to join the team. Comforting and communicating with the players will bring about cooperation or sharing, and connection occurs when they begin functioning as a whole as opposed to individual players.

Uncontrollable mood swings are an example of what happens when the players are not working together as a team. Jean, Linda, and Nancy all spoke of rapid fluctuations in mood that they couldn't control when some hidden part took center stage. People may be misdiagnosed as having bipolar or manic-depressive illness when in fact they may have dissociated parts that break loose with their own feelings and steal the spotlight from time to time instead of staying connected to the team.

One of the most effective ways of forging a connection between yourself and a hidden part or among the hidden parts themselves is to apply the skills you practice in the working world to this task. When Jean had trouble accessing Cave Girl—the part of herself that was still in shock from the violence and sexual abuse of her childhood—I asked her to apply the skills she used with her battered women clients to herself. She made an assessment of Cave Girl's needs, identifying her withdrawal and silence as signs of depression. Of Cave Girl's history, she said that whenever there was trouble at home she would retreat into her cave. The little girl had remained there throughout the rest of Jean's life, frozen in time and unapproachable because of her distorted belief that she had to stay away from adults. Jean's letters established a link between Cave Girl and Knowledge. As a trained counselor, she enlisted Knowledge's help in approaching the little girl in the cave and getting her to join the team.

INTEGRATION

The natural by-product of successfully working through all of the phases of treatment—comforting and communicating with one's separate parts and helping them to cooperate with each other and connect as a team—is integration. The more a person has experienced respecting and accepting the memories and feelings bound up in each part, the less need there is for the symptoms that maintained their disconnection, and they are all reduced:

Amnesia: With the flow and sharing of feelings and memories and skills and knowledge back and forth, amnesia has outlived its usefulness as a retaining wall and gradually diminishes.

Depersonalization: Once people can accept that the abuse or trauma happened to them, not to some stranger they've detached from themselves, they don't have the same need for depersonalization when some trigger reminds them of the abuse or trauma. Like Linda, who doesn't have to go outside her body anymore during intimacy with her fiancé and can allow herself to feel positive emotions, people who have inner team-work are aware that this situation is different from past situations and feel safe now.

Derealization: People who are able to distinguish the present from the past and feel safe no longer need to disconnect from familiar people or their home environment. For an abused child, derealization was use-ful because mental detachment from the perpetrator was the only way that the child could escape. For an adult, having an internal system for preventing this automatic trauma response from going off inappropri-ately reduces disconnection from people who are close. Linda doesn't have to disconnect from Ted, for example, and think of him as the rapist. He can be who he is, and she can acknowledge him and love him as he is today.

Identity confusion: When identity fragments within a person are con-nected, identity confusion is necessarily reduced. The reason people who dissociate have identity confusion isn't that they lack an identity—it's that they have many parts of their identity that are disconnected and attempt-ing to have lives of their own. This is the inner struggle that dissociatives speak of so often. Once a person has connected with these inner parts and they've connected with each other in a supportive way, as opposed to a way that denies, disavows, or wants to get rid of, identity confusion is replaced by a feeling of unity. Moods stay on a more even keel and deci-sion making doesn't pull a person apart in a million different directions, because now there's a team with a coordinator in charge.

Identity alteration: Seizing of control by different parts occurs much less frequently, if at all, as a result of inner teamwork. An exercise in inner teamwork before making an important decision or at some turning point in a person's life is mentally calling a meeting of the different parts that have been identified and assigning the most functional part to chair the meeting. The chair asks the other parts to express their opinions so that everyone's voice can be heard, acknowledged, and understood. In Jean's case, for example, Knowledge might chair the meeting and have a discus-sion about dating after the divorce. Anger might want to get back into drinking and promiscuous sex. Sexuality's healthy part might want to hold out for a relationship with a caring, responsible man who is not a sub-stance abuser. Cave Girl might want to shrink from going out with any-one. Knowledge would make the ultimate decision, but at least everyone's feelings would be made known and attended to so that the decision would not result in a mutiny by any particular part.

As functioning cooperation of this kind proceeds forward, all five dissociative symptoms further diminish or disappear entirely. Integration of the separate parts into a unified whole is a natural consequence, and the person whose identity was once a collection of estranged fragments is made whole. Alters are not "killed off," as most people with DID initially fear; instead the dissociated memories, feelings, and behavior become integrated, eliminating the need for the five core dissociative symptoms. Internal struggle gives way to relative peace, and people who have suffered so much are now able to end abuse in their current life and build relationships with loving, supportive people.

HYPNOSIS

Hypnosis can be useful for people with a dissociative disorder in a number of ways. As an adjunct to psychotherapy, hypnosis can help abuse survivors reduce guilt feelings associated with the abuse, as well as teach them how to identify, express, and nurture their dissociated feelings or hidden aspects of themselves.

One of the techniques I find particularly helpful with trauma or abuse survivors is Spiegel's "split-screen" method, which teaches how to integrate one's dissociated memories and feelings. The therapist instructs the patient to picture a traumatic memory on one side of a mental screen while visualizing positive or assertive responses to the trauma on the other. As a result, the patient comes away less weighted down by the trauma and is eventually able to have a more balanced view of it. For example, a woman suffering from posttraumatic symptoms following a violent attack might be instructed to project on her "screen" her courageous defense of her life whenever she was overwhelmed by intrusive memories of her brutal assault. This technique can also be used to recover pleasant memories from the past so that people can visualize "safe places" to go to during episodes of depersonalization or derealization.

Hypnosis by a clinician specifically trained in it can be a particularly effective way of reducing stress, anxiety, depression, and phobias, as well as managing pain. Because the full SCID-D evaluation usually elicits spontaneous memories of abuse, and traumatic memories also occur spontaneously throughout the treatment with the Four C's, I generally do not use hypnosis for recovery of abuse memories. Having said that, I do believe hypnosis can be useful to someone with a dissociative disorder for a wide variety of associated symptoms.

DRUG THERAPY

Medication is a useful adjunct in the treatment of people with dissociative disorders. I often find that it temporarily alleviates such symptoms as severe anxiety or depression. Whether these symptoms are related to a coexisting disorder or are secondary to underlying dissociative symptoms, medication may provide some symptomatic relief.

Although there are few controlled studies of drug therapy for dissociative symptoms, many people with these symptoms find that medication relieves associated anxiety, depression, mood changes, and irritability. Antianxiety medications, used as needed, may be effective in reducing associated anxiety. There are many new antidepressants with minimal side effects that can reduce feelings of depression. Mood stabilizing and anticonvulsant drugs may reduce the severity of mood shifts. Hypnotic agents can help people suffering from insomnia. Stimulant medication, frequently used for coexisting ADHD, can help some dissociative people not only improve attention and memory, but have fewer shifts in moods. Medication may also help take the edge off the volatility in people with a dissociative problem, mitigating temper outbursts that occur with the uncontrolled emergence of angry feelings.

Finding a physician who understands dissociation is extremely important, because you will want to discuss the effect of a medication on all of your symptoms. People with a dissociative disorder may fluctuate in their need for medication, as well as in their sensitivity to it, depending upon which aspect of themselves is in control. If you haven't been on medication before, it's impossible to predict which medication will be most effective for you, so it helps to be flexible and see whether a particular medication prescribed by your physician works or not. Beware of using many different medications at the same time, though, because this often occurs when you are getting a different medication for each of your external symptoms, and in the meantime your dissociative symptoms are not receiving the specialized psychotherapy they need. Since people with dissociative disorders are not psychotic (out of touch with reality), antipsychotics should be used primarily for severe agitation that does not respond to antianxiety agents.

Medication for someone with an underlying dissociative syndrome should always be used in conjunction with psychotherapy; it is never a substitute for it. Pills can make the road less bumpy, but the long-term resolution of external symptoms like depression and anxiety depends upon getting specialized psychotherapy focused on treating internal dissociative symptoms.

15

~

ALIENS FROM INNER SPACE:
UFO ABDUCTIONS, PAST LIVES,
NEAR-DEATH EXPERIENCES

"THE BOOK THAT started it all," according to its publishers, with "revelations of alien-human contact" was *Missing Time* by Budd Hopkins. The author created a sensation with the accounts related by seven people under repeated sessions of hypnosis. They told how they were temporarily abducted by aliens and taken aboard UFOs, where they were held captive and violated with bodily intrusions that left mysterious scars. The similarities in the victims' descriptions of their alien abductors and the experiments they endured led the author to conclude that what the people had described was exactly what happened. And yet even the jacket copy on the back of the book offers a clue to a different explanation:

> *Hopkins could not have told the stories of those victims without having first discovered the one experience common to all who report alien encounters—the phenomenon known as missing time.* Missing Time *tells how the people who have experienced abductions retained no memory of them— all traces of the trauma were effectively erased from their memory.*

Amnesia was the one experience common to all of the victims, and only under hypnosis were they able to recall the "trauma." But what trauma was it? Were they remembering an actual abduction by aliens from outer space or a previous trauma of childhood abuse that their own inner aliens—their dissociated hidden parts—had reconstructed into a less stressful memory? Were these real images or symbols of a reality from which they had disconnected?

The SCID-D holds an answer to their symptoms. Absolutely everything in the transcripts of the people describing alien abductions has analogies to what abuse survivors report on their experiences of the five dissociative symptoms on the SCID-D. The conclusion is clear: *alien abduction stories are probably screen memories, partial or implicit memories, of feelings and sensations associated with early childhood trauma that block the actual memory of the trauma.* They are a symbolic form of dissociated traumatic memories of childhood sexual or other abuse—a psychological event rather than explicit memories of a real occurrence.

INTERPRETING THE SYMBOLS

Howard Rich, one of the abductees in *Missing Time,* recalled under hypnosis seeing an incredibly bright "blue light"—not unlike Jean's "green light"—one night while he was visiting his mother and was alone in a ground floor bedroom. Impelled by fear and an intense feeling of being in danger, he went outside to investigate and was gone for what he thought was a few minutes, but what the clock later revealed was more than an hour. During this period of amnesia Howard claimed that he saw dark, shadowy figures he couldn't identify—"just black—the shapes—the figures"—and felt a muscular paralysis that rendered him helpless.

Floating outside his body, Howard moved into a thick black cloud and onto a high, flat table and was subjected to an "examination." While he continued to feel that he was floating and that everything around him was dreamlike, the kind of pleasant numbing of an anesthetic, the shadowy figures probed him with bright lights that were all around the room and touched him everywhere. Howard's breathing became agitated and his muscles tensed at this point in the hypnosis session. He said that he felt "something happening down there." Reliving the experience, he arched his back and bent his neck as if in sudden pain and cried out, "Oh, God! It hurts—it hurts—Oh!" Emotionally he felt there was a struggle going on inside him to dispel his fear of his captors and prove to himself that he was stronger. Without remembering his legs' walking, Howard returned to the bedroom in his mother's house and awoke in the morning with a few droplets of blood on his pillow.

It took Howard a week to recover from the anxiety that the traumatic memory provoked. He told Hopkins that he had suffered from "a powerful sense of having done something forbidden, of having betrayed an important injunction not to remember and not to tell what happened to him."

Remember Vince, the former football player in Chapter 5 who suffered from severe dissociative amnesia and saw "dark people" or shadowy figures who accosted him during his daily episodes of lost time? They held him down, stuck needles in him, or tried to strangle him. When Vince relived their assaults during his trances, like Howard, he arched his back and stretched his neck until he was in pain. Vince was originally diagnosed as having DDNOS, a milder dissociative illness than DID. But that diagnosis was changed to DID when he later began to describe the different people who existed inside him and recovered memories of being sexually abused by priests in Catholic school during his childhood. This abuse was the actual trauma for which the attacks by the shadowy "dark people" in his trances were screen memories.

If Howard had been given the SCID-D, he would have shown moderate to severe levels of all five dissociative symptoms:

Amnesia: Howard had significant periods of time that he couldn't account for by memory.

Depersonalization: He had also experienced bodily floating, automatic moving, a feeling of being anesthetized, and self-injury he had no awareness of (probably caused by inserting his finger inside his nose, as other alien abduction reports indicate).

Derealization: Howard had the feeling of being in a dream in which the surroundings were strange and unreal and having perceptual distortions like the "blue light," the "black cloud," and the lights inside the cloud.

Identity confusion: Howard had the feeling of having his identity stripped from him while his body was being used for experimentation and had sensed an internal struggle over his own physical strength and his sense of helplessness.

Identity alteration: Howard had the feeling of having no will of his own and the perception that other personalities (externalized as aliens) were taking control of his behavior.

Howard's physical movements during hypnosis and his crying out in pain are analogous to the behavior of DID patients reliving traumatic events of childhood sexual abuse in flashbacks. Many other abductees report having nasal or anal probes inserted into them and having semen or ova withdrawn from them with some kind of instrument. A ubiquitous tool that appears in the accounts is a "bullet-shaped" or cylindrical object with a rounded bulbous end, seven or eight inches long, and "over twice as thick" as a man's thumb—an obvious phallic symbol. One of the male abductees reported having his legs raised by round metal loops on the table so that he was forced into the same kind of posture as a woman in obstetrical stirrups. All of the people in *Missing Time* spoke of feeling strong, externally imposed fear or waking up paralyzed by a sense of a strange presence in the room; of being in a hazy, dreamlike, out-of-body state; of being held captive on a high, flat table or bed by humanoids with mechanical limbs reminiscent of the Tin Man in the *Wizard of Oz;* of having something painfully implanted in them and a sample taken from them, usually in the groin or lower abdominal region; and of being used in a single-minded, unfeeling way by these creatures, who, as one man put it, "were just out to do their job."

All of this can be seen as an emerging partial memory of sexual abuse by exploitative perpetrators whom the victims feel compelled to hide because they are usually threatened with bodily harm or death if they reveal the truth. Howard's sense of having disobeyed an important injunction not to remember and not to tell what happened to him is a common feeling among survivors of childhood sexual abuse who've dissociated from the trauma and are loath to report it.

PERPETRATOR PROTECTION

What better way to dissociate from one's trauma and the perpetrator of it than to attribute it to someone else, some imaginary figure—in this case, an alien that no one can find or identify? This concealment is very consistent with Jennifer Frye's betrayal blindness theory. The majority of adults who recall alien abduction experiences under hypnosis remember being abducted before as children, often when they were six or seven years old. As Jennifer Frye has explained, young children who are betrayed by people who are supposed to be their primary caretakers have to turn a blind eye to it or they won't survive.

Breaking Down the Wall of Silence by Alice Miller, a lay analyst who blocked out her own abuse for some sixty years, points out that society also makes it very difficult for people to retain explicit memories of childhood abuse. People who go public with their experiences may run into resistance by skeptics in the media. Or they may meet with a reluctance to get involved among people they tell, who act like bystanders stolidly walking, eyes averted, past an accident victim lying on the sidewalk. Psychoanalysis itself is a system that suppresses the truth about abuse in childhood, Miller says, dating back to Freud's time in 1897 when the subject of child abuse was banned from psychoanalytic circles. Freud, perhaps unable to confront his own childhood, proclaimed that childhood sexual abuse existed only in his patients' fantasy lives and made his students suppress any hint of such abuse whenever it appeared.

Today teachers, social workers, child protection agencies, and law enforcement officers are becoming increasingly aware of how widespread and devastating child abuse is, but too many people are still looking the other way. The societal wall of silence may no longer be impenetrable, but it is still standing tall.

We have an ever-growing number of people who are now able to identify that they've been traumatized—but by "aliens." The screen memories they've created to explain what they've been forbidden to remember shows the extent of their disconnection, a very fundamental problem that occurs in dissociative disorders. Implicit memories, instead of being taken figuratively as metaphors for the actual trauma, are being taken literally by an entire subculture in our society who believe in alien abduction.

Virginia Horton, one of the abductees in *Missing Time,* actually saw a resemblance between her imaginary abductor and the real perpetrator who wanted to take "a little itty bitty piece of her"—her grandfather. Her hypnosis sessions also provide concrete evidence of the existence of alternate personalities within Virginia. Much of the time she spoke like a six-year-old girl, at other times like a sixties teenager, and the rest of the time like a contemporary highly intelligent adult.

Described as a happily married thirty-five-year-old lawyer with a major corporation, Virginia recalled under hypnosis that her family was living on her grandfather's farm when she had her first episode of memory loss as a six-year-old girl. She was in the barn gathering eggs and arrived in the yard of the house with a deep gash on the back of her calf, having no memory of going from the barn to the yard and no idea how she had cut herself. There was no tear in her jeans or other sign of a mishap. At age sixteen on a family picnic in France Virginia had another lengthy memory blank while playing in the woods. She returned to her family with blood on her blouse and no explanation for it.

Under hypnosis after expressing considerable fear of remembering these incidents, Virginia recalled that the cut on her leg was made by aliens using a tubular instrument that resembled "a long electric massager"—easily a symbolic penis. She remembered lying on a couch surrounded by shadowy people performing experiments in a room full of silver-colored objects sparkling like crystals (perceptual distortions common in derealization). She felt the presence of the people more than she could see them, as if they had to remain hidden or their appearance would scare her. The one person she spoke to, she said, reminded her of her grandfather—"somebody who's older and whom I'm very comfortable around." She later added that he wouldn't tell her how old he was, "and that reminds me of my grandfather, too, who used to lie about his age."

As for the wound in her leg, Virginia says that she didn't feel any pain because she was told that she wouldn't feel it—another way of describing how a self-injurer numbs feelings of pain during a depersonalization episode. "It was like the pain was inside and the pain wanted to come out," Virginia said, "but I don't think it hurt at the time."

Under hypnosis Virginia attributed the mysterious blood she found on her blouse when she was a teenager at a family picnic in France to an alien abduction. The humanoid abductors who carried her aboard the UFO and set her down on the couch had an outer layer that was not skin, but a gray, skinlike fabric that masked their faces. Again the captor who communicated with her reminded her of her grandfather, a very patient old man who wouldn't reveal his age and liked to explain things.

During this abduction Virginia encountered a pretty deer with a personality of a female schoolgirl, close in age to Virginia at the time, who seemed to be her best, long-lost friend—a description that sounds very much like a hidden part of herself, possibly an animal alternate personality. Speaking like a teenager, Virginia recalled that she floated out of her body and was taken for a ride by the deer, flying above the earth. But Virginia admitted that she might have invented the deer or that it might have had a "hypnotic cover." Like all abductees, she was not sure how much of her story was speculation to "fill in" for feelings or circumstances she couldn't account for because of her amnesia. The author himself asks, "Was Virginia's trip the recollection of an actual event or was it, perhaps, something else—an interpolated dream or an artificially induced image like the nonexistent deer?"

The blood on her blouse, Virginia said, was the result of a probe that was inserted into her nose so that it wouldn't leave a mark like the scar on her leg. For a reason she couldn't understand, this "research mission" was very exciting for her abductors and a cause for celebration. Her attempt to explain this excitement on the basis of an award for "extraterrestrial biology," the author notes, "clearly implies a guess, an approximation that is metaphorical rather than literal." That can be said for the entire alien abduction account—it's an attempt to make sense of blurred memories of childhood sexual abuse that are only half understood. Hypnosis puts survivors in touch with the hidden parts of themselves that are stuck in time and still reliving the experience symbolically.

All of the alien abduction accounts make a point of the captors' having metallic limbs or using metallic instruments to take what they need in a cold, self-serving manner—"a one-way transaction," as Budd Hopkins puts it. He reports that for reasons that are vague to them, abductees say that they were singled out and were made to feel "special, loved, members of the 'select.'" Hopkins likens this technique to the "love bombing" used by religious cults to weaken the opposition of their potential converts and set them up for unusual demands that will be made of them. If you read between the lines in this dialogue excerpted from a male abductee's account, the seduction seems much more personal. The alien abductor professing love can be seen as a child's useful metaphor for a sexually abusive caretaker trying to relax the child standing paralyzed with fear before him:

> He wants—to hug me—says—says, "Why are you scared?"
>
> "Someone loves you very deeply, and they want to see you. Close your eyes and be still."
>
> A "painful operation of some kind" follows, and the terrified victim asks, "What are you—what are you putting me in? What? It hurts—oh! Can't see—can't see—can't see—can't breathe."
>
> Told to relax, the captive says, "OK, OK, OK, I'm relaxed. I'm relaxed! Help! Help!" Another painful process follows, and the victim complains of cramps in his hands and arms and says, "Oh, my body is vibrating—I'm just standing here. I can't see. Something is above me—and it makes me vibrate."
>
> Afterward, the captor flatters his victim with words that imply some kind of mind control: "We are working with your mind. We know you have very strong mental abilities."

To abuse survivors this supposed alien seems deplorably all too human.

WHY ALIENS?

What about the argument that there must be some truth to alien abduction because of all the similarities in the descriptions of the aliens, their space ships, and the nature of the experiments? This is the argument advanced not only by Budd Hopkins, but by the prestigiously credentialed John E. Mack, M.D., a tenured professor of psychiatry at Harvard Medical School, who wrote his own book on the subject, *Abduction: Human Encounters with Aliens*. The anecdotes in Dr. Mack's book were criticized for a lack of scientific methodology, but the similarities raised the question of an overall pattern. How is it that the aliens are all between four and five feet tall in stature and look the same—fetuslike with large hairless heads, soft whitish gray skin, big black eyes? And why do the UFOs all resemble the ones we saw in *ET* or *Close Encounters of the Third Kind*?

Carl Sagan, a longtime acquaintance of Mack's, had an answer for this. He pointed out that the fantasy life of people has always been influenced by prevailing cultural images in all times and places. When everyone believed that gods regularly came down to earth, gods were what people envisioned as fearsome otherworldly beings. In the Middle Ages, when demons were in vogue, it was incubi and succubi. Later, when fairies were widely believed in, it was fairies that were said to paralyze and rape human victims. Now, in the space age, when we are sending space ships to Mars and have begun to think that aliens might exist, aliens descending from space ships are the imaginary predators that people see in their dreams and flashbacks.

What I find most consistent about these humanoid figures is that the people who see them can't identify them. Their strangeness is their overriding feature—the "strangeness" of familiar people that occurs in dissociative episodes. Abductees have the same dissociative symptoms as the trauma survivors that I see in my psychiatric practice. Part of what defines a posttraumatic disorder is that there are consistent, reliable ways that people respond to trauma. The consistency of the abductees' symptoms, including the derealization of their abusers into strange or unfamiliar beings, fits in perfectly with the clinical picture of a dissociative disorder.

Dorene, a patient I first saw about ten years ago, has been living alone for seventeen years since her divorce and is now in her sixties. She began treatment convinced that burglars were breaking into her home. What were they taking? Nothing valuable—they were moving her underwear around. Personal items that she had placed in certain locations weren't in them, and then she would find them in places that she had never put them. She was so paranoid about these intruders that she went to the managers of her apartment building and asked them to change her locks numerous times, and they did. But this problem continued, causing her much distress and prompting her grown daughter to think she was crazy. The clinic she went to for treatment asked me to evaluate her, and I suspected that she had a dissociative disorder. Dorene, however, was convinced that intruders were breaking into her home, and no one could talk her out of it. She was as certain of that as people who insist they were abducted by aliens.

Recently Dorene went back into treatment at the clinic, and once again I was asked to evaluate her. The SCID-D showed that she had each of the five core symptoms:

She had memory problems concerning things she put away and couldn't find although she believed that somebody else was moving them. She also said that her head was in a "fog" at times and that she once found herself in a different city and couldn't remember anything about herself—a classic example of amnesia.

Depersonalization manifested itself about four times a month when Dorene felt that she became a "spirit" watching herself, or felt that her hand was disconnected, or looked in the mirror and said, "Who's that? That's not me."

In terms of derealization, Dorene reported going home sometimes and thinking, "This is not my house. This place is strange. Where am I?" She'd think that a door should be in a certain place, and it wasn't, or she didn't know where her bedroom was.

She expressed identity confusion this way: "I've always felt I wasn't me—I've felt it for years." She once told a priest that she was possessed because she felt as if someone else was making her do things. Recalling an experience she had when she was in the hospital, she said, "I would feel and see someone on top of me, and I felt like someone was making love to me." After she left the hospital, this feeling of being possessed recurred for months.

Dorene manifested identity alteration in several ways. A gifted pianist, she volunteered to play at a senior citizens' home and would find every so often that she was unable to play at all. "What's wrong?" the man who accompanied her on the violin would ask. Dorene had no answer, not realizing that an alternate personality who couldn't play the piano had taken control. Another manifestation was Dorene's automatic writing—a very common occurrence among DID patients when alters take over. She recalled that it was a little girl named Doris—a ten-year-old who had been sexually abused and wanted retribution—who was doing the automatic writing. Dorene did not identify Doris as part of herself. Feeling frightened by the angry childish writing by her own hand, she would tell Doris, "Don't come back!"

In addition to these symptoms Dorene suffered from migraine headaches and a fear of choking—two physical symptoms that are very common among people with a dissociative disorder related to childhood sexual abuse. Earlier in her life Dorene had worked at a variety of jobs. A bright, attractive woman, she had no trouble finding work, but she was fired again and again. She'd do well on the job for a while, until one day she would abruptly stop going to work because "something happened inside of me"—apparently one of her alters took control.

I was able to identify a few personalities within her. There was Doris, for one, the little girl who came out during her automatic writing. And there was another hidden part she called by a completely different name from hers—Vanessa Langdon—who was very extroverted. Dorene said that she felt she was playing a role when she acted like Vanessa. She herself tended to be more introverted, having grown up in a violent home with a brother who was a drug addict. Although she didn't remember being sexually abused, she thought it was possible that she had been.

I explained to Dorene how the human mind uses dissociation to cope with trauma. The intruders moving her personal belongings around in her home might be internal parts of herself she had dissociated from as a child, I told her, and had dissociated from a second time by thinking that they were external intruders. When I asked her what Vanessa Langdon might say about that if she could speak to me, she said, "I'm glad the doctor's really getting to the bottom of this."

ABDUCTEES VERSUS SIGHTEES

A distinction needs to be made between people who believe they have been abducted by aliens and sightees who report witnessing unidentified flying objects (UFOs) but do not recall extraterrestrial contact. A study undertaken in 1994 by Susan Marie Powers, Ph.D., a research psychologist, assessed the dissociative symptoms in three groups of people: abductees, sightees, and sexually abused persons who had good recall of their experiences involving penetration but did not recall any extraterrestrial contact. Dr. Powers found that posttraumatic stress disorder (PTSD) symptoms were manifested by 45 percent of the abductees, none of the sightees, and 70 percent of the sexually abused subjects. Dissociative symptoms were demonstrated by 70 percent of the abductees, 10 percent of the sightees, and 100 percent of the sexually abused subjects. Neither of the two screening inventories that were used was specifically designed to evaluate dissociative symptoms. Had the SCID-D been available at the time and administered, it might have found an even higher prevalence of all five dissociative symptoms among the abductees.

The study by Dr. Powers confirmed previous findings that there are important differences between the person who alleges that he or she saw a UFO and a person who says he or she was physically violated by aliens. *Sightees who do not report any subsequent contact with extraterrestrials or abduction tend to produce normal scores on psychological tests, whereas abductees do not.* It is beyond the purview of this book to make any assumptions one way or another about the reliability of UFO sightings. What can be said with certainty is that people who claim to have had contact with alien abductors experience dissociative symptoms that are virtually identical to those found in people with dissociative disorders.

Dr. Powers cited research by Ring and Rosing (1990) indicating that people who claim contact with aliens often have a childhood history of physical and/or sexual abuse. Why then did the sexually abused population produce higher scores on the screening inventories than the abductee group? Dr. Powers suggested that as screen memories for early childhood trauma such as sexual abuse, the alien abduction narratives may function as "coping mechanisms that mitigate the experience of re-lived trauma." Remembering the "reconstituted memory" in the form of alien abduction, she said, "might be less stressful than confronting the trauma of childhood abuse perpetrated by relatives or family friends."

SOLVING THE PUZZLE

One facet of alien abduction that Budd Hopkins found perplexing was the "externally induced amnesia." He thought that the aliens probably forced this amnesia upon the abductees by posthypnotic suggestion, but then asked, "Why is it done, especially if the UFO occupants know it can in many cases be broached by our own terrestrial hypnotic techniques? And why have there been cases where it was apparently not used at all?"

Hopkins speculated that the traumatic experience was blocked from conscious memory for the good of the abductees—talking about it to others would invite doubts about their sanity and compromise their role as "human specimens" being studied over a period of years. He also thought that amnesia failed for some people because they fainted and could not have posthypnotic suggestions implanted while they were unconscious. But why wasn't the externally enforced amnesia more successful when, supposedly, it was implanted?

Dissociation is the piece of the puzzle that solves this mystery. Amnesia was enforced not by posthypnotic suggestion, but by verbal threats (Steven Kilburn, one abductee, actually recalled under hypnosis being told not to remember anything or he might die). And it was also self-imposed by the victims—child victims who were not violated by aliens, but by abusive caretakers and had to dissociate from the trauma and be blind to the perpetrators as a matter of survival. Abductees remembered the trauma not because posthypnotic suggestion failed to block their memories of alien abduction, but because hypnosis succeeded in temporarily dispelling the amnesia that hid their dissociated screen memories of childhood abuse.

Dr. Aphrodite Claymar, a psychologist who hypnotized a number of the subjects in *Missing Time,* admitted that after spending more that fifty hours with a dozen subjects who were under hypnosis, she still could not say whether the alien abduction experience was real or not. She further admitted that the subjects had not been subjected to "the kind of psychological testing that might provide a deeper understanding of their personalities." Budd Hopkins had hoped that Dr. Claymar would be able to provide a final answer by inducing hypnosis in the abductees. But the evidence that would establish these similar experiences as something more than fantasy, she said, remained "disturbingly elusive." She concluded, "The answer to the question has not yet been devised, the key to unlock the secret not yet found."

Dissociation, identified by the presence of the five core symptoms, is that key.

PAST LIVES

Imagining that one's childhood trauma occurred in a previous historical period is another way of dissociating from it. A belief in past lives allows people to externalize abuse to a different century and maintain attachments to family members who may have abused them in *this* life—a necessary disconnection because it's too threatening to confront that abuse even in adulthood. It's easier to think that one was a slave in ancient Egypt, for example, than to accept that one was oppressed and exploited in this life by loved and trusted caretakers. Again the narratives of past lives that are recalled under hypnosis are, like alien abduction narratives, metaphorical rather than literal accounts of what happened. People with past lives are not ready to say that they have different people inside them, but they can instead say that they themselves had different lives.

The ability of people with past lives to recall under hypnosis accurate descriptions of countries and cultures in previous times, or to speak languages they didn't know they knew, or to demonstrate extraordinary intuition can be explained by dissociative amnesia. This fluctuation in knowledge and skills is very characteristic of people with a dissociative disorder. They have talents and information they're unaware of that might have been acquired by an alternate personality—skills or knowledge they don't remember having acquired in another personality state, as opposed to having learned them in another life.

The man who is credited with giving legitimacy to past life experiences is Brian Weiss, M.D., a psychiatrist who is a graduate of Yale Medical School and author of the book *Many Lives, Many Masters* (Simon and Schuster, 1988). Dr. Weiss's book tells the story of Catherine, a twenty-eight-year-old patient of his, who suffered from severe anxiety and panic attacks and phobias. She feared choking and darkness, as well as water, airplanes, being trapped, and dying. Her father was an alcoholic, and her mother was hospitalized for depression and had shock treatments when Catherine was eleven. As the middle child she never enjoyed the freedom that her older brother had and the favoritism showered on her younger sister by both parents. At the time Catherine started therapy she had been involved in a six-year affair with Stuart, a married doctor who emotionally abused and manipulated her. Catherine was a lab technician at the same hospital where Dr. Weiss was chief of psychiatry, and she went to see him because she felt she was losing control over her life.

After eighteen months of unfruitful conventional therapy, Dr. Weiss decided to try hypnosis. Catherine remembered "amazingly few" traumatic events from her earlier years under hypnosis other than being pushed from a diving board into a pool when she was five. Reliving the experience, she started to choke and gag, but the gagging stopped when Dr. Weiss suggested that the experience was over and she was out of the water. Then she recalled "the worst event of all," which occurred at age three: her father, reeking of alcohol, entered her dark bedroom at night and molested her. When the terrified child began to cry, he covered her mouth with his hand, and she could not breathe. Catherine began to sob in Dr. Weiss's office, and again he comforted her by suggesting that the experience was over.

During the next few months of weekly hypnotic regressions, Catherine accessed hidden parts of herself that she recalled as different personalities in past lives. Their stories are quite revealing. There is Aronda, a young woman in 1863 B.C., who, together with her baby (recognized by Catherine as her niece in real life), drowns in a flood. In a subsequent lifetime Aronda reappears in the Royal House as a servant, and her death this time is peaceful—she floats out of her body. Johan, a young man in America in the days when bows and arrows were used, goes on a scouting expedition in a canoe and is killed when an enemy fighter grabs him from behind and slits his throat with a knife. Catherine catches a glimpse of the killer's face and sees Stuart—her real-life lover. She next finds herself floating above her body, observing the scene below, and being pulled into a "tiny, warm" space, about to be born. The mother holding her is, Catherine says in surprise, "the *same* mother I have now!"

There are many other incarnations, during some of which Catherine speaks in voices and speech patterns that are different from her own. As Elizabeth, speaking as a child might, she becomes frightened when she recalls her father's fighting with her mother and pushing the children. Eventually Elizabeth marries happily and dies peacefully in old age, again floating out of her body. As Abby, a black servant on a plantation in the South in the 1880s, Catherine sleeps with a man without being married to him. She dies of a fever in her sixties and floats out of her body, drawn toward the light to be reborn. In all of Catherine's hypnosis sessions she experiences or reexperiences lifetimes of poverty, physical pain, servitude, and abuse within her family. When she dies, she always floats out of her body toward a new incarnation in a different lifetime.

In one session Catherine enters her present lifetime as herself at age five. Whining like a child, she complains that her father is beating her with a heavy stick and forcing her to eat food she hates that is going to make her sick. When asked why he is punishing her like that, she says, "He hates me for what he did, and he hates himself. So he must punish me. . . . I must have done something to make him do that." Dr. Weiss points out why this deep guilt she has carried with her since she was a baby is unreasonable and tells her that she has to relieve herself of it.

In one of her past lives Catherine looks at her father's face and sees Stuart—both think she is a nuisance. In an ancient lifetime her father and her brother die, and a spiritual entity called a Poet Master, speaking in a different voice, says that we must have patience: "A life cannot be rushed, cannot be worked on a schedule as so many people want it to be." When Catherine's body is burned in a fire in a past life, another spiritual part of herself, a Master Spirit, explains that we don't need our bodies: "Our body is just a vehicle for us while we're here; it is our soul and our spirit that last forever."

Dr. Weiss thought that the information Catherine imparted about previous times and the spiritual and intuitive insights of the "Masters" or "spirit entities" were beyond Catherine's conscious capacities. The conscious Catherine, when awake, he said, was much more limited and comparatively superficial—"oblivious of the genius within her." He concluded that she was not herself but in a "superconscious state" when she relayed the messages from the Masters about such concepts as patience; trust and forgiveness; eradication of fears, especially fear of death; not judging others or halting anyone's life; and, most of all, our immortality.

Dr. Weiss had no scientific explanation for the disparity between Catherine's conscious personality and her "superconscious" one. Although he recognized that her repeated experiences of floating out of her body were akin to "near-death" experiences described by others, he did not identify this as a sign of the dissociative symptom of depersonalization. Several times in his book he ruled out a dissociative basis for Catherine's condition without evaluating her for dissociation in a systematic manner. Once he said flatly that she did not have dissociative tendencies because "she was generally aware of what she was doing and thinking, did not function on 'automatic pilot,' and had never had any split or multiple personalities."

Actually the people Catherine became in her trances were all alternate personalities or dissociated parts of herself with their individual qualities. The sagelike poet or Master Spirit that surfaced in her "superconscious state" was similar to Jean's alternate personality that she called Knowledge. In Catherine's conscious state her other personalities with their particular memories and knowledge were kept out of her awareness by amnesia, and they could be accessed only under hypnosis. In the same way that Dorene experienced automatic writing, Catherine was on "automatic pilot" the whole time that the Masters issued their wisdom through her mouth.

Catherine, in fact, exhibited all five core dissociative symptoms to a significant degree. Besides identity alteration, amnesia, and depersonalization, she repeatedly experienced derealization—the distortion of her home environment into strange places, for example, or times when she looked at her father's face or her killer's face and saw Stuart, her married, emotionally abusive lover. As for identity confusion, Catherine began therapy complaining of having no control over her life, of feeling confused by all the anxiety and fear overwhelming her—a common complaint initially presented by DID patients. An accurate assessment based on her symptoms would have shown Catherine to be one of them.

Dr. Weiss was surprised at how soon after the first hypnosis session—three and a half months—Catherine's symptoms of anxiety, panic attacks, and phobias virtually disappeared. He admitted feeling frustrated that he was not able to be a bridge between her insightful state, in which she realized that she needed to break away from Stuart, and her state in the real world: "These insights needed to reach her conscious mind and needed to be applied to her conscious life. Superconscious insight was fascinating, but by itself it was not enough to transform her life."

The remarkable progress that Dr. Weiss had in reducing Catherine's fear of death and her other phobias came about because his past-life therapy acknowledged and worked with her hidden parts and did not discount them. He was able to reduce her fears, anxiety, and panic attacks by getting her to do two of the four C's—comfort her different parts and communicate with them—at least under hypnosis. Since he did not recognize Catherine's underlying dissociative disorder, he was unable to help her fully integrate the hidden parts of herself into a unified whole by means of cooperation and connection with each other. Without that inner teamwork her alternate personalities were still externalized to different lifetimes, and she remained disconnected from the "genius within her" on a conscious level.

Alien abduction and past life narratives are useful as coping mechanisms that lessen the pain and terror of relived childhood abuse. Once the trauma is externalized to that extent, full recovery can be a slow process. It requires a therapist who is skilled in dissociation to identify what's happening. People who believe that these experiences are real are suffering from a double dissociation. First, they dissociated the original trauma from their conscious awareness; then they disconnected once again by masking the trauma—either by assigning it to an imaginary perpetrator or by assigning it to a different historical period. Getting people to connect their fragmented traumatic memories to themselves when they've doubly dissociated from them is extremely challenging.

Dr. Powers concluded her study of dissociation in alleged extraterrestrial abductees with a caution against challenging their belief system prematurely. A person who has been traumatized by horrific memories, she pointed out, should not be further traumatized by a therapeutic approach that undermines the individual's sense of sanity. An abuse survivor who believes in the alien abduction experience or past lives need not *immediately* abandon that belief. As Dr. Weiss showed, listening to the patient's subjective experience and empathetically taking the same point of view can ameliorate the person's confusion and terror and help her move on with her life. But we've also seen that there are limits to this approach, and in some cases it might even strengthen the cognitive distortions in destructive ways.

After a person becomes comfortable with both the memories and the therapist, other possible explanations for the origin of the trauma can begin to be considered. Is it possible that it was perpetrated by a human or that it happened in this life? When an alternative explanation is accepted, dissociated material may eventually become conscious and accepted, too, and the person can begin to incorporate her personalities in different lifetimes into a coherent sense of self.

NEAR-DEATH EXPERIENCES

Religious or mystical phenomena often accompany the transient deper-sonalization episodes that occur as a universal response to life-threatening trauma. The first study of near-death experiences was undertaken in 1892 by Albert Heim, who accumulated the accounts of over thirty survivors of falls in the Alps. Heim found that "the person falling often heard beautiful music and fell in a superbly blue heaven containing roseate cloudlets."

Spiritual perceptions were found to be common in a later analysis of 114 accounts of near-death experiences obtained from 104 people by Russell Noyes, Jr., M.D., and Roy Kletti, M.A. A twenty-four-year-old mountain climber who lost his footing and found himself exposed to a two-thousand-foot drop reported: "I felt closer to God. I developed an understanding of death as something beautiful, a realization that stands out yet today as profoundly important." A fourteen-year-old boy who accidentally shot himself in the chest reported a religious feeling that "strength came from a force outside myself. It affected my mind as well as my body, and I think it enabled me to hold onto life." A fifty-five-year-old man who was certain he had died when his Jeep was blown up by a German mine during World War II reported experiencing a mystical sense of transcendence over time and space. He felt that he had entered a state in which only his mind existed in one moment of total serenity and peace that never altered. "I cannot stress strongly enough," he said, "the feeling of . . . total blissful acceptance of my new status, which I knew would be never-ending."

Transient depersonalization episodes involving visions of guardian angels or other religious figures can persist for a while in normal people after an acute trauma. We all need to develop a way to nurture ourselves when we're tenuously hanging on to life. The angel appearing at our bedside in the hospital, assuring us that we're going to make it, may actually be an internal helping part of ourselves that we've projected into an external source of support in this time of desperate need. This kind of apparitional experience would not constitute a psychiatric problem if the apparition went away in due time. If it developed an independent life and visited us recurrently and we began to lose time or have distress or dysfunction as a result of our ongoing dialogues with it, this out-of-body experience would be a symptom of a dissociative disorder. It would then have to be evaluated in the context of the other four symptoms.

Such popular books as *Life After Life* by Raymond Moody, *Closer to the Light* by Dr. Melvin Morse, and *Embraced by the Light* by Betty J. Eadie contain accounts of near-death out-of-body experiences. One of the most detailed and extensive personal accounts is found in Eadie's book. As thirty-one-year-old Betty hovered between life and death of complications after surgery, she felt herself floating out of her body and through the closed window of her hospital room. She experienced herself as moving at incredible speed through a tunnel toward a brilliant light and into the arms of a man surrounded by a golden halo who received her with "the most unconditional love I have ever felt." Recognizing the man as Jesus Christ, Betty proceeded to have an extended dialogue with him during which he answered all of her questions about God, the meaning of life, healing and dying, the laws that govern human beings, the importance of forgiveness and trust, and the supreme power of love. Like Catherine's Master Spirit, he assured her of our immortality: "The grave was never intended for the spirit—only for the body."

During her near-death experience Betty meets other spiritual beings and is taken on a tour of a breathtakingly beautiful garden, a library, and a room where happy souls are working on looms. She returns to earth after a tribunal lovingly reviews her life and tells her she must go back. Among the many lessons that Betty has learned on her journey is this one: "I understood that life is lived most fully in the imagination—that, ironically, imagination is the key to reality." By this she means that we are to use our free will to create our own lives and find joy in our creations. The belief in life after death is surely one of the most joyful and comforting creations of the human mind and allows us to live our lives more abundantly.

Betty Eadie was separated from her parents at the age of four and placed in a Catholic boarding school. She had a harsh childhood devoid of the unconditional love that she found in her depersonalized near-death experience. Once before, in her first winter at the boarding school when she almost died of whooping cough and double pneumonia, she had a religious vision of "a man with a beautiful white beard" who cradled her in his arms and comforted her. Through her depersonalization episodes Betty created a symbolic source of nurturance denied her in childhood and tapped into the spiritual insights lying dormant within her that lay outside her conscious awareness.

No matter how persuasive they are, narratives of alien abduction, past lives, and an afterlife should not be confused with proven, objective statements of fact. This is not to rule out the possibility that there is extraterrestrial life or that we have had past lives or that there is life after death. We should keep an open mind and continue to draw comfort from our religious beliefs but also be open to alternative explanations. If these experiences can be explained by a conceptual model in this life and in this world—the scientific model of dissociation—it seems unnecessary to extrapolate to any other life or world in order to understand them.

Before the advent of the SCID-D, clinicians were faced with a dubious choice regarding patients who spoke of past lives or abductions by aliens: either proclaim these people crazy or accept their accounts as descriptions of real events. Today, the SCID-D assessment process shows that these people are attesting to symptoms of dissociation and could benefit from therapies designed to treat dissociative disorders. The phenomena they elaborately describe are, most likely, not events that actually happened, but yet another example of the power of the human mind to protect itself by creating imaginative metaphorical symbols for memories of unthinkable childhood trauma.

16

UNNECESSARY LOSSES

THE CURRENT EPIDEMIC of dissociation is a senseless one. Here is an illness that can be treated and cured and yet is so widely undetected or misdiagnosed that the waste, in terms of both human dysfunction and money misspent on inappropriate health care, is tragic. This book is a first step toward ending these *unn*ecessary losses.

The three in-depth case histories have shown how a dissociative disorder often underlies a presenting problem and, because it is not recognized or treated, reaches a point where the patient needs to be hospitalized or suffers some other serious consequence. The first case history patient, Nancy L., had been treated for attention-deficit hyperactivity disorder for nine years before she broke down completely. She was taken to an emergency room in a crisis state and was spared hospitalization only because her psychiatrist suspected a dissociative disorder and referred her for a SCID-D that resulted in a diagnosis of DID and appropriate treatment. The second case history patient, Linda A., had received therapy for a long history of anxiety and panic attacks. Not until a violent overreaction to a police incident almost landed her in jail was she diagnosed with DDNOS and for the first time treated successfully for her dissociative tendencies associated with being raped in adolescence. Jean W., the third case history patient, had been treated for anxiety and drug and alcohol problems earlier in her life and wound up in the ER with a severe panic attack at the age of forty. Had her real illness, DID, not been diagnosed and treated, in all likelihood she eventually would have found herself in the ER again.

Stories like this abound. One of my DID patients, a first-time mother in her late twenties and wife of a physician, was given electroshock therapy over my objections for what her husband thought was postpartum depression. The shock treatments worsened her condition and caused a six-month setback with uncontrollable flashbacks of a gang rape she suffered when she was a young schoolgirl. And then there was Dorene, who was written off as "crazy" by her own daughter for seventeen years because she thought intruders were breaking into her home and moving her personal belongings around. Originally misdiagnosed as having a paranoid disorder, she was finally referred to me for a SCID-D that confirmed my earlier suspicions of DID. Now in her sixties Dorene is being treated at the clinic by a therapist who has been advised of her dissociative disorder, and she is finally receiving the therapy she needs.

A wrong diagnosis can result in keeping a person immobilized—remaining in therapy for years and years without being able to make appreciable progress. Antidepressant and antianxiety drugs can help the person function in a going-through-the-motions state of chronic depersonalization—a kind of permanent "stuckness"—but the ability to engage fully in nurturant relationships and in the development of one's own talents will be seriously compromised.

Meredith, the woman mentioned in the chapter on the four C's of treatment as an example of someone who had a distorted belief about gender and developed a male alter, fell victim to this predicament. At the age of thirty-eight, after ten years of treatment with a psychiatrist, she had two master's degrees in biology and was working at a dead-end job, was still living with her parents, and had never been intimate with a man. Concerned about her lack of progress, she volunteered to participate in my field study on dissociation. The SCID-D revealed that Meredith had severe dissociative symptoms that started in her childhood. She had a little boy, Donny, inside her who went to an imaginary psychiatrist because he kept cutting himself. Meredith herself wasn't a cutter, but Donny was. Her real psychiatrist, a kindly man who didn't believe in dissociative disorders, dismissed Donny as simply a figment of her vivid imagination.

When Meredith's psychiatrist retired, I began seeing her regularly. I discovered that although Meredith hadn't been sexually abused, the emotional abuse she'd suffered had severely impaired her sense of self. Her mother constantly flailed away at her for being fat and homely—actually she was a bit overweight, but had a cute face and sweet demeanor—and forced her to be her nursemaid for a variety of ailments, terrifying young Meredith by screaming in pain whenever she attended her. Her mother was also one of those people who believed that boys could do everything, but girls could not, and gave her brother free rein while holding her back. As a consequence Meredith developed Donny, a blond-haired, good-looking little boy who was self-assured at times but who also had a great deal of pent-up rage and aggression that he turned upon himself by being a cutter. He was an elaborate invention that protected Meredith from self-mutilation and severe depression.

From the start Meredith's alter, Donny, a child who was afraid to be on his own, became an integral part of therapy. By learning how to comfort Donny and other childlike parts of herself, Meredith was able to overcome her terror of living on her own as an adult. Within six months of treatment—after ten years of being immovably stuck—she was able to move out of her parents' home into her own apartment, enter a doctoral program in her field, make many friends, and begin navigating the possibility of an intimate relationship with a man.

One of the most tragic and common clinical mistakes is misdiagnosis of a person with DID as a schizophrenic. People with DID perceive the voices of alters as internal phenomena and are oriented in reality, whereas schizophrenics are out of touch with reality and may hear voices of others—CIA agents, for example—perceived as emanating from outside sources and invading their brains. Silencing a multiple's separate parts with antipsychotic medication instead of working to integrate them can reduce a person whose illness has a good rate of recovery to a nonfunctioning zombie. One such woman, among countless others, a skilled nurse who had DID, was so badly mistreated as a schizophrenic that she stopped working, lost her house, and ended up totally incapacitated in a psychiatric institution.

By contrast, Albert, a mild-mannered man in his early fifties, entered a clinic near me with a diagnosis of schizophrenia, and I was called in to consult on the whopping dose of four different antipsychotic medications that he'd been taking for twenty years. Albert said his doctor had prescribed these drugs for him to get rid of an angry man he had inside of him—someone he called Son-of-a-Bitch—who drove him out of control whenever he came out. I evaluated Albert and, on the basis of my findings, told him that he was not schizophrenic and that I would work with him in a different way. The objective was slowly to reduce the medications he'd become psychologically dependent on after so many years by learning more about Son-of-a-Bitch instead of trying to get rid of him.

The first step, I told Albert, was to begin to refer to the man inside him in a much more respectful way if he didn't want this angry person to cause such havoc when he came out. I suggested that he consider a different name for Son-of-a-Bitch and sent him home in the care of a social worker. Two weeks later I saw Albert, and the name he'd come up with was Bad Temper. That was an improvement, I acknowledged, but it still wasn't completely respectful. Albert thought for a moment and said, "Okay, how about Temper?" I told him that was much better.

Albert continued therapy with the social worker, learning more about Temper. When I saw him several months later, the name had changed once again. It had become *Mr.* Temper. A year later, after several reductions in Albert's medications, his social worker told me that Mr. Temper no longer existed separately within him.

The rapidness of this progression was remarkable, but the treatment probably worked so well for Albert because it was such a radical departure from the grossly incorrect treatment he'd had. His case shows how we can prevent the tragic waste of life of many creative people with DID by teaching them how to communicate with their different sides and integrate them instead of trying to suppress them with drugs alone. Research has shown that patients spend *seven to ten years or more* in ineffective treatment, often shunted haplessly from one therapist to another until their dissociative disorders are correctly diagnosed. This is a fate that you can prevent for yourself or a loved one simply by asking to have the SCID-D assessment done.

In addition to sparing needless human suffering, proper diagnosis and treatment of dissociative disorders can prevent a shameful waste of public money. A 1984 study revealed that 47 percent of patients with inaccurate diagnoses required hospitalization before their DID was discovered, compared with only 19 percent who needed to be hospitalized during treatment after an accurate diagnosis. The average cost of a two-week psychiatric hospitalization is fifteen thousand dollars. Since misdiagnosed people may require several hospitalizations, it is easy to see that taxpayer-supported hospitalizations and insurance costs could be greatly reduced by early diagnosis and proper treatment.

As an informed individual you have the power to prevent these unnecessary human and financial losses. Now you can identify dissociative symptoms, whether in yourself or someone you love, and seek out a professional who is qualified to make an accurate diagnosis and provide the care that can make the difference between bare subsistence and a life abundantly lived.

Beyond that, you can help put an end to our current epidemic of dissociation by striking a blow at its root cause—the inexcusably high incidence of childhood abuse and trauma in our society. The sexual, physical, and emotional abuse of helpless children by those entrusted with their care is an evil that no one should turn away from any longer. We cannot continue to tolerate a system that protects abusers and denies or downplays the mistreatment of children. We collude in this atrocity by our silence or skepticism. Decency demands that we speak out for all those mute survivors whose childhood, a time that should be filled with happy memories to cherish in the mind's eye, is instead a shameful secret that they dare not see at all. Our disconnection from the truth, like theirs, is waiting to be healed.

REFERENCES

~

INTRODUCTION

p. xi. F. R. Schreiber. *Sybil*. New York: Warner Books, 1973.

p. xi. C. H. Thigpen & H. Cleckley. *The Three Faces of Eve*. New York: McGraw-Hill, 1957.

p. xvii. M. Steinberg. *Structured Clinical Interview for DSM-IV Dissociative Disorders-Revised (SCID-D-R)*. Washington, DC: American Psychiatric Press, 1994.

To date, there are more than 65 scientific publications documenting the reliability and clinical utility of the SCID-D-R. Its reliability for detecting and distinguishing patients suffering from dissociation from those with anxiety, depression, and other disorders has been replicated and published by clinical investigators worldwide. For a review of SCID-D-R research, see:

M. Steinberg. Advances in the clinical assessment of dissociation: the SCID-D-R. *The Bulletin of the Menninger Clinic* (2000) *64*(2), 146–163.

p. xix. Y. Aderibigbe, R. Bloch & W. Walker. Prevalence of depersonalization and derealization experiences in rural population. *Social Psychiatry and Psychiatric Epidemiology*. In press. The investigators asked 1,008 adults about experiences of depersonalization and derealization in the past year. The reported prevalence rates were 19.1 percent for depersonalization, 14.4 percent for derealization, and 23.4 percent for either dissociative experience. A majority of those reporting depersonalization (54 percent), and 10 percent of the total sample met Steinberg criteria (1995) for severe or recurrent depersonalization (resulting in dysfunction or distress).

I. IN THEIR OWN WORDS

p. 7. E. R. S Nijenhuis et al. Dissociative pathology discriminates between bipolar mood disorder and dissociative disorder (letter). *British Journal of Psychiatry* (1997) *170*, 581.

2. A HEALTHY DEFENSE GONE WRONG

p. 10. R. Noyes, Jr. & R. Kletti. Depersonalization in response to life-threatening danger. *Comprehensive Psychiatry* (1977) *18,* 375–384.

p. 10. R. Noyes, Jr. & R. Kletti. Panoramic memory: a response to the threat of death. *Omega: The Journal of Death and Dying* (1977) *8*(3), 181–194.

p. 14. J. LeDoux. *The Emotional Brain: The Mysterious Underpinnings of Emotional Life.* New York: Simon & Schuster, 1996, as reported by Stephen S. Hall, The anatomy of fear, *The New York Times Magazine,* February 28, 1999, 42, 44–47, 69–70, 72, 88–89, 91.

p. 15. D. Fink. The comorbidity of multiple personality disorder and DSM-III-R Axis II disorders. *Psychiatric Clinics of North America* (1991) *14,* 547–566.

p. 15. J. P. Wilson, Z. Harel & B. Kahana (eds.). *Human Adaptation to Extreme Stress: From the Holocaust to Vietnam.* New York: Plenum Press, 1988.

p. 16 J. A. Chu & D. L. Dill. Dissociative symptoms in relation to childhood physical and sexual abuse. *American Journal of Psychiatry* (1990) *147,* 887–892.

p. 16 J. Goodwin. Post-traumatic symptoms in abused children. *Journal of Traumatic Stress* (1988) *1,* 475–488.

p. 16. A. Miller. *Thou Shalt Not Be Aware: Society's Betrayal of the Child.* New York: Meridian, 1984.

p. 17. D. Finkelhor, G. Hotaling, I. A. Lewis & C. Smith. Sexual abuse in a national survey of adult men and women: prevalence, characteristics, and risk factors. *Child Abuse & Neglect* (1990) *14*(1), 19–28.

p. 17. J. L. Herman. *Father-Daughter Incest.* Cambridge, MA: Harvard University Press, 1981.

p. 17. D. Russell. The incidence and prevalence of intrafamilial and extrafamilial sexual abuse of female children. *Child Abuse & Neglect* (1983) 7(2), 133–146.

p. 17. U.S. Department of Health and Human Services. *The Third National Incidence Study of Child Abuse and Neglect.* Washington, DC: U.S. Government Printing Office, 1996.

p. 17. U.S. Department of Health and Human Services. *Child Maltreatment 1995: Reports from the States to the National Child Abuse and Neglect Data System.* Washington, DC: U.S. Government Printing Office, 1997.

p. 18. W. J. Ray & M. Faith. Dissociative experiences in a college age population: follow-up with 1,190 subjects. *Personality and Individual Differences* (1995) *18,* 223–230.

p. 18. M. Strong. *A Bright Red Scream.* New York: Viking, 1998.

3. DEBUNKING THE MYTHS

p. 19. K. S. Pope & S. Feldman-Summers. National survey of psychologists' sexual and physical abuse history and their evaluation of training and competence in these areas. *Professional Psychology: Research and Practice* (1992) *23,* 5, 353–361

p. 20. C. Classen, D. Spiegel & C. Koopman. Trauma and Dissociation. *Bulletin of the Menninget Clinic* (1993) 57, 2, 178–194.

p. 20. E. Cardena & D. Spiegel. Dissociative reactions to the Bay Area earthquake, *American Journal of Psychiatry* (1993) *150,* 3, 474–478.

Numerous investigations during the past decade, both in the United States and abroad, have confirmed that dissociative disorders are common in the general population as well as among patient populations. Following are prevelance studies of dissociative disorders in general and outpatient populations:

p. 21. D. Davis & M. Davis. The prevalence of dissociative disorders within the mental health services of a British urban district. In: International Society for the Study of Dissociation (ed.), *Proceedings of the Fourth International Conference of the International Society for the Study of Dissociation.* Chester, UK (1997). The estimated life prevalence rates for a British sample as 15.2 percent for dissociative disorders in general and 5.7 percent for dissociative identity disorder.

p. 21. S. Graves. Dissociative disorders and dissociative symptoms at a community mental health center. *Dissociation* (1989) *2*, 119–127.

p. 21. M. Poustovoyt et al. Epidemology of the dissociative disorders in the conventionally healthy persons population. *Acta Psychiatrica, Psychoterapeutica et Ethologica Tavica* (2000) *5*, 2–13. The authors surveyed 1,056 people in the Ukraine using a screening tool. They found that 12 percent had scores indicating considerable dissociative experiences.

p. 21 C. A. Ross. Epidemology of multiple personality disorder and dissociation. *Psychiatric Clinics of North America* (1991) *14*, 503–517. Ross surveyed 454 adults from the general population in Canada and found that 10 percent had a dissociative disorder of some type and 1 percent had DID.

p. 21. W. J. Ray & M. Faith. Dissociative experiences in a college-age population: Follow-up with 1,190 subjects. *Personality and Individual Differences* (1995) *18*, 223–230.

p. 21. V. Sar et al. Frequency of dissociative disorders in the general population: an epidemiological study in Turkey. In: International Society for the Study of Dissociation (ed.), *Proceedings of the International Society for the Study of Dissociation*, 1998. p. 21. Based on a survey of 624 women in the city of Sivas, Turkey, the authors estimated that 1.1 percent of women in the general population of Sivas had DID and 18.3 percent had a dissociative disorder.

p. 21. V. Sar et al. Frequency of dissociative disorders among psychiatric outpatients in Turkey. *Comprehensive Psychiatry* (2000) *41*, 216–222. In this study, dissociative disorders were common among 150 outpatients in Turkey. Twenty-three (15.3%) were found to have significant dissociative symptoms and eighteen (12%) were diagnosed as having a dissociative disorder.

p. 21. J .R. Vanderlinden et al. Dissociation and traumatic experiences in the general population of the Netherlands. *Hospital & Community Psychiatry* (1993) *44*, 786–788. These authors found that dissociative experiences were in their sample of 378 individuals in the Netherlands.

p. 21. J. R. Vanderlinden et al. Dissociated experiences in the general population in the Netherlands and Belgium: A study with the Dissociative Questionnaire (DIS-Q). *Dissociation* (1991) *4*, 180–184. Vanderlinden et al. surveyed 235 Dutch and 139 Flemish people using a screening tool and found that 3 percent reported serious dissociative symptoms and 1 percent showed scores as high as those seen in individuals with multiple personality.

p. 21. R. C. Kessler et al. Lifetime and 12-month prevalence of DSM-III-R psychiatric disorders in the United States: results from the National Cormobidity Survey. *Archives of General Psychiatry* (1994) *51*:8–19. Kessler and colleagues report on the prevalence of a variety of psychiatric disorders, based on interviews of a national sample of 8,098 respondents. They found the twelve-month prevalence of major depressive episodes to be 10.3 percent and generalized anxiety disorder, 3.1 percent.

p. 23. For a scholarly review of research in this field, see D. Brown, A. W. Scheflin & D. C. Hammond. *Memory, Trauma Treatment, and the Law: An Essential Reference on Memory for Clinicians, Researchers, Attorneys, and Judges.* New York: W. W. Norton, 1998.

p. 23. International Society for the Study of Dissociation (ISSD). *Guidelines for Treating Dissociative Identity Disorder (Multiple Personality Disorder) in Adults.* Skokie, IL: ISSD, 1994.

p. 23. D. Schacter. Memory distortion: history and current status. In D. L. Schacter et al., eds. *Memory distortion: How Minds, Brains, and Societies Reconstruct the Past.* Cambridge, MA: Harvard University Press, pp. 1–43. Schacter notes (p. 28): "A further question concerns whether people can falsely create an entire history of traumatic abuse when none occurred. There is no hard scientific evidence that shows such a phenomenon uniquivo-cally."

p. 23. E. Bernstien & F. W. Putnam. Development, reliability and validity of a dissociation scale. *Journal of Nervous and Mental Disease* (1986) *174*, 727–735. This study describes the reliability and validity of a widely used screening tool, the Dissociative Experiences Scale.

p. 23. K. Riley. Measurement of dissociation. *Journal of Nervous and Mental Disease* (1988) *176*, 449–450. This investigation describes the reliability of another useful screening tool, the Questionnaire of Experiences of Dissociation.

p. 23. J. LeDoux. *The Emotional Brain.* New York: Simon & Schuster, 1996.

p. 23. M. B. Stein et al. Hippocampal volume in women victimized by child abuse. *Psychological Medicine* (1997) *27*, 951–959.

p. 23. B. A. Van der Kolk, J. Burbridge & J. Suzaki. The psychobiology of traumatic memory: clinical implications of neuroimaging studies. *Annals of the New York Academy of Science* (1997) *821*, 99–113.

p. 23. P. Coons. Confirmation of child abuse in child and adolescent cases of multiple personality and dissociative disorder not otherwise specified. *Journal of Nervous and Mental Disease* (1994) *182*, 461–464.

p. 23. P. Barach. Therapeutic techniques used by therapists treating their first patient with dissociative identity disorder: diagnostic indicators, memory recovery techniques, therapeutic boundaries. In: The International Society for the Study of Dissociation (ed.) *Proceedings of the International Society for the Study of Dissociation.* San Francisco, 1996.

p. 23. J. Herman, & M. Harvey. Adult memories of childhood trauma: a naturalistic clinical study. *Journal of Traumatic Stress* (1997) *10*, 557–571.

p. 23. Kenneth V. Lanning. *Investigator's Guide to Allegations of "Ritual" Child Abuse.* National Center for the Analysis of Violent Crime, Federal Bureau of Investigation, Quantico, VA, 1992. Ken Lanning, the FBI agent in charge of ritual-abuse investigations, has written: "I believe that the majority of victims alleging 'ritual abuse' are in fact victims of some form of abuse or trauma" (p. 39).

p. 25. L. Silvern et al. Retrospective reports of parental partner abuses: relationships to depression, trauma systems and self-esteem among college students. *Journal of Family Violence* (1995) *10*(2), 177–202.

p. 25. L. M. Williams. Recall of childhood trauma: a prospective study of women's memories of child sexual abuse. *Journal of Consulting and Clinical Psychology* (1994) *62*(6), 1167–1176. Dr. Williams's follow-up of 129 women seventeen years after they were treated at an ER for sexual assault revealed that 38 percent of the women had amnesia for their abuse. She found that the factors relating to having amnesia included earlier age at onset of abuse, more violent abuse, and longer duration.

p. 25. D. Elliott & J. Briere. Post-traumatic stress associated with delayed recall of sexual abuse: a general population study. *Journal of Traumatic Stress* (1995) *8*, 629–647. Drs. Elliot and Briere found that of 505 people who had been sexually abused 42 percent experienced some form of amnesia for their abuse. The factors influencing the delayed recall of the abuse included threats by perpetrators and a high level of distress associated with the abuse.

p. 26. L. C. Terr. *Too Scared to Cry: Psychic Trauma in Childhood.* New York: Harper & Row, 1990. Dr. Terr found that children under age three at the time of exposure to documented trauma almost always experienced behavioral memory—including fears, dreams, and reenactments—of the trauma.

p. 26. L. C. Terr. Childhood traumas: an outline and overview. *American Journal of Psychiatry*

(1991) *148*, 10–20. Dr. Terr summarizes the relationship between frequency of trauma and memory as follows: "Verbal recollections of single shocks in an otherwise trauma-free childhood are delivered in an amazingly clear and detailed fashion. Children sometimes sound like robots as they strive to tell every detail as efficiently as possible" (p. 14), where memories of prolonged abuse develop into amnesias.

p. 26. J. Briere & J. Conte. Self-reported amnesia for abuse in adults molested as children. *Journal of Traumatic Stress* (1993) *6*(1), 21–31. Drs. Briere and Conte found that of 450 adults with sexual abuse histories 59 percent had experienced amnesia as a result of their abuse at some time prior to age eighteen.

p. 26. J. Herman & E. Schatzow. Recovery and verification of memories of childhood sexual trauma. *Psychoanalytic Quarterly* (1987) *4*(1), 1–14. Drs. Herman and Schatzow found that of 53 female incest survivors in group therapy 74 percent had been able to corroborate their abuse experiences from various sources, including perpetrator admissions and the discovery that another sibling had also been sexually abused.

p. 26. M. Steinberg, P. Hall and D. Cicchetti. Recognizing the validity of dissociative symptoms and disorders using the SCID-D-R: Guidelines for clinical and forensic evaluations. *The University of Southern California Interdisciplinary Law Journal*. In press. The authors present systematic guidelines for detecting the validity of dissociative symptoms and disorders.

p. 27. S. Boon & N. Draijer. Diagnosing dissociative disorders in the Netherlands: a pilot study with the structured clinical interview for DSM-III R Dissociative Disorders. *American Journal of Psychiatry* (1991) *148*(4),458–462.

p. 27. T. Kundaker et al. The reliability and validity of the Turkish version of the SCID-D. In: *Dissociative Disorders: Proceedings of the International Society for the Study of Dissociation*, ed. The International Society for the Study of Dissociation. Chicago, 1998.

p. 27. F. W. Putnam: *Diagnosis and Treatment of Multiple Personality Disorder*. New York: The Guilford Press, 1989.

p. 27. G. Fraser et al. Contrasts between DID, paranoid schizophrenia, non-psychiatric controls, and a non-patient group simulating DID as a factitious disorder on normed tests and interviews. In: International Society for the Study of Dissociation (ed.). *Proceedings for the 16th International Conference of the Society for the Study of Dissociation: Integrating Dissociation Theory into Clinical Practice and Psychological Research*, pp. 12–13. Miami, FL: ISSD, 1999.

Another investigation conducted by Kluft found no malingerer able to be consistent in the characteristics of an assumed personality; the assumption of alters was polarized along good/bad or innocent/guilty personalities. See R. P. Kluft. The simulation and dissimulation of multiple personality disorder. *American Journal of Clinical Hypnosis* (1987) *30*, 104–118.

A study purporting to show that people can readily enact a multiple personality when given "appropriate inducements" was conducted by Spanos, Weekes, and Bertrand on 48 college students role-playing accused murderers—not a typical DID case to begin with. The study involved simulated hypnotic interviews during which the "hypnotized" subjects were told that the interviewer wanted to communicate with another part of them. Subjects were then asked four questions: (1) Who are you? (2) Can you tell me about yourself? (3) Do you have a name I can call you by? (4) Tell me about yourself [repeating the alternate name]. What do you do?" See N. P. Spanos, J. R. Weekes, and L. D. Bertrand. Multiple personality: a social psychological perspective. *Journal of Abnormal Psychology* (1985) *94*, 362–376.

Although Spanos et al. reported that some subjects used an alternate name and said they could not remember anything beyond the initiation of the hypnotic procedure, there was no evidence that the researchers were able to elicit the full range of symptoms necessary for a diagnosis of DID. In fact, the use of an alternate name and the claimed presence of amnesia (based on yes/no responses) are insufficient to meet the DSM-IV criteria for such a diagnosis.

p. 27. G. Gleaves. The sociocognitive model of dissociative identity disorder: a re-examination of the evidence. *Psychological Bulletin* (1996) *120*(1), 42–59.

p. 28. R. P. Kluft. An overview of the psychotherapy of dissociative identity disorder. *American Journal of Psychotherapy* (1999) *53*, 289–318.

p. 28. F. W. Putnam et al. The clinical phenomenology of multiple personality disorder: 100 recent cases. *Journal of Clinical Psychiatry* (1986) *47*, 285–293.

p. 28. J. Allen. *Coping with Trauma: A Guide to Self-Understanding.* Washington, D. C. : American Psychiatric Press, 1995.

4. THE FIVE CORE SYMPTOMS

The following two publications provide a review of the five core symptoms:

M. Steinberg. *Handbook for the Assessment of Dissociation: A Clinical Guide.* Washington, DC: American Psychiatric Press, 1995

———. Advances in the clinical assessment of dissociation: the SCID-D-R. *The Bulletin of the Menninger Clinic* (Spring 2000) *64*(2) 146–163.

The following two audiotapes provide a review of these symptoms and the assessment process:

M. Steinberg. *A Clinician's Guide to Diagnosing Dissociative Symptoms and Disorders: The SCID-D.* Toronto: Multi-Health Systems, 1996, Audiocassette and manual.

———. *Tips and Techniques for Assessing and Planning Treatment with Dissociative Disorder Patients: A Practical Guide to the SCID-D.* Toronto: Multi-Health Systems, 1996. Audiocassette and manual.

The SCID-D-R has been translated into French, Spanish, Japanese, Portuguese, Hebrew, Russian, Dutch, Norwegian, German, and Turkish. Numerous investigations in the United States and abroad have found that the SCID-D-R is a reliable tool for the identification of the five core dissociative symptoms and disorders, and that these symptoms are universal manifestations of the ways individuals survive trauma. Guidelines for clinicians in the administration and scoring of the SCID-D-R can be found in M. Steinberg. *Interviewer's Guide to the Structured Clinical Interview for DSM-IV Dissociative Disorders-Revised (SCID-D-R).* Washington, DC: American Psychiatric Press, 1994.

5. THE BLACK HOLE OF LOST MEMORIES

p.42. D. Laub & N. Auerhahn. Knowing and not knowing massive psychic trauma: forms of traumatic memory. *International Journal of Psychoanalysis* (1993) *74*, 287–302.

p. 42. R. Joseph. The neurology of traumatic "dissociative" amnesia: commentary and literature review. *Child Abuse & Neglect* (1999) *8*, 715–727.

p. 42. L. Nadel & W. Jake Jacobs. Traumatic memory is special. *Current Directions in Psychological Science* (1998) 7(5), 154–157.

p. 42. B. D. Perry, L. Conroy & A. Ravitz. Persisting psychophysiological effects of traumatic stress: the memory of "states." *Violence Update* (1991) *1*(8), 1–11.

p. 43. P. M. Coons & V. Milstein. Self-mutilation associated with dissociative disorders. *Dissociation* (1990) *3*(2), 81–87.

p. 43. D. Miller. *Women Who Hurt Themselves.* New York, Basic Books, 1994.

p. 43. M. Strong. *A Bright Red Scream.* New York: Viking, 1998.

See also chapters 3 and 4 in M. Steinberg, *Handbook for the Assessment of Dissociation: A Clinical Guide.* Washington, DC: American Psychiatric Press, 1995.

6. WATCHING YOURSELF FROM A DISTANCE

p. 54. R. Noyes Jr. et al. Depersonalization in accident victims and psychiatric patients. *Journal of Nervous and Mental Disease* (1977) *164,* 401–407.

p. 58. J. P. Cattell & J. S. Cattell. Depersonalization: psychological and social perspectives. In *American Handbook of Psychiatry,* 2nd ed., ed. S. Arieti. New York: Basic Books, 1974, pp. 766–799. Cattell and Cattell found that depersonalization is the third most common clinical symptom among psychiatric patients, after anxiety and depression.

p. 58. M. Roth. The phobic anxiety-depersonalization syndrome and some general aetiological problems in psychiatry. *Journal of Neuropsychiatry* (1960) *1,* 293–306.

See also chapters 5 and 6 in M. Steinberg, *Handbook for the Assessment of Dissociation: A Clinical Guide.* Washington, DC: American Psychiatric Press, 1995.

p. 59. F. Miller & E. A. Bashkin. Depersonalization and self-mutilation. *Psychoanalytic Quarterly* (1974) *43*(4), 638–649.

p. 61. R. J. Lifton. Understanding the traumatized self: imagery, symbolism, and transformation, in *Human Adaptation to Extreme Stress: From the Holocaust to Vietnam,* ed. J. P. Wilson et al. New York: Plenum Press, 1988.

7. A VISIT TO THE LAND OF OZ

p. 68. G. Florio & M. Matza. Gunshots, blood and chaos, *The Philadelphia Inquirer,* April 21, 1999, pp. A1, A16.

p. 71. V. Siomopoulos. Derealization and déjà vu: formal mechanisms. *American Journal of Psychotherapy* (1972) *26,* 84–89.

p. 77. E. Pooley. Portrait of a deadly bond. *Time* May 10, 1999, pp. 26–32.

p. 78. Nancy Gibbs et al. Special report: the Littleton massacre. *Time,* May 3, 1999.

See also chapters 7 and 8 in M. Steinberg, *Handbook for the Assessment of Dissociation: A Clinical Guide.* Washington, DC: American Psychiatric Press, 1995.

8. WHEN YOU DON'T KNOW WHO YOU ARE

p. 82. J. Palmer. A new leaf: how a Wall Streeter turned restaurateur. *Barron's* May 10, 1999, pp. 25–26, 28.

p. 83. K. Gergen. *The Saturated Self: Dilemmas of Identity in Contemporary Life.* New York: Basic Books, 1991.

p. 83. E. H. Erikson. *Identity: Youth and Crisis.* New York: W. W. Norton, 1968.

p. 83. American Psychiatric Association. *Diagnostic and Statistical Manual of Mental Disorders,* 4th ed. (DSM-IV). Washington, DC: American Psychiatric Association, 1994.

p. 92. C. Gilligan. *In a Different Voice: Psychological Theory and Women's Development.* Cambridge, MA: Harvard University Press, 1982.

See also chapter 10 in M. Steinberg, *Handbook for the Assessment of Dissociation: A Clinical Guide.* Washington, DC: American Psychiatric Press, 1995.

9. ONE PERSON, MANY SELVES

See chapters 9 and 11 in M. Steinberg, *Handbook for the Assessment of Dissociation: A Clinical Guide.* Washington, DC: American Psychiatric Press, 1995.

10. MEN, ABUSE, AND DISSOCIATIVE DISORDERS

p. 118. M. Landsberg. Memories of molestation recovered by men, too. *The Toronto Star,* March 4, 2000.

p. 118. M. Hunter. *Abused Boys: The Neglected Victims of Sexual Abuse.* New York: Fawcett Columbine, 1990.

p. 119. E. Griffin-Shelly, L. R. Benjamin & R. Benjamin. Sex addiction and dissociation. *Sexual Addiction and Compulsivity: The Journal of Treatment and Prevention* (1995) *2,* 295–306.

p. 119 G. Kolodner & R. Frances. Recognizing dissociative disorders in patients with chemical dependency. *Hospital and Community Psychiatry* (1993) *44* (II), 1041–1043.

13. JEAN W.: NIGHTMARE VISIONS

p. 216. G. Dunn et al. Dissociative symptoms in a substance abuse population. *American Journal of Psychiatry* (1993) *150,* 1043–1047.

p. 238. For further reflections on forgiveness, see A. Miller, *Breaking Down the Walls of Silence: The Liberating Experience of Facing Painful Truth.* New York: Dutton, 1991.

pp. 247–48. The technique used to treat Jean was adapted from the nonhypnotic chair technique as described in J. G. Watkins & H. Watkins, *Ego States: Theory and Therapy.* New York: Norton, 1997.

p. 249. J. Ford. *Wonderful Ways to Love a Child.* Berkeley, CA: Conari Press, 1994.

14. A DIFFERENT APPROACH: THE FOUR C'S

P. 256. J. L. Herman. *Trauma and Recovery.* New York, Basic Books: 1992.

p. 256. R. P. Kluft. The initial stages of psychotherapy in the treatment of multiple personality disorder patients. *Dissociation* (1993) *6*(2/3), 145–161.

p. 259 The following are recommended books for adults that focus on comforting and parenting techniques:

A. Domar & H. Dreher. *Self-Nurture: Learning to Care for Yourself as Effectively as You Care for Everyone Else.* New York: Viking-Penguin, 2000.

J. Ford. *Wonderful Ways to Love a Child.* Berkeley, CA: Conari Press, 1994.

J. Gray. *Children Are from Heaven.* New York: HarperCollins, 1999.

C. D. Kasl. *Finding Joy: 101 Ways to Free Your Spirit.* New York: HarperCollins, 1994.

J. Louden. *The Woman's Comfort Book: A Self-Nurturing Guide for Restoring Balance in Your Life.* New York: HarperCollins, 1992.

———. *The Couple's Comfort Book: A Creative Guide for Renewing Passion, Pleasure and Commitment.* New York: HarperCollins, 1994.

W. H. Missildine. *Your Inner Child of the Past.* New York: Simon & Schuster, 1963.

N. J. Napier. *Getting Through the Day: Strategies for Adults Hurt as Children.* New York: W. W. Norton, 1993.

V. Vienne. *The Art of Imperfection—Simple Ways to Make Peace with Yourself.* New York: Clarkson Potter, 1999.

p. 260. The following are some of my favorite therapeutic books for children of all ages:

A. Gash. *What the Dormouse Said: Lessons for Grown-Ups from Children's Books.* Chapel Hill, NC: Algonquin Books, 1999. This book summarizes the "wisdom from more than two hundred best-loved children's books."

M. Gerstein. *The Wild Boy—Based on a True Story of the Wild Boy of Aveyron.* New York: Frances Foster Books, 1998.

C. Myers. *Wings.* New York: Scholastic Press, 2000.

S. Greenlee. *When Someone Dies.* Atlanta: Peachtree Publishers, 1992.

M. Itoh. *I Want to Tell You About My Feelings.* New York: William Morrow, 1992.

M. K. Shanley. *She Taught Me to Eat Artichokes.* Marshalltown, IA: Sta-Kris, 1993. This wonderful story of friendship and growth asks the following question: "We are most comfortable with the things we know the best. But if we always avoid the unfamiliar, how will we ever know what riches may be waiting for us, deep within the heart?"

p. 261. J. Viorst. *Rosie and Michael.* New York: Simon & Schuster, 1988.

p. 261. M. Waddell & B. Firth. *Can't You Sleep, Little Bear?* Cambridge, MA: Candlewick Press, 1988.

p. 267. J. Frye. *Betrayal Trauma: The Logic of Forgetting Childhood Abuse.* Cambridge, MA: Harvard University Press, 1998.

p. 268. M. Torem. Therapeutic writing as a form of ego-state therapy. *American Journal of Clinical Hypnosis* (1993) *33,* 267–276.

p. 273. Hypnosis can be useful during the course of therapy for a variety of symptoms, including stress reduction, phobias, and anxiety. The following studies provide additional information about the applications of hypnosis:

C. D. Hammond. Hypnosis in the treatment of dissociative identity disorder. In *Multiple Personality Disorder: Continuum of Care,* ed. B. M. Cohen & J. A. Turkus. New York: Brunner/Mazel. In press.

p. 273. D. Spiegel: Hypnosis in the treatment of victims of sexual abuse. *Psychiatric Clinics of North America* (1989) *12,* 295–305.

p. 273. Y. M. Dolan. *Resolving Sexual Abuse: Solution-Focused Therapy and Ericksonian Hypnosis for Adult Survivors.* New York: Norton, 1991.

p. 273. J. G. Watkins & H. Watkins. *Ego States: Theory and Therapy.* New York: Norton, 1997.

For further information about treatment of the five core symptoms, see the following two studies: P. Hall & M. Steinberg. Systematic assessment of dissociative symptoms and disorders in a clinical out-patient setting: three cases. *Dissociation* (1994) *7,* 112–116; idem, The SCID-D diagnostic interview and treatment planning in dissociative disorders. *Bulletin of the Menninger Clinic* (1997) *61*(1), 108–120.

The treatment of individuals with dissociative disorders also requires familiarity with unique parenting, couples and family issues, as well as spiritual issues. For further information, see the following three studies:

L. R. Benjamin & R. Benjamin. An overview of family treatment in dissociative disorders. *Dissociation* (1992) *5,* 236–241.

———. Various perspectives on parenting and their implications for the treatment of dissociative disorders. *Dissociation* (1994) *7,* 246–260.

E. S. Bowman. Understanding and responding to religious material in the therapy of multiple personality disorder. *Dissociation* (1989) *2,* 231–238.

15. ALIENS FROM INNER SPACE: UFO ABDUCTIONS, PAST LIVES, NEAR-DEATH EXPERIENCES

p. 275. B. Hopkins. *Missing Time.* New York: Ballantine Books, 1988.

p. 278. J. Frye. *Betrayal Trauma: The Logic of Forgetting Childhood Abuse.* Cambridge, MA: Harvard University Press, 1998.

p. 278. C. McLeod, B. Corbisier & J. Mack. A more parsimonious explanation for UFO abduction. *Psychological Inquiry* (1996) 7(2), 156–168.

p. 278. A. Miller. *Breaking Down the Walls of Silence: The Liberating Experience of Facing Painful Truth.* New York: Dutton, 1991.

p. 278. J. Takhar & S. Fisman. Alien abduction in PTSD. *Journal of the American Academy of Child & Adolescent Psychiatry* (1995) 34(8), 974–975.

p. 282. J. Mack. *Abduction: Human Encounters with Aliens.* New York: Charles Scribner's Sons, 1994.

p. 284. S. Powers. Dissociation in alleged extraterrestrial abductees. *Dissociation: Progress in the Dissociative Disorders* (1994) 7(1), 44–50.

p. 285. K. Ring & C. Rosing. The Omega project: a psychological survey of persons reporting abductions and other UFO encounters. *Journal of UFO Studies* (1990) 2, 59–98.

p. 287. B. Weiss. *Many Lives, Many Masters.* New York: Simon & Schuster, 1988.

p. 291. R. Noyes, Jr. & R. Kletti. Depersonalization in the face of life-threatening danger: a description. *Psychiatry* (1976) 39, 19–27.

p. 292. R. Moody. *Life After Life.* New York: Bantam Books, 1985.

p. 292. M. Morse. *Closer to the Light.* New York: Villard Books, 1990.

p. 292. B. Eadie. *Embraced by the Light.* Placerville, CA: Gold Leaf Press, 1992.

16. UNNECESSARY LOSSES

p. 296. M. Steinberg et al. Distinguishing between multiple personality disorder and schizophrenia using the Structured Clinical Interview for DSM-IV Dissociative Disorders. *Journal of Nervous and Mental Disease* (1994) 182, 495–502.

p. 297. R. P. Kluft. Treatment of multiple personality: a study of 33 cases. *Psychiatric Clinics of North America* (1984) 7, 9–29.

INDEX

abuse. *See also* sexual abuse
  alien abduction experiences and,
    275–86, 290–91, 293
  cognitive distortions from, 266–67
  depersonalization and, 59, 61, 62, 261
  derealization and, 71, 75–77, 78
  dissociation in, xi, 16–18, 114, 298
  feeling invisible and, 123–24
  identity confusion and, 93–95
  men and dissociative disorders and,
    118–24
  mental clouding from, 61
  past life experiences and, 286–90, 293
alcohol abuse, 15, 17, 18, 62, 107, 119
alien abduction experiences, xvi,
  275–86, 290–91, 293
alteration of identity. *See* identity alteration
alter personality. *See* multiple personalities
American Psychiatric Association, 83,
  84
amnesia, 37–51
  alien abduction experiences and, 276,
    277, 283, 285–86
  common signs of, 44
  compensatory techniques for, 44–45
  as a core symptom, 31, 34–36, 37–51
  definition of, 31
  derealization with, 70
  dissociative disorders in men and, 122
  as a dissociative symptom, xvi
  distorted sense of time in, 45
  examples of, 44
  factors influencing propensity toward,
    26
  identity disturbance dimensions and,
    101
  integration and, 272
  mild, 37, 38–40
  moderate, 40–41
  multiple personalities and, 46–47
  normal versus abnormal dissociation
    and, 13
  myths about, 24–26
  past life experiences and, 289
  questionnaire for evaluation of,
    48–51

amnesia *(continued)*
  self-injury and, 43
  severe, 41–42
  surface versus hidden symptoms and,
    254–55
  trauma triggers for, 46
anger, 118–19
antianxiety medication, 28, 274, 295
antidepressants, 28, 274, 295
anxiety, xvi, xviii
  depersonalization with, 56–57, 58–59
  derealization with, 70
  in dissociative disorders, 6, 15, 113
  dissociative disorders in men and, 119
  drug therapy for, 28, 274
  normal versus abnormal dissociation
    and, 13
  parental rejection and, 267–68
attention-deficit hyperactivity disorder
    (ADHD), xv, xviii, 119, 134, 262,
    274

bipolar disorder. *See* manic-depressive
    illness
blanking out. *See* amnesia
body perception, 62, 114
borderline personality disorder, 106
brain, physiological basis for dissociation
    and, 14–15, 25–26
burning behavior. *See* self-injury

case histories
  Jean W., 207–50
  Linda A., 169–206
  Nancy L., 129–68
childhood
  abuse in. *See* abuse
  identity formation in, 85–89, 102–3
  mild amnesia about, 40
children of alcoholics, 17, 135–36
Cicchetti, Domenic, xvii
Claymar, Aphrodite, 286
cognitive distortions, 266–67

cognitive theories
  of derealization, 71
  of identity formation, 85
comfort (four C's approach), 258–64,
    271
communication (four C's approach),
    264–69, 271
compulsive behavior, 7, 17, 119. *See also*
    obsessive-compulsive disorder
    (OCD)
connection (four C's approach), 270–73
cooperation (four C's approach),
    269–70
coping (defense) mechanism, dissocia-
    tion as, xix, 5, 8–18, 56–57
creative visualization, 263–64
cutting behavior. *See* self-injury

DDNOS. *See* dissociative disorder not
    otherwise specified
defense mechanisms. *See* coping
    (defense) mechanism, dissociation
    as
denial, 21
depersonalization, 18, 52–67
  alien abduction experiences and, 277,
    283
  compartmentalizing emotions and,
    57–58
  as a core symptom, 31, 34–36, 52–67
  creative visualization and, 263–64
  definition of, 31
  derealization with, 69–70
  identity disturbance dimensions and,
    101–2
  integration and, 272
  internal dialogues in, 55–56, 62–63
  manifestations of variations of, 53
  mental clouding (feeling foggy) and,
    60–61
  mild, 53, 54–55
  moderate, 53, 56–57
  near-death experiences and, 292,
    293

surface versus hidden symptoms and, 254–55

three dimensions of, 101–2

workplace and, 96

imaginary friends, 16

incest, 87–88, 95–96. *See also* sexual abuse

integration, 271–73

internal dialogues, 268–69

International Society for the Study of Dissociation, xiv–xv, 23

invisibility, sense of, 59, 123–24. *See also* depersonalization

Jean W., case history of, 128, 207–50, 294

Kletti, Roy, 291

Kluft, Richard P., xi, 256

learning theories of identity formation, 85

letter-writing exercises, 268–69

Linda A., case history of, 128, 169–206, 294

Louden, Jennifer, 259–60

Mack, John E., 282

manic-depressive illness, xv, xviii, 106

memories

and occurrence of false memories of sexual abuse, 22–24

replaying of, 14–15

retracting, 23, 24

memory

flashbacks and, 13

gap in. *See* amnesia

impairment of, in DID, 17

normal versus abnormal dissociation and, 13

panoramic memory, 10, 13

physiological basis for dissociation and, 14–15

self-image and, 38

trauma and, 42

memory lapses. *See also* amnesia

as a coping mechanism in trauma, 10, 13

as a dissociative symptom, xv, 13

identity alteration and, 108

normal experiences of brief, mild episodes of, 16–17

self-descriptions of, 4, 5

men

abuse and dissociative disorders and, 17, 118–24

compartmentalizing emotions by, 58

feeling invisible and, 123–24

sex ratio in DID diagnosis and, 118

symptoms of dissociative disorders in, 119

warrior personality and, 120–22

mental clouding, 13. *See also* amnesia

depersonalization and, 60–61

Miller, Alice, 278–79

mission statements, 264–66

mood swings, 4, 7, 15, 106, 119, 271, 274

Moody, Raymond, 292

Morse, Melvin, 292

movie, feeling that one is watching a, xv, 4, 53. *See also* depersonalization; derealization

multiple personalities, xii–xiii

amnesia and, 46–47

circumstantial evidence for, 111–12

faking or exaggerating, 27

four C's approach to, 255–74

functioning of individuals with, 22

incidence of, xiii–xiv, 21

keeping separate parts hidden, 21–22

memory gaps and, 42

myth about, as freaks of nature, xi–xii, 22

naming of alters in, 110

reports from others on, 112–13

DSM-IV Dissociative Disorders), 19,
23, 27. See also questionnaires for
self-evaluation
development of, xvii–xviii
five core symptoms on, 32–33, 34–36
screening, questions used for, xv, xviii.
See also SCID-D
self, feeling of detachment from. See
depersonalization; derealization
self-comforting strategies, 259–64, 271
self-destructive behavior. See self-injury
self-injury (self-mutilation)
amnesia and, 43
depersonalization and, 59–60
in dissociative disorders, 15, 18
trauma and, 42
sex change, and identity confusion,
95–96
sex differences. See gender, negation of;
men; women
sexual abuse. See also abuse; incest
alien abduction experiences and,
277–81
association between dissociative disorders and, xi
confusion about sexuality and, 95–96
depersonalization and, 69
derealization and, 76–77
dissociation as a defense in, 16–17
identity confusion and, 93–95
incidence of, xix
myths about forgetting details of,
24–26
myths about occurrence of false
memories of, 22–24
past life experiences and, 286–91
reporting, 24, 25
retracting memories of, 23, 24
as a risk factor for developing dissociative disorders, 17–18
sexual behavior, compulsive, 17, 119
sexual identity, 32, 91–92
shame, and derealization, 73
social anxiety disorder (social phobia),
119, 120
splitting off, 14. See also derealization

state-dependent learning, 42
Steinberg Clinical Interview for DSM-IV
Dissociative Disorders. See SCID-D
stress
depersonalization and, 54–55
dissociation as coping mechanism for,
xix, 5, 12, 14–15, 20
students, dissociative disorders in, 18
Sybil, xi, xvi, 21, 27
symptoms, xiv, xv–xvi
continuum of dissociation and,
xvi, 6
coping (defense) mechanism and,
8–9
denial of, 21
five core, 31–34
inability to identify, 6–7
myths about, 20–21, 22
normal versus abnormal, 11–13
self-descriptions of, 3–5
surface versus hidden, 254–55

therapy. See psychotherapy;
treatment
Three Faces of Eve, The, xi, 21
time sense, xv. See also amnesia
as a coping mechanism, 10, 11, 20
gaps and distorted sense of, 39–40,
42, 45
trances, 41, 46–47, 110–11
trauma. See also abuse
amnesia triggered by, 46
depersonalization and, 54, 58, 60
derealization and, 68–69, 71, 72,
74–75, 76, 78
dissociation as coping mechanism to,
xix, 8–11, 14–15, 20, 26, 298
memory and, 42
as a risk factor, 17–18
treatment. See also four C's approach;
psychotherapy
drug therapy in, 274–75
hypnosis in, 273–74
myth about ability to cure DID,
27–28

treatment *(continued)*
  time frame for, 28
unreality, feeling of, xvi, 10, 18. *See also*
  depersonalization; derealization

violence, and dissociative disorders in
  men, 119, 121, 122
Viorst, Judith, 261
visualization, 263–64
visual perception changes, in derealization, 69

Waddell, Martin, 261
warrior personality, 120–22
watching oneself. *See* depersonalization
Watkins, Helen, xi

Watkins, John, xi
Weiss, Brian, 287, 289, 291
Wilbur, Cornelia B., 27
women
  childhood abuse experiences of, 17
  depersonalization and, 58
  identity confusion and, 92–93
  self-mutilation among, 18
  sex ratio in DID diagnosis and, 118
  shame and derealization in, 73
workplace
  compartmentalization of emotions in,
    270
  depersonalization and, 57–58
  identity alteration and, 105
  identity confusion and, 84, 99

About Our Web Site

If you or someone you know suffers from symptoms of dissociation or would like to learn more about resources, please visit our Web site:

http://www.strangerinthemirror.com

Proper diagnosis and treatment offers much hope for dissociative disorders. The first step is to obtain appropriate help.